Four days . . .

It was a frightening thought. *If Burnside crosses quickly, en masse, he might very easily break through and head directly for Richmond before Jackson's men ever arrive.*

Again Lee looked to the sky, still obscured by the fog, and he started to pray for bad weather to hold Burnside in place, but rain, sleet, and snow would also further delay his own reinforcements coming in from the valley. And so Robert E. Lee prayed his most comfortable prayer—the one he whispered every day, a hundred times a day.

"Thy will, O God, be done."

Books by Richard Croker

NO GREATER COURAGE:
A NOVEL OF THE BATTLE OF FREDERICKSBURG

TO MAKE MEN FREE:
A NOVEL OF THE BATTLE OF ANTIETAM

No Greater Courage

A Novel of the
Battle of Fredericksburg

RICHARD CROKER

HARPER

An Imprint of HarperCollinsPublishers

This is a work of fiction. Any references to real people, events, establishments, organizations, or locales are intended only to give the fiction a sense of reality and authenticity, and are used fictitiously. All other names, characters, and places, and all dialogue and incidents portrayed in this book are the product of the author's imagination.

HARPER

An Imprint of HarperCollins*Publishers*
10 East 53rd Street
New York, New York 10022-5299

Copyright © 2006 by Richard Croker
Maps by Robert Croker
ISBN: 978-0-06-122806-3
ISBN-10: 0-06-122806-0

First Harper paperback printing: April 2007
First William Morrow hardcover printing: March 2006

Printed in the United States of America

Visit Harper paperbacks on the World Wide Web at www.harpercollins.com

10 9 8 7 6 5 4 3 2 1

No greater courage was ever shown by soldiers than by our boys at Fredericksburg.

—RICHARD B. LOOMIS,
21ST MASSACHUSETTS INFANTRY

CAST OF CHARACTERS

ARMY OF THE POTOMAC
Maj. Gen. Ambrose Burnside, *Commanding*

50th New York Volunteer Engineers
Brig. Gen. Daniel Woodbury, *Commanding*
Maj. Ira Spaulding
Capt. Wesley Brainerd
Johnny Jones (Civilian)
Pvt. Billy Blakesley

RIGHT GRAND DIVISION
Maj. Gen. Edwin Summer, Commanding

SECOND CORPS
Maj. Gen. Darius Couch

1st Division, Brig. Gen. Winfield Scott Hancock
1st Brigade, Brig. Gen. John Caldwell
2rd Brigade, Brig. Gen. Thomas Meagher
   116th Pa. (The Irish Brigade)
   Sgt. J. Stretchbok
   Pvt. Bill McCarter
3rd Brigade, Col. Samuel Zook

2nd Division, Brig. Gen. Oliver O. Howard
3rd Brigade, Col. Norman Hall
   20th Mass. (The Harvard Regiment)
   Capt. George Macy
   Capt. Oliver Wendell Holmes, Jr.
   Capt. H. L. "Little" Abbott
   Lt. Leander Alley
3rd Division, Brig. Gen. William H. French
1st Brigade, Brig. Gen. Nathan Kimball
   24th N.J.

George McClernan

James McClernan

2nd Brigade, Col. Oliver Palmer

14th Conn.

  Pvt. Augustus Foote

  Pvt. Benjamin Hirst

3rd Brigade, Col. John Andrews

10th N.Y. Zouaves

CENTER GRAND DIVISION
Maj. Gen. Joseph Hooker, Commanding

THIRD CORPS (To Franklin)
Brig. Gen. George Stoneman

1st Division, Brig. Gen David B. Birney
114th Pa. (Collis's Zouaves)
"French" Mary Tepe

2nd Division, Brig. Gen. Daniel E. Sickles

FIFTH CORPS
Brig. Gen. Daniel Butterfield

1st Division, Brig. Gen. Charles Griffin
1st Brigade, Col. James Barnes
  118th Pa. (Corn Exchange Regiment)
  Lt. Col. James Gwyn
  Capt. Francis A. Donaldson
  George Slow (Civilian)
3rd Brigade, Col. T. B. W. Stockton
  20th Maine
    Lt. Col. Joshua L. Chamberlain

3rd Division, Brig. Gen. Andrew A. Humphreys
2nd Brigade, Col. Oliver Palmer

LEFT GRAND DIVISION

Maj. Gen. Wiliam B. Franklin, Commanding

FIRST CORPS

Maj. Gen. John F. Reynolds, Commanding
Col. Charles Wainwright, Chief of Artillery

1st Division, Brig. Gen. Abner Doubleday

2nd Division, Brig. Gen. John Gibbon
1st Brigade, Col. Adrian Root
    16th Main (The Blanket Brigade)
      Lt. Will Stevens
      Sgt. Ned Stevens
2nd Brigade, Col. Peter Lyle
3rd Brigade, Brig. Gen. Nelson Taylor

3rd Division, Maj. Gen. George G. Meade
1st Brigade, Col. William Sinclair
    13th Pa. (The Buktails)
    2nd Pa.
      Lt. Evan Woodward
2nd Brigade, Col. Albert L. Magilton
3rd Brigade, Brig. Gen. C. Feger Jackson

ARMY OF NORTHERN VIRGINIA
Gen. Robert E. Lee, *Commanding*
Maj. Gen. J. E. B. Stuart, *commanding cavalry*
Maj. John Pelham, *cavalry artillery*
Jean, *cannoneer*

Lt. Col. Edward Porter Alexander, *Chief of Artillery*

The Washington (Louisiana) Artillery
Col. J. B. Walton, *Commanding*
Lt. Wiliam Miller Owen, *Adj.*

FIRST CORPS
Lt. Gen. James Longstreet, Commanding
Maj. Moxley Sorrel, Chief of Staff

McLaw's Division, Maj. Gen. Lafayette McLaws
Barksdale's Brigade, Brig. Gen. William Barksdale
Cobb's Brigade, Brig. Gen. T. R. R. Cobb
Kershaw's Brigade,
Brig. Gen. Joseph Kershaw
2nd S.C.
Sgt. Richard Kirkland

SECOND CORPS
Lt. Gen. Thomas J. Jackson, Commanding

A. P. Hill's Division
2nd Brigade, Brig. Gen. Maxcy Gregg
4th Brigade, Brig. Gen. J. H. Lane
5th Brigade, Brig. Gen. J. J. Archer
6th Brigade, Brig. Gen. William Dorsey Pender

Ewell's Division, Brig. Gen. Jubal Early,
Commanding

CIVILIANS

Jane Howison Beale
Martha Stephens
T. S. Barton
Clara Barton
Frederick O. Douglass

IN WASHINGTON

Salmon P. Chase, Secretary *of the Treasury*
Kate Chase (his daughter)
William H. Seward, *Secretary of State*
Edwin Stanton, *Secretary of War*
Brig. Gen. Herman Haupt, *Military Director of Railroads*
Gideon Welles, *Secretary of the Navy*
Maj. Gen. Henry Halleck, *General in Chief*
Senator Benjamin F. Wade *(R), Ohio*
Senator Charles Summer *(R), Massachusetts*
John Hay and John Nicolay, *Personal Secretaries to
    President Lincoln*

THE NEW YORK TRIBUNE

Horace Greeley, *Publisher*
George Smalley, *Editor*
Sydney Howard Gay, *Editor*
Henry Villard, *Special Correspondent*
Sam Wilkeson, *Washington Bureau Chief*

The preceding list is in no way intended to be a complete account of the units involved at the Battle of Fredericksburg. It is only a guide to help locate the major characters of my story. For a complete "Order of Battle" see *Fredericksburg! Fredericksburg!* by George Rabel.

For a picture gallery of Fredericksburg or to contact the author, go to www.rcroker.com.

PROLOGUE

"General Lee, sir."

"Yes, Colonel Taylor."

"We have confirmation, sir. General McClellan has been relieved."

"And with whom has he been replaced?"

"Reports indicate that it is General Burnside, sir."

Robert E. Lee looked at Longstreet and Stuart, both of whom were smiling. He shook his head and said, "I fear they may continue to make these changes till they find someone whom I don't understand."

He walked over to the large table set up in the middle of the room and examined his map intently for a while before speaking again. "General McClellan was not relieved due to incompetence, but inactivity. That means that General Burnside will be coming south—quickly and perhaps recklessly."

There was another silence while Lee mentally put himself in command of the Army of the Potomac and inside the mind of Ambrose Burnside. He considered his options and laid out all of the lines on the map—lines of communication and lines of supply and retreat and, most importantly, the lines of attack formed by all of the rivers, railroads, and roadways that could carry the Union army to Richmond.

"By some route or another, Richmond will be his target, gentlemen," he said. "The Northern press is pressuring Lincoln to take Richmond and he will pass that same pressure on to General Burnside." He sighed lightly, almost feeling sorry for the new Union commander. "He is a modest man and independent command will not come naturally to him. He will not be strong enough to resist. So we shall wait for him to tip his hand. General Stuart's cavalry will keep a close eye, reporting every movement of every corps. And whatever route he may choose, gentleman, we shall challenge him."

"He has options," Longstreet said.

"A few." Lee nodded. "He could come at us almost anywhere along this line." Lee drew the line on the map with his finger and looked up as everyone else looked down. "He could move against us here at Culpeper or Gordonsville or he could make a sprint directly south—along the shortest route—and try to surprise us by crossing the Rappahannock here . . . somewhere near Fredericksburg."

Accustomed to the textbook planning and cautious movements of the enemy under McClellan, no one in the room thought that to be a likely scenario, not even Lee.

"Gentlemen, General Burnside would love nothing more than a winter siege of Richmond." The unthinkable spoken. Each man had his own vision of the cruelty, the fevers, and the famine—the horror of Richmond racked with plague. "As improbable as it may sound, Fredericksburg is his shortest route to get there before the weather sets in and he must consider it, and if he considers it, then so must we."

They all studied the map with the images of a famished Richmond still fresh in their minds. "Well, General Longstreet, if all goes well it looks as though you could finally get your wish."

"And what wish is that, General Lee?"

"I distinctly remember you saying to me, 'I wish we could just let the Yankees come to us,' and an opportunity may present itself here that will require us to do just that."

Longstreet smiled. He remembered the occasion quite

well now. He remembered well enough to know that Lee had edited out the "damned" Yankees, but that wasn't all that brought on Pete's smile. He knew now that he might have the opportunity to prove that a defensive plan would win more battles than any number of reckless assaults. *Let's keep the army all together for once,* he thought.

Lee continued to think out loud. "If we pull back to the North Anna River line it will make little difference where they cross the Rappahannock." The words just hung in the air. It was not an order, everyone knew—only an option. "But we will wait for now until we know better what General Burnside has in mind."

The hour was late and Lee was tired. He needed to pray and to make just a single private moment to grieve for his beloved daughter Annie, just a month in the grave. The thought of Annie sent his heart out to Jeb Stuart as well, who had just learned last week of the passing of his own five-year-old daughter. Mrs. Stuart had come here to grieve with her husband and only last night she had wept on General Lee's shoulder. *It is all so very, very hard,* Lee thought. *And now, so soon, I need General Stuart more than ever before.*

"General Stuart, I know it is difficult for you, sir—no one knows *how* difficult better than General Longstreet and myself." Now it was Longstreet's turn to remember the three children he and his wife had lost last winter. "But I need you now, General, to report to me every movement of every division of the Union army. The slightest divergence may offer us the key we're looking for. For the moment General Jackson will continue to operate out of Winchester and General Longstreet out of Culpeper until we have some better notion as to Burnside's plan."

He saw Longstreet grimace but he brought his smile back very quickly. "When we know more, we will come together quickly, as it is my intention to meet him with every man, rifle, and gun we've got. He cannot be allowed to besiege Richmond—the capital would never survive."

On that ominous note the junior generals saluted and returned to their duties. Lee watched them go and looked back down at his map. His eyes went directly to Richmond and his heart quickly followed.

Mary's in Richmond. Into his mind came a heartbreaking image of his grieving wife mourning alone. And Mary was just one of many. *A siege cannot be allowed.* A thought? A prayer? At these times it's hard to tell the difference. The men will stop them. Not me. The men will do whatever we ask.

He prayed for courage as he took off his boots, and when his head finally touched the pillow, Annie came to him just as she had every night since God had taken her home— fresh and beautiful and vibrant and alive. He smiled sadly, he wept briefly, and then, at last, he slept.

CHAPTER 1

Honest Johnny Jones was Wes Brainerd's manservant and oddly enough this unassuming, toothless little Welshman had a voice that could wake an army, and on this particular day the voice was not a happy one.

"I'm not understanding it a lick, Captain. The Good Lord and Abraham Lincoln's got something in mind for these lovely bridges, but I'm thinking sittin' around in the mud don't suit neither of their purposes."

"Well, that's all General Burnside's problem now, Johnny. He's in charge."

"If anybody in this infernal army had the God's good sense to put you in charge then we might have some kind of notion where these bridges ought to be headed! It seems Ol' Sideburns went to the Little Mac School o' War. We waited two months for McClellan to tell us to go nowhere and do nothin,' and now Burnside's givin' the same damned orders." Johnny puffed himself up like a make-believe Caesar shouting commands for the legions. "'Look you now! Muck around in the mud for a bit and we'll holler for you right *after* we needs ya.'"

Wes Brainerd loved Johnny Jones. He was worth his salary for the entertainment value alone. "Congratulations on your promotion, General Jones. That is precisely what we shall do until told otherwise. And speaking of promotions, I think *Major* Spaulding deserves a cigar."

"*Major* Spaulding, indeed . . ."

Brainerd put up his hand and stopped Johnny in mid-sentence. "Save it for another time, Johnny. Right now I need to go over and congratulate Ira."

He put on his coat and braved the snow to give his old friend a pat on the back.

"Well, *Major* Spaulding, you don't look any less confused to me than Captain Spaulding did but congratulations anyway."

"Thanks, Wes—I guess. It's not official yet." It was just a bit of an uncomfortable moment for Spaulding since both men knew the promotion should rightfully have gone to Brainerd. Spaulding considered broaching the subject but right now he had slightly more pressing issues. "Looks like we're packing up our bridges and heading off to Washington—finally."

He handed Brainerd the orders that had just been delivered.

"Ouch."

"What?"

"Did you notice the date?"

"I was just handed them a minute before you came in. What's the date?"

Brainerd handed the orders back and pointed to the very top line.

Spaulding blinked a couple of times and shook his head. "November 6? That's almost a week ago!"

"Yeah—and a week ago McClellan was still in command."

Spaulding continued to blink while he considered all the ramifications. Jeb Stuart and his cavalry were doing too good a job of taking down the telegraph lines and keeping them down, so there was no good way to get quick confirmation.

"Well, the orders are old and they come from a guy who just got fired, but other than that they seem sound."

Brainerd laughed but the joke wasn't intended. "Seriously, Wes, the army is entirely in Virginia now. There's little chance that Burnside has any plans to move back into Maryland, so the bridges are not likely to be needed here.

The war is moving south and we need refitting. Hell, there's not a fit horse left in the herd, and if Washington's not where we need to be, it's sure as hell on the way."

"Well thought out, *Major* Spaulding! With a little hard work we can put some miles behind us before the sun sets."

WASHINGTON, D.C.

"I can't tell you how long I stood at the bottom of those stairs, Sam." Henry Villard signaled the bar boy for another round. The *New York Tribune*'s Washington office was ever-so-conveniently located directly across the street from the Willard Hotel, where the chairs at the bar were much more comfortable.

"Whoa! Not for me, Henry!"

"You're getting soft, Sam. Washington Bureau chiefdom is making you citified. I remember when Sam Wilkeson could out-drink Sam Grant!"

"More than Grant maybe, but never more than, what is it, Ferdinand Heinrich Gustav Whatever-the-hell-your-name-used-to-be."

Villard laughed. "Hilgard and I regret the day I ever told you that." The drinks came and Wilkeson accepted his just as though he had never considered refusing it. "Why in hell would I tell my most closely guarded personal secret to a reporter?"

"*Dummkopf,* maybe?"

"*Dummkopf—ja.* Anyway, I can't tell you how long I stood there because I don't know."

"I've stood there too. We all have. Climbing up those steps to Greeley's office is like climbing into hell."

"Yeah—at least you get to *fall* into hell—at the *Tribune* they make you *climb*! Sam, I rode into Rebel artillery fire at Perryville without a second thought, but I was scared piss-less to climb those damned steps."

"That's because you'd rather get fired *at* than get fired." Grins from both men.

"*Var.*" The beers were taking their toll on Villard, and exhaustion, elation, anger, or drunkenness sometimes caused him to lapse back into German. "I mean, 'true.'"

"They very well might have fired you that day. The old man was humiliated at having to reprint the *Gazette* story about Shiloh in the *Trib*." Wilkeson sipped his whiskey. Villard gulped his beer.

"Lost in the mail. I couldn't hop on a horse and 'spur' my way to New York like Smalley did after Antietam."

"He spurred a horse for a minute and then he spurred a train for the rest of the trip."

"And he'll be more than happy to tell you about it too."

"What was it like at Shiloh, Henry? Was it as bad as they say? Was it as bad as Bull Run?"

"Sam, you really need to get back into the war. Bull Run—First Bull Run—was a goddamned picnic! Our soldiers ran at Bull Run because they could! We had the river at our backs at Shiloh. We couldn't run. And the Rebels just kept on coming!"

"How did Grant do? Really?"

"Great story. Cool as a cucumber. They say Sherman told him after the first day, 'We had the devil's own day today, Sam,' and Grant just shook his head and said, 'We'll lick 'em tomorrow.'"

"And he did."

"But he wouldn't have if Halleck hadn't showed up."

"Halleck. That may be the best example ever of winning the battle and losing the war. Rewarded for just showing up at Shiloh and now he's the damned general in chief of the whole damned army. Your boy Abe may have really messed up there."

Villard didn't like it much when folks blamed Lincoln for things, but Wilkeson might be right this time. He ignored the comment and went on with his story.

"'Shiloh' means 'Place of Peace.' Maybe the greatest irony in the history of the world." Another gulp of beer. "It was a brutal fight there, Sam, and then they were all just left on the field. Dead and wounded, Rebels and Yanks all mixed together, piled on top of each other. I went to the church after the battle and the pews had all been torn out and there were dead and wounded Rebels just lying there, officers and men just groaning and crying and waiting to die. Not a doctor anywhere. All the doctors were taking care of our guys and any Rebels they found were just piled in this little church. 'Shiloh.' "

The memories got mixed up with the beer and Villard just couldn't stop talking. Wilkeson, good reporter that he was, had no intention of interrupting.

"But it didn't stop there, Sam. That wasn't the worst of it. Those bodies at least were still warm and looked human." Another wave at the bar boy. Villard was going to need another beer—or two—before he could screw up the courage even to remember, much less repeat, all he had seen. Wilkeson stayed as quiet as a sleeping rabbit just waiting for Villard to get on with it.

"I've seen murder, Sam. The Rebs captured this wounded man riding in an ambulance and they just shot him to death in his sleep. Hell, I've seen one of *our* generals murder *another* one of our generals standing in the lobby of a hotel in Louisville! I've seen wanton destruction of farms and families. A kid shot a Union soldier who was taking a pee and then got away, so we burned the nearest farm, stole their cattle, and confiscated their slaves. Women and children left behind just to starve to death. But even that's not the worst."

The drinks came—and went—very quickly.

"Let me tell you about Perryville."

"Please do."

"That wasn't a battle for the Union or for emancipation or for anything else 'political.' Perryville was about water. It was hot and dry, like a desert—there's a horrible drought going on in Kentucky now, and people on both sides were dying of thirst. Literally. And there was this damned dirty little creek there. Ten drunk Germans could have pissed more water than this damned little stream had in it. But we had it and they wanted it. They took it and we took it back. Some little Irish squirt of a general named Sheridan rallied the men and sent 'em back in and took it back, but I'll tell you this, Sam, when men are fighting for water, they fight like hell. Now it's a personal fight between me and you and that makes men mean! So, anyway, the Rebs moved out that same night. Buell didn't have the heart, or the guts—or the water—to chase 'em very far and just gave up after a week. So I headed back for Louisville."

The lobby of the Willard Hotel was filling up now, but neither of the *Tribune* reporters paid any attention, either too drunk or too engrossed in the story to notice.

"It was on this ride, Sam, that I saw things that no man on this earth should ever have to look at. I *smelled* it before I saw it. It was the smell that made me pull off of the road and go looking. Had to put a wet 'kerchef' over my face to keep from throwing up. There were bodies lying on this field that had been there for over a week—in the sun. All Rebels. Must have been fifty of 'em."

He didn't look at Wilkeson any more but stared into his nearly empty beer glass as he finished the story. "Did you hear what I said? 'All Rebels.' That means they had cleared our boys off and buried them and had just left the Rebels there to rot in the sun. They were black and bloated. Some of 'em were swollen up to three times the size of a normal man." He had to stop when the sickening images returned to his mind. He took a deep breath and drained his glass before going on. "And there were pigs, Sam. More pigs than corpses."

Wilkeson thought he was going to lose whatever was in his stomach because he knew what was coming.

"The pigs were . . ."

"Don't tell me, Henry!" Sam looked at his friend and thought he saw tears. "Don't tell me, Henry. I don't want to hear it."

"Thank you, Sam. I don't want to tell it either."

A long silence. Even though the room was now full and raucous, neither man heard a sound. When the silence became awkward, Sam finally said, "You never finished telling me about your meeting with Greeley."

"And Gay and Smalley."

"George was there too?"

"Yeah. *He's* had enough, he said. George Smalley can't bear the thought of looking at another dead man. So, instead of firing me, they gave me Smalley's job." The irony wasn't wasted on either man. "*He* can't look at another corpse, so they hired me. I guess because I'm a German I'm supposed to be immune to this shit."

"How did they talk you into it?"

"They offered me a raise, and a three-man staff, and a title—but none of that was the reason I took it."

"Why did you?"

"My dispatch from Shiloh was lost in the mail, Sam, and my reputation was lost along with it. I've got to catch up with the Army of the Potomac and get it back."

CULPEPER
NOVEMBER 13
9 A.M.

The handwritten fliers were posted throughout the camp, escaping the notice of absolutely no one—including James Longstreet.

"What the hell is the 'Literary and Dramatic Association'?"

Moxley Sorrel read the fine print for his general. "The Washington Artillery, that New Orleans outfit, is having a literary reading tonight." Sorrel performed grand gestures, doing his best impersonation of a bad Shakespearian actor. It was just good enough to make Longstreet laugh and, for Sorrel, that was good enough. Old Pete's notorious sense of humor hadn't survived the loss of his children.

"Is that what's going on over on the other side of the hill?" Longstreet asked.

"Think so, sir. They're building an amphitheater out of logs and blankets."

Odd, Longstreet thought, *but good, clean fun—and good for morale when boredom is their worst enemy.*

Sorrel was amused. "I'll tell you what, sir—people from Louisiana seem to be either pirates or poets and nothing in between."

"Or priests," Longstreet added. "But when the shooting starts they all fight like hell."

"My guess is that they're gonna have a big turnout tonight."

"How's that?"

Sorrel pointed at the big print at the bottom of the flier: " 'Big fire.' They'll show up for the fire."

"Might have to drop by myself." Longstreet smiled. "My literary education is wanting a bit—and my feet are cold."

WARRENTON

Most of the businesses in Warrenton were boarded up. The residents, those who hadn't fled south to escape the humiliation of Union occupation, ventured out from their homes only occasionally to search for rare scraps of food or firewood or to tend the hallowed grounds of the Confederate cemetery. As for the occupiers, the army's supply lines were so broken down that even the short jaunt from Washington proved impossible, and the valiant soldiers of the *Grand Armée* had become little more than a gigantic band of petty thieves, stealing anything that might be killed and cooked just to feed themselves for one more day. Buildings were being pulled apart one plank at a time to make coffins for the dozens of men who died every day from dysentery or the fever.

They called it "Camp Death."

One look at this dilapidated, depressing, well-guarded ghost town and all Henry Halleck wanted was to get back on the train and head back to Washington, but the general in chief took his orders directly from President Lincoln and he had a job to do. His orders were to help Burnside pick a plan, kick him hard in the pants, and send him on his speedy way. After two futile months of pushing, prodding, pleading, and flat out ordering George McClellan to pursue the Rebels after Antietam, the administration was bound and determined that their new commanding general would do as he was told and attack, attack, and attack again without question or complaint until Robert E. Lee's Army of Northern Virginia was totally destroyed. Now.

On this night a single Rebel artillery round fired into the lobby of the Warrenton Hotel would have mutilated the entire command structure of the Army of the Potomac as every man with a blue coat, a gold star, and a tablespoon of ambition in the whole state of Virginia had gathered there to kiss General Halleck's pompous butt. Especially those who wanted Burnside's job—which was most of them.

Halleck was the major topic of conversation on this night. One group might be saying that his books on strategy and military history were still in publication and used at West Point, or that his "victories" in the West were about the only bright spot in the whole damned war. Two steps to the right and the conversation might revolve around how every army in the country, East and West, had ground to a halt under his "leadership." The general consensus was that this soft and balding little man was a top-notch scholar and a second-rate general.

Edwin Sumner stood alone in a corner and neither gossiped nor eavesdropped. Two months away from his sixty-sixth birthday, he had served in the army since 1819 and was already a major when Burnside was a West Point plebe. He commanded one of Burnside's brand-new "Grand Divisions"—two corps lumped together to cut down on the number of people who reported directly to the commanding general. Even though he commanded nearly forty thousand men, it seemed like people of all ranks wanted to avoid being seen with him. He was the senior man in the whole damned army but the papers had crucified him after Antietam. "Cautious" they called him. Cautious—of all things! He fumed at the very thought of it. *That damned* New York Tribune *ought to be burned to the ground with Horace Greeley in it!* The papers had no idea how many Rebels had been hiding in those damned woods and Sumner knew it first damned hand. He had marched an entire division right into the heart of 'em and lost over three thousand men in fifteen minutes! *Cautious, my ass*.

His forty-four years of gallant service against the Mexicans, against the Indians, and against the Rebels at Seven Pines had all been forgotten in fifteen disastrous minutes. His impeccable reputation for courage and tenacity, built up over a lifetime, was torn down and lay in ruins near a churchyard in Sharpsburg, Maryland. The strain of it showed plainly on the proud man's face. In the two months since Antietam he had lost weight that he could ill afford to lose. His face was drawn and his beard had bleached itself from salt and pepper to solid white, all in the matter of a handful of weeks. The man they called "Bull" was, at last, showing his age.

Glancing across the room Sumner noticed that Hooker had sidled up next to Halleck closer than a jealous wife in a room full of camp followers. It almost looked as though the two men didn't hate each other. There was no doubt in Sumner's mind that Hooker had been responsible for the newspaper articles. Just the kind of thing Joe would do. The man would shoot his mother in the back and kiss the devil on his fiery butt for just one day in command of the Army of the Potomac. *"Fightin' Joe,"* my ass, Sumner thought. The papers were responsible for that too.

Right now all Sumner wanted was to get up next to Burnside to plead his case just one more time. He knew that before long the "excess personnel" would be ushered out of the room leaving only Burnside, Halleck, and the other Washington boys. General Meigs, the quartermaster general, and Brigadier General Herman Haupt, the Military Director of Railroads, were in Halleck's entourage and would be included in the inner sanctum, but the riffraff of grand division commanders and other lesser beings would soon be dismissed like women after dinner. Tonight the plan of attack would be determined and Sumner wanted to have a say. Even though he and Burnside had discussed it at length, he wanted to push it just one last time but Burnside was never left alone. As the hour grew late, Sumner grew desperate for just one word—literally "one word"—with his old friend and new commander. Finally, as the lesser men began to ease their ways out the door, Sumner made eye contact and managed to mouth that all-important single word.

"Fredericksburg" he said and Burnside nodded. Sumner felt better. He had a war to win—and a reputation to salvage.

As he rode back to his own headquarters, his head was filled with the Fredericksburg plan. McClellan would never have been able to make it work, Burnside might. Mac would have arrived at a leisurely pace, giving Lee plenty of time to get there first and lie in wait. Then he would have sent the army into battle one corps at a time—just as he had at Antietam—one after another in pathetic little driblets. But McClellan was gone and, with rivers and railroads to keep them supplied, a swift and massive assault directly into the heart of the rebellion would finally get this damned war over with. Fredericksburg. Swift and massive. Then, finally, on to Richmond.

Cautious, my ass.

BOSTON, MASSACHUSETTS

"The Emancipation Proclamation is newspaper fodder—and nothing more!"

Henry Abbott had never seen his old friend so perturbed, and that was saying something because Oliver Wendell Holmes, Jr., was perpetually perturbed. He had grown up in the shadow of one of Massachusetts's most prominent men and, like father, like son, nothing got him more riled up than good, old-fashioned politics. As for "Little" Abbott, nothing gave *him* more pleasure than infuriating Oliver Wendell Holmes the Younger.

"But, Holmes, old boy, aren't you one of our state's foremost abolitionists?"

"Yes, of course. 'Emancipation is the demand of civilization. All else is intrigue.' "

Abbott could hear the quotation marks.

"Ah—the universe according to Uncle Waldo." He knew that would get Holmes even more fired up.

"*Professor Emerson.* And don't ridicule him, Little. He is a tribute to Harvard University."

Abbott didn't much care for his nickname, but he too had grown up in the shadow of a great man, and every gentleman in Massachusetts continued to call him what his daddy called him. So "Little" it was and "Little" it would always be. "But isn't the President doing exactly what 'Professor Emerson' suggests? Isn't he freeing the slaves?"

"He has freed *no one*! What do you think the Southern states are going to do? Bow down and say 'Yes, sir, Mister Lincoln. Whatever you say, sir.' "

Holmes was so agitated by now that only the rocking of the train kept him in his seat. "And the Border States get to *keep* their slaves! Slavery is an insult to humanity no matter *where* it exists!" He patted the holster containing his pistol. "But *this* is the tool of emancipation, Little—this and an amendment to the Constitution—*not* some weak and unconstitutional proclamation!"

Holmes was on the verge of an apoplectic fit and Little Abbott couldn't keep the smile off his face. "You sound like Horace Greeley. I'm surprised your daddy hasn't taken you out back and whipped you like a borrowed mule!"

Both men laughed. They hadn't seen each other since before Antietam and had some serious catching up to do. Abbott had missed the fight—down with typhoid fever—and Holmes had dodged death by less than an inch when a Rebel bullet grazed his neck during Sumner's disaster in the West Woods, only a stone's throw from the Dunker Church.

They were old friends, these two young captains. Harvard graduates. Both from the upper tier of the Boston aristocracy. Both could trace family lines back to Revolutionary War heroes. There was no bluer blood in Boston than the Abbotts's and the Holmes's, but their personal brotherhood was much deeper than that by now. Both had been with the 20th Massachusetts since the very first call-up. Holmes had enlisted filled with the patriotic zeal of the day and was off to free the slaves, while Abbott was more concerned with "what people would think" if he *didn't* enlist. The 20th Mass. quickly became known as the "Harvard Regiment" because so many of its officers were graduates. The regiment had seen its first action in October of '61. They had ferried across the Potomac in clumsy pontoons, climbed a cliff known as Ball's Bluff, and found what seemed to be the whole damned Rebel army waiting for them in the bushes. Holmes was one of the first to fall with a bullet to the chest. They fought well for as long as they could, but when it came time to retreat, they had nowhere to go. Their only option had been to tumble back down the cliff to where the Rebs just sat on the ridge shooting down on them like wounded ducks on a pond. In an absolute panic hundreds of men from other platoons plunged into the currents of the Potomac, where many of them drowned. Thanks to Little Abbott that was not the plight of his men. He had stood his ground well that day and retreated in good order. When he found his platoon trapped on the shoreline, he ruled out the Potomac as an escape route and moved his men safely upstream where they found a tiny boat at an abandoned mill. From there he rowed his men to safety five at a time.

His next major engagement was on the Peninsula, where he took a bullet to the arm and refused to abandon his men. The boy who had been afraid of what people might say had grown to be a man who was afraid of nothing.

After Antietam, Holmes had returned to Boston to recover from his wounds and Abbott, likewise, to recuperate from the fever. But both were better now and en route to Virginia to rejoin the Harvard Regiment and to fight another day.

The train ride from Boston to Washington was taking forever, but that was okay because Holmes was a man who could *talk* forever—his Antietam neck wound notwithstanding.

"If it's not all about slavery, then it's about nothing at all."

Holmes was winding down, and Little couldn't allow that. It just wasn't in his nature. "The irony is that our President says that he's fighting to preserve the Constitution, and then he abolishes habeas corpus with the stroke of a pen!"

And Oliver Wendell Holmes, Jr., was off again on another political diatribe.

WARRENTON

"I must first say again that I believe that President Lincoln has made a serious error in appointing me to this position. I did not seek . . ."

"General Burnside . . ." Halleck was already in a bad frame of mind and in no mood to hear again about the general's reticence. ". . . your modesty is well known, and even refreshing, but you have been given command of this army, you have accepted that command, and now, sir, it is time for you to *assume* command. We are here to hear your plans, so please, let's get on with it."

"This plan is generally General McClellan's, with a few

significant changes, and portions of it have already been put in motion," Burnside announced. "We shall steal a march on General Lee, move this entire army to Falmouth in under three days, and cross the river there into Fredericksburg . . ."

Haupt interrupted. "It was my impression that McClellan abandoned that plan when I informed him that the O&A Railroad would be insufficient to supply the army."

Meigs nodded. "That was my understanding as well."

Halleck couldn't believe what he was hearing. "Gentlemen! In the event that any of you may not have gotten the word, General McClellan is no longer in command of this army! General Burnside is!"

His outburst stunned the room. "Now, if you please, we have before us a new commanding general, a clean sheet of paper, and we must come away from here with an effective plan of attack. The President favors an assault on Culpeper."

The three Washington insiders all looked to Burnside and waited for him to speak as though he had just returned from Mount Sinai armed with tablets from God. He decided to stick with what he knew.

"Fredericksburg is the shortest route from where we are to where we need to be. Lee's army is divided and we can easily feint toward Culpeper to hold him precisely where he is while we make a rapid forced march to Falmouth, cross the Rappahannock there into Fredericksburg, and move quickly against Richmond from there."

"I will tell you the same thing I told Geo—" Haupt stopped himself in mid-'George.' ". . . the same thing I told the previous commanding general, that the O&A Railroad is not adequate to furnish even half of the supplies your army will require."

"I have anticipated that, General Haupt, and have ordered that the docks at Aquia Creek be fully reconstructed so that we will be able to supply the army over water. I understand that the rail lines between there and Falmouth are in acceptable working order."

The railroad man nodded. "They can be made so."

From that moment forward, the flow of the conversation never veered too far away from Fredericksburg. For every argument against it, Burnside had an answer. He knew the routes each of his new grand divisions would follow. He had planned for winter quarters should the weather halt the movement. He even had plans to supply the army between Fredericksburg and Richmond. There was only one detail left missing.

"General Halleck. It is my understanding that the pontoon bridges have moved from Harpers Ferry to Washington."

Halleck shrugged his shoulders.

On this point Burnside needed to be certain. With no way to cross the Rappahannock the whole plan would be futile. "Orders were issued by General McClellan a week ago, so I must assume they have been in Washington for some time now, but the wires around Harpers Ferry have been down and I have been unable to get verification. We shall need those pontoon trains at Falmouth at the earliest possible moment, sir. Enough bridges to span the Rappahannock twice."

"Very well."

"Will you see to that for me, General Halleck?"

"I shall send you the pontoons, General Burnside. We shall send out the orders tonight. But make no movement until the plan is approved by the President. I will meet with him in the morning and will notify you of his decision."

"Very well, General, but I will *need* those pontoons."

11:30 P.M.

The engineers had spent the better part of the day poling their pontoons down the C&O Canal from Harpers Ferry toward Washington. The water in the canal was roofed with a not-so-thin sheet of ice and the going was agonizingly slow. With total darkness they finally halted for the night and Private Billy Blakesley huddled under one of the pontoon boats that had been pulled from the canal for repairs and was leaning against a tree. The poor boy was frozen to the core of his spine. His boots leaked and his socks were wet and he had no gloves at all. The feeling in his fingers and toes had been gone for hours and his cheap excuse for a government blanket seemed cleverly designed to let heat out and water in. His teeth chattered con-

stantly as a brutal night wind angrily spat frozen pellets of
rain into his face. The ground beneath his boat was ice on
top with mud beneath but at least he had a roof and some
solitude where he could be miserable alone. He drew his
knees up to his chin to try to warm himself and cursed the
road that had led him to this place. Only two months in the
50th New York Volunteer Engineers and Billy wanted to
go home, curl up in front of his daddy's fire, and pretend that
he had never been so stupid as to enlist in the army. He tried
desperately to feel the warmth of his imaginary fire while
he fumed about all the lies he'd been told.

This ain't the war the papers are fighting, he whimpered
to himself. Lyin' damned New York Republican bastards.
Save the Union! Free the Slaves! They didn't say Freeze to
Death! Starve to Death! It's the Rebels they said who are
freezing to death—marching barefooted and surviving on
hardtack and coffee. The recrutin' guy had said the Army of
the Potomac was the "best supplied army in the history of
the world." Another lie. Pity all those *other* poor bastards.
Damn. *We don't even* have *coffee and even if we did there's
not a stick of dry firewood within a hundred miles of here*.

He hated being cold; he hated being away from home; he
hated the army already; and he hadn't even been shot at yet.
There's the good part, he thought. At least nobody shoots at
engineers. We build our floating bridges, watch the army
march across them, and then we tear them down again.
We're as wet and cold and lonesome as everybody else, but
at least nobody shoots at us.

Somewhere during the night exhaustion finally over-
came the cold. He had no idea how long he had managed
to sleep before the Welsh brogue of Honest Johnny Jones
woke him up.

"I'll be telling' ya this, Mr. Brainerd, sir, those major's
leafs is rightfully yours."

Billy almost forgot the cold feet and muddy clothes for a
moment. He had to smile at Johnny's accent and his total
devotion to Captain Brainerd. This man genuinely believed
that if Wesley Brainerd of Rome, New York, were given
command of the Army of the Potomac that the war would
be over tomorrow.

"The oak leaves belong to Major Spaulding, Johnny, and mine'll be along shortly."

"If there's a God in heaven, sir."

Billy began to feel more than just a little bit guilty for eavesdropping and decided it was time to let his presence be known. He tried to crawl out from under the pontoon and his hand slipped on a patch of icy mud sending him sliding face-first against Brainerd's boots. Trying to stand up and snap to attention before his surprised commanding officer only made matters worse as his feet slid out from under him and little Billy Blakesley sat flat on his cold, muddy butt and saluted as best as he could.

"What the . . . ? Who the hell are you?"

"Billy Blakesley, sir. Private, Bill . . ."

"Where's your goddamned coat, Private?"

"Coat, sir? They never gave me no coat, sir."

"Goddamn those fat-ass quartermaster sons of bitches!"

Brainerd grabbed the startled private by the back of the neck, helped him to his feet, and stormed up the hill to the nice warm house where the officers and some of the sergeants slept. He virtually broke down the door with his foot and headed straight for the regimental quartermaster, who had just dozed off after a hard day's work. Brainerd grabbed the sergeant's coat that he was using for a blanket and threw it at Blakesley.

"*That* coat now belongs to *that man,* and you'll not have another of your own until every soldier in the 50th New York is as warm as a mother's hug! Do you understand me, Sergeant?"

"I, ah."

"Do you *understand* me?"

"Ah, yes, sir."

"Very well. Now, Johnny . . ." The Welshman beamed with pride at his employer's outburst. ". . . get this man a hot cup of coffee and a warm bath—and I'm sure the quartermaster here won't mind rustling up a dry uniform."

CHAPTER 2

WASHINGTON, D.C.
NOVEMBER 14

Lincoln examined Halleck's map thoroughly and tried to figure out why he had such a bad feeling about Burnside's new plan. It was similar to the plan he had recommended to McClellan a month or more ago. He remembered asking McClellan why the most direct route was not the best. Why could our army not march faster down the "cord" of the circle than Lee could march around the "arc"? Yes, even though it was basically what he had tried for a month to get the "Young Napoleon" to do, Lincoln studied the idea with a sense of foreboding that he simply could not explain.

"McClellan had objections about the 'vulnerable' and extended supply lines."

"General Burnside believes he can supply the army over water by using the facilities at Aquia Landing."

"Do you agree?"

"If the rails are in working order from there to Falmouth, I believe he can."

"Can he steal a march on Lee and arrive at Fredericksburg ahead of him?"

"He believes he can."

The President tried again to put his finger on the problem that plagued him but he could not. "*He* believes he can. Do you?"

"It's possible, I suppose. Weather permitting."

"But *he* believes he can steal a march on Lee. I have to say, that is more than a little bit refreshing. McClellan sat in the mud for a month telling me every day why he *couldn't*."

Lincoln closed his eyes and took in a deep breath and held it for a moment before slowly letting it out. "Very well, General Halleck. I do not want to stifle General Burnside's enthusiasm at the very outset. It's the very thing we've been lacking. Wire General Burnside that he has my approval but that he must move quickly in order to be successful. Otherwise . . ." He didn't finish the sentence. He didn't have to.

I P.M.

Henry Villard had met Lincoln on several occasions over the years. He had reported on the famous debates with Steven Douglas back when Moses was a child. On their first meeting he and Lincoln were standing on a train platform when a cloudburst chased them both into an empty freight car parked nearby. They had spent the better part of an hour together that day. Lincoln told him that Mary had much more faith in his ability to govern than Lincoln himself did. "I'm not quite as certain that I'm qualified to be a senator as she is." Lincoln had laughed out loud on that day when he told Villard that Mary wanted him to be President. "My highest office has been one term in Congress! And she wants me to run for President!"

But now the man *was* President and Villard decided it was time to renew old acquaintances. A walk up the stairs and a knock on the door was all that it took. Lincoln didn't recognize him at first, but when reminded of the freight car story he remembered quite well. "And you're the man who wrote that report on the army in the West that was in the *Tribune* the other day!"

"I am."

"Well then, please do come in and have a seat! Did I do well in relieving Buell?"

"Well, Mr. President, but late."

"That seems to be the way of things these days. He seemed to be such an astute military man."

"Perhaps too astute."

For half an hour they talked about the army in the West and its erstwhile commander. Villard explained that Buell was a textbook tactician but that the Rebels had thrown that book away long ago. He told the President that the reports of Buell being a States Righter at heart and unenthusiastic about the Union were false but that it was true that he adamantly opposed the Emancipation Proclamation.

"Not a surprise there," Lincoln said. "It's easier to find teats on a bull than to find a supporter of the proclamation in our army. Now, tell me about Rosecrans and the others."

"I suppose Rosecrans may surprise me, but I believe Grant may be your man in the West when all is said and done."

"Does he drink as much as they say?"

"He drinks when he's bored, Mr. President, but he's never bored when his army is on the move."

"So, if I keep him moving he'll keep himself dry?"

"I believe that to be so, Mr. President."

Villard had come here to grill Lincoln about the Army of the Potomac and ended up *being* grilled instead, but he couldn't stop it. The conversation moved like a river and he was powerless to change its course. Finally, and far too soon, Lincoln stood and began to usher the reporter out the door while he asked, "Where to from here?"

"The Army of the Potomac. As soon as I can get passes."

"Very good, Henry," and then with a big smile and a too hard slap on the back, "Come and see me again after you've had time to scrutinize *those* men!" And with that Henry Villard found himself standing in the hallway looking at a closed door. He was so exasperated that he just stood there trying to figure out what had just happened.

I came here to get information from him! *That's my job!*

He shook his head in disbelief and then smiled to himself. *That man is a natural-born reporter.*

WASHINGTON, D.C.
8 P.M.

Brigadier General Daniel Woodbury was astounded when he looked up to see Ira Spaulding standing before him, hat in hand, and looking for all the world like he'd lost a fistfight in a mud hole. His uniform was caked with nearly dry muck and he could barely stand at attention.

"Well—report, Major."

"We're here, sir, and in bad need of refitting."

"Are you aware of the fact that you were ordered to Falmouth two days ago?"

Spaulding almost fell over. "Falmouth, sir? I just got orders day before yesterday to come here!"

"Well, you're ordered to Falmouth now. I got two telegrams from Burnside already today. Not *one,* but *two*! Both of them asked *where* you were and *when* you'll be there. So, when can you move out?"

Spaulding was dazed by now. They had sat in Harpers Ferry and Berlin doing nothing for a month and had begun to think the army had forgotten they were there. Then a week-old order sent them scurrying to Washington only to find out they weren't supposed to be there at all, but fifty miles south.

Goddamned army, he thought. *All I want is a hot bath, some old Scotch, and a clean bed at the Willard Hotel, and I'm being told it's time to move out.*

"Major?" Woodbury thought Spaulding had fallen asleep standing. "When can you move out?"

"Sir, we don't have any horses! We don't have any wagons. We don't have any food for the men *or* for the horses if we *did* have any horses—which we *don't*!"

Woodbury felt sick. The absolute last thing he wanted to do was march himself into Halleck's office and inform him of yet another delay, but that was exactly what he was going to have to do.

"Very well, Major. Place your pontoons in depot, get some goddamned horses, and report back here tomorrow. In the meantime, I'll go and get yelled at by the general in chief."

WARRENTON
NOVEMBER 15
4:30 A.M.

It was well before first light when the Irish Brigade formed up, ready to bid farewell to the mud/hellhole of Warrenton, Virginia. Friendships were beginning to take hold in the new 116th Pennsylvania, and by now Bill McCarter was inseparable from the sergeant everyone called "Stretch." His name was Stretchbok and they called him Stretch and that's all there was to it. For all the Irish Brigade knew he had no first name. Heck—he'd been "Stretch" for so long that even *he* might not be able to recall his real name.

When they had first met, the odd-sounding name had caught McCarter's attention just as it did everyone else's. But Stretch had a standard and well-rehearsed response to anyone who questioned him about it. Always with a smile wider than the Allegheny he'd say, "My name is Stretchbok and my people are from Germany. I live in Pennsylvania where the folks there call us 'Dutch,' and I've joined up with the Irish to free the Africans, and if that ain't America in a nutshell, then I don't know what the hell is."

Stretch and McCarter were the 116th in microcosm. A burley, brash German and a frail, genuine son of Erin. Born in Derry, Ireland, McCarter's brogue was doubly difficult for Stretch to understand because of the stammer that had plagued the young Irishman all his life. This was the 116th—Ireland and Germany come together to fight for America, and they couldn't wait for their very first brawl.

As prescribed by a military tradition a thousand years old, the 116th stood around for three or four hours before they finally moved out.

"Warrenton is a lovely sight—when you're l-looking *backward* at it!"

Stretch did just that. He turned and looked back at Warrenton and gave the town a crisp, one-fingered salute. "And so we bid *adieu* to you, Mudville, and to all of the lovely, gentle ladies of Southern lore."

"Gentle ladies, my Irish arse. N-n-nothin' but a foul-mouthed horde of secessionist m-murderers if you're askin' me."

"Foul-mouthed whats?"

"I said 'hordes' lad. But now that you mention it, I was givin' 'em the b-benefit of the doubt."

RAPPAHANNOCK STATION

James Longstreet's corps was stretched out along the upper Rappahannock River from Rappahannock Station northward to Warrington Springs, and early on this cold November morning Union artillery opened at key points all along that fifty-mile front.

The day wasn't old before the reports of skirmishing began to filter into Longstreet's headquarters at Culpeper Courthouse. All indications were that this would be Burnside's target, but Lee and Longstreet both knew that indications lied. Lee had proven himself to be a master of such deceptions at Second Manassas, and neither he nor Longstreet was about to fall for any of their own tricks.

Longstreet knew, of course, that there was still a chance that Burnside was *not* bluffing; that the entire Army of the Potomac might be massing to pour over his pitiful little corps, through Culpeper and directly on to Richmond, but only if Burnside had become a believer in the Gospel according to John Pope—to hell with lines of supply and communication and retreat—if that had happened, then Culpeper might well be the real target. But while none of that was likely, it was still possible, so orders were sent to the rearguard as well—just in case: *Be ready for battle at a moment's notice. Officers, take care of your men. Soldiers, obey. Take good aim. Keep steady in your ranks.*

WASHINGTON, D.C.
7:30 P.M.

Salmon Chase smiled across the crowded room at his beautiful daughter. Of all the things Chase hated, paying for Kate's dresses ranked high on the list—until he saw her in one. Then the pain went away. His beautiful little girl was the queen of Washington City and she absolutely dressed the part. Tonight the gown matched her eyes and her jewelry matched her gown, which revealed just enough cleavage to attract attention without creating a disturbance.

Kate was frustrated that their residence was humble compared to where they were headed, but that was no reason for the entertainments to be any less lavish. Her parties were smaller but always far more elegant than the garish and tawdry backwoodsy events Mrs. Lincoln hosted. If Kate knew anything, it was how to give a party. She knew how to dress, who to invite, what to serve, and where to direct the conversations. Her schooling had begun in the governor's mansion back in Ohio when her daddy was chief executive there and she had served as the adolescent First Lady of the Buckeye State. She now used this respite between elective offices to buff and polish her skills for the time when they would be most needed, for the time when she and her father would move the ten blocks from 6th and E to 16th and Pennsylvania.

Her father was being wholly wasted as Secretary of the Treasury and everybody in town knew it. Mostly it was Seward's fault. The Secretary of State had *become* Lincoln's cabinet. The other secretaries were nothing more than bureaucrat errand boys. Seward and Lincoln would dine together, tell jokes, and sneak off for God-only-knows how many private meetings. That is where policy is decided; between courses at dinner at Seward's house. The cabinet meetings were few and far between and most often used to announce decisions already made by Lincoln and Seward. This is why McClellan had been able to hang on for so long. It is why the Emancipation Proclamation was so laughably weak and it is why the Republicans had taken such a horrible beating in the November elections, and she knew it was all Seward's fault. All that is wrong is Seward's fault. All that is holding her daddy back is William Henry Seward and Seward must go.

Kate knew all of this when she sent out the invitations for tonight's soiree and the room was filled with the powerful men of the so-called "radical" wing of the Republican Party. These are the men who have known all along that the war is about slavery and nothing more. All of the other issues, "Union," "states' rights," and all of the other excuses, were nothing more than window dressings. When all of the nonsense is boiled away, it all comes down to the absolute and immediate abolishment of the vile institution. So it was these men whom Kate invited, and tonight the conversation would be directed at ridding the nation of Seward.

Senator Wade would be a problem. Benjamin Wade was always a problem. The gentleman from Ohio was far and away the most radical of all the radicals, and not only on the issue of slavery. He advocated such extreme notions as votes for women and equal civil rights for blacks. He wanted the lands of all former slaveholders confiscated and divided up among the slaves themselves. But none of these were the issues he elected to lecture the room about tonight. Tonight his topic of choice was economics.

"His name is Engels," Kate heard him say. "Friedrich Engels. A brilliant man. An economist and philosopher in England. He and a Mr. Karl Marx have written a manifesto—*Manifest der kommunistischen Partei,* it's called—the *Communist Party Manifesto*."

"I've heard of it," Chase said. "I've heard they're trying to stir up a social revolution over there, and frankly, it scares the hell out of me. Seems to me that they're leading the people to another French-style revolution, except this time it will be capitalists' heads that will roll."

"Perhaps not so drastic as that, Mr. Secretary, but on many points I am in full agreement with them. An economic system which degrades the poor man and elevates the rich, which makes the rich richer and the poor poorer, which drags the very soul out of a poor man for a pitiful existence, is wrong."

Kate saw her father's telltale signs of anger rising. First the veins in his neck began to throb visibly, and then he began to clench and unclench his fists in a rhythm. His skin began to turn red just above his collar and in only a matter of seconds his entire face would be as red as a cherry. On many things Salmon P. Chase favored radical change—but there was no greater capitalist in the world than America's Secretary of the Treasury. Wade was an old friend, a fellow Ohioan, and their greatest ally, and Kate knew it was time to step in.

"Be that as it may, Judge Wade, those people may be enslaved, in a manner of speaking, by their lot in life, but they are not chattel, not up for sale, and not used for breeding stock as are millions of people right here in America." She handed the senator a brandy and stood just a bit too close, offering him perhaps too lovely a view. "And *that* is a wrong that such powerful men as yourselves can actually set right."

"You are absolutely correct, Miss Kate. But, unfortunately, His Majesty, King Abraham, stands in our way."

Chase had to smile, not an easy chore for the dour secretary whose face had been locked in a perpetual scowl since childhood. His daughter was beautiful and brilliant and, in one sentence, she had readjusted the senator's aim in the general direction of the proper target, but he would have to wait for Wade to take a breath to get the conversation aimed precisely at the bull's-eye.

"Our President's views on slavery could only come of one born of poor white trash and educated in a slave state," Wade said, and Chase jumped in before the senator could get cranked up again.

"It may not be the king so much as his prime minister," Chase said. "I believe that Mr. Seward is the evil genius who is holding us back."

Hours later, when the guests had gone and her father had retired, Kate sat alone in front of the dwindling fire feeling very pleased with herself. The evening had been a huge success, socially and politically. The powerful men gathered there had discussed many of the obstacles to immediate abolition. They agreed that Burnside was nothing more than McClellan with funny muttonchops—Democrat at heart and fully willing to sacrifice the slaves on the altar of "Union." They also agreed that until Burnside, Porter, Franklin, and all of the other McClellan-Democrat generals could be drummed out of the army, very little progress would be made on the battlefield. And finally, and most importantly, they had agreed that Seward must go. The sooner the better.

Kate smiled. The deed was done. The plot was hatched and Seward would soon be gone. On this night, Kate knew, the anchor had been raised, and the 1864 Chase for President campaign was finally under way.

NOVEMBER 16

It began as a light, cold drizzle. Private McCarter, Sergeant Stretch, and the rest of the 116th Pennsylvania trailed the veterans of the Irish Brigade, making their road even muddier and less navigable. They were miserable enough trying to march through the mud and light rain, but it soon came down as if it was being poured out of heavenly cauldrons. The veterans of the Irish Brigade quickly taught the new kids of the 116th to look out for their rifles first. Gum blankets, which might have been used as ponchos, became raincoats for muskets, covering the locks and barrels to keep them dry. The old-timers knew very well what it was like to be under attack by the Rebels and to face them with wet powder. Might as well just throw the damned guns at 'em once they get wet.

Adding insult to misery, the Irishmen were detailed to herd seven hundred head of cattle this day. The mud, mixed with cow manure, made their march more treacherous and, if possible, even less pleasant. The cows didn't want to march in this weather any more than the men did, and Stretch and McCarter had to keep prodding the cantankerous animals with bayonets to try to keep them moving.

Stretch was such a clumsy giant of a man that he had

trouble walking on dry, flat land on a sunny day, so he spent most of this march on his knees. Or on his butt.

McCarter reached down to help his buddy up, but Stretch waved him off, preferring to rest in the cold mud for a time.

"And how are you this fine day, Mr. McCarter?" he said, looking up and imitating the brogue of his new Irish friend.

"Quite well, Mr. Stretchbok, but it appears the saints are cryin'."

Stretch struggled to get to his feet and almost fell again before he caught himself. "Well, I wish your darned saints would cheer up a bit then. It can't be as bad as all that!"

WASHINGTON, D.C.

The doors to Secretary Chase's office were suddenly and inexplicably open to the press again. At one time he had been easily accessible but back during the Second Bull Run debacle he had withdrawn. The rumors at the Willard were that these days a good reporter—"good" meaning "Republican"—could walk right in again. Villard was not one to pass on an opportunity and showed up at the secretary's office just as he had at the President's— totally unannounced. Chase was reluctant at first until he found out that the reporter who wanted to see him was from the *Tribune*.

"My friend Mr. Greeley's rag, huh? Whatever happened to that other reporter, Mr. Little or whatever?"

"Smalley, sir. He's an editor now and I've replaced him as the special correspondent with the Army of the Potomac."

"Smalley—right! Good man. If it hadn't been for him we might not have heard a lick about Antietam to this day! Mc-Clellan sure as hell wasn't going to tell us he let the Rebs off the hook!"

Villard respected Smalley's work as much as anyone. His story about Antietam was an absolute masterpiece of reportorial skill. But Henry was already tired of living in the shadow of a fledgling legend. Smalley had scooped the world on Antietam and Villard's report on Shiloh had been lost in the goddamned mail.

"Yes, sir. Mr. Greeley only hires the best."

"Mr. Greeley *is* the best, Mr. . . . ?"

"Villard, sir. Henry Villard."

"Yes, well, as I was saying, your employer is among the greatest men in the country. A great Republican and as great an enemy of slavery."

"It is his passion . . ."

"As it is mine! And you may deliver a message to him for me if you will." Chase stood up and walked around his desk to close the door. "Your word, first, Mr. Villard, that this is not for publication—at least not that you heard it from me."

All reporters hate this dilemma, but it is always best to be told up front. Chase noted Villard's hesitation.

"It is a personal message on a political matter—not official business at all."

Villard still hesitated. The obvious questions came to mind. Then why don't you tell him yourself? Why the secrecy? Then the arguments pro and con: agree and you at least get something. Refuse and you get nothing and possibly make an enemy in high places in the bargain.

"Very well, Mr. Secretary, but I reserve the right to stop you if I feel you are putting me at a disadvantage with my competitors."

"Understood, Mr. Villard, and agreed. You tell Mr. Greeley this for me. You tell him that while we are all pleased that the President has at last taken some kind of stand against slavery, if he had listened to me the document would have freed all slaves everywhere immediately!"

Villard was trapped now. Privy to inside-the-cabinet intrigue. Stopping Chase now would be just plain stupid.

"I'm sure Mr. Greeley will want to know who argued otherwise."

"Seward mostly. And of course the ones from the Border States but they don't matter. Seward is the only one who counts. He's become a cabinet of one, Mr. Villard. The rest of us are never consulted on any matter of importance until the issue has already been decided by Masters Lincoln and Seward." Chase wanted Villard to show shock and amazement, but the reporter was barely even surprised. Jealousies among strong-willed men are more the rule than the exception in any line of work. Disappointed, the treasury secretary tried again. "William Henry Seward is the President of the United States, Mr. Villard, and his lanky friend from Illinois is merely his puppet."

Now Villard was surprised. Not surprised that Chase would *think* such a thing, but that he would *say* it. Too surprised, in fact, to respond.

"You tell Mr. Greeley that. And tell him as well that as long as Seward sits at the right hand of the throne that blacks will never be allowed to fight, that the war will continue to be about the nonsense issues, and that the beating we took in the last elections will be only the beginning of the end of the Republican Party."

Villard had now heard enough and said so.

"Very well, Mr. Villard, I understand. But you tell Mr. Greeley what I have said."

As he stepped out into the cold rain, Villard tried to remember every detail so that he could write it all down as soon as he was able to find a dry place. He was thoroughly amazed that Chase of all people would confide all of this in a reporter until he remembered something that had been said very early on. It seemed not to matter much at the time but became hugely important the more he thought about it.

"*. . . at least not that you heard it from me.*"

He doesn't mind if the story is told as long as he is not the source.

Very interesting, Villard thought. Salmon P. Chase is running for President again, against his own boss.

FREDERICKSBURG
NOVEMBER 17
NOON

Colonel Ball knew what his Mississippians were up against. With fewer than 1,500 men, it was their job to keep the entire Second Corps of the Army of the Potomac on the northern shore of the Rappahannock. Behind the Second Corps as many as five more may be following. More than 100,000 men. Behind Ball there was no one.

The boys of the 42nd Mississippi had left Oxford early in July and had been training in Richmond ever since. They had witnessed McClellan's withdrawal from the Peninsula from the sidelines. They had read about Cedar Mountain, Second Manassas, South Mountain, Harpers Ferry, and Sharpsburg in the papers and cursed and swore at every word. They'd lived in the monotonous drudgery of drill, drill, drill, while others got the glory. But now, by God, it was their turn.

Ball called only one company of the untried men together at the anticipated fording point and gave them not a hint as to the desperate straits they were about to find themselves in.

"Soon the lead elements of the Yankee army will come marching up over those hills with an eye toward crossing the river and taking Fredericksburg." He paused long enough to allow the men to look and imagine the Yankees cresting the hill in force. "The women and children who greeted you so generously only two days ago are still there, gentlemen. They're still in their town and in their homes. It's our job to keep them safe and keep the Yankees out of Fredericksburg."

Another pause allowed the men to envision the grand ladies of the town falling into the hands of the Huns. "The ford is narrow and passable only for mounted troops. I do not believe they will be able to mount a grand charge across the river."

He was now thinking out loud, putting the finishing touches on his plan as he made his speech. "We shall place our artillery on that high ground there. The remainder of the regiment will be held in the rear and ordered forward if needed."

If needed, he thought. *When needed is far more accurate, and when that time comes, we will have to call forward every man and gun in Virginia.*

"You will hold your fire until they are about midway across the river," he told them, "and you will hold this position at all hazards."

With that he took the unsullied regimental flag from the young bearer, held it above his head, and shouted, "Today you will make Mississippi proud!"

Suddenly their days of tormented inactivity were over.

Pent-up frustration blasted out of these boys like a ball from a cannon. Their cheers for their commander echoed along the valley as he galloped off to place the guns Longstreet had been kind enough to send him. At long last the boys of the 42nd Mississippi were going to have a real fight against real Yankees and not a man among them cared a hoot about how many there might be. Send 'em on.

WASHINGTON, D.C.

C hase was furious.

"There is no explanation for this!"

Kate was afraid he was moments away from a stroke.

"Now, calm down, Daddy. You can't do anything about anything if you're dead!"

"I'm not gonna die—but I just might *kill* somebody!"

With her best smile Kate jokingly prodded, "Oh, really? Who?"

Chase had no choice but to calm down. Kate could do that.

"Now—what has got you so riled up this time? What has our friend in the big house done to set you off?"

"Morrison from Illinois resigned his commission to serve in the Congress and Grant refused to accept the resignation."

"He's a Democrat—so that's good, right?"

"Except that 'our friend' overruled Grant to let the little Democrat turd take his seat!"

"Why in the world would he do a thing like that?"

"The President says Morrison is a 'war Democrat,' whatever the hell *that* is! He's a 'hero,' wounded at Fort Donelson, and I say, so what?"

"If they kept him in the army, might we get a Republican elected to that seat?"

"We might."

The treasury secretary fumed in silence until he finally said, "Senator Wade is going to be fit to be tied when he finds out."

"And when might that be?"

Chase smiled as he got Kate's meaning. "In about a half an hour," he said as he put on his coat and walked out the door.

FALMOUTH

As the men of the 57th New York crested the hill, the spearhead of the Army of the Potomac came upon a genuinely lovely sight. The Rappahannock River twisted its way through the valley below with Fredericksburg nestled in a gentle bend on the opposite shore. The only flaw in the picture was the ruined rail bridge that had been destroyed by one army or the other a long time ago. But the rest was a perfect portrait of America. A few patches of snow decorated the fields, soft clouds of white smoke drifted up from the chimneys, and most of the men felt an immediate longing for home. As they stood there, enjoying the view, a distant thud attracted their attention to the ridges across the river and a more ominous plume of white smoke floated up from the trees. Three seconds later an iron ball exploded overhead and the men of the 57th New York quickly scurried down the backside of the hill.

Colonel Samuel Zook rushed forward to determine the extent of the resistance and was more than pleased with what he saw. It looked to him to be a single battery of artillery posted just outside of the town. The infantry that had to be nearby might be another issue, but for the moment his decision was an easy one.

He looked all along the ridgeline on his side of the river and for as far as he could see in either direction were miles of natural artillery emplacements, all well protected and offering coverage of the plains and the heights and the town on the opposite side. "Yes, sir, these hills were *made* for artillery, by damn! Bring up the guns and knock the tar out of those bastards on that hill! Courier!"

"Sir."

"Report back to General Hancock that we have been welcomed to Falmouth by not more than a battery or two of Rebel guns. Tell him I shall know the infantry strength within the hour but the enemy does *not* appear to be here in strength! That's hugely important, Captain. Tell him that a crossing in force is likely to be largely unopposed. Now, ride."

Zook's guns were placed and the artillery duel quickly began.

Fredericksburg

Jane Howison Beale, a widowed schoolteacher, sat reading in her parlor when the sound of the guns brought her quickly to her feet. Martha, the parlor maid, a slave really in name only, remained calm and appeared almost immediately with Jane's two youngest sons in tow—both clinging tightly to Martha's dress.

They sat still in the house for a while, just to make sure it wasn't Ball's boys doing some target shooting, but soon shells began bursting over the town itself. They went to an upstairs window to see what could be seen and hadn't been there for more than a minute before a round exploded almost directly overhead. The boys began to scream and cry and the whole group ran down the stairs and onto the porch where they found the streets jammed with panicked women and children herding themselves as fast as they could toward the safety of Marye's Heights up behind the town. Another Union shell exploded into the paper factory and the poor women who worked there poured out of the building. Jane stood calmly on the porch and watched the terror unfold before her.

"We've gotta go, Miss Jane," Martha said and she took the children by their hands and started to lead them out into the panicked crowd but Jane grabbed her by the sleeve.

"No, Martha!" She almost had to yell to be heard. "This is a stampede. We'll all be safer right here for the moment. We'll go when the streets are safe."

"Miss Beale, Miss Beale! Have you heard?"

"Heard what, Sally?"

Sally was terrified. Her dirty-faced toddler cried louder than the cannons and wiggled almost violently to get free—to get away—to get down so he could run.

"Colonel Ball's boys are running away and the Yankees are coming along right behind 'em!"

"Don't be silly."

"I'm not being silly, Miss Beale! I saw some of 'em myself. They're running, sure enough."

Jane couldn't believe that things could have gone so badly so quickly and she just stood there waiting for some verification before she would risk the lives of her boys to the crushing crowd. It didn't take long.

The father of one of her students guided his horse slowly up next to her veranda. Slowly so as not to trample some poor, stray child.

"Mrs. Beale," he said as he touched the brim of his hat, "It's time to leave, I'm afraid. That's the whole Yankee army over there and Ball's boys just can't hold 'em back. They're on the run already."

Calmly, as always, Jane Beale returned to her home, carefully packed a carpet bag before she walked back out onto Lewis Street. The crowd was gone, most of them were already halfway up the hill. The artillery had fallen silent and the streets were as quiet as a Sunday afternoon.

The reports hadn't been wrong. Exaggerated a bit, but not wrong. In less than fifteen minutes Colonel Zook's experienced gunners had chased Ball's artillerymen off the hill. They had been in such a panic that they neglected to bring their guns along.

The Rebel artillery unit wasn't from Mississippi. They were arrogant Virginians. Or at least they *had been* arrogant fifteen minutes ago. Now, to Colonel William Ball, they were just plain old cowards.

"Grab those yellow bastards by the hair if you have to and drag 'em back to their guns!" Ball was about to explode with anger. "If they won't stand and fight, *shoot 'em*! Right here on the spot! Won't nobody say nothin'!"

The Mississippi boys were more than happy to follow these orders and a few of them may have been just a little disappointed that the gunners all complied and nobody got to shoot any of them.

The experience taught Ball an important lesson. If the Yankees are coming there's not a regiment in Virginia brave or determined enough to stop them. He did his best to warn the residents remaining in Fredericksburg that it was time to seek safer ground. He moved his Mississippians back into town and hauled cotton bales out onto the streets and set them ablaze, and, while he was about it, he ordered 150,000 pounds of tobacco dumped into the Rappahannock. "There's no way the damned Yankees are going to get the town and the tobacco too!"

Across the river General Edwin Sumner was up by now and watched the smoke from the burning cotton bales rising high above Fredericksburg. For a moment he thought the Rebs had torched their own town. The old veteran now commanded two corps—part of Burnside's reorganization. Grand Divisions Burnside called these two-corps units, with Sumner, Franklin, and Hooker commanding.

Convinced now that Fredericksburg was not on fire, Sumner waited impatiently for instructions from Burnside. More impatient still were Darius Couch, commanding general of the Second Corps, and his feistiest division commander, Winfield Scott Hancock. After almost a full day of skirmishing, both men were convinced that few Rebs held the town and were equally convinced that no more were coming. At least not yet.

Couch nudged his horse up next to Sumner's for a "brief word."

"General Sumner—if I may, sir."

"Go ahead, General."

"In the vernacular, sir, 'There ain't nobody over there.' A battery or two and a worn-out regiment is all they showed us today and we're sitting here with a full corps already up and another here by morning."

Sumner continued to gaze through his field glasses at the cotton fires burning around Fredericksburg, but he said nothing. He'd heard almost these same words from another general—Franklin—not many weeks ago. At Antietam he and Franklin had almost come to blows over how many Rebs might be waiting just a hundred yards ahead, on the other side of the Boonsboro Pike. Thank God McClellan had put a stop to that. The last thing Sumner had needed was to march into a second trap in one day. Thank God for that at least. He knew that on this day Couch was more than probably right, but still, with the disaster at Antietam still fresh in his mind, Sumner remained silent.

"Sir—we can cross—at least the cavalry can. We can

take that town and the heights beyond it tonight or first thing in the morning at the latest."

Sumner now took down his glasses and looked at Couch and then back across the river at the town. It looked to Couch as if he was about to issue an order to move forward when a courier galloped up the hill and came to a stop at Sumner's side.

"A response from General Burnside, sir."

"Go ahead, Captain."

"General Burnside begs to inform you, sir, that the pontoons have been delayed again and he has no notion as to where they are or when they will arrive at Falmouth. He also suggests, sir, that the recent rains may swell the river to the point where it is unfordable at any point, and that if you cross ahead of the pontoons your corps might well become trapped on the southern side of the river with no lines of retreat, supply, communications, or reinforcement."

Sumner glanced at Couch in time to see the disappointment register on his face. He nodded and the courier continued. "General Burnside orders, sir, that you hold your ground here and await further instructions."

"So be it," Sumner said, "but I hope to hell those pontoons get here before Bobby Lee does."

WASHINGTON, D.C.

"D amn!"
Wesley Brainerd simply shook his head in absolute amazement. He was certain his old friend, Ira Spaulding, was on the verge of tears.

"How do you like being a major now, Ira?"

"Ask me again on payday, but right now I don't like it worth a damn."

The bridge builders knew the tragedy that was waiting in the wings for this latest comedy to play itself out. Their orders to move to Washington had reached them six days late. Not only that, but they were orders from McClellan, who was no longer in command. The new orders from the new commanding general hadn't reached them until they were already in the wrong place—late. But all that could no longer be helped. Those acts of the comedy had already been played. Right now the two men stood on a hill watching a bunch of bumbling engineers trying to catch five hundred unbroken mules that had been sent to them in lieu of horses by some genius in the quartermaster corps. Mules were kicking, men were falling down, and a handful of Negro teamsters sat on the hill laughing themselves silly at the sight.

Spaulding was livid.

"Do you boys think that you could do this job any better?" He was just trying to shut them up. Burnside was waiting for these damned bridges and it really wasn't a laughing matter.

"Well, yes, suh. I reckon we could do it a tolerable bit better."

"Well then, help yourselves!"

The black teamsters marched themselves down the hill, began manhandling and cursing the bewildered animals while staying clear of their backsides, and in fairly short order had most of them calmed and corralled and many of them harnessed.

Only darkness halted their work, and as they walked back up the hill, the lead man made a point of reporting back to the irate major. With a grin he said, "I reckon by this time tomorrow we'll have 'em pulling wagons for you, Major. Hope that'll do."

Spaulding was embarrassed, but there was no way he was going to show it. "That'll be fine, Mr. . . . ?"

"Marshall, sir. Anthony Marshall, but folks call me 'Bone.' "

"Bone?"

"Bone*headed* I suppose, sir. Reckon that's why I'm so good with mules."

"That'll be fine, Mr. Marshall. Thank you."

"Happy to be of assistance, suh." He offered Spaulding a sarcastic bow and smiled. "Happy to be of assistance."

After Marshall was out of earshot, Brainerd said, "Well,

Ira, if that wasn't a hell of a show I've never been to a circus."

"Don't start in on me, Wes. General Burnside needed these bridges at Falmouth yesterday and we're still fifty miles away and twenty-four hours from starting out."

"More than that, Ira."

"What?"

"We're twenty-four hours from having mules trained to pull wagons if those boys are good to their word. By then it'll be dark and we won't be able to leave till the next morning—and that's if everything goes perfectly."

Ira Spaulding, who was never at a loss for words, was at a loss for words. Finally, he said the only word he could say.

"Damn!"

CULPEPER
NOVEMBER 18

Longstreet found Lee at his desk with a fresh stack of dispatches laid out in front of him like the parts to a puzzle.

"General Burnside is doing his job a bit too well, General Longstreet."

"What news, General?"

"It appears that at least one corps has already arrived at Falmouth. Colonel Ball engaged them there yesterday."

The tone in Lee's voice was concerned but then he glanced at one last dispatch and brightened. He stood up quickly, as though he had been prodded somehow, and went directly to the map. Longstreet often marveled at Lee and his map. The old man would just stand in front of it for long, quiet moments as though he were mesmerized by it. Unmoving, unblinking, and totally absorbed by whatever it was he saw there. Longstreet knew better than to interrupt his concentration and stood by patiently waiting for Lee to rejoin him in the room.

"The supply base will be the key, General," said Lee. "If General Burnside shows signs of moving his supply base to Aquia Creek Landing, then we can be almost certain that he will be moving the bulk of his army in the direction of Fredericksburg."

"Has he shown any signs of that?"

Lee shrugged his shoulders. "Some gunboats and transports have arrived there but that's the most recent information I have. I believe we should instruct General Stuart to cross the Rappahannock and move to the Federal rear." He pointed to a spot on the map and tapped it about five times with his finger. "We should also determine the scale of activity at Aquia Landing. If they've abandoned Warrenton and Manassas and are fully reconstructing the wharves at Aquia then we will know that Fredericksburg is his target."

"Have they attempted a crossing at Fredericksburg or made any attempt to take the town?"

"Not when Ball sent his latest dispatch, but that was last night. Very interesting that General Burnside should come so far so fast and simply come to a halt there."

Lee turned his attention back to the map and once again fell under its spell. After a minute he spoke almost in a whisper. "He has moved very quickly." Another moment of silence and another observation intended only for himself. "In this weather, over those roads, his men have performed admirably." Only then did he take his eyes off the map to address Longstreet directly. "Ball has only a regiment at Fredericksburg and Burnside is moving quickly. He will not stay on that side of the river for very long." He moved back to his desk and studied the dispatches for one last time before issuing his orders.

"Send two divisions to Fredericksburg, General. If they arrive there quickly we may gain some time."

Longstreet's heart began to pound, afraid that Lee was about to split the army again as he had before Sharpsburg. He started to warn him—to remind him about the disaster at Antietam that had very nearly destroyed the army, but Lee interrupted him even before he began to speak.

"Do not concern yourself about that," Lee said. He looked up at Longstreet and smiled. He almost laughed. "We will bring the army together when the time and place are right."

Longstreet did laugh. It wasn't a magician's parlor trick

and there was no reason for him to be surprised that Lee knew what he was thinking. It was the same thing he was always thinking: *Let's bring the army together and let the damned Yankees come to us.* The gospel according to Longstreet.

"I understand, General. McLaws and Ransom to Fredericksburg then, sir, if that meets with your approval."

Lee nodded and moved on. "A brigade of cavalry and a battalion of artillery as well, but once Burnside decides to cross we will not be able to stop him even with that."

Lee walked slowly to his favorite chair and sat down, leaned his head back, and closed his eyes. Longstreet was uncertain whether he had been dismissed until Lee said, "I may have underestimated this man, General. Certainly General McClellan never pushed his army like it has been pushed over the past few days and they seem to have responded magnificently."

"That they have, sir." Now it was Longstreet's turn to examine the map. The Union soldiers had made a truly amazing march in genuinely deplorable conditions. "That they have."

FREDERICKSBURG

"Colonel Ball, they ain't comin', sir."

Ball's Mississippians were packed up and ready to move out and abandon Fredericksburg to the Yankees, their enthusiasm spent in yesterday's encounter.

"I believe you're right, Captain." Ball wiped the grime off the glass on his telescope as though a cleaner lens might be more honest.

"Sir, they're putting up tents and building fires. The cavalry reports that there are no preparations for a crossing being made anywhere along the river."

"I agree, Captain. The river's up and our scouts don't report any bridge builders or pontoon trains anywhere nearby." He closed his telescope and returned it to its case. "So it looks like we'll be staying here for another day or so, just to see what happens."

WASHINGTON, D.C.

Yesterday Ira Spaulding had viewed his black teamsters with disdain. Today, after watching them break
almost five hundred of the army's most ornery mules
in less than a day, he was significantly more respectful. The
beasts had been not much better than wild animals only
hours ago and now they were trained and harnessed and
ready to pull some pontoon wagons.

The man who seemed to be the teamster's leader approached Spaulding and Brainerd beaming with pride.
"Major. Captain. How's that? We did what we promised,
and them mules is ready for some serious wagon pullin'."

Spaulding shook his head in amazement. "I'm sorry, sir,
but I've forgotten your name."

"I'm Anthony Marshall, sir, at your service."

"Well, right now, Mr. Marshall, I'm at *your* service. Is
there anything I can do—anything I can get for you and
your men?"

"Well yes, sir, there is one thing." The smile on Marshall's face vanished. He instantly turned deadly serious.
"Sir—you can get us some of those fine blue uniforms and
a stack of muskets and let us go out and fight for our people.
But I don't s'pose you can do that, can you, Major?"

It was at this moment that Spaulding first realized just
how ludicrous it was that Marshall, and a million other
strong and intelligent men like him, the very people who
had the most to gain, were denied the right to fight. The
wrongheadedness of it was suddenly too idiotic to comprehend. He desperately wanted to say something to the man,
but there was simply nothing he *could* say. Marshall waited
for some kind of response but when none came he decided
to press the point.

"You know President Lincoln's freed the slaves down
South. He's signed that paper. There ain't no reason in the
world why we shouldn't be able to join the army and go
down there and help set those people free . . ." He leaned in
just a little bit closer to the bewildered major to make sure he
would be heard clearly. " . . . 'Cept some folks don't think

we're good enough to die." He paused a second, just to let the bitter irony sink in just a little bit deeper. "Now, ain't that something?"

Spaulding still didn't know what to say, and the silence was awkward until Marshall's smile returned. "So get us some uniforms and some rifles . . ." He winked at the officers. ". . . and some coffee too. Some coffee'd be real nice."

CHAPTER 3

At long last the 50th New York Engineers was outfitted and more or less ready to roll. They were fully equipped with forty wagons specially designed to carry big, clumsy pontoon boats filled to the gunwales with gear. Major Spaulding and Captain Brainerd shepherded their train across the Long Bridge, headed out of Washington.

Somebody, somewhere, had decided that one train was to go by land and another over water. Brainerd sidled his horse over to the side of the bridge to look out over the Potomac and when he saw what was going on down there, he leaned over in his saddle and shook his head.

"Ira! Come over here and take a look at this!"

Spaulding joined Brainerd and simply could not believe his eyes. There, below them, in the middle of the Potomac River, was the second pontoon train bound for Aquia Creek Landing. The barge pulling them had run aground on a sandbar and the trailing pontoons were tangled all around her in a rat's nest of boats and ropes. Both men wanted to laugh, but they just couldn't.

At that moment, it began to rain.

Near U.S. Ford

J oe Hooker was "fightin'" mad. First of all, his Center Grand Division, two full corps with almost forty thousand men, had been placed last in line en route to Fredericksburg, but that wasn't the worst of it. What had him genuinely riled was that he was headed toward Fredericksburg at all!

"The man's a fool!" he yelled for all to hear. "I've got solid supply lines, the United States Ford is four miles from here and passable *without* any goddamned pontoons, the Rebel army is spread out like a bucket of spilt milk, and he's done everything but send Lee a telegram telling him where we're headed so he can meet us there!"

He stormed around his headquarters camp cursing himself blue. He cursed Burnside, he cursed Sumner, and he cursed the damned Rebel sharpshooter who shot him in the foot at Antietam, costing him a victory over Stonewall Jackson and probably the command of the Army of the Potomac. That was the only conceivable reason why Lincoln would have passed him over in favor of Burnside of all people.

The next change of command is coming soon, he thought, *and this time there will be no question.*

He sat at this desk and prepared two documents. The first was a respectful recommendation to Burnside, suggesting that the United States Ford option was far and away the best. While maintaining reliable supply lines, he could get behind the divided Rebel army and have a clean shot at Richmond. He knew full well that Burnside's movement was a virtual avalanche at this point, and the commanding general probably couldn't stop it now even if he wanted to. But he also knew from his friend Salmon Chase that Senator Wade and his Committee on the Conduct of the War would soon be looking for Burnside's head—and a replacement. This communiqué was to serve one purpose and one purpose only—it would soon be documentary evidence of Fightin' Joe Hooker's "I told you so," all tied up neatly with a bow and ready to deliver to Senator Wade's esteemed committee.

But that alone was not enough. Another document repeated the proposed line of attack and added a few gratuitous slurs to the reputation of George McClellan, as he knew that attacks against the Young Napoleon were always well received. Urging haste, Hooker said, "The enemy, it seems, has counted on the McClellan delays for a long while," and made it clear that they would regret it if they did so facing an army commanded by Joe Hooker.

He folded the document, sealed it, and addressed it—to Edwin Stanton, Secretary of War, Washington, D.C.

It was almost dark by the time Ambrose Burnside arrived at Falmouth to assume command of his army at the front.

It was almost midnight by the time Ira Spaulding ordered his pontoon train to a halt for the night. The rain had turned to sleet, the roads had turned to mud, and, as he and his men bedded down for the night, they had put only eight miles behind them.

MORRISVILLE

Colonel Charles Tilden of Augusta, Maine, stood in front of his pitiful band of frozen Yankees, dreading what he was about to tell them. Most were wrapped in blankets—because blankets were all that they had. Their shoes had long since worn through, and they had no warm shirts, no greatcoats, and no tents. They hadn't had any of these things for over two months! When they were ordered out of Washington on September 7 it was still summertime. They had been told to leave their heavy equipment behind. Wagons would be along shortly to pick it all up, and they would get it back when they needed it. Well, the wagons never showed up, the equipment vanished, and the paperwork at the quartermaster bureaucracy indicated that the 16th Maine was well equipped and requests for replacements were routinely turned down. So they marched through the sleet on bare feet, slept in the open in rain and snow, and wore their blankets as overcoats. The 16th Maine looked more like refugees than soldiers, they had suffered months of ridicule from the other regiments in Root's

Brigade, and now their commanding officer had to announce that there was yet another delay.

The boys of Company D had it no worse nor any better than any of the others. One private had deserted weeks ago, but beyond that ugly mark on the company's record, there was very little grumbling. They had heard it all before, and they were Maine men. Hardy and stubborn stock. While the delays were inexcusable and the weather intolerable, there was little a soldier could do about either.

Many of the boys from Company D were from Waterville, Maine, a small, prosperous riverfront town nestled between the Sebasticook and the Kennebec rivers below the Ticonic Falls. The Stevens boys were the sons of a prominent merchant there, a powerful and respected deacon in the biggest church in Waterville. On the occasions when Deacon Stevens was called upon to take the pulpit, the pews were always packed because the whole town knew they were in for some serious hellfire and brimstone and a God-inspired lecture on how slavery was the work of the devil and all slave owners were bound for hell with no more questions asked.

Will was the older of the Stevens brothers at twenty-two and a proud graduate of Waterville College. He had attended his commencement exercises back in August wearing his new, blue Federal uniform and had marched off the platform and directly to the camp of the 16th Maine Volunteers where, thanks to his stellar performance in school and the fine reputation of Deacon Stevens, he was immediately appointed second lieutenant. Ned, at eighteen, hadn't earned his degree as yet, but just being his daddy's son was worth a couple of stripes. Ned had two heroes in his life—Jesus Christ and his big brother, Will. Will was strong and smart and as devout a Christian as could be found anywhere in the world. The people of Waterville knew him and loved him and admired him. Will would follow in his father's footsteps and be a fine preacher someday. Ned was the typical little brother. Never far from his big brother's sight. A shadow.

Deacon Stevens had brought them up right. Lieutenant Will and Sergeant Ned were good boys. Never in any trouble. They never swore or whored or smoked or gambled. Those were one-way tickets to hell. They had a sense of duty and a Maine-born dedication that drove them to become good and disciplined soldiers. These young men saw themselves as soldiers in God's army. Not the Union army—not Abe Lincoln's army—but God's army, the "terrible swift sword" unleashed to set right the greatest evil of all time. With an evangelistic fervor that made their father proud, the Stevens boys were Christian soldiers, out to free the slaves, and if God wanted them to march barefooted through the snow to fight that fight—then so be it. Thy will be done.

EIGHT MILES SOUTH OF WASHINGTON, D.C. NOVEMBER 20

The night had been a short one, and Ira Spaulding's engineers awoke wet and cold. It wasn't light yet but it wasn't raining. Every man coughed first, peed second, and looked to the sky third. They hoped for a nice, clear sky full of stars shining around a bright silver moon, but it was not to be. Not a single star could be seen and that was almost a certain sign that the rain wasn't over.

Billy Blakesley still had made no friends. He almost worshipped Captain Brainerd, but of course he was an officer and could never be a friend. So Billy went about his business alone. He tried not to break his teeth on his hardtack, the brick-hard bread the men had started calling "Lincoln Biscuits," drank his coffee, and tried to wash the mud off of his boots. He cleaned his boots every morning knowing full well that they would be caked with slime again after his very first step, but for some reason he did it anyway. Something his daddy had taught him. He always kept to himself and spent his days thinking about how he was going to beat the hell out of that recruitin' guy whenever he got home. If he ever got home.

He also took great care of his coat—the one Captain Brainerd had given him. He only had two things to love now: letters from home and his beautiful, heavy blue coat.

He put it on and strapped his belt around the outside and then he retrieved his pickax. The infantry got to march with rifles, looking all manly and brave. Engineers marched with shovels or axes on their shoulders and looked like some weird kind of "make-believe" soldiers.

He was almost ready to move out when he heard the distinctive Welsh accent of Honest Johnny Jones. "At least we don't have to do like Noah and build a boat! Abe's done give us a mess of 'em." Jones's voice was so loud and unique that it carried for miles and always—always—pinpointed Captain Brainerd on the map. Wherever Brainerd was, Johnny was within ten feet. Billy was ready to go and had nothing else to do, so he ambled over closer just to watch and listen to whatever his hero might be saying. They were talking about Brainerd's horses.

"He's a fine enough–looking horse," Brainerd said, "but I'm afraid Old Bill is a terrible hard rider."

"Aye, but he's got a fine heart, don't he, Captain?"

"Grand, Johnny. You picked me out a fine one, but he wore a blister on my rear yesterday, so I think I'll exchange the style of the bay for the ease of the gray today." Brainerd's smile and Johnny's laugh lightened Billy's mood more than just a little and now, at last, he was ready for the march. Not happy. Far from it. But at least ready. For Captain Brainerd, Billy Blakesley would do anything.

The pontoons were carried by special wagons pulled by six mules and it was Billy's spot to walk alongside the lead pair of one of them. More than once he thought about just jumping on the mule's back and riding until someone made him get off. He thought about sneaking into one of the pontoons and hitching a ride that way too. He thought about these things, but he never had the nerve to try them.

The weather prognosticators of the 50th New York had obviously been right. With the light came the rain—again—and in buckets. No. Not in buckets. In barrels and mixed with heavy-hitting sleet thrown into their faces by a relentless wind. To make matters worse, if matters could be made worse, their line of march paralleled Hunter's Creek. It was a harmless enough stream under normal circumstances but in this unrelenting downpour the creek rose and escaped the banks and assaulted the train quicker than Jeb Stuart. It wasn't long before the creek was a river and the road was a memory, and there was nowhere for men, wagons, mules, and pontoons to go. Finally Billy's mule lost its footing and slid into the torrent, pulling its teammates and wagon in behind. Of course the wagon was attached to a twenty-one-foot-long boat that had a mind and mission of its own once it hit the water. Several men jumped in behind to get the mules and the wagon back to high ground. Billy had never been a swimmer and tried his best *not* to volunteer for that heroic duty, but God and the mud beneath his boots had a different plan. Once neck-deep in Hunter's Creek he had no alternative but to hang on to the panicky mule to keep from drowning. Drowning had to be the worst possible way to die so he kicked for all he was worth and managed to grab the limb of a fallen tree. He used every muscle that wasn't frozen to steer the animal toward an incline just downstream. The nearly exhausted mule miraculously found its footing and pulled the rest of the team along behind until suddenly there were dozens of men gathered around to help pull the whole package to safety.

Billy turned loose of the mule's neck and fell ass-first onto the ground. He was breathing in quick, shallow gasps and his entire body chattered both from the fear and the horrible, unbearable cold. There was a roar in his ears that he couldn't figure out. Someone threw a blanket around him and lifted him up, and he realized that the roaring in his head was the sound of cheering. Every soldier in the 50th had watched what had happened and decided that Billy was a genuine hero—the guy who had batted in the winning run in an extra-inning championship game. Billy beamed like a lantern and waved at his hundred new friends and was finally able to take a very deep breath because he wasn't nearly so cold any more.

FALMOUTH

"Damnation! Where in the hell are my damned bridges?"

Ambrose Burnside had been educated by

Quakers, and such language did not come naturally to him, but on this day nothing less would do. He slammed his telescope closed and stormed out of the Phillips house. His heart pounded with anger and frustration. His entire plan hinged on getting across the river before Lee could fortify Fredericksburg, but the damned engineers couldn't follow simple orders. The whole army was lining up along the banks of the Rappahannock, a hundred thousand strong— complete with stores and ammunition and hundreds of artillery pieces, and the goddamned engineers couldn't even row a couple of bridges downstream. And now the lead elements of Lee's army were marching unopposed into the town. There weren't many yet, maybe a single division, but Burnside knew full well that thousands more followed.

"Where are the goddamned bridges?"

It had taken a full week for Little Abbott and Wendell Holmes to find their way back to the Harvard Regiment. The train ride from Boston was delayed time and again by snarled traffic north of Washington. They made their way on foot to Warrenton only to find the army gone. Rumors had Sumner's Right Grand Division encamped at Falmouth, so the two Boston bluebloods had sloshed through the rain and mud alone until they finally found their camp. Wet, cold, miserable, and exhausted, they had arrived late last night and made time to speak with no one. They sought out only Lieutenant Leander Alley, who managed to find them real beds in a real room in a real house where they had slept until noon.

But today, bone dry and fully rested, they were anxious to catch up on all the news of the regiment since Antietam, and Lieutenant Alley was more than anxious to give it to them.

Here was a man who most certainly was *not* a graduate of Harvard. If he had a drop of blueblood, it was seawater blue. He had been a whaler before the war and he very much looked the part. The man was built like a mast; tall and thin but sturdy and unbendable. His whalebone pipe was permanently affixed to his right hand, his manner of speaking was crusted with sea salt, and he commanded respect equal to any ship's captain. To him disobedience was a mortal sin and nothing less, and he punished the transgressors with a hand-carved plank he kept at his side at all times. His company knew it as "Alley's spanker." The whaling man had been a private in camp, a second lieutenant after Ball's Bluff, a first lieutenant just prior to Antietam, and Abbott and Holmes, the Boston bluebloods, loved him like a brother.

"The first thing you should know is that our Colonel Lee has gone madder than a March hare."

Abbott laughed, expecting this to be the set up for a joke of some kind.

"No, sir. 'Tis not a laughing matter. I mean the devil's own madness. After General Dana went down in the big fight in Maryland, Colonel Lee was next in line to command the brigade, but he just clammed up, sirs. Never said another word. Never issued a command. Nothing."

Little Abbott came to the defense of the old West Pointer. "Men respond to that kind of pressure differently, Leander. That kind of news in the middle of a disaster such as . . ."

"Aye, but then he vanished. Without so much as a 'by your leave,' the man just disappeared. Macy here's the one what found him—almost a *month* later."

Captain George Macy was eavesdropping on the conversation and was ready to jump in on cue.

". . . Still wearing the same clothes he wore at Antietam. You may believe this or not, but I swear to you that the old man had soiled himself and didn't even care."

Abbott was almost ready to cry. William Lee had been a friend of the family for years and had acquitted himself well in command of the regiment through the battle at Ball's Bluff and all the engagements on the Peninsula. Abbott simply couldn't believe what he was hearing. "What did you do?"

Macy shrugged. "I cleaned him up, changed his clothes—threw the old ones away—and found him a place to sleep and left him pretty much where I had found him."

"Are you sure he wasn't just on a drunk. He's been known to do that, you know."

"No. His soul is gone, Little. The 'divine spark,' as they call it, is nowhere to be seen. The look on his face is as stupid as a cow."

"Where is he now?"

Alley had finished reloading and lighting his ever-present pipe and was ready to retake the floor. "That's the thing, my hearties. He's back with us, but not with us, if you get my meaning. He's a body without a man inside."

"And so who commands the regiment?"

"Until such time as something better comes along," Captain Macy said, "that would be me."

FREDERICKSBSURG

The field glasses felt good in Robert E. Lee's hands. This was the first time he had been able to use them since he'd injured his wrists after Second Manassas—almost three months ago. His boots had been wet and an artillery round spooked Traveler just as Lee tried to mount. He'd fallen backward and landed square on both wrists and spent the entire Battle of Sharpsburg being led around the field like a child on a pony, but the primary irritation had been his inability to use his glasses. There was still pain, an almost constant ache, but it was no longer debilitating. Only a nuisance. He could button his own shirt now. He could write and ride again. And he could grip his glasses—and it felt good.

Lee panned left to right along the hills across the river, taking in whatever he might glimpse through the mist that followed the rain. He couldn't see everything, but fall was over and the trees were bare, so he could see enough. The rain had stopped and the Army of the Potomac made no attempt to hide. He saw tents and fires and men by the thousands over on the Falmouth side. He saw the beautiful Lacy house, high on the hill directly across the river, and it angered him briefly to see blue soldiers hurrying in and out of the home where he had been a guest on many occasions. And all along the line, for as far as he could see in either direction, he saw canons. Probably more than a hundred if anyone bothered to count. Guns that thoroughly commanded the town and all of the approaches to the heights on the other side. What he saw was exactly what he had expected to see—nearly perfect defensive ground held by the enemy.

He returned his glasses to their case and looked upward at the flat, gray clouds above. *Snow,* he thought—or prayed. Maybe the winter will blow in cold and fast and there will be no fight here at all. Maybe we will be able to pull back to the North Anna River and fight on ground of our choosing—on ground where we might win a significant victory—because no such thing is possible here. Maybe it will snow tonight and continue to snow for a month.

Maybe.

MOUNT VERNON
NOVEMBER 21

Years ago, seeing the first President's home would have been the thrill of a lifetime for Wesley Brainerd, but not today. Today Mount Vernon was only a magnificent reminder of how little progress they had made in getting Burnside his precious pontoons. On a nice day, over dry roads, Washington to Mount Vernon was a comfortable day trip. For the 50th New York Engineers, in deplorable conditions, it had taken them the better part of two days to move their cumbersome train fewer than ten miles, and they still had forty to go.

Nevertheless it was impossible for him to view the mansion without admiring the man who had lived here—the man who had fathered a nation that was now torn apart. The rain had turned to snow and it was beginning to accumulate, so Valley Forge came easily to mind. While the outbuildings had been vandalized for firewood, the house itself was untouched—far too sacred for any man from either side to defile. Brainerd took a moment to enjoy the view that must have given Washington so much pleasure, looking down the valley at the graceful bend in the mighty Potomac. It was a spectacular sight to see—even on a miserable day like today.

FALMOUTH

Marsena Patrick was late. The provost general of the Army of the Potomac had been dispatched from the Phillips house to Fredericksburg hours ago in a rowboat and under a flag of truce. His mission was to demand that the mayor of Fredericksburg surrender the town or suffer bombardment. Sumner had complained of random musket fire aimed at his men from the town and railroad cars full of army stores that were being evacuated south to Richmond.

Surrender the town by 5 P.M. tonight or we will give you sixteen hours to evacuate the women and children before we bomb Fredericksburg to rubble. That was all he was supposed to say before returning to the Phillips house to await the response. But hours had passed and Burnside and Sumner were only a moment away from sending a boatload of infantrymen over to rescue him when the missing general walked quietly through the door.

"Where in the hell have you been?" Sumner blurted out. "We expected you back hours ago."

Burnside was more interested in the results than the timetable. "What did they say?"

Patrick was momentarily struck dumb. He had to figure out where to start. "Well, sirs, they just promised not to do it anymore, but the reason it took so long is that the mayor insisted on involving the military and I had to wait while a Colonel Ball went to confer with his superiors. He was gone for quite some time and returned with Moxley Sorrel, sirs."

"Sorrel?"

"Yes, sir. And after I repeated our demands he too left for a while and when he came back he told me that there would be no more firing from the town—on orders from General Longstreet."

"*Longstreet?*"

"That's what he said, sir. He requested time to evacuate the civilians and warned that they would resist any efforts on our part to occupy the town."

"You're absolutely certain he said 'Longstreet'?"

"Absolutely certain, sir."

Sumner and Burnside just looked at each other. Neither

spoke a word. It was as though they had just learned of a
death in the family.

OCCOQUAN CREEK
7:30 P.M.

The snow had stopped and the engineers were heading
downhill now and naturally thought their trek might be
easier. Not so. The approach to the Occoquan Creek
was a steep, rocky road with narrow ruts and sharp cutbacks.
The pontoon wagons were over thirty feet long and almost
six feet wide. When they finally reached the "creek," they
found it just like Hunter's Creek, which had almost swallowed up the entire train yesterday. It was raging and over its
banks and fording it was simply out of the question.

"What do you think, Wes?" Spaulding was at his wit's end.
Brainerd could tell that his young friend was ready to snap,
so he kept his obligatory smart-aleck response to himself.

"Well, thank God and Ambrose Burnside we've brought a
bridge along. We'll bridge it, cross it, haul it back in on the
other side, and continue on our merry way," Wes said.

He noticed that Spaulding was shaking, but he couldn't
tell if it was from anger or fear or just from the cold.

"That's another half day lost, Wes! And Burnside *himself*
is hounding me now! Hurry up! Hurry up! Hurry up! Two
and three times a day I'm getting messages and every time I
turn around there's another damned thing going wrong!"

"If you've got a better idea, Ira, I'd love to hear it."

Spaulding closed his eyes and went into himself for a
moment. He was very quiet for a long while, and when he
opened his eyes again he wasn't shaking anymore. "Yeah,
I've got a better idea," he said. "To hell with these damned
muddy roads! I'm going to send Captain McDonald back to
Alexandria and have him send a tugboat down here and
we're gonna *float* these damned things to Aquia Landing!
To hell with General Woodbury."

"Great decision, Ira! There's only one problem."

Spaulding obviously didn't want to hear it, but Brainerd
had to say it nonetheless. "When you get to Aquia, you're

still going to need the animals and wagons to pull them to Falmouth, and in order to do that we've still got to get them across this damned river."

Spaulding was pleased with himself now that he had actually assumed command and he was simply not going to allow Brainerd's observation to become an obstacle.

"We'll construct the bridge and move the wagons and animals across first thing in the morning. The pontoons will be lashed together and remain in the water until the tug arrives and be ready to go from there. You will take the cavalry escort with you overland. The wagons will be lighter and easier to handle empty, and we'll meet at Aquia Landing."

After it had all sunk in, Brainerd gave a broad, beaming, proud smile, nodded his head, and said only, "Yes, sir."

NOVEMBER 22

Things had gotten no better for the men of the Irish Brigade. The "new kids" of the 116th Pennsylvania were still learning the rigors of army life the hard way. For the last week it had been hardtack and water for dinner, long, cold nights spent digging emplacements along Stafford Heights for the artillery, and hardtack and water for breakfast. Their supply wagons, it seemed, had slipped off the road into a ravine and their precious coffee allotment had floated downstream in a perfect downpour.

Such misfortunes did not relieve them from taking their turns on the picket lines, and today would be Stretch and Bill McCarter's turn.

" 'Tis a darned sight b-better than d-diggin' holes for the artillery guys to hide in," McCarter said, his natural stutter made worse by the cold.

His evening shift was even entertaining as the Rebels across the way put on a show or two for his amusement. A pair of borrowed field glasses enabled him to enjoy the final two innings of a baseball game, and when that was over a primitive ring was constructed and two feisty Rebels climbed in and proceeded to beat each other senseless.

Crowds gathered, men cheered, and bets were taken and paid on both sides of the river.

HEADQUARTERS, ARMY OF THE POTOMAC
NOVEMBER 22

General Halleck:

By reference to my plan of operations, submitted by order of the Commander-in-Chief, it will be found that one of the necessary parts of that plan was to have started from Washington at once with pontoon trains sufficient to span the Rappahannock at Fredericksburg twice; and I was assured that at least one train would leave as soon as the General in Chief and General Meigs returned; and I proposed that if an escort was required and I was informed by telegraph, I would furnish it from my cavalry. It is very clear that my object was to make the move to Fredericksburg very rapidly, and to throw a heavy force across the river before the enemy could concentrate a force to oppose the crossing and supposed the pontoon train would arrive at this place nearly simultaneously with the head of the column. Had that been the case, the whole of General Sumner's column—33,000 strong—would have crossed into Fredericksburg at once over a pontoon bridge, in front of a city garrisoned by a small squadron of cavalry and a battery of artillery which General Sumner silenced within an hour after his arrival.

Had the pontoon bridge arrived even on the 19th or 20th, the army could have crossed with trifling opposition. But now the opposite side of the river is occupied by a large rebel force under General Longstreet, with batteries ready to be placed in position to operate against the working parties building the bridge and the troops in crossing.

The pontoon train has not yet arrived, and the river is too high for the troops to cross at any of the fords. You can readily see that much delay may occur in the general movement, and I deem it my duty to lay these facts before you, and to say that I cannot make the promise of probable success with the faith that I did when I supposed that all the parts of the plan would be carried out. Another very material part of the proposition, which I understand to be approved as a whole, was that all the surplus wagons that were in Washington were to be loaded with bread and small commissary stores and sent to this place at once, which would probably have supplied our army with from five to ten days' provisions.

I do not recall these facts in any captious spirit, but simply to impress upon the General in Chief that he cannot expect me to do as much as if all the parts of the plan had been carried out. In fact, a force can be arrayed against us at this place that would very materially retard us.

I am not prepared to say that every effort has not been made to carry out the other parts of the plan; but I must, in honesty and candor, say that I cannot feel that the move indicated in my plan of operations will be successful after two very important parts of the plan have not been carried out, no matter for what reason.

The President said that the movement, in order to be successful, must be made quickly, and I thought the same.

I have the honor to be, very respectfully, your obedient servant,

A. E. BURNSIDE

FREDERICKSBURG

It was a pathetic parade that clogged the roads leading south out of Fredericksburg. Old men, women, and children from every station in life carried whatever they could as they followed General Lee's advice to evacuate the town. Some traveled in wagons or carriages stuffed to overflowing with the valued accumulations of a lifetime. Of course their furniture and works of art were too large to carry and had to be left behind, but they had the family silver, jewelry, and heirlooms with them. Some had a cow or two leashed to the back of their wagon, or a slave or two to drive them.

But then there were the others. The ladies from the paper mill whose husbands were off to war or already killed in it. These were the hardest to watch. For those who weren't widows, many of their husbands were camped somewhere near the town, but might as well have been in Georgia for all the help they could give. Hundreds of these poor women walked up the hill toward Marye's Heights with their children in tow—sometimes a great many children—carrying a single valise or carpet bag that contained virtually nothing. Unlike the upper crust of Fredericksburg, these people had nowhere to go. They had no friends in nearby towns or relatives in Richmond who would put them up until the issue was settled. They were just told to leave and so they left, hoping that on this freezing cold night someone would be kind enough to lend them a blanket—just until tomorrow when the battle would be fought, the Yankees would be beaten, and everyone could go home.

It became such a heartrending show that the army began to pitch in with whatever wagons could be spared to ferry the masses at least to the outskirts of the town.

Of the very rich and the very poor, Jane Beale was neither. While the Army of Northern Virginia was kind enough to offer her an ambulance, she really had no place to go. All of her friends and relatives were in the very same boat. They all lived somewhere between the lines being formed by the two great armies and were headed south along with her. She eventually threw herself on the mercy of a kindhearted soul, a Mrs. Temple, who lived in a modest home a mile or two behind the Rebel lines. The good lady apologized for the accommodations, but closed her door to no one. By the time night had fallen, there was not a square foot of floor space that did not form a bed for some dispossessed citizen of Fredericksburg.

FALMOUTH
NOVEMBER 23

Bill McCarter was in the middle of his third shift on picket duty and he was no longer being entertained by the frolicking Rebels across the river. It was 3:30 A.M., pitch dark, brutally windy, and agonizingly cold. He wrapped the cape of his overcoat around his face and tied it in place with a string. Every part of him was covered but his eyes, but it still wasn't nearly enough. The part of his coat that covered his nose and mouth got wet from his own breath, quickly turned white, and formed itself into a frozen death mask of his face. The only thing he had to keep him warm was the memory of his first hearty dinner in days: a half of a raw turnip graciously given him by a man from another regiment. He tried to smile as he remembered his feast, but he was just too damned cold.

The wind assaulted him directly off the nearly frozen river and pierced his body like a hundred needle-sharp arrows, so he sought refuge behind one of the stone pilings that had once supported the railroad trestle. He pounded his feet against the ground and jumped up and down and blew on his hands and tucked them under his armpits. Anything to get warm. He did everything he could think of until it all just became too much trouble for too little relief. It was against regulations to sit down, so he leaned against the stones of his sheltering column and closed his eyes to pray. Maybe Jesus would help.

7 A.M.

Thomas R. R. Cobb sat on his horse and tried to will his brigade to move faster. He prayed for them to move faster. He pleaded with them and ordered them and threatened them and even kicked a few of them in the butt, but still they plodded along through the mud at slower than a snail's pace. Darkness had come just an hour too soon last night with his destiny waiting just over the next hill, and there he came to a halt, impotent and frustrated and stuck in the damned mud. A brigadier general for less than a month, he was champing at the bit to lead an entire brigade in glorious battle. For days he'd worried that the Yankees would cross the river before he got there. He'd worried that the fight would be over. He damned the mud and the stuck wagons and the lame horses. He cursed the cold and the rain and he mercilessly prodded his miserable, shoeless soldiers who struggled with every exhausting stride through the knee-deep slime. He did all of that, but mostly he prayed.

Tom Cobb was personally responsible for the secession of the state of Georgia, at least in his own mind. He had served for only a matter of weeks in the first Confederate Congress before it dawned on him that "Confederate Congress" was an oxymoron. A national government was the very thing they were fighting against! Plus he was bitter that a Mississippian had been elected President over his much more deserving brother. He resigned his seat to raise a cavalry regiment and had seen action with Jeb Stuart but now he had his own brigade and he was spoiling for a fight.

Things had finally begun to go right for the firebrand general. He had spent his entire army experience railing against the West Point boys who ran the army—Robert E. Lee included. "Pompous," "arrogant," and "ignorant" were just a few of the words he assaulted them with. But then everything had changed. The men at the top had finally recognized his worth, promoted him to brigadier, and promised to reassign him to Georgia where he could fight for his own country. But first, one last opportunity for glory on the fields of Virginia, and then, hopefully, home by Christmas, made famous by a gallant charge and perfectly poised for a trip to the statehouse in beautiful Milledgeville, Georgia.

He was days late when he finally pushed his half-dead horse to the top of the last muddy hill and Fredericksburg came into view. The valley was colored by the magic light of the early morning sun, and he was happy to see the columns of white smoke from thousands of cook fires just being lighted on the Falmouth side of the river. They told him that his prayers were answered. The Yankees were still on their side of the Rappahannock. He also knew that he was the lead element of forty thousand men put here by God to send the damned Yankees to hell should they decide to come over.

One more prayer: "Thank you, Jesus."

Thomas Reade Rootes Cobb was a very happy man.

TELEGRAPH HILL

Robert E. Lee was incensed. President Davis was trying again to command his army from the capital. At least he was a military man—a West Point graduate, a gallant and wounded veteran of the Mexican War and Secretary of War under President Pierce. But, in Lee's mind, Presidents are Presidents and generals are generals, and military decisions should be left to the commanders in the field. The only consolation Lee had in the meddling of politicians was that he knew that Burnside faced the same difficulty. Burnside's problem was probably even worse because Lincoln was *not* a military man. But Lee also knew that democracy depended on the rule of law, and that generals had to follow orders, just like any other soldier.

Lee was still fuming over his most recent telegram from Richmond when Longstreet joined him on Telegraph Hill. It was the highest point on the Fredericksburg side of the river, where they could see virtually the entire line.

"It looks as though we will be defending Fredericksburg, General Longstreet. Orders from the President."

"It's a good line, General."

"I know, General. 'Let the Yankees come to us.' " Both men smiled. "It is a good line if he chooses to cross here and only if he gives us the time to get our entire army up and in place . . ." Lee turned his attention to Prospect Hill off to his right and the railroad line that ran in front of it. ". . . And even then our right may be vulnerable."

"Do you believe that those are his plans, sir—to cross here?"

"Not definitively. General Stuart reports that Warrenton and Manassas have been abandoned and that every corps except portions of Sigel's are stretched out from here to the Potomac, but he is showing no signs of forward movement. It's simply impossible to tell just yet."

Lee's wrists still ached from the fall back in August and the cold only made them worse. He turned and headed back toward his tent to be near the fire. "But the thing that concerns me most is that there will be no opportunity to counterattack here. Even if we are able to come together here before he attacks, there will be no opportunity to destroy the enemy and the time has come, General Longstreet, when they must be destroyed. Nothing less will do." He stopped and turned toward Longstreet so he could face him; so that he could look into his eyes to make his point. "Mr. Lincoln's proclamation takes effect in little more than a month, but its damage has already been done because we are no longer waiting for England to join us, General. With that document Mr. Lincoln has made slavery the issue and because of that the British are not coming. Not now—not ever."

Lee rarely talked politics but this was not a political issue. The Emancipation Proclamation was a military strategy, Lee knew, and a brilliant one at that.

"If they continue to wait until you are fully up and Jackson is fully up, and if they choose to cross here, we may be able to kill them, maybe by the thousands, but when they do decide to pull back, they will be fully under the cover of those guns and we will not be able to pursue. No, sir. We may be able to win a battle if one is to be fought here, but it will be of no strategic consequence, and the war will go on."

They entered Lee's headquarters tent where Colonel Taylor had stoked the stove so full that it was as warm as a baker's kitchen. The two men removed their coats and the commanding general found the chair closest to the fire and eased himself into it. He leaned forward and held up his hands until they were almost touching the camp stove and his wrists soon felt better.

"I want to pull back to the North Anna River line and fight them there and then push them back and trap them against the river, and then we would be able to destroy those people, General—the whole lot of them." He leaned back and rested his head against the back of the chair and closed his eyes. His wrists felt better, but his heart did not. "Without the British we must win a total victory. We must destroy their armies completely and kill their will to fight on. We might be able to do that at the North Anna, but the War Department doesn't want to risk a fight so close to Richmond. Not if we can stop them here, and that, of course, is the question."

Both men remained silent for a while and enjoyed the warmth. Longstreet broke the silence.

"McLaws's division is up, sir. And more are on the way."

"It will not be enough, General. Under the present circumstances General Jackson does not threaten the enemy in his current position, regardless of what General Burnside's intentions might be." One quick glance at the map. "We'll have him come east where he will be able to threaten Burnside's flank and respond more quickly to whatever might arise."

Longstreet was thrilled, but tried not to show it. "Are you ordering him to Fredericksburg, General?"

"Not just yet, General Longstreet, but I will start him on his way."

FALMOUTH
8 A.M.

"BILL!"

The voice was desperate but a hundred miles away. McCarter tried to answer, but his sleep was too deep.

"BILL!" A little louder this time, a little more frantic, but still not near.

Then he felt warm hands on his face—rubbing him—slapping him. He wanted to be left alone. He wanted to sleep. *Dammit, stop!* But they just wouldn't leave him be.

"BILL! WAKE UP, you stuttering little Mick!"

Through the dense fog of an almost comatose sleep it finally dawned on the tough little Irishman who it was that was yelling at him. *Stretch. That's who it is.* He fought to open his eyes just enough to get his friend to shut the hell up and suddenly there were cheers all around him. A dozen or more men raucously laughed and shouted and patted one another on the back.

"Atta boy, Bill." Stretch beamed like a proud poppa, like this was the happiest moment in his entire life. He lifted McCarter's head and put a steaming hot cup of coffee to his lips. "Now, sip on this, Bill boy. Let's start warmin' ya up from the inside out."

McCarter tried to speak, but Stretch wouldn't let him. "Hush up now. First you'll drink, and then you'll walk. You can talk tomorrow."

Another sip of coffee. "You came damned close to never walking or talking again, young fella. The boys here was ready to bury you last night, as God is my witness, and they would have too if they hadn't all been tired of digging entrenchments!" There was laughter in the room followed by another sip of coffee. "That's right! Three men froze to death last night and Doc said you'd d'ave gone with 'em in about twenty more minutes."

Stretch held his stuttering little friend in his arms and rocked him as gently as a mother. He couldn't fight back the tears—even if he'd wanted to. "Yup. That's what the man said."

THE PHILLIPS HOUSE

Ambrose Burnside scribbled an order, ripped it from the pad, and virtually threw it at General Erasmus Keyes.

"There," Burnside said, "see to it!"

Keyes was surprised. "You want me to *arrest* General Woodbury?"

"I do. General Halleck accepts no responsibility and says Woodbury is to blame for the bridges being late—one solid *week* late I might add—and the entire operation is in jeopardy! And I want the man responsible court-martialed! Now—find him and place him under arrest!"

Keyes left on his unhappy mission, leaving Burnside and Sumner alone in the room. It was a very long time before either man spoke. Their mood was funereal. It was finally Sumner who said what both men were thinking—what both feared.

Quietly, almost secretively he said, "We can't cross here, Burn."

Burnside pounded his fist on the table. "We can't cross anywhere *else* either! From U.S. Ford all the way down to Port Royal, we haven't been able to find a single spot that isn't either impassable, heavily defended, or spills out onto bad ground. Not a single spot."

"That may be true, General, but here is the worst." He felt like he was telling a friend that his child had died, but it had to be said. "If we throw our bridges directly into the town the losses will be unbearable. Every house within musket range will be filled with Rebel infantry, and if we manage to make it beyond the town, their artillery covers all the approaches to the heights."

"I cannot abandon the attack. The pressure from Stanton and Halleck is constant. Halleck has told me to make a battle even if it is one we *can't* win. That's what the man said! If the bridges had arrived on time we would be halfway to Richmond by now, and do you want to know the rub? By this time tomorrow I'll have enough pontoons to bridge the Gulf of Mexico!"

"There is a place, General, just a mile downstream. It is guarded but only lightly. If we cross there, a determined attack might be able to turn his right."

NOVEMBER 24

Wesley Brainerd, now escorting only empty wagons to Aquia Landing, had his best day in over a week. The weather improved, Spaulding's tug had arrived on schedule to float the pontoons down the Occoquan, and his land train was hampered only by bands of Rebel cavalry who seemed only interested in watching—and perhaps wondering where Brainerd had left his boats. From first light to total darkness he had moved his empty train sixteen miles.

Not bad—for once.

Aquia Creek Landing

"Well, well, well . . . if it ain't the 'Blanket Brigade'!"

The 16th Maine—still wrapped in blankets because their coats and shoes and tents were tied up in a bureaucratic boondoggle—had just sloshed their way to Aquia Landing and were in no mood for "light ribbing." Sergeant Ned Stevens broke ranks and grabbed the Massachusetts man by the collar of his nice, warm coat. "We ain't the 'Blanket Brigade'! We're the 16th Maine, by God, and don't you ever call us that again!" Without a second's hesitation the Massachusetts man sucker-punched Ned square in the face. Ned went quickly to the ground, his nose broken and bleeding. Big brother Will tackled the Massachusetts man to the ground and began to beat him with a fury. Within a minute the entire "Blanket Brigade" tore into the 12th Massachusetts like they were fighting the Stonewall Brigade. Colonel Tilden went in to break up the fight, but found himself toe-to-toe with a Massachusetts man and proceeded to pummel him to a pulp. The fight lasted for ten minutes or more before officers from the 12th Mass. were finally able to break it up.

It was the 16th Maine's first battle. And they won it. Or at least they thought they had.

That night, as the Maine men began to look for a dry spot to lay their filthy blankets, Will looked at Ned with his swollen, busted nose and started to laugh. Nobody in the 16th had laughed in weeks, but tonight Will started to laugh . . . and Ned started to laugh . . . and another man joined in . . . and another . . . and pretty soon the laughing turned to bragging. It was as though they had taken on Bobby Lee's whole darned army and whupped 'em bad, all by themselves.

On this night a regiment was born.

CHAPTER 4

"Flabbergasted." It's the only word in the entire English language that can describe the reaction of Stonewall Jackson's staff when he stepped out of his tent. The "ragamuffin general" was downright festooned. He had metamorphosed from drab private soldier caterpillar to flamboyant cavalier butterfly and looked for all the world as though he were bound for a costume ball disguised as Jeb Stuart.

It was Stuart, in fact, who had provided Jackson with the coat, adorned with enough gold to make an emperor jealous. The worn old kepi from VMI was replaced with a tall black hat and his sword was worn over a gold sash of command. Jim Lewis, Jackson's body servant, had spent the entire night polishing buttons, swords, and boots. Yes, the staff was flabbergasted, and Jackson loved it.

"What are you smiling at, Douglas?"

"Ah, nothing, sir." Kyd Douglas, Jackson's fun-loving young assistant adjutant, was having a terrible time not bursting into laughter.

"Didn't I sign an order that would rid me of you?"

"Ah, yes, sir, you did, sir, but not just yet, sir."

"Is there nothing we can do to speed those orders along?"

Douglas was having so much fun now that he surrendered to the urge and broke into his hallmark grin. "Believe me, sir, I've tried!"

Jackson smiled and patted Douglas on the arm and then turned to the gathered officers to make his announcement.

"Young gentlemen! This is no longer the headquarters of the Army of the Valley." His expansiveness matched his attire. "We are now the Second Corps of the Army of Northern Virginia!" Those gathered had little notion as to what it might mean, but if it made Jackson happy it must be good—so they cheered.

"Prepare everyone to move out—we'll be heading east."

Aquia Creek Landing
2 p.m.

The pontoons were back on the wagons and, at long last, on the final leg of their plagued odyssey to Falmouth. Now Spaulding had an answer to the neverending inquiries from Burnside.

"Tell the general we'll be there tonight."

Major General Burnside;
Falmouth, Virginia

If I should be in a boat off Aquia Creek at dark tomorrow (Wednesday) evening, could you, without inconvenience, meet me and pass an hour or two with me?

A. Lincoln

November 26

In person and in writing, General Woodbury defended himself before General Burnside. The commanding general sat in a rocking chair at the Phillips house, head back and eyes closed, while Woodbury went into all the painful details of why the bridges had taken so long. He told him about McClellan's orders arriving a week late. He told him that the bridges had begun their trek from Harpers Ferry and not from Washington as Burnside had thought. He told him about the mules and about the lack of urgency in Halleck's orders. He told him about the storms and the floods and he told him that his men had performed nothing less than a miracle to get the bridges here when they did.

"Very well," Burnside said. "You are restored to duty. Now go out and find me a place to cross the river."

BLUE RIDGE MOUNTAINS

For the lead elements of Jackson's corps, the going was slow and treacherous up and over Fisher's Gap. The switchbacks were tiring and tedious, forcing the men to struggle over a hundred yards of frozen road to gain only ten feet of elevation.

But their just rewards awaited them at the summit. The mountain folk in these parts concocted some of the finest homemade brandy in all of Virginia, and they were more than happy to accept Confederate scrip in exchange. The urgent and well-ordered forward movement of Stonewall Jackson's corps degenerated very quickly into a confused, drunken stagger. The men began to giggle and sing and stumble and fight. Many broke ranks to throw up in the woods or, worse yet, just to take a little nap.

Brigadier General Jubal Early was appalled. He dismounted and approached one of the larger stills shouting angry orders to post a regiment around it. Not another man was to taste so much as a sip. All the while he was bellowing instructions to close the thing down, he was filling his own canteen to overflowing with the splendid golden brew.

He tested the concoction as he headed back to his horse and stopped dead in his tracks after only one sip. He found a young member of his staff and pulled him aside for a private talk. He handed the captain a handful of Confederate dollars and instructed him to "purchase a keg, and put it in my ambulance."

It wasn't long before the guards placed around the still were far too drunk to keep anyone else away, and the liquor flowed on.

Jackson was not amused. His adjutant, Sandy Pendleton, was, but Jackson most certainly was not. The normally cantankerous Jubal Early, weaving in the saddle and singing along with his men, was as happy as a puppy at supper time. He was so happy, in fact, that he thought it was incredibly funny when he was placed under arrest.

FALMOUTH

The fine dining they were accustomed to at home was a long-lost memory, but the officers of the Harvard Regiment always found a way to keep alive the elegant tradition of after-dinner cigars and political conversation.

George Macy held the floor—for the moment. "McClellan wasn't cashiered from the service. He retains his commission and he's come back before. Once this disaster has played itself out, my wager is that he'll come back again. This time forever!"

Little Abbott smelled a good verbal brawl brewing and couldn't resist egging it on. "Not so long as Mr. Lincoln is involved, which we all hope will not last very much longer."

Macy refused to give up hope—it was the last hope they had. "It was Lincoln who brought him back before."

"But he won't do it again," Abbott said. "Stanton and Halleck won't let him. The only way we'll ever get Mac back is to elect him President—mark my words."

To everybody's surprise, including Abbott's, Wendell Holmes remained perfectly quiet, leaving the floor to George Macy. "We can't wait for the next election, that's over two years away. A lot of brave men are going to die in two years."

Abbott's role on all of these occasions was to stir up trouble. It was his forte—his absolute joy in life. It had almost gotten him kicked out of Harvard as a matter of fact and, at the time, he wouldn't have cared much if it had. "The war *could* end before '64. It's possible."

Much to Abbott's delight every other man in the room began speaking at once, most of them calling him a dozen different kinds of idiot. This was particularly amusing to Little, as these same men were arguing just as vociferously a year ago that the whole affair wouldn't last six weeks. As usual though, the room eventually surrendered to Holmes.

In an uncharacteristically soft tone, Holmes finally spoke. "Little is right, gentlemen. This war is almost over, but it is *not* going to have a happy ending. If McClellan doesn't come back, and if Burnside continues to insist on this harebrained scheme of his, Mr. Lee is going to give us a whipping *right here* that could win the South its independence." The room fell ominously quiet as many considered for the very first time the nauseating possibility of total defeat. "I believe we may be only weeks away from total and permanent separation."

Holmes shook his head. "We just can't lick these guys. They're too tough, too well led, and one more thing we often choose to forget—they've got too much to lose."

After reflecting on that piece of doom for a moment, Macy put forth another view, perhaps even more depressing than Holmes's. "I disagree that the end is near. Say what you will about Abe, he's not going to give up this fight. But you're right about them having too much to lose. This emancipation nonsense has guaranteed absolutely nothing except that this war will go on forever—or at least until every Southern man in this nation is dead or conquered."

Abbott saw an opportunity to stir up just a little bit more trouble and couldn't resist. "But it's our job to *enforce* the Emancipation Proclamation, as officers in the United States Army. We're under direct orders from the commander in chief himself *and* we've sworn an oath."

"I've sworn an oath to follow all *legal* orders, Little!" Macy was getting angry now. "The Emancipation *Abomination* is not only unlawful, it's unconstitutional, and I, for one, shall play no role whatsoever in enforcing it."

Rather than launching into his well-rehearsed sermon on the evils of slavery, as Abbott hoped he would, Holmes stood up and abruptly bolted from the house. Not in anger but in sudden desperation, taking everyone by surprise.

"He's got the flux," Alley said. "Hasn't been able to keep anything inside him since he got here."

Little had suspected it but hadn't said anything. Dysentery was a serious matter in the Army of the Potomac. Dozens, if not hundreds, of men died from it every day, and it didn't give a damn whether its victim was from Harvard or Kentucky. The mood in the room turned somber, each man sympathizing with Holmes but at the same time glad not to be in the same boat. There but by the grace of God . . .

"Young Holmes is off to see the surgeons," Alley said, "and I'm afraid we'll not be seeing him for a while."

Aquia Creek Landing

An odd, mongrel navy floated around the Aquia Creek Landing. Gunboats, tall ships, stern-wheelers, and barges of all shapes and sizes floated at anchor, waiting to be told what to do. Abraham Lincoln was on the steamer *Baltimore,* waiting for Ambrose Burnside.

Burnside stood by the gangplank for several minutes before climbing aboard. He had nothing against Lincoln. A lot of the men in the army resented him—even hated him—for firing McClellan. Burnside himself had tried to talk the President out of it, not once, but three times. He had told Lincoln that he could never be half the general Mac was, but he wasn't surprised at all when McClellan was sent packing. The Young Napoleon, as he was called, would never move an inch unless he was absolutely certain of a quick and easy victory. Problem was—he was never certain. Lincoln said he had "the slows." Once he had said, "If General McClellan isn't going to use his army, I should like to borrow it for a while."

The fight between McClellan and the administration had raged for over a year until Lincoln had finally had enough. He had pushed and pushed and pushed until he had gotten sick and tired of pushing and, when McClellan had failed to pursue the Rebs after Antietam (and after the November elections), the hammer had finally fallen.

Burnside had turned down the job on several occasions. He remembered one time last August, when he stood in the President's office and pleaded with him to give Mac just one more chance. Lincoln had shown him the Emancipation Proclamation—sworn him to secrecy—and told him that with the next victory the slaves would be freed. When Lincoln announced it after Antietam, that had been the end of McClellan. From that moment on the whole thing had degenerated into pure, ugly, despicable politics. Burnside firmly believed that serious consideration had been given to a coup d'état, but thank God, that had never come about.

So Lincoln had offered the army to Burnside again and Burnside had refused it—again. Until he was told that if he didn't take the job this time it would be offered to Hooker. It was like putting a gun to his head.

So now, as he stood on the dock, readying himself for another meeting with the commander in chief, Burnside remembered all of that, especially the incessant prodding, and he was not looking forward to whatever the next hours might bring.

MARYE'S HEIGHTS

It was Edward Porter Alexander's job to place Longstreet's artillery for him, and he was having a wonderful time doing it. It was such beautiful ground for a defensive stand. He had the luxury of viewing it at leisure and bringing in the engineers to dig pits— a lavish treat in an age when so many battles happened by accident when the two armies just bumped into each other and had to fight on a spot chosen by gods rather than generals. Here he could plan his placements and conceal and protect his guns. Here he had the high ground and a field below that was as open as a pasture.

Colonel Alexander was proud of his work.

General Lee was not.

Captain Sam Johnston, the bearer of bad tidings, came running down the hill, trying to catch up with Alexander.

"General Lee has just told me that he is not pleased at all with your placement of the guns on Marye's Heights." Johnston was sweating as though it were the dead of summer. The young chief of engineers wasn't happy about being in Robert E. Lee's doghouse. "He wants to know why we put 'em on the downside of the hills instead of up on the highest point, or over on the backside to get more elevation so we can fire on the hills across the river." Johnston desperately wanted to say, "I told you so," but he hadn't, so he said the next best thing. "You made me put 'em there, so now you can come along and help me take the cussin'."

Lee and Longstreet were riding the highest point of Marye's Heights, looking across the river at the long line of ridges where Burnside's artillery was being dug in. "Ah, Colonel Alexander," Lee said, "I'm afraid Captain Johnston has misplaced your guns. They're too low to have any effect on those people across the river."

"I told him to put them there, General, and, if I may, sir, I'd like to tell you why."

"Go on, Colonel."

"I placed these guns to repel an infantry assault." Alexander was now like an artist, showing his patron the fine details of a recently completed masterpiece. He demonstrated how they were perfectly arranged to cover virtually every inch of ground for two hundred yards in front and a thousand yards along the length of a long stone wall that ran along a sunken road. "Loaded with shot and canister, and positioned as they are, General, a chicken could not live on that field when we open on it."

Longstreet smiled. Lee did not. "And how shall we respond to those guns over there"—Lee pointed toward Stafford Heights—"when they open on the town?"

"We shall not, sir. Nothing we can do from here will do anything more than give those men a headache, and the town will be bombarded anyway. Placed there, sir, the guns will gain us nothing and will cost us our view of the field below. I prefer the latter, sir."

"You were my student at West Point, were you not?"

"I was, sir."

"Well, I'm not certain that I taught you very well."

With that, Lee spurred Traveler and the two generals rode away, headed for Telegraph Hill.

Johnston was humiliated. Every man in the Army of Northern Virginia would rather die than suffer even the slightest reprimand from Marse Robert, and he felt as though he had just been severely chastised. "Well. I guess we have to dig some new emplacements."

"No, we don't."

"I beg you pardon, sir."

Alexander smiled. "Did you hear him order us to move them?"

"No—but he said . . ."

"He said I wasn't a very good student, but he *didn't* say to move the guns, and, until he does, these guns are going to stay right where they are."

THE PHILLIPS HOUSE
NOVEMBER 27

Burnside was up well before dawn and sitting alone on the porch of the Phillips house staring out into the darkness. The headquarters was still so asleep that the commanding general had to commandeer a cup of coffee from the pickets outside.

Of course he couldn't see a thing this early, but he didn't really need to. He'd been there for over a week now and the town of Fredericksburg and the heights beyond were etched deeply into his imagination. So he sat alone and pictured it in his mind and he thought about what Sumner had said, and about what Hooker had said, and about what Lincoln had said last night on the boat.

Sumner wanted to cross below Fredericksburg and Hooker wanted to cross above, and now Lincoln had chimed in with a plan of his own requiring an additional fifty thousand men—half positioned upstream and half down—ready to spring a trap or march on Richmond the moment Lee began his retreat.

It was all just too hard. He looked down at his tin cup still half full of long-ago-cold coffee and noticed that his hand was shaking. *Cold,* he thought, but he didn't really feel cold. Pity the poor boys out on picket duty tonight. Cold—lack of sleep—there were lots of reasons why a man's hands might shake.

But deep down, Ambrose Burnside knew why his hands shook. He was scared.

Ambrose Burnside, he thought . . . failed businessman, ticket-taker for the railroad, and now commanding general of the largest army in the world. He had pleaded with Lincoln not to give him the job. He had told the President he wasn't qualified. Hell—he had told *everyone* he wasn't qualified. And yet, here he was, with the lives of two hundred thousand men in his hands if you count both sides of the river. Two hundred thousand soldiers, three million slaves, and the future of an entire nation rested in the trembling hands of Ambrose Burnside, and he was just plain scared.

It was still an hour before sunrise when he heard the sound of horses approaching. He threw the remaining coffee out onto what used to be Mr. Phillips's lawn and walked down the steps to greet his guest—Edwin Sumner.

Without so much as exchanging salutes, Burnside gave Sumner the good news—what there was of it.

"I met with the President last night."

Sumner was taken aback. "What did he say?"

"He said Halleck isn't in charge—he is. And he told me not to go until I was ready."

"Well, *there's* a switch. He's been pushing his generals into battle ever since McDowell at First Bull Run."

"He says he and the nation are prepared to be patient. He wants us to get it right."

"The way things stand right now that might be easier said than done."

"Maybe so, General, but at least we're not crossing those bridges today, which is what I thought he was going to order me to do."

Sumner cringed at the thought, but at the same time he

knew they couldn't wait too much longer. "Be that as it may, General, but I believe that Longstreet is fully up now . . ." The old soldier hesitated. He was reluctant to pile worse news on top of bad, but, as it turned out, he didn't have to. Burnside knew what was coming and finished Sumner's thought for him.

". . . And Jackson's on his way."

It was time for the sun to rise, but it couldn't break through the thick morning fog. All it could do was turn the pitch-black night into a dreary gray day.

"General Burnside, sir?"

"Yes?"

Sumner sighed. "Happy Thanksgiving."

The vast majority of the men in the Army of the Potomac had very little to be thankful for. They lived in squalor, they were constantly wet and cold, and many suffered from dysentery or diarrhea brought on by a constant diet of hard-tack and coffee. Individual units made some concessions to this unofficial holiday by scheduling concerts, Bible readings, and speeches from officers telling them how grateful they should be to be here. Most of the men spent their Thanksgiving Day wishing they were home. They pictured their families, warm and safe and gathered together around a bountiful table piled to the sky with turkey and ham and bowls filled to overflowing with potatoes and corn and piping hot fresh baked bread soaked with butter. It all made hardtack hard to look at. It was a stale, inedible, bug-infested slap in the face. Homesick on the best of days, this horribly cold Thanksgiving Day was a hundred times worse.

For the McClernan brothers Thanksgiving was made either better or worse by the fact that they were together. They were nine-month enlistees from Camden, assigned to the 24th New Jersey. Their father was probably around here somewhere too, but he was an artilleryman and didn't travel with his boys.

James and George McClernan had enlisted back in August—after Malvern Hill, but just before Second Bull Run. They had only just begun their training when Lee marched into Maryland, so they missed South Mountain and Antietam as well. But now they had caught up with the Army of the Potomac and had been assigned to Kimball's Brigade along with some other New Jersey boys and some veterans from Ohio, Delaware, and Virginia—what some were calling "West" Virginia these days.

The brothers were so far untouched by an outbreak of the measles that had plagued the 24th for the past couple of weeks, but were no less cold and hungry and miserable. "Camp Misery" they called their current home.

Early on this Thanksgiving Thursday they were summoned to their commanding officer's tent. Neither had a notion what it could be about, but both doubted it was anything good.

"You boys the McClernan brothers?"

"We are, sir," they answered simultaneously.

Colonel Robertson examined the two and never would have figured them for brothers. James was obviously the older, but he was also larger, darker, and had a much rounder face. George was not much more than a boy and was almost frail compared to his older brother.

"I've called you in here to do a favor for your momma."

The boys were more confused now than ever.

Robertson grinned for a second, but then he gave them the news that he knew they wouldn't like. "I'm busting you boys up."

They were second-generation Irish, but Irish nonetheless. Both faces went beet red with anger at precisely the same moment.

"Don't worry—you'll both stay in the 24th, but I'm moving one of you out of Company D and into Company I."

James was about to burst, and even though he had not been invited to speak, he couldn't help himself.

"Why, sir?"

"Several reasons. One is just a numbers game, but I would have made this change anyway. I'm doing it with as many families as I can." He hesitated a minute before going into his well-practiced speech.

"Neither of you has ever seen battle before, and you have no idea what it can be like. I have. And I've seen what happens when a single shell blows a hole twenty-men deep in a company of men. And I've seen what happens to a family when brothers fall, side by side at the very same instant. I am the man who has to write the letters, and it's hard enough to tell a mother that one of her sons has died. I hate writing two names in the same letter. For those people back home, it makes the worst day of their lives twice as bad."

Robertson paused to give them a moment to understand. "So, James, effective immediately, you have been reassigned to Company I. You will still be able to watch out for each other—only with some interval."

The McClernan brothers moped their way back to their tent and tried to find some little something to be thankful for. They supposed they should be thankful for Colonel Robertson. His heart was in the right place. Good intentions and all. What he had done for them—for their mother and sister and all—wasn't by the book. The boys had never heard of such a thing, but after some rational thought it made sense. They would still much rather have stayed together, but they finally understood.

It was dinnertime before the sadness and homesickness of the holiday really hit them, when it came time to fry some pork fat for the hardtack to soak up.

"Ummmm," George said as he almost broke a tooth on his stone-hard Lincoln Biscuit. "Nothing better than a golden brown turkey leg."

The Bucktails, however, were not content with a make-believe feast. They, by God, were going to have a *real* one. These men were a pack of sharpshooting frontiersmen from the "wildcat district" of western Pennsylvania. Before the war they had been lumberjacks who had hunted for their food and lived by their own rules in the rugged Pennsylvania wilderness. They got their name from the deer tails that adorned their hats, their symbol since the day they signed up. They had been fighting almost since day one. They battled gallantly on the Peninsula, in the Shenandoah Valley, at Second Bull Run, South Mountain, and Antietam, and there weren't nearly as many Bucktails as there used to be. Regardless of their heroism, the army constantly tried to tame them—and constantly failed. These men remained frontiersmen—adamantly unruly and totally undisciplined. They not only ignored the rules—they flaunted them, and any punishment they might suffer was worn as a badge of honor. They were a sharp thorn in the side of General George Gordon Meade, who now commanded their division. They despised him and his short temper and his disciplinarian tactics. They called him "that damned old goggle-eyed snapping turtle," and he called them undisciplined riffraff.

The Bucktails were bivouacked a mile and a half downriver from Falmouth and hadn't been there long before they named the place "Camp Starvation." They put up a sign. Meade tore it down. They put it back up. They tore up fence rails for firewood and Meade punished them, and they burned more fence rails. Whenever the general rode anywhere near he was followed by the humiliating chant of "crackers and hardtack," coming from the loathed Bucktails—an affront that only last week had resulted in the entire regiment being forced to stand at attention all day long in a cold, driving rainstorm. But that was long ago and long forgotten. Damned if they would spend Thanksgiving Day eating brick-hard Lincoln Biscuits dipped in coffee, the men of the Bucktail Regiment, the 13th Pennsylvania Volunteers, went out, against orders, as usual, and took a Rebel hog prisoner. They held a trial, found the pig guilty, and executed him for treason. The perpetrators of this dastardly act were subject to be hanged, but they all knew that not even George Meade would hang a soldier for stealing a pig on Thanksgiving Day. Besides—the evidence had been consumed.

Once again Colonel Tilden called his "Blanket Brigade" together for another announcement.

"I'm colder than a pig in an ice house," Ned Stevens told his brother—as though Will needed to be told.

"Well, never you fret, baby brother. Colonel Tilden is about to warm us all up with a fresh list of excuses."

The 16th Maine gathered around as they had a dozen times before, waiting to be told again that their shoes and coats and tents were "on the way."

Tilden ordered them to attention and marched them a quarter mile to a clearing just north of their bivouac. The clearing was loaded with about a dozen wagons filled with new, warm coats, shoes, and tents.

He said only two words. "Happy Thanksgiving."

MADISON COURTHOUSE

"He did *what*?"

Kyd Douglas was ready for the wrath of Maxcy Gregg. He knew that the aristocratic general from South Carolina needed very little provocation to spit fire at Stonewall Jackson, and now Gregg felt legitimately provoked.

"He released General Early without charges."

"That old man was as drunk as a skunk while leading a march, and Jackson lets him go! Our men were heroes at Manassas, and we very nearly got wiped out, and the very next day he arrested General Hill for being five minutes late starting a march! My entire regiment would have been killed that day if it hadn't been for General Hill."

"General Gregg. . . ."

"Hell—if it hadn't been for Powell Hill this whole damned army would have been destroyed at Sharpsburg, and still that madman harps on being five minutes late on the march so that our men could fill up their damned canteens! And now he finds another general *drunk* on the march for cryin' out loud—fallin' down, slobberin' drunk I might add—and he just lets *him* go!"

Douglas gave up on making any rational arguments on Jackson's behalf. It was best at this point to just let Gregg blow off steam and be done with it.

"Thomas J. Jackson isn't fit to lead schoolboys on a playground, and that's what I think of our precious Stonewall."

For Thomas J. "Stonewall" Jackson, this was the best

Thanksgiving Day ever, for on this day he received the long-awaited news. His wife was well, and he was the father of a beautiful, healthy baby girl.

FALMOUTH
NOVEMBER 28

Bill McCarter shivered once again, but not from the cold this time. This time it was from fear.

Everyone had been so nice to him since the night he had almost frozen to death. The Catholics in the Irish Brigade were convinced that he was nothing less than a favored child of the Blessed Virgin—rescued from purgatory directly by the hand of God. The men had told him they really had been ready to put him in the earth that night, to bury him alive, absolutely convinced that the stuttering little Irishman was as dead as a frozen mackerel.

So McCarter had spent the last few days enjoying his new celebrity, until someone handed him a note.

Look up McCarter, the order read, *and send him forthwith to my tent. Fill his place in line with another man.* The order was signed General T. F. Meagher.

Asleep on duty. It was the first thing—the only thing—that came to McCarter's mind. He came very close to tears.

So now he waited outside of Meagher's tent—waiting, he was certain, to be called in and shot, right there on the spot. His regimental commander had told them all about a thousand times that a man could be shot for sleeping on picket duty. Nobody ever had, but there's always a first time. Okay. Probably not shot, but surely some kind of horrible punishment, some public humiliation for the entertainment of the Irish Brigade.

He sat on a trunk and tried to write a letter home. He was most proud of his penmanship, but not today. Today his hand shook uncontrollably and there was no help for it.

"So this is the famous Private McCarter." The brogue was so think you could smell the whiskey on it. McCarter looked up to see General Thomas Francis Meagher looking down at him. McCarter leaped to his feet, letting pencil and paper fall to the ground in front of him so that he could come to attention and salute.

"Yes, sir! Private William M-M-McCarter, sir!"

Meagher smiled. "Whoa. Calm down a wee bit, lad. I'm not gonna bite ya."

It helped a little but not much.

"I hear that you are a man who's come back from the dead."

"A bit of an exaggeration, s-sir." He hated his stutter. Standing right here, in front of one of the most respected and important men in the world, and the poor boy couldn't even say "sir" without stammering.

"Be that as it may, Private, it's quite a feat. I know of only one man who's ever done it before!" He laughed and patted McCarter on the back, and the general's permanent entourage laughed along with him.

Meagher pointed down at the piece of paper on the ground. "And what might that be?"

"I was writing a letter home, sir." There. An entire sentence without a stutter. Much better.

"It's okay, Private. You can pick it up before it blows away."

McCarter did as he was told, but felt a little awkward doing it. He came right back up to full attention.

"I don't want you to think I'm pryin' now, but it has come to my attention that you've got a beautiful hand."

A beautiful hand? McCarter was astounded. The man's about to court-martial me and he wants to talk about my handwriting? "Ah, a lot of people think so, sir. Some of the men get me to write their letters h-home for 'em."

"The good Lord works in mysterious ways, Private. It just so happens that I'm in need of a new assistant adjutant. The man I've got now writes like a chicken tracking over paper. Might you want to do some writin' for me?"

McCarter couldn't believe it. Two minutes ago he feared for his life and now he was being offered a job writing things down for General Meagher. He glowed.

"Surely, sir!"

"Done then." He turned to a nearby captain. "See to it."

And that was that. The captain told him to make himself comfortable and that his first assignment would be coming along in an hour or so, and just like that, everyone vanished back into the tent.

A man come back from the dead, McCarter thought. *Twice.*

SKINKER'S NECK

For the second night in a row, Wesley Brainerd was behind enemy lines, scouting for a crossing site.

Last night had been a disaster. He and his men had damned near drowned when they got across the river and went to set foot on "dry land." Brainerd sank in well over his knees and had to be pulled out of the high tide marsh.

But on this night, he had higher hopes. He and his small squad of men rowed across the river at a spot called Skinker's Neck, more than a dozen miles downstream from Falmouth. The approaches were wide and solid. There was plenty of room to bring in the pontoons and maneuver troops. It offered a firm footing for the artillery. Only two questions remained: Was the ground on the other side solid enough to support a parade of soldiers, horses, and big guns; and were there any Rebels there? It was Brainerd's job to find out.

Remembering the misstep of the night before, Brainerd was a little more cautious this time while climbing out of the boat. No need. The ground beneath his feet was moist from all the recent rains, but just under that it was as unyielding as brick. They spent virtually the entire night wandering through the woods and along the roads. Once they had to dash for cover as a Rebel cavalry squad trotted by, but Brainerd saw this as good news—where there are cavalry patrols, there is seldom any infantry.

FREDERICKSBURG
NOVEMBER 29

Through the thick morning fog Robert E. Lee could see only the silhouette of the man approaching him on horseback. From the outline he was certain that it was

Jeb Stuart and was amazed when the man got closer and he realized that it was actually Stonewall Jackson—he was only dressed up like Jeb Stuart. He wore a big, black, fully festooned hat and a new, gray frockcoat lavishly trimmed in gold. The regalia of a cavalier. He also wore something else uncommon to him—a smile.

"Good morning to you, General Lee, sir!"

"And to you, General Jackson. You have made good time, and I hope your corps is close at hand."

"The roads are in deplorable condition, sir, and we've come almost two hundred miles. The vanguard should begin arriving here tomorrow, but I see no way that they will be up in force before Tuesday night or Wednesday morning. And that only with God's guidance."

"Three or four days hence," Lee said. He didn't need to say any more. Jackson knew full well what the man was thinking. *Dear God, please let it be soon enough.*

Jackson waited long enough for Lee to finish his short prayer. "What plans do you have for them, sir, when they arrive?"

"General Longstreet has established very fine positions on the heights just beyond the town, but he is spread very thin to our right. If the fight is to be here, you will pull your men into line near Hamilton's Crossing, in front of Prospect Hill, just behind the rail lines there. If you place the bulk of your corps there, it will allow General Longstreet to shorten and strengthen his lines on our left."

"The bulk, sir?"

"Yes. I am not yet certain as to General Burnside's plans. If what we have before us is a feint, it may be the largest in history, but it still may be. There seems to be some activity in the vicinity of Port Royal. A crossing there might threaten our flank or steal a march on us to Richmond. We'll need some strength there as soon as possible, General. At least enough for a delaying action until we know better what those people have in mind."

Jackson nodded and saluted. "With your permission, sir, I will have a quick look at the ground."

"Of course, General Jackson."

Stonewall went on about his business, leaving Lee alone for the moment.

Four days. It was a frightening thought. *If Burnside crosses quickly,* en masse, *he might very easily break through and head directly for Richmond before Jackson's men ever arrive.*

Again Lee looked to the sky, still obscured by the fog, and he started to pray for bad weather to hold Burnside in place, but rain, sleet, and snow would also further delay his own reinforcements coming in from the valley. And so Robert E. Lee prayed his most comfortable prayer—the one he whispered every day, a hundred times a day.

"Thy will, O God, be done."

SKINKER'S NECK

General Henry Hunt was Burnside's chief of artillery and on this day his job, along with the recently unarrested Daniel Woodbury, was to reconnoiter the crossing site at Skinker's Neck with Wesley Brainerd's reconnaissance squad. Brainerd reported to the generals what he and his men had found the previous night, and he couldn't contain his enthusiasm. A small shed occupied by three or four "contrabands" and a single squad of Rebel cavalry was their only sighting of human beings. He reported solid roads (considering the recent snow and rain) and favorable terrain on the southern banks.

Hunt took the captain's word for it on the south side, but he also had to consider long-range artillery placement on the northern side as well for covering fire. He had to examine all of the roads between there and Falmouth to determine if they could be traveled, quickly and safely, by a grand division of men and horses and fifty or more heavy guns. This was going to take some time.

It took the rest of the day.

FREDERICKSBURG

Stonewall Jackson quickly studied the terrain around Prospect Hill, just off to Longstreet's right flank. The hill itself was wooded, ideal for concealment, and at its base stretched thousands of acres of open land, broken by the tracks of the Richmond, Fredericksburg & Potomac Railroad and the Old Richmond Stage Road, both of which ran generally parallel to the river.

Jackson didn't believe for a moment that the Yankees would attempt a crossing there because it was too wide open. Good for maneuvering, but vulnerable and clearly visible from Lee's position on Telegraph Hill. Nonetheless, it was the Confederate army's right flank, and whether the Yanks crossed here or farther downstream didn't really matter. He would kill them no matter where they came from.

As the day grew late, Jackson headed for the house arranged for him by the staff. The owner had slammed the door in their faces until they mentioned that his honored guest would be none other than Stonewall himself and the reluctant host had quickly become convinced to open that door widely. After a long day, a good meal and a warm bed awaited.

Jackson had ridden all night and worked all day, but he was not the least bit tired. He offered a long prayer before the meal and joined in boisterous and lighthearted conversation during. Many of those gathered actually heard the pious general laugh for the very first time. While everyone else wanted nothing more than to drag themselves to bed, Stonewall seemed to want to talk all night. He finally realized that he was keeping everybody up and allowed himself to be escorted to the master bedroom. He thanked his host graciously and sat down to the desk to jot off a personal note home.

"Oh, how thankful I am to our kind Heavenly Father for having spared my precious wife and given us a little daughter!"

On and on he wrote, giving endless thanks to God and assuring his wife that no little girl in the world would ever be loved more. But then, perhaps failing to note his own contradiction, he added: "Do not set your affections upon her, except as a gift from God. If she absorbs too much of our hearts, God may remove her from us."

WASHINGTON, D.C.
NOVEMBER 30

The fire was warm and the men were quiet. Lincoln loved this room. The rooms in the White House were all so pretentious and Mary had decorated them far too lavishly back in her happier days—before Willie had passed away. Seward's house was much more a home. The President frequently came here just to sit and talk, away from the endless lines of office seekers and the mountainous piles of documents that seemed to chase him from room to room in the Executive Mansion.

In Seward's well-worn, overstuffed favorite chair, Lincoln sat and rested while his secretary of state read the President's message to Congress for about the tenth time in as many days. The whole procedure was a presidential pain in the neck, but it had to be done. The Constitution said so. Two copies would be delivered to the Capitol tomorrow, one to the Speaker of the House and one to the president of the Senate, to be read aloud in each chamber.

While the secretary read, the President studied his face and slid into a frenzy of remembering. He remembered the very early days—before Fort Sumter—when Seward thought he could hold the South in the Union by declaring war on England. It was the first, but not the last, of Seward's grandiose, harebrained schemes. Mary had hated him for years, ever since the 1860 Republican Convention, or maybe even longer than that. She hated him then, and she hated him still. Seward's nomination as Secretary of State was the cause of her very first tantrum as First Lady–elect. She had stamped her feet and clenched her fists, shrieking at the top of her tiny voice, "Seward in the cabinet? *Never!* That dirty abolitionist sneak will take credit for everything that goes right, and he'll blame Abe for anything that might go wrong!" She wanted none of the presidential candidates from that convention in the cabinet, but her husband had a contrary view. He knew from the moment he accepted the nomination that Seward, Chase, and Bates would begin their '64 campaigns the minute the election of 1860 was decided. So he appointed them *all* to the cabinet—regardless of Mary Todd's adamant and boisterous objections.

"Keep your friends close," he'd told her, "and your enemies closer."

But William Seward was no longer an enemy. He had become Lincoln's closest friend and adviser. Politically, he balanced off against Chase and Stanton, the radicals in the cabinet, very nicely. Personally, and maybe most importantly, the New York sophisticate, the onetime leader of the "silk hat Republicans," actually seemed to enjoy Lincoln's homespun humor—a very rare thing in Washington Town. He was the only man in the cabinet capable of a good, joyful belly laugh and Lincoln couldn't bear to think what he would do without him.

He continued to study the face that he had once found so devious. *If ever any man ought to have a beard,* he thought, *it's Seward.* The man has no chin! A hook nose, gigantic ears, bushy eyebrows, and no chin at all. But the secretary remained completely clean shaven, regardless of the fashion of the day.

Finally Seward sighed, as he had every time he'd read the message.

"Senators Wade and Sumner are going to go apoplectic when they hear this," he said.

"And Secretary Chase."

"Has the treasury secretary seen it yet?"

"He has." Lincoln smiled. "His face turned so red he looked like a tomato with ears!"

"Compensated emancipation?"

"Primarily. I think that's what he hated most." The President chuckled. "It's hard to tell what Chase hates *most*."

Seward smiled too, but shook his head at the same time. "Mr. President, when the new Congress is seated in March, we will have only a sixteen-vote majority in the House, and you're asking for a constitutional amendment, actually *three* of them, not a one of which has a snowball's chance in hell of getting a two-thirds vote. Hell—we won't even be able to get all of the *Republicans* to vote for 'em."

"But the moderate Republicans and the war Democrats together might add up to two-thirds."

"Moderate Republicans?" Seward shook his head. "Now there's an oxymoron! You'll find more virgins in a whore-house than moderates in our party these days. The majority of our party wants to free all the slaves immediately and give them full citizenship and even let them *vote*! And you're ask-ing them to *buy* slaves and ship them off to some colony somewhere. That's going to cost a pretty penny as well."

Lincoln was getting tired of making the same arguments over and over again, and he almost lost his temper. "It will cost a darned sight less than fighting this *war*! Why can't *anybody* understand that?"

He had overreacted and he knew it. There was a moment of embarrassed silence before the President took a fresh piece of paper out of his pocket and handed it to Seward.

"I rewrote the closing paragraph last night."

Seward took the new page and read it to himself.

IN GIVING FREEDOM TO THE SLAVE WE ASSURE FREE-DOM FOR THE FREE—HONORABLE ALIKE IN WHAT WE GIVE AND WHAT WE PRESERVE.

WE SHALL NOBLY SAVE OR MEANLY LOSE THE LAST, BEST HOPE OF EARTH. OTHER MEANS MAY SUCCEED; THIS COULD NOT FAIL. THE WAY IS PLAIN, PEACEFUL, GENEROUS, JUST—A WAY WHICH, IF FOLLOWED, THE WORLD WILL FOREVER APPLAUD AND GOD MUST FOR-EVER BLESS.

Seward looked at Lincoln and said nothing.

Lincoln gathered up the pages from Seward's table as he prepared to leave. "It is the only way. We are giving the slaveholders until the year 1900 to free their slaves and get their money. That's plenty of time for them to adjust their economy—*and* plenty of time for the slaves to receive an education and learn a trade. By shipping them off to South

America, we've taken away the fear of the Northern cities that millions of black men will migrate North to take their jobs, and the whole kit and caboodle taken together may very well bring a quick and easy end to the war."

As tired as Lincoln was of making these arguments, Seward was equally tired of hearing them. He sighed deeply. "Not a snowball's chance in hell, Mr. President, and I'll wager a quart of hazelnuts that these amendments never even come to a vote."

The President smiled one last time. "A quart of hazelnuts it is."

CHAPTER 5

Henry Villard soaked in his very first view of the Army of the Potomac, and it was a magnificent sight. By the time he awoke, the fog had burned away and the morning was as clear as crystal and the hill on which he stood overlooked what must have been the whole vast Army of the Potomac. There were more tents on the ground than stars in the heavens. The legions of Rome could never have been so grand as this.

A dreadful beauty, he thought. It reminded him of the terrifying majesty of a magnificent predator. A colossal tiger waking before the hunt. The Army of the Potomac was a spectacularly beautiful killing machine.

He broke a layer of ice off the water in a nearby bucket so he could splash his face. It was bitterly cold but felt so good he did it three times. But now it was time for business, and Villard headed off to make the acquaintance of Major General Joseph "Fightin' Joe" Hooker. George Smalley's old friend was as good a place as any to start.

While he stood outside Hooker's tent waiting to be announced, he heard a stream of profanities that would have shocked Satan.

"Bad time?" he asked the adjutant.

The man responded with a shrug and a smile, "No better or worse than any other."

It was only moments later when he was ushered into the general's tent. Villard noticed immediately that Hooker was still red-faced with anger, but at the same time he was a fine-looking general. He stood straight and tall. He had blond hair and commanding eyes that were neither blue nor green. *This is a man who was born to lead,* Villard thought, *or at least one who expected to be obeyed.*

Villard handed him a letter of introduction that Hooker scanned briefly, barely noticing the glowing reports of Villard's talent and skill and trustworthiness. He got quickly to the signature.

"Smalley! That man did brave work at Antietam."

Villard was over it by now. *Everybody loves George Smalley and I've just got to live with it and prove that I'm just as good.*

"He thinks the world of you, General Hooker."

"Yeah, that young reporter put on a uniform at Antietam. I personally saw him climb off a dead horse and keep on going to deliver an order for me. Good man."

"We think so . . ."

"Hell of a story he wrote too!"

"Best ever."

"He might have had a *better* story to tell if I hadn't gotten my foot damned near shot off. I was *this* close. One damned charge away from licking that damned son-of-a-bitch Jackson once and for all! Now *that* would have been a story!"

Villard had long since decided that he had no hope of being any more than a listener in this conversation, but what the hell, that's what reporters are supposed to do anyway.

"I'll tell you another thing . . ." Hooker peeked at Smalley's letter to remind himself of the reporter's name, ". . . Henry. That same bullet cost me the command of this army and gave it to that bungling idiot Burnside!"

"Bungling idiot, sir?"

"That's what I said. It took him all day long to get across

that damned bridge at Sharpsburg—'Burnside's Bridge' they call it now. He was held up all day long by a couple of dozen Georgia clod farmers throwing rocks at him. If he'd gotten across that damned bridge when he was supposed to I'd'ave whipped Jackson before I got shot!"

Hooker paused, but it was only to take a breath.

"And the crime is that he's not much worse than any of that bunch of McClellan-lovin' bastards he's got around him."

"Like who?"

Hooker still used a cane and used it now like a saber, aimed directly at Villard's heart. "Franklin. Same thing. At South Mountain he had a whole damned corps and got held up for a day by a handful of dismounted cavalry and a couple of lousy light guns. All damned day! And Sumner— well, that old man just lost his nerve."

"So are we gonna get whipped again? The same people are in charge."

"Damned right we are! The Rebels are pouring into that town like ants to sugar, and if Burnside thinks he's going to be able to go through 'em, well, a lot of men are gonna have to die to prove him wrong. Mark my words."

"Well, I hope you're wrong, sir."

"Well, I'm not! Hell, I've heard that Lincoln even made a special trip down here to try to talk him out of it, and Lincoln ain't exactly Napoleon himself."

This pause was to light a cigar. "Let me tell you this, Henry, and I've told it to old Abe himself. I'm the best damned general he's got in his whole damned army, and until he puts me in command we're gonna just keep on getting whipped, and I don't care who you tell."

FALMOUTH
DECEMBER 2

Bill McCarter stood just behind General Meagher and watched as the regimental color guards marched into the hall under the proud green flags of the Irish Brigade. He knew what was happening only because he'd been told. The veterans *felt* it at the very core of their being. Most of them were the Irish Catholics from New York City. Bill was a Protestant from Philly and knew nothing of the "Know-Nothings."

Only a year or two ago the Know-Nothings would have loved nothing more than to beat the stuffing out of any Irish Catholic caught walking the streets alone, but as the fame of General Meagher's boys grew, many of the "natives" of New York decided it was time to mend fences. "Give us your glorious green flags," they told Meagher, "stained, torn, and bullet-riddled, and we will restore them to their old glory and bring them back, mended, clean, and better than new."

Meagher had agreed. To him it represented a glorious victory. But to his Irish Catholic men, handing over their flags to the Know-Nothings felt more like surrender. For those who had followed the green flags with the golden harps into battle from Bull Run to Antietam, it tore their brave hearts to tears to see the glorious standards handed over to anyone. Most didn't even want them mended. Every hole was a badge of honor, every rend melded them closer together, and every drop of blood that stained the green satin was nothing less than a sacred icon.

But the new regiments were there as well, and McCarter easily spotted Stretch standing at the head of his column and his heart broke just a bit. It seemed a century ago and it seemed a minute ago that Stretch had warmed him back to life, and he couldn't help but feel just a little bit ashamed. It had been little more than a week since he had abandoned the 116th for the luxury of headquarters life. He remembered the weeks when he had had nothing but hardtack and coffee for days on end. These days he dined with the general on such delicacies as salt-boiled salmon and fresh potatoes. He even got condensed milk to lighten his coffee and fine Virginia tobacco for his pipe and he slept on the soft sofa in the general's warm tent.

The band struck up "Garryowen" as the colors were struck, rolled, and returned to their cases for a trip to New York and a date with a seamstress.

As the regiments filed out of the room, Stretch caught

McCarter's eye and smiled and winked at him. *It's all right,* the old German told him with that one, quick look. *Go about your business. We're all proud of you.* It helped—but not much.

THE PHILLIPS HOUSE
DECEMBER 3

For the first time in weeks, things were finally going right for Ambrose Burnside. He was almost his old, affable self as he announced his new plans to his grand division and corps commanders, whom he had gathered at the Phillips house.

"The engineers and General Hunt have reconnoitered a crossing point at a spot called Skinker's Neck, twelve miles from our present location. I am assured that it is adequate for mass movements of men and artillery."

He looked at Woodbury and Hunt and waited for them to confirm this with emphatic nods.

"Most importantly, it appears that General Lee has failed to guard it—and for this oversight we shall make him pay. A speedy crossing here will place us between Longstreet and Richmond. Gentlemen, from this point we can do some very serious damage to the rebellion."

Burnside shot a quick glance at Joe Hooker that told him in an instant to shut up and do as he was told. Hooker said nothing.

Burnside nodded. "Generals Franklin and Hooker will be prepared to move at dawn, day after tomorrow. In the meantime, prepare three days' cooked rations and issue each man sixty rounds of ammunition."

FREDERICKSBURG

On the road now for almost two weeks, with 175 miles of frozen or muddy roads behind them, Stonewall Jackson's corps began to struggle into Fredericksburg, one exhausted regiment, one famished company, one barefooted soldier at a time. But much to James Longstreet's dismay, the Army of Northern Virginia was still spread out over more than thirty miles—from the confluence of the Rapidan and the Rappahannock in the north, all the way south to Port Royal on the Potomac.

"General Burnside has too many options," Lee told Longstreet, "and until he tips his hand, we have to guard against them all."

Longstreet grudgingly had to agree, but he knew full well that eighty thousand men, stretched along a front this long, formed a line as thin and brittle as a dried-out twig, and just as easily broken.

WASHINGTON, D.C.
DECEMBER 4

Fitz-John Porter went pale as he watched his inquisitors enter the chamber. He had seen their names on a list, but this was the first time he had seen them assembled together. They were announced and paraded themselves into the room. It was all Porter could do to force himself to stand as they entered.

A modern-day star-chamber. It was the only thought that came to Porter's mind as his eye moved down the line. It looked like the assembled guest list for one of Salmon Chase's Republican soirees. One man was actually a regular houseguest at the Chase home. Another was an officer Porter had refused to accept in his command and had sent packing back to Washington—thoroughly humiliated. An epileptic drunk who was far more responsible for the defeat at Second Bull Run than Porter had been sat alongside a personal friend of the Lincoln family.

These pompous inquisitors looked so solemn and arrogant as the charges against Porter were read, as though these ludicrous complaints should be taken seriously and that a fair and impartial verdict was certain to be reached.

Before the first witness was called, Porter had given the

proceedings a name of his own making: *The Republican Inquisition,* he called it.

PORT ROYAL

"FIRE!"

The explosion echoed across the valley and the round splashed into the brown water of the Rappahannock just three feet short of the ugly Union gunboat. John Pelham grinned as the Yankee sailors who had been napping on deck scurried for cover.

Pelham was a skinny, freckle-faced country boy from Benton County, Alabama. He was either blessed or cursed with soft blue eyes, thin red lips, and fine blond hair that he had to keep cut short so as not to be mistaken for a sixteen-year-old girl. In a word, John Pelham was "pretty." But his cherubic appearance was a perfect irony. As a boy he broke bulls—for riding—for fun. At West Point he championed in fencing and boxing, and at twenty-five he was a major in the Confederate army, where he commanded Jeb Stuart's artillery—and his respect. He had won the admiration of both sides for his fearless actions at Manassas, on the Peninsula, at Manassas again, at Sharpsburg, and while covering Stuart's crossing of the Potomac after his most recent circumnavigation of George McClellan's army—a humiliation that turned out to be the last blow to the final nail in the Young Napoleon's coffin.

For his courage and skill on the field of battle, Stuart called him "brilliant."

For his pretty-little-girl good looks, everyone else called him "Sallie."

For the past ten days Pelham and his men had been pestering a flotilla of Federal gunboats that were hanging around Port Royal, trying to position themselves for a run up the river to Fredericksburg. He couldn't do a lot of damage, but he did the best he could. Basically, he was being a pest. He would toss them an exploding calling card two or three times a day, just to let them know he was there and force them to lift anchor and move someplace they didn't want to be.

But today was going to be different. D. H. Hill of Jackson's corps had arrived last night from the valley, and now there were enough Rebel guns to do some serious damage to the pesky Federal gunboats.

Sallie Pelham's favorite crew was a unit of French-speaking Cajuns from Mobile who shared Pelham's lust for life and joy of fighting. They played army every day and loved it every minute. Pelham called these men his Napoleon Detachment, after both the gun and the emperor, and the pun was intended. Sallie Pelham loved his Frenchmen. Particularly he loved Jean.

Jean had no last name. Jean was all there was and all he needed. He was a little wisp of a Cajun whose accent was an odd merger of French with a Haitian tilt blended with a distinctive pronunciation borrowed from the *Hommes du colour libre* —the free men of color—he grew up with. The English language was a distant third, but it was in there somewhere.

From upstream and around a bend in the river, Pelham heard the unique sound of Hill's newly acquired Whitworth Rifle. It was a British breachloader and its projectile whistled a loud, continuous, ominous note for the entire duration of its flight. After only a couple of these threatening high notes and the resounding explosions that followed, four more Union boats came chugging around the bend, headed directly for Pelham's three-inch Blakelys—just as planned. Pelham's guns were hidden in the trees about three hundred yards from where he knew the boats would have to pass.

"Darn, those things are ugly," he told Jean as they came into view. "They look like something from the nether regions—which is precisely where I intend to send them."

His guns were already loaded and pricked. As the USS *Jacob Bell* came into range, Pelham only nodded and the men of the Napoleon Detachment began to sing.

> *Allons enfants de la Patrie*
> *Le jour de gloire . . .*

The lanyard was pulled, the powder exploded, and the ball was on its way.

. . . *est arrivé!*

Pelham liked fighting the navy, because he could always see just how close his rounds fell to the target. This one was long, but only by a matter of feet.

He turned the elevation screw and ordered "tail right," to adjust for the movement of the boat. Once again the boy major ordered "fire," this time launching a direct hit. He watched as "all hands" (as they say in the navy) scurried "below decks" to check and repair the damage. All four gunboats put on full steam and headed for safety, but not before unloading their guns on Pelham, costing Private Harrison a leg. Much to Pelham's dismay, the *Jacob Bell* survived—but Burnside's gunboats were gone, and probably gone for good.

With that little issue cared for, D. H. Hill had some serious work to do. He had more than five miles of riverbanks to guard, and barely a division to do it with.

STAFFORD HEIGHTS

The Corn Exchange Regiment was the most miserable bunch of soldiers in the entire Army of the Potomac, and Captain Francis Donaldson was the most miserable of the lot. He had not enlisted in the Corn Exchange Regiment in the first place, but had been captured, exchanged, and when he returned, his old unit had been so beaten down that they required no more officers and Donaldson found himself commanding a company in his present regiment known officially as the 118th Pennsylvania Volunteers.

His men were an unhappy lot for the usual reasons: bad food, awful weather, slow pay, unbearable boredom, Draconian punishments, and lice. Donaldson was unhappy because he hated Lieutenant Colonel James Gwyn, the uncivilized lush who commanded the regiment. The two men had hated each other from the moment of their very first meeting. Donaldson thought Gwyn was a drunken, dictatorial, worthless excuse for a leader, and Gwyn thought Donaldson was an arrogant, pigheaded, "holier-than-thou" pain in the butt. Both men were right.

Only a couple of weeks ago Gwyn tried to blow past one of Donaldson's pickets without offering the proper countersign. He became abusive to the young guard who finally let the drunken colonel pass. Captain Donaldson ordered them *both* arrested. He proffered charges against the private for failure to follow orders, and against the colonel for "conduct unbecoming an officer."

Cooler heads eventually prevailed, at least in the colonel's case, and Donaldson withdrew the charges, but the damage was done, and Colonel Gwyn's primary role in life became making the haughty young captain's life a living hell. The tougher Gwyn was on Donaldson, the tougher Donaldson was on his men.

There was one, single bright spot in Donaldson's otherwise wretched existence, and that was his "man," George Slow. Slow had been a slave all of his life until his master, a man named Pendleton, had enlisted in the Rebel army back in the early days of the war. He simply couldn't keep slaves on his new salary of twelve dollars a month, even if he got paid on time, which was never. So rather than sell them, he set his slaves free, and George Slow found himself on his own for the first time ever. The Pendletons were good people, and Mrs. Pendleton continued to care as best she could for the few of their former slaves who had nowhere to go.

Donaldson had more or less just come across George one day leaning against a fence post watching the army march by, and offered him a job to come along and serve him for the duration of the war. George accepted and proceeded to make himself invaluable.

Donaldson was more than a little surprised to discover that Slow was literate and self-motivated. This was simply not the *Uncle Tom's Cabin* image of the poor, beaten, downtrodden slaves that was prevalent in the North. George had to explain to the Yankee officer that the plight of slaves differed from master to master. That a few encouraged their charges to read and to think for themselves, while the master next door might well flog his slaves just for fun. It was worse, Slow told him, the farther South you went, down to the 'land of cotton,' but here, in northern Virginia, Donaldson was told, there weren't very many Simon Legrees.

Donaldson was totally astounded by one of George's favorite stories. "One time a man got so mean to one of his slaves he kilt him, and they had a trial and found the master guilty of murder and took him right out and hung him in the courthouse square. That happened, Master Donaldson, it truly did."

George had taken off for a day or two to visit his families—both the black one and the white one—and came back to camp with a passel of spring chickens, homemade bread, and the greatest gift of them all, two pounds of fresh butter, along with a note from Mrs. Pendleton thanking the Yankee officer for taking such good care of George, and for the moment at least, Captain Francis Donaldson wasn't quite as miserable as he'd been before.

FALMOUTH
DECEMBER 5

It was a full two-thirds of the Army of the Potomac that moved out precisely at dawn on Friday morning, headed for Skinker's Neck, the starting point for what Ambrose Burnside was now certain would be the last battle of the war. Bands played "Yankee Doodle" as the men stepped off in good spirits, ready, at last, to get across the river and meet the enemy and, hopefully, to decide this thing once and for all.

Before the lead elements of Franklin's grand division had marched more than a mile, it started to rain, and well before noon the rain turned into sleet. The wagons and artillery pieces began to slide off the road and stick in the mud, and the "speedy" march Burnside had ordered quickly slowed to a sloppy crawl.

"General Burnside, sir. Beg to report, sir."

"Go ahead."

"General Gibbon reports, sir, a brigade at least of Rebel infantry gathered along the southern heights at Skinker's Neck, sir. He believes it to be Early's Brigade of Ewell's division, sir. And that's just what he can see, General. He begs to inform the general that he no longer believes a crossing there to be practicable."

Burnside said nothing. There was nothing he could say. He heard a commotion and looked down the road ahead just in time to see one of General Hunt's prized cannons—a Parrott rifle—slide down an embankment pulling six terrified and screaming horses tumbling down behind it.

Then, just at sunset, it started to snow.

Near Skinker's Neck
December 6

The bulk of the Army of the Potomac awoke trying to recover from yesterday's painful and pointless march. They had slept where they halted, with mud as a bed and snow for a blanket, and well before sunrise were trying to turn the whole parade around and head back for Falmouth.

Falmouth

While Joshua Lawrence Chamberlain's 20th Maine had been spared that particular torture, he still awoke that morning feeling like he had never been so cold in his entire life. And this coming from a Maine man. He stepped out of his tent and saw the pale, blue glow of fresh fallen snow in the predawn light. *Better than sleet,* he thought, *but not by much.* He wasn't the first up this morning. Even though there was only the softest blush of sunrise, some of the men were already up and building fires. Maybe not. Maybe they had been up all night, tending last night's cook fires. More likely. He smelled the cooking

pork fat the men dowsed over their hardtack and his mouth
demanded some. He had to check on Prince first though.
Without ever having been tested in a fight of any consequence, the 20th Maine and Chamberlain were already famous because of Chamberlain's amazingly beautiful white
stallion. Generals had offered to buy him, but Professor
Chamberlain would have none of it. The animal was part of
his show. He was a college professor and not a soldier and
he knew it. The game was to keep the men from knowing it.
He studied every manual, every book, and every pamphlet
ever written about war and made a point of showing off
what he had learned, quoting Napoleon and speculating
about what Frederick the Great might have done. He
wanted his men to think he knew what he was talking
about, and Prince made him look and sound more like the
soldier he was pretending to be.

Of course Prince was fine. Cold and hungry like all of the
other soldiers in the 20th, but he was fine. Chamberlain patted his snout and gave him a bite of an apple.

"Some sabbatical, huh, boy?" *Other professors take their
sabbaticals in Rome or Athens,* he thought. He briefly envi-
sioned himself exploring ancient ruins or reading priceless
manuscripts on the veranda of an elegant Grecian villa. He
tried to feel the warm Aegean breeze blowing gently against
his face, but he couldn't. "Not us though, boy. Not you and
me. We've gotta spend our sabbatical in Virginia sleeping
outside on nights when bears need a blanket. We've gotta
spend our sabbatical freeing the slaves, don't we, boy?"

Prince nudged him, demanding the rest of the apple. "All
right, fella. I guess I'll just have to settle for pork fat again
today."

He gave the horse the rest of the apple, patted him one more
time, and headed for the group of men huddled around the
largest fire. He noticed something peculiar about this group as
he walked up the hill. Everyone was perfectly still and quiet.
Odd. When he reached the fire he started to say something but
caught himself when he realized that the men were praying.
He stopped a few paces short of the group so as not to intrude
and one of the men noticed him and walked out to meet him.

"Have you heard, sir?" the private whispered.

"I've heard nothing, Private. What is it?"

"Two more men died last night, Colonel, sir. Froozed to death, sir. Stiffer 'n boards."

FREDERICKSBURG

Two divisions—close to ten thousand men—stood face-to-face across an open, snow-covered field. The two opposing generals glared at each other across the lines as their men prepared for a brawl.

John Bell Hood was one of Lee's most aggressive generals, so he was not about to stand timidly by and let the other man start the fight. He drew his saber and held it high over his head. At the very top of his lungs, he ordered, "CHARGE!"

At that instant his men let loose with over two thousand snowballs. Seconds later Lafayette McLaws's division answered in kind, and the greatest snowball fight of the century had begun.

For many of the boys from the Deep South, this winter was the first snow they had ever seen, and they laughed and hurled their harmless weapons and sometimes just rolled around in the unfamiliar wet, white stuff—to hell with the bare feet and cold hands. It was all just too much fun.

DECEMBER 7

Clara Barton's bandaged hand, rough, red, and swollen from her brush with frostbite, had at last healed itself to the point of being only a constant nuisance. Her respite in Washington Town had been a blessing. She was well rested and resupplied now and anxious to catch up with her boys at Falmouth. She had looked forward to sleeping on the train ride from Aquia Creek, but the closer she got to the Army of the Potomac the more wide awake she became. She had seen this landscape before. She had taken the same ride only a year or so before, but nothing was the same. What had been lush now was desolate. Where there had been grass, there was mud. Where there had been pristine forests, now there were only gnarled and ugly stumps. A year ago there had been houses, pleasant little working farms, dotting the countryside. But armies had passed this way, and today only the chimneys survived, standing alone like towering headstones left behind to honor the memory of homes and to mark the remains.

Rebels, she thought. Never forget that these were the homes of murderers. Slaveholders probably, who have brought this all on themselves.

These angry thoughts always disturbed her. It isn't the people really who are at fault—it is the culture that makes them the way they are, and it is the culture that must be destroyed.

As though God Himself controlled the timing as these thoughts filled her head, the train passed what must have been an elegant plantation house not so very long ago, but on this day it stood in shambles. Not a window was unbroken. The surrounding trees and fences had been hacked down for firewood and the gardens trampled down to mud. All the way around the first story of the house, boards had been pulled off, probably to make coffins. *Coffins for "my boys,"* Clara thought, her emotions moving from sad back to angry. This house was once the very symbol of the arrogant aristocracy that brought the whole war about. Now it is nothing more than a pathetic eyesore, but it still remains a symbol. A symbol of God's wrath unleashed against cruelty.

Barton smiled, hummed the tune, and remembered the words:

> *He has loosed the fateful lightning of His terrible*
> *swift sword,*
> *His truth is marching on.*

It wasn't long before Clara saw the first of the tents; the outskirts of a gigantic canvas city with a population double the size of Washington. As the train moved closer to Falmouth, the number of canvass homes grew from hundreds to thousands, to tens of thousands, taking up almost every available square foot of mud. An ambulance awaited her at the station with orders to take her directly to General Sturgis's headquarters at the Lacy house.

Sturgis now commanded the division that included her beloved 21st Massachusetts, the men she had been caring for from the very first. These were the men whose wounded had been piled on the Senate floor after an early run-in with Rebel demonstrators way back in '61, while they were en route to Washington. Sturgis was grateful for Barton's work there and at Antietam and understood her awkward position as a single woman traveling with an army. He took care of her men and her supplies and he also took great care of her.

He beamed when he saw her climbing down from the ambulance and reached out for her hand for the traditional kiss. She offered it to him out of habit and immediately regretted it when she remembered the bandages.

"Miss Barton. It's so good to have you back."

"It's good to be back, General. I was lost back in the city."

He held her hand longer than necessary trying to examine her wounds.

"Not exactly 'ladylike,' are they?"

"Are they healing at least?"

"Much better, thank you."

"Physician, heal thyself."

She smiled and finally took the hand away. "How are the men?"

"Your men are fine. I have them stationed right out behind the house."

First duty, she thought, *to check in with Welles and the boys before dinnertime.*

"As for the others, there have been some improvements, but we continue to lose hundreds of men every week to disease."

A sigh was Barton's only response. The Sanitary Commission was working hard to clean up the army, but a hundred thousand men housed in tight quarters, badly fed, and constantly filthy—it's almost an impossible undertaking.

The city boys were pretty good about their hygiene; as good as they could be under the deplorable circumstances. They at least took care of their business downstream. The country boys and the Westerners, it seemed, simply could not be trained. They went pretty much wherever they were standing when the urge hit them.

Sturgis took Clara by the arm and began walking toward the big house up on the hill. An enlisted man took her personal bags and followed along.

"Letterman has been doing some good work of late."

"He's a good man, and the right man to be medical director."

"I think so. He's set up hospital tents! One for each brigade. Hopefully, there will be no more dragging men into the nearest barn to perform amputations."

"Hopefully."

"The ambulances are now assigned to specific units and will follow them wherever they go. The idea is that the wounded will no longer have to wait for a caisson to empty its chest before men can be carried out. And the drivers and crews have been trained to apply tourniquets and the like."

"Steps in the right direction at least."

"At least."

"Sam? Why are we headed for the house?"

"I've arranged quarters for you there."

Uh-oh. Barton was sick to death of the defenseless female thing. "I had hoped to be able to stay with my men."

"Out of the question, Clara."

The argument was over. Sturgis had used his "general's voice." It was an order. Another sigh.

"You will have company in your room, another volunteer, but you'll be warm and safe and you'll still be close to your men."

She had a hundred arguments against these arrangements, not the least of which was that she simply preferred to stay in a headquarters tent to accepting even the involuntary hospitality of Mr. Lacy, a slave-owning plantation owner. But the arguments would be useless and she was allowed to be here only at General Sturgis's pleasure. No point.

"The corporal here will see you to your room, and dinner

will be served at seven." He clicked his heels together and took her bandaged hand and kissed it once again.

"Thank you, Sam."

"Thank you, Clara."

MARYE'S HEIGHTS

Lieutenant Owen of the Washington Artillery observed as the emplacements for their guns were being improved. They had arrived over two weeks ago and the luxury of making "improvements" was one that no one was accustomed to.

He and his boys couldn't wait for the Yankees to come marching up that hill. He watched the redoubts being meticulously designed with earth piled muzzle-high for their guns to hide behind but with space to turn and adjust fire. *For the first time,* he thought, *we are actually going to be able to fight from behind dirt instead of standing out in the open.*

The engineers had quit for the day and Owen's boys were doing a little work of their own, raising up the spaces between the guns for the protection of the crews.

He looked out over the river at the Army of the Potomac and wondered when they would come. "Y'all come on over, boys!" he yelled. "We're just about ready!"

He didn't know that Longstreet and his staff were only about fifty feet away and could hear his taunts.

Old Pete rode up next to the young captain. "Yell all you want to, Captain. They ain't coming up this way."

"Hope they do, sir. They come up this way, there ain't many of 'em going back the other way. What you see down there, sir, is a perfect slaughter pen, sir. Nothing else."

"What are your men doing over there?"

"Making some more improvements, sir. Just raising 'em up a bit here and there. The engineers don't want us messin' with 'em, but we don't see no harm. Hope you don't mind, sir."

"If we only save the finger of a man, that's good enough."

When the work on the gun emplacements was done for

the day, Owen moved over onto the other side of the heights to supervise the construction of the Literary Guild's new theater. The men were in rehearsal for a new performance and this time everything was going to be exactly right. They were in winter quarters, everybody hoped, so this theater could be more permanent. The stage was surrounded on three sides by blankets and they even had a stage curtain, the "grand drape" they called it, made from a canvas tent with the initials "ANV" and "WA" with the crossed cannon barrels of the artillery drawn on it in charcoal. Their slogan was there too: "Try Us." The seating was made of half-hewn logs placed in a large semicircle around the stage with occasional pits dug for fire building—all for the pleasure and comfort of the theatregoers of the Army of Northern Virginia.

Seeing that the preparations were going along well enough, Owen excused himself for dinner. He and a few of the officers from the Washington Artillery were the guests of Mr. T. S. Barton. His house in Fredericksburg was old but grand. He kept his table full and his door open to the gunners of the Washington Artillery. T. S. had always been fond of New Orleans and apparently had some hospitality to repay the Crescent City.

He welcomed Owen and his friends like long-lost family and led them into his dining room, where a slave stood guard over a long table loaded with cold saddle of mutton and fresh-baked bread. Soft bread would be worth a small fortune back up on the hill and more than a few pieces found their way into pockets rather than stomachs. T.S. didn't care.

"Help yourselves, boys. Better you have it than the damned Yankees!" He showed them all a yellow-toothed smile that must have been charming on a young man's face. "If they're coming I want 'em to find this old house emptier than Satan's heart."

After Barton asked God's blessings on Robert E. Lee and all those gathered here, the slave opened a dusty bottle of wine. And another. And another.

"Where they got you fellas positioned?" he asked the Louisianans.

"Up on Marye's Hill, just behind the stone wall."

Barton sneered. "Up there by old lady Stephen's house?"

"That's right. She's . . ."

"She's a whore and a nigger lover! That's what she is."

The boys from New Orleans were taken aback by Barton's outrage at the poor old woman on the hill.

"Well," Owen said, "she's poorer than Job's turkey, that's for sure."

"Don't let her fool you! She sells liquor to the darkies up there and lets any piece of white trash that stumbles onto her doorstep stay the night. She's got little parcels of property all over the county, so she's making some money someway, if you know what I mean."

There was silence around the table. The soldiers gathered on the heights had actually grown fond of Martha. She took care of anybody who got hurt. She shared her well with anyone in need. To the Confederate soldiers on Marye's Heights, Martha Stephens was a kind lady and no one in the group had a bad word to say about her. So they said nothing and just continued to eat.

"Do ya think they're coming across?" Barton asked the soldiers.

Tongues were loose enough by now and the men were so happy with the change of subject that none had any hesitation to share their opinions with the old citizen. "Hope they do, frankly."

Everyone heartily agreed. Their faces beamed with wine and anticipation.

"We're so dug in up there on that hill that as long as they keep comin' we'll keep sending 'em to hell."

Barton was the happiest of the lot but he still had the same problem everybody else in Fredericksburg had. He didn't know whether to stay or go.

"I suppose you're safe enough here for the moment, but if you hear two cannons fire back to back, real quick-like, that's the signal," Owen told him. "That's when the boys are supposed to roll their guns into place real smart-like. You hear those guns go off like that, then it's time to skedaddle."

Barton sipped some more of his finest Madeira and thought about it for a minute. He looked around the house he had been born in and had lived in for most of his life and made up his mind. "You know what, fellas? I ain't goin' nowhere." He pounded his fist on the table and nodded his head. "That's it. If I die here then that's all there is to it. I was born here and I'll die right here if need be."

Owen tried to talk some sense into the old man's head but he would hear none of it. After three bottles of wine he was ready to die for the cause. "Well, Mr. Barton, you just think on it again in the morning when the wine's not talking for you. When you hear those two guns, you get on out of town."

The evening was ending on a sour note until their host brightened his own mood and handed out bottles of wine as parting gifts for his guests from the venerable Washington Artillery. They stumbled up the hill to their camp, singing and laughing as they went.

Regardless of the wine, Owen knew that sleep would not come easily this night—again. It will be spent mostly trying to stay warm and listening carefully for the sound of two cannons fired back to back.

CHAPTER 6

Captain Francis Donaldson and Lieutenant Jonathan Thomas rode the perimeter of the brigade, performing their duties as officers of the day. They checked guard posts and made certain the camps were properly policed and orderly. Donaldson loved the duty only because it took him out from under the direct command of Colonel Gwyn for a night, and made him momentarily safe from the never-ending harassment he received at the hands of his perpetually inebriated and belligerent inferior.

There was one more thing he liked about it—he had a captive congregation of one who had no alternative but to listen to his never-ending sermon on the deadly sins of the army. It was always the same. The First Deadly Sin—James Gwyn, his regimental commander, was a drunken tyrant. He always began with that. Then, Fitz-John Porter, his beloved former corps commander, was in Washington being court-martialed by a panel that would make the star-chamber look like an honorable tribunal, and, finally, Deadly Sin Number Three: George McClellan, the greatest American general of all time, was sucking his thumb in Trenton, New Jersey, because the fools in Washington would rather let Republican generals lose the war than let a Democrat general win it.

But tonight the sermon had a new ending—a Fourth Deadly Sin—the transgression of putting an idiot like Burnside in charge.

"Burnside hasn't got the talent or the guts Mac had to stand up to those fools in Washington. He's nothing more than Edwin Stanton's obedient little lapdog."

"Give Old Sideburns a chance, Frank. We haven't seen him in action yet."

Donaldson couldn't believe Thomas could be such a fool. "Jonathan! I'm no prophet but even I can predict the beating we're going to take if Burnside tries to attack Lee now."

Thomas, along with everybody else in the Corn Exchange Regiment, was tired of listening to Donaldson's incessant ravings about George McClellan and Company. Virtually all agreed with him, but they were tired of hearing it nonetheless. Normally he would have just gotten up and walked away, but tonight he was alone with the angry young captain and had no choice but to listen.

"Why not move the army to one flank or the other and make them let go of Fredericksburg and its entrenchments and come out and fight us?"

"What makes you so certain that that is not precisely what he intends to do? Have you been invited to the general's councils of war?"

As usual, Donaldson moved right along just as though Thomas had not spoken. "It seems to me that just because the enemy builds fortifications right in our path, that is no reason why we should attack them. I'll tell you this, Jonathan, if we suffer the kind of defeat that I expect we will, then the nation had best watch out for a second Cromwell to step in, take charge, and dissolve our rotten Congress."

Their tour was over and Thomas was glad of it. They rode into the camp of the Corn Exchange Regiment and returned their horses to the quartermaster. Thomas was about to bid his captain good night when Donaldson suddenly went red in the face and stormed to his tent, where an officer had dragged all of his belongings out into the mud and was rummaging through them.

"What do you think you're doing?" Both Jonathan Thomas and George Slow thought the captain was going to assault the culprit—who was a major on Colonel Gwyn's staff.

"Following orders from Colonel Gwyn, Captain."

"What orders?"

The major didn't even look at the captain but continued calmly about his chore. "The colonel's stove has been stolen, and he believes you may have it."

Donaldson was shocked. He was insulted and humiliated and furious. He blew out of the camp like a storm and went directly to Gwyn's tent, where he didn't even bother to knock. There was no announcement, no salute, and certainly no respect intended.

"I demand to know the meaning of this insult!"

It wasn't until after he had spoken that he noticed that the colonel had guests. But by the amused looks on their faces Donaldson knew that he had been expected. The colonel didn't even pretend not to know what he was talking about.

"No insult is intended, young man. I understand that a Sibley stove intended for me was mistakenly delivered to you, and I simply sent my orderly to retrieve it."

A lie. Donaldson knew it was just another in a long line of insults and harassments, but there was little he could do. "And do you not believe, *sir* . . ."—the word dripped with disrespect—". . . that if such an event had occurred that I would not have sent the stove to you?"

"I have no way of knowing what you would do—I never have any way of knowing what you would do."

The colonel's guests made a show of trying to hold in their laughter. It was, finally, more than Donaldson could bear.

"Colonel Gwyn, sir, I respectfully request a transfer—as is my right."

"Request all you want, Captain, but you are going nowhere!" He looked around at his equally drunk friends for approval, which was quick in coming. "I don't know how I would entertain myself were it not for your presence among us."

This time the gathered audience didn't even try not to laugh. They burst out.

Donaldson stood at attention, his fists clinched, his face red, trying to decide what to do—what to say. But there was nothing.

"Captain Donaldson—you are dismissed."

FREDERICKSBURG
DECEMBER 9

The modesty was gone. Ambrose Burnside absolutely exuded confidence as he burst into the room where Sumner, Hooker, and Franklin waited. The three grand division commanders all stood (Hooker very reluctantly) as Burnside entered.

"As you were, gentlemen." The generals took their seats and waited to be told that the Army of the Potomac was about to be ordered into winter quarters.

"What was bad news last week appears to be good news today. It appears that the Rebels are heavily reinforcing their positions guarding Skinker's Neck. Reports indicate that as much as half of General Jackson's corps is either there or headed in that direction. This is where they expect us to cross."

The air in the room grew thick as the commanders realized that winter quarters was the furthest thing from Burnside's mind.

"I see no reason to disavow them of that belief." He smiled broadly, as though he had just made a joke, but there was not a man in the room who saw the humor. They were all too anxious to find out precisely what the commanding general had in mind.

"We will feint at Skinker's Neck, to hold Jackson in place and perhaps draw even more men in that direction. General Sumner will cross right here—directly into the heart of the town and precisely where they least expect it. At the same time, General Franklin will cross downstream at Deep Run and attack Jackson's corps at the soft spot between the two

Rebel corps. General Hooker's grand division will move into position behind Stafford Heights and be ready at a moments' notice to march to the aid of whichever effort shows the earliest signs of success."

Burnside, at long last, was certain that his initial plan had been salvaged. He was in command and fully expected his highest commanders to join him in his enthusiasm. They did not and Burnside could see it in their faces.

"Gentlemen, General Lee's army is stretched out along a thirty-mile front. He is totally unprepared for the quick and massive assault that I intend to launch against him. The attack will commence as soon as the bridges are completed, and the engineers will begin laying those bridges under the cover of darkness on the day after tomorrow."

5 P.M.

The Lacy house was a wonder to behold. The two-story, red-brick Georgian-style plantation stood high on the heights overlooking the Rappahannock. It dominated the landscape around it by its commanding size and strength and stateliness. As he walked up the hill toward the massive mansion, Wes Brainerd imagined George Washington as a young man walking up this same hill. He took time to envision it as it must have been in those days, before the armies had marched back and forth over the land, ruining the roads and trampling the gardens that must have been elegant in Washington's day. They were all mud now. He looked back down at the river and his recent visit to Mount Vernon came to mind. He remembered the first President's grand mansion and how it stood on a hillside overlooking a wide and graceful bend in the Potomac. Designed from Washington's memory of this place? Maybe so.

Glad he isn't here to see it today, Brainerd thought. *Or worse yet, tomorrow.*

"Wesley!" It was Major Spaulding running up the hill to catch up.

"Jeeze, Wes," Ira gasped while he tried to catch his breath, "you couldn't wait for five damned minutes?"

"Sorry, Ira. I figured you were already up here."

"Well, that's some mighty sorry figuring!" Brainerd slowed his pace to let Ira catch his breath a bit, but even though he was gasping for air Ira kept talking. He could never stop talking. "So what do you think's gonna happen?"

"I think General Woodbury's gonna tell us that we've scared the pants off Bobby Lee and he's agreed to surrender and we can all go home."

"Criminy. When am I gonna learn not to ask you questions?"

"I've often asked myself that very same thing, Ira. When *are* you gonna stop asking me questions?"

"You know what I mean, though. Where are they gonna tell us to put the bridges?"

Brainerd knew full well the seriousness of the question. He too had been thinking of little else. "I wish I could tell you, Ira, but there just isn't a single place along this whole damned river where there ain't about a half a million Rebels dug in and waiting for us."

"You think they might just call the whole thing off and go into winter quarters?"

"I think Jeff Davis might be a horse's butt."

Spaulding shook his head and looked to the heavens for help.

The two engineers finally made it to the porch of the mansion and waited for General Woodbury to come out from his meeting with Sumner. They leaned against a column and looked back down at the river.

"Must have been a beautiful place before we showed up," Spaulding said. Brainerd was going to tell him his revelation about Washington patterning Mount Vernon after the place, but the door opened and Woodbury came out and interrupted the thought. He didn't look well.

"Gentlemen," he said, casually returning their salutes, "we have our orders."

"Are we going to take another stab at Skinker's Neck?"

Woodbury shook his head and took a breath. "There will be a diversion there to make Lee think that's the spot, maybe make him move some guns over there, but it's only a diversion." The general looked like he was about to throw up. "General Franklin's grand division will cross about a mile downstream at Deep Run." He took another deep breath and pointed down toward the river and the town of Fredericksburg. "And General Sumner will cross right there."

Spaulding's knees almost buckled. He felt faint. "Excuse me, sir? Right there? Right into the town and under all those guns?"

"Those are our orders."

Spaulding was stammering mad. "D-did anybody tell him that that's suicide? Did you tell him we can't . . ."

"*We* are not in a position to tell him *any*thing! He still blames us for the bridges not being here a month ago!"

"That was *not* our fault and he should know that by now!" Brainerd nudged Ira to try to get him to calm down a bit. He got the hint and shut up for once in his life.

"Those are our orders, men," Woodbury said. "All that's left is for you to figure out how to get it done."

Spaulding, Brainerd, and a couple of other officers strolled down to the river and studied the slopes of the hill that the pontoons would have to be carried down. They studied the footings and the currents and did all the things that engineers do, but they were just going through the motions. There was little conversation. Finally they found themselves just standing there looking across the river at the buildings that they all knew full well were packed to the rafters with Rebels.

"Well, gentlemen," Brainerd said at last, "I've got a will to write, and after that, a bridge to build."

6 P.M.

Evening approached as the corps and division commanders of Sumner's Right Grand Division convened at the Lacy house for a council of war. As they arrived, there were a few comments about the grand home but no one was in much of a mood for small talk. The rumors of a frontal assault against Marye's Heights had become far too commonplace and persistent to be entirely false. Winfield Hancock didn't speak to anyone, afraid of what he might say. Afraid he would use words like "reckless," "suicidal," and "idiotic."

Hancock sat in a chair in the back of the room while Sumner confirmed Burnside's plan to cross the Rappahannock directly in front of Fredericksburg. The generals listened in stunned amazement—their worst fears confirmed.

"The enemy will not expect us to cross there," Sumner told them. "Lee's army is thinly spread along a thirty-mile front from Port Royal to the Rapidan River, and the town is the hinge—the weak point between his two corps—and he will have weakened his position there to reinforce his right after Franklin attacks downstream."

Silence. Sumner thought it signaled agreement and was about to move on when Hancock couldn't contain himself any longer. He was a half a second away from spitting a string of insults and profanities into the face of his commander when another, calmer voice interrupted.

"If I may speak freely, sir." Hancock thanked God that it was someone else who stepped forward to say what had to be said. He had been a division commander for less than two months—only since Antietam—and had already had a brief run-in with Sumner on that very day. So it needed to be a senior man who started the fight. Thank God for Darius Couch.

"Of course, General."

Even Corps Commander Couch had to take a moment to frame his words. He had to speak his mind without crossing over that nebulous line between "speaking freely" and insubordination.

"With all respect, sir, even if we are able to bridge the river there, Lee could defend that line above the town with a company and a cannon. The way I see it, we could send the whole damned army up that hill . . ." He paused again, trying to defeat his own barely contained anger long enough to select exactly the right phrase to make his point without landing himself under arrest. Hancock, by this time, had no such fear.

". . . and the whole damned army would die there!"

Now Sumner grew angry. "Do you have something to say, General Hancock?"

"With all due respect, sir, we can walk out onto the porch of this house this minute and look up at those heights and see the redoubts the enemy has constructed there. Left, right, and center. When we start crossing that river there will be a hundred guns placed along those heights! Every square inch of the field will be covered by those guns alone. He doesn't even need any infantry."

"We all know that, General, but General Burnside believes, and I concur, that most of those guns will be called away when Franklin presses his right."

"We know that is the plan, sir"—Couch now resumed the argument, pulling Hancock back from the brink—"but what if Franklin fails? Or what if Lee simply decides to hold fast?"

Silence again, but this time it was Sumner who hesitated. He looked around the room, hopeful that someone would come to his defense, but not a man spoke. They all looked to their commander, anxiously waiting for the answer. At that moment Edwin Sumner realized that every general under his command was scared to death to assault Marye's Heights. Something else occurred to him as well. He scanned the room and looked into every face and everyone he saw was a McClellan man. Couch had been McClellan's classmate at West Point. Hancock had been promoted time and again ahead of ranking officers. "Superb," McClellan had dubbed him even before he had ever seen his first battle, and the newspapers had gotten hold of it and anointed him as some kind of *wunderkind*.

Sumner bristled at the thought. *This room is filled with McClellan Democrats who are bound and determined to get their hero back and fully willing to lose the fight to do it.*

Finally a voice. A demanding voice. "What do we do then, General?" Couch wanted to know. Hancock wanted to know. Every man in the room wanted to know the backup plan. But still Sumner remained silent, stewing at the political game being played at the expense of the Union. For everyone else Sumner's silence was perfectly articulate. It said to all of those gathered that there simply was no backup plan. There was barely any plan at all.

When Sumner finally did speak he said only, "These are General Burnside's orders. I believe the plan will work, and I know that when the time comes, you and your men will cross those bridges and take those heights."

Another silence followed. There was nothing more to say until Sumner finally nodded emphatically and, with a tone of disgust in his voice he said, "Gentlemen, report back to your commands and await your orders. You are dismissed."

The generals rose and departed, leaving the old soldier alone in the room with his thoughts. He didn't want to admit what he knew to be true—what he had told General Burnside over two weeks ago. *Hancock is right,* he thought. *We outnumber them six corps to two, but still, if Franklin fails to do his part . . .*

He didn't finish the thought. He couldn't.

MARYE'S HEIGHTS
7:30 P.M.

The moment the sun dipped below the horizon the temperature dropped fifteen degrees and Moxley Sorrel reminded Longstreet of the performance being staged by the men of the Washington Artillery—and of the promised "big fire." They arrived after the opening curtain and all of the "warm" seats closest to the fire were taken, but they were so amazed by what the boys from New Orleans had accomplished they had to stay and watch. Captain Owen saw them standing at the rear of the crowd and offered to move them forward but Longstreet refused.

"I've never seen this play before, Lieutenant," Longstreet whispered. "What have we missed?"

"It's the *Lady of Lyon,* sir. By Lytton. It was quite the rage in New Orleans before the war."

About this time a burly soldier strolled onto the stage wearing a blond wig and a hoop skirt complete with petticoats. The theatregoers of the Army of Northern Virginia roared with laughter. He was obviously willing to make some sacrifices for "art," but shaving the beard would have been above and beyond the call of duty. A few catcalls from the "orchestra" brought a curtsy followed by a playfully obscene gesture only partially obscured by an ornate hand fan.

"That's Sergeant Wood, sir. A lawyer in New Orleans, but he did some professional acting there as well."

"And a lovely thing he is too," Longstreet said with a giant smile. "And where, may I ask, did he come by his 'costume'?"

"I've sworn a gentleman's oath never to tell, sir, but obviously a lady of the town is quite generous."

"In every sense of the word, I'd say. Jackson could conceal a division under those hoops."

DECEMBER 10
THE PHILLIPS HOUSE

Burnside was half angry and half hurt. His plan had consumed every waking moment for a month and everything, it seemed, conspired against him. Hooker was first, but he had expected that from Hooker. Then the weather and then the damned pontoons. He had moved an entire army to Falmouth in three days and the damned pontoons took two weeks. As though all of this weren't bad enough, now every officer in the whole Right Grand Division was on record against it. The weather he couldn't control. The military bureaucracy, if that was at fault for the pontoons, was apparently beyond his control as well. But he could put down a mutiny, and on this night that was precisely what he intended to do.

For the second night in a row Sumner's corps and division commanders gathered for a meeting, this time at the Phillips house. Few if any in the room had ever seen Burnside angry, so they were almost startled when the commanding general exploded into the room. They all came to immediate attention and expected the "as you were" command that normally followed. Not tonight.

Burnside marched to the front of the room and turned to face his reluctant commanders. "The plan of attack has been determined. Is that clear?"

"Yes, sir," they all answered like a squad of fresh cadets.

"Is it clear, General Hancock?"

Hancock was shocked to hear his name singled out. He clenched his fists and continued to look straight ahead. "It is clear, sir, and I want to assure you that whatever you may have heard, I meant no disrespect to the general, sir. I only . . ."

There was an audible gasp in the room as everyone anticipated that Hancock was poised to cross the line yet again.

"You only what?"

"I only wanted to be sure that everyone was aware just how difficult an assignment it will be to take those heights against those guns. And again, sir, I assure you that I meant no discourtesy."

"I do understand. We all understand. But the plans are made, gentlemen, and I will have no more cold water thrown on them. All I want now is the total devotion of you and your men. May I count on you, General Couch?"

Couch had been surprised that Burnside had so attacked Hancock when it was he who had most opposed the plan last night, but as the conversation had focused on the division commander, he was equally surprised to hear his own name now.

He gave a soldier's response in a soldier's voice. "Sir, I assure you that if I have ever done anything in any battle, I will do twice as much in this."

Burnside nodded and the tension in the room began to fade when General William French, whom no one had missed, opened the door, marched in, looked around, and said, "Is this a Methodist camp meeting?"

Burnside's face broke into a grin and he had to put up a fight against laughing out loud—as did most of the others in the room. He shook his head and said, "Very well, gentlemen. The President and the people are counting on you. Good luck." And with that, he left.

General Andrew A. Humphreys could not understand for the life of him why so many professional soldiers were moping around Falmouth like a bunch of damned pallbearers. For him the days leading up to a fight were like the day before Christmas, and like a nine-year-old boy, he couldn't wait. The only thing that hampered his spirits was that the plan called for Hooker's grand division to be held in reserve. A. A. Humphreys was a man who wanted to lead the charge in every battle—to be the first to win or the first to die, and either way was fine with him.

His son, Henry, served as his adjutant, and peeked into his tent.

"General Tyler requests an audience, sir."

For some sons and brothers it was difficult to maintain professional decorum while dealing with close kin in superior positions. It was not so with Lieutenant Henry Humphreys. All the time he had been growing up his father had always been "Major" or "Colonel"; he had always been "sir." The only difference these days was the grade.

General Humphreys stood and straightened his frockcoat and adjusted his tie.

"Very well, Henry. Send him in."

A moment later two men entered . . . General Tyler, the commander of one of his brigades, and a colonel Humphreys didn't know.

"General Humphreys, I would like to introduce you to Colonel Matthew Quay, sir. He has a small problem and a special request."

The colonel saluted smartly—always a good sign in Humphreys's eyes.

"What can I do for you, Colonel?"

"General, I have developed a bit of a cough, sir. I'm sure it's nothing, but—"

General Tyler interrupted. "The doctors think it's serious, sir."

"Only on occasion!" Quay desperately wanted Tyler to shut the hell up. There was nothing to be gained by making matters worse. "And well, sir, last week, thinking that we were going into winter quarters, I foolishly allowed the doctors to convince me to resign my commission—just planning on going home to recover until the spring or summer."

His lungs began to ache and he knew another coughing fit was coming on. *Jesus, God,* he thought. Not *now*! He tried to fight it back, but his body wouldn't let him. Humphreys and Tyler looked at each other knowingly, but waited politely for the colonel to recover.

"Sorry, sirs. It really is just an occasional thing. All the wet and snow and sleeping under the stars and all. It really is nothing."

"Go on, Colonel."

"Thank you, sir. Well, now that the fight is coming, well, I just can't leave *now,* General, but I have no command. If you would just allow me to march alongside General Tyler tomorrow . . . well, it would mean a great deal to me, sir."

It took the colonel three or four seconds to inhale enough breath to go on.

"If I had thought for a minute that General Burnside was going ahead with this plan I would never have . . ."

Tyler couldn't listen any longer. Only talking was wearing the poor man out. "They told him he would be foolish not to go home, sir."

Now Quay was furious at his old friend. His anger gave him the strength to fill his clogged lungs and almost to shout, "I would rather *die* and be called foolish than *live* and be called a coward!"

The words almost sent Humphreys reeling. They were perhaps the most gallant words ever spoken in his presence. They were epitaph words. No. They were words worthy of being engraved at the base of a statue. A moment ago he had felt sorry for the tired and sickly man, but now he loved him. Here was a kindred soul.

"Allow me to take your hand, sir. I will be proud to have so eloquent a person ride with me any time—anywhere."

Quay was overcome with relief, almost to the point of tears. He had postwar ambitions and having the word "coward" attached to his name would end his political career before it ever got started. He gratefully took Humphreys's hand. Another cough began to rise up from his chest, but this was a struggle he had to win. Fighting it back he said, "Thank you, sir. I shall be forever grateful."

FALMOUTH
7:30 P.M.

His writing chores done for the day, Bill McCarter was left with nothing to do but sit and watch. It was like a punishment for him, watching the Irish Brigade prepare for battle while he just stood there. This was to be his first chance to "see the monkey show" and he found himself armed with only pen and paper.

Heavy siege guns, pulled by six horses, rumbled through their encampment at breakneck speeds. Cavalry regiments hurried forward, kicking up mud as they galloped through. The men cooked "salt horse" and fresh beef in cauldrons suspended over thousands of campfires that glowed along a twelve-mile front. They cleaned their rifles, said their prayers, and did whatever had to be done to prepare for tomorrow.

"Hey there, young fellow. Is General Meagher about?"

McCarter looked up and was surprised to see a civilian on horseback.

"No, sir. Not at the moment."

"Didn't really suspect he would be, but figured I'd give it the old college try nonetheless." He dismounted and offered Bill his hand. "I'm Henry Villard of the *New York Tribune,* and who might you be?"

"William McCarter of the 116th Pennsylvania Volunteers."

They watched together the spectacle going on before them. Couriers moved about in a hurry, carrying important documents from one general to another. Just down the road several regiments marched toward their assigned places in the line.

"Hell of a show, ain't it?" Villard said.

"Nothing like the one we're g-gonna see tomorrow."

"You're right about that. I understand the men are being issued eighty rounds this time—double what they got back at Antietam."

McCarter tried to impress the reporter by looking unimpressed, but if it was true, it was a very bad sign.

Villard offered his card to the young private and said, "Give this to General Meagher when he returns and tell him

I came by." He mounted his horse and before he rode away he said, "And good luck to you and the 116th."

"Thank you, sir."

Villard was gone before McCarter realized what had happened. He had introduced himself as *William McCarter of the 116th Pennsylvania Volunteers. The 116th. Hell.* At this moment he didn't even know where the 116th was.

Winfield Hancock's meeting with the brigade commanders was over. They all knew the plan and the parts they were to play in it. Their corps would lead the assault up Marye's Heights. French's division would lead and Hancock's would follow—Zook's Brigade first, Meagher's second, and Caldwell's third.

Meagher and Caldwell left the room, neither particularly happy. Caldwell was upset because he thought the plan was insane, and Meagher was angry because his Irish Brigade wasn't picked to lead the charge. Sam Zook hadn't said a word and waited behind after the other two had left.

"You're amazingly quiet tonight, Sam." It wasn't like him at all. Samuel Zook was a profane, arrogant, headstrong man, never reluctant to let his opinions be known. He was almost an exact copy of Hancock, and for that very reason, the men had trouble getting along. But tonight it was obvious that something was bothering the 3rd Brigade commander, and Hancock needed to know what it was.

"What is it, Sam? You may speak freely."

There was an uncomfortable silence before Zook finally responded.

"I'm not coming back from this one, Win."

Hancock was surprised. He wasn't surprised that Zook would have such a premonition—he *was* surprised that he would talk about it out loud.

"We all have those feelings from time to time, Sam, and ninety-nine times out of a hundred, we laugh about them later."

Zook forced a smile and chuckled. "Yeah, I know. But not me. I've never once even been the slightest bit worried about myself in a battle—but every time I look up that hill and see those guns . . ." A sigh. He shook his head and smiled . . . genuinely this time.

"You're right, Win. It's just weird, the feeling I've gotten a couple of times."

"Just stop right there, Sam. Don't dwell on it. The more you think about it, the more likely it is that something bad will happen. And besides, you *can't* die." Hancock put on a mockingly serious face. "I won't allow it. Therefore it would be going against orders."

It was exactly the right thing to say. Zook laughed and accepted a draft of fine Irish whiskey (courtesy of General Meagher) from Hancock's flask.

"Now, do your duty, Colonel Zook. Give 'em hell and come back safe."

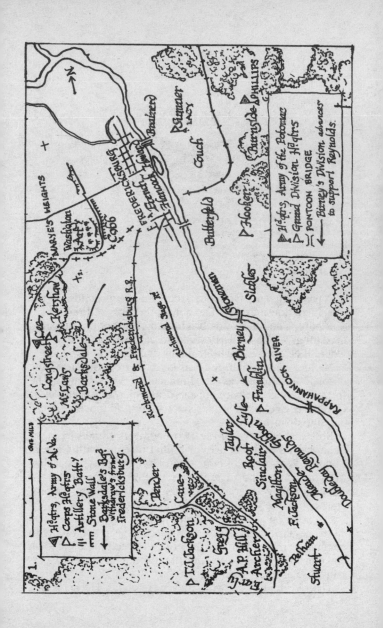

CHAPTER 7

Spaulding and Brainerd stood on the grounds of the Lacy house and looked across the river at Fredericksburg. The moon was bright and clear but on the verge of setting. Moonset was estimated at 1 A.M. and only then would it be dark enough for the bridge building to begin.

Neither man spoke. A fresh layer of frost disguised the desolate landscape as an immaculate wonderland. The fortress across the way appeared as quiet and peaceful as Christmas Eve. Both armies slept and not so much as a bird dared to disturb them.

Still without a word the two engineers turned to make their way up to the house for a final meeting with General Sumner. With only an hour to go Brainerd prayed one last time for some kind of reprieve. A return to sanity. A last-moment change in orders moving the bridgehead or procrastinating the whole plan until the spring.

"Gentlemen . . ." Sumner returned their salutes.

"General Sumner, sir, we are about to issue the orders to commence the building of the bridges directly into the town and considered it wise to consult with you first to make certain there have been no changes."

The old man knew what they were about. He knew full

well that they were hoping for a cancellation. He found it almost amusing but at the same time sad.

"There are no changes, gentlemen." The two young officers tried not to let their disappointment show. "You are to begin at one A.M. under the cover of darkness. Keep it as quiet as you can." He smiled. "No need to wake up Bobby Lee too early. Us old men need our sleep."

Brainerd and Spaulding both laughed and actually did feel better, infected with the old general's optimism.

"Good luck to you now. We are about to achieve a great victory here that could not be had without you."

And so, at one o'clock in the morning, the trek down the slopes began and, for the first time in months, something was going smoothly for the 50th New York Engineers. Brainerd watched as his men wrestled their heavy boats down fifty feet of steep and muddy slopes to the banks of the Rappahannock. "Quiet" was the order of the day but it wasn't necessary. The men knew their jobs well and went about them without need for orders or instructions. The boats went into the water one at a time and it wasn't long before Brainerd's bridge began to take shape. There were four other bridges being constructed at the same time, but Brainerd's was the one in the middle—the one that would spill out directly into the heart of Fredericksburg.

The artillerymen above on Stafford Heights rolled their guns into place, and Sam Zook ordered two regiments of infantry into position along the riverbank to provide support in case the Rebels offered any resistance. With Zook's guns standing guard, the quiet construction finally got under way as a thick fog began to rise off the river.

"Mac!"

"Yes, sir!" McCarter was at General Meagher's side in an instant. It had torn a hole in the young man's soul to watch the 116th march out of the compound on their way to the heights—on their way to the fight—leaving him behind to copy papers. He couldn't tolerate it and this might be his only opportunity to ask the general's permission to rejoin his old unit.

The old Irish revolutionary was limping badly as he

moved around in his tent, packing books and papers into a large steel box. The last item packed was the scrapbook, complete with the poems McCarter had copied. The general held it up so McCarter could admire it one last time.

"Soon this will be back home in Ireland," Meagher said, "and I'll be not far behind. When we're done with this little scrape here, when this issue is settled, I'm headed back there to fight a war that *needs* fightin'."

He sat down and placed the book in the box and took a moment to rub his ailing knee before he closed the lid and locked it tight.

"Now, young Private McCarter, I'm placing this in your charge." He handed Bill the key as though it were a relic of the true cross. "Tomorrow you'll be goin' nowhere. You'll be guardin' my own personal property here, and if it is my fate to fall, you'll be givin' that key to General Hancock. Am I clear?"

McCarter's golden opportunity was gone. A direct order had been given—general to private—and nothing could be done about it.

"Yes, sir."

There was a commotion outside and soon one of the brigade surgeons entered the tent. "Are you ready, General Meagher?"

The old Irishman sighed and shook his head. "As ready as I'll ever be I suppose."

Bill didn't know what was going on, but he knew he had no business watching it whatever it was. He started to leave but Meagher stopped him.

"No—stay on, lad. This is likely to be a helluva show."

Meagher dropped his trousers and lay down face-first on his cot while the doctor removed some tools from his bag. A glass syringe with a long silver needle and some clean rags. Meagher was a general, so he got *clean* rags.

The procedure hadn't even started yet when Bill began to feel ill. On the back of the general's knee was a lump the size of a baseball.

MARYE'S HEIGHTS
2 A.M.

Lieutenant Owen was exhausted. It had taken all day and well into the night to get old man Barton loaded up and on his way to Richmond. Several cases of the old Rebel's wine had found their way to the campsite of the Washington Artillery and were being put to good use in a fine New Orleans recipe for piping hot punch. It eased the cold and soothed the body aches at the same time.

A card game had lasted well into the morning. Many of the men and their guests from town had fallen asleep where they lay, warmed from the inside by the punch, but in spite of it all Bill Owen slept only fitfully. *If they're coming, they're coming soon.* He knew they were coming either this week or next year and he didn't hold out much hope for taking the winter off.

THE LACY HOUSE

Clara Barton wrapped herself in a shawl and walked out onto the balcony just outside her room to see what might be seen. The candle still burned in General Sturgis's tent and her heart went out as she imagined him writing a farewell to his wife and children. A muffled sound caught her ear and she tried to make out what was happening down by the river. Too dark. Too foggy. But she didn't really need to see. She knew what was happening. The engineers were at work. The bridges were being laid.

She looked one more time toward Sturgis's tent and beyond it to the place where her Massachusetts boys lay sleeping.

Thy will, O God, be done. And please give me just one hour's sleep. Only one, and I'll be ready for tomorrow.

3 A.M.

Brainerd stood on the end of his bridge quietly supervising his engineers and cursing the cold. The lashers had it the worst. When all was said and done, the bridges were held together by boards and ropes, and it was the lasher's job to tie them together . . . and you can't tie knots with gloves on. On a warmer night they might have been finished by now but with the temperature in the low twenties their nearly frozen fingers just couldn't handle the job.

The span was less than half done when a quick breeze blew down the valley lifting the fog for just an instant. Brainerd glanced toward the town and saw a long line of Rebels, armed with muskets and moving quickly along the streets, and his blood ran as cold as the night.

A private tapped him on the shoulder and whispered, "Captain Brainerd, sir, General Woodbury is standing on the shoreline and wishes to speak with you."

Brainerd walked over the two hundred feet of completed bridge and saluted his commanding officer.

"What progress are you making, Captain?"

"Halfway or a little better, sir. It's cold and the currents are playing havoc with us here."

Woodbury did the quick and easy calculation and said, "You seem to be ahead of the others, but you're not going to be across by sunup." The tone in his voice was resignation. Brainerd felt awful for him. He was no longer the man he had been only a month ago. He had been a proud and competent veteran commander until his orders were delayed by carelessness; the quartermaster sent him a herd of unbroken mules; and a winter storm and floods the likes of which northern Virginia hadn't seen in decades mired his trains in chest-deep mud, and it was all blamed on him. The man had suffered the trials of Job and the humiliation of arrest, and now he was beaten down to the point where he spoke only in whispers—almost to himself.

The general looked out over Brainerd's bridge and couldn't see the men working on the far end. "Maybe the fog will last and keep you hidden."

"I pray so, sir, but just a moment ago I caught a glimpse

of some Rebels moving through the town. I'm afraid they know we're coming already."

Woodbury stooped his shoulders, closed his eyes, and shook his head. "Do the best you can, Captain, and when they open fire on you, retire to the shore in as good order as possible."

"That you can count on, sir."

Woodbury continued to stare across the river as though he might be able to glimpse the future through the darkness and the fog. Finally he sighed deeply and said, "Maybe they're having better luck downstream."

A mile downstream the 15th New York Engineers had yet to launch a single boat. It had taken them three hours to move their bridge trains through the darkness and over the wet, rutted roads to the point where they were supposed to begin, and now Lieutenant Cross stood on the heights and looked down at the river. He scanned the opposite shore through his glasses but could see nothing.

"This is it then," he said. "Let's get some boats wet."

FREDERICKSBURG

General William Barksdale closed his eyes. They were useless to him anyway. He wanted to focus all of his senses on hearing. A bump here and an occasional muffled thud there had been coming across the river for an hour or two, but they were never enough to be sure. Too distant, too faint, too few and far between to know for certain. But in the last few minutes they had become more frequent and, most significantly, closer.

"Courier—a message to General Longstreet."

5 A.M.

The first blast from Longstreet's warning shots was enough to wake everybody up but it was the second that had the entire Army of Northern Virginia up and about—in a hurry. It was only seconds later when buglers all along the Rebel lines began blowing "Reveille" and "Boots and Saddles," ordering Lee's army up and to arms.

Bill Owen was at Colonel Walton's side almost immediately as they supervised the rolling of the Washington Artillery's guns into position behind the redoubts along Marye's Heights. The roads were slippery and the night was freezing, but the wine-fogged heads from the night before were suddenly crystal clear and finely focused. It took them only minutes to position their guns. The ammunition boxes were left in easy reach of the cannoneers while the horses and caissons were removed to the rear, into the safety of a nearby ravine.

Only feet below the muzzles of the newly placed guns, just on the other side of the stone wall, Owen noticed the candles being lighted in Martha Stephens's house. It was only seconds later when the lady herself came out to have a look. Totally unflustered, she lighted her pipe and leaned against the wall to watch while all hell broke loose around her. She didn't blink as T. R. R. Cobb's men marched into the sunken road and took up positions behind the stone wall, ten feet behind her house. Owen grinned as the infantrymen filed into position behind that impenetrable shield. It stood four or more feet high and looked as though it had been constructed specifically for a man to stand behind to rest his musket on the top to take careful aim at his prey below. It was the perfect fort.

Bring 'em on, Owen thought. *Poor, dumb Yankee bastards. Bring 'em on.*

FREDERICKSBURG

Jane Beale was almost a veteran by now. The firing of two guns in rapid succession at this hour was uncommon but not particularly alarming. What was alarming was Martha knocking on the door at five o'clock in the morning.

The house slave tried to contain herself, to sound calm

and in control, but her voice registered about an octave higher than usual. "Miss Jane—the Yankees are coming. They've got two bridges nearly across the river."

Now Jane's voice was an octave or two higher as well, and her words were staccato. "Wake the children and any of our guests who may still be sleeping. Everyone is to gather in the basement!"

Beale dressed quickly, grabbed an armload of clothes, not knowing how long they would be forced to stay in the cellar, and then began to round up her herd. Fighting her own panic was her first priority until she found her children, dazed and confused, standing on the landing, still more asleep than awake and trying to figure out what to do and where to go. Julian was slowed by fever and his younger brother Sam had his trousers still around his knees and at that moment Jane realized that panic was a luxury she couldn't afford. She didn't have time. She had to get her boys dressed and down the stairs to the safety of the cellar.

Robert E. Lee was astounded at the audacity of Burnside's plan. An assault directly into the heart of his strongest line was not like Burnside at all. Lee had all along considered it a possibility, but Longstreet's defensive line on Marye's Heights had been designed to discourage just such a plan. Of course it might all still be a ruse, but if so it was an elaborate one.

It was his right flank that concerned him most, however. Jackson's line was thin and weak. A concerted effort on that side of the line today might turn him and enable Burnside to approach Fredericksburg from the right. Two corps might set up shop there and hold the Army of Northern Virginia helplessly in place while as many as four corps of Union troops marched almost without opposition to Richmond.

A. P. Hill would be here in time—the fiery redheaded general had developed a habit of showing up just in the knick of time. But Jubal Early and Harvey Hill were still as far as thirty miles away—a time-consuming trek even for Jackson's "foot cavalry."

"You sent for me, General Lee?"

"I did, General Barksdale. I need to impress on you the importance of your mission."

Barksdale was a little irritated. He needed to be with his men right now, and he knew full well the importance of the mission. Or so he thought.

"General Barksdale, General Burnside has over a hundred thousand men on the other side of the river, and now it appears he intends to cross them over right here. General Jackson has fewer than twenty thousand men guarding our right flank—but with twenty thousand more on the way. Those men will not arrive here before tomorrow at the earliest."

The numbers turned Barksdale's stomach.

"You will not be able to stop them, General. We do not expect anything of the sort. But we must have time to get those soldiers up and in their ranks at Prospect Hill or all could be lost."

"I understand, sir."

"Give me a day, General Barksdale. I must have this day."

On the Rappahannock

B rainerd could see the Fredericksburg landing now. In fact he couldn't take his eyes off of it. *Less than a hundred feet to go, but if I can see them . . .*

"Fire!"

The voice was from a distance and muffled by the fog but Brainerd heard it clearly enough only an instant before the precious silence was ruined by the furious growl of hundreds of muskets. Men fell all around him. One into a pontoon, another into the water, and a third died on the bridge. From peaceful quiet to absolute pandemonium in one hellsent instant. It had been almost serene only seconds before and now the roar of muskets and the sounds of screaming men and footsteps drumming on the planks of the bridge added up to bedlam as the engineers who were still able all broke hell-bent for leather back to the shoreline.

Zook's regiments stationed along the shore fared little

better. They too were defenseless and even though they weren't clearly visible yet, the Rebels had the range. Everyone looked for someplace to hide, but for most, what little cover there was had already been taken. Most of the men just lay facedown in the snow and mud with their hands over their heads and prayed for the shooting to stop.

"Wes!"

Brainerd, lying in the mud like everybody else, looked behind him to try to find where the voice was coming from. Ira stuck his head out from behind the only tree within a half mile and signaled him to come. The captain had never run so fast in his life.

"Perkins is dead, Wes."

Brainerd said nothing.

"What are we going to do, Wes?"

"Well, Ira—here comes the man whose job it is to tell us."

General Woodbury was walking almost casually down the hill from the Lacy house, seemingly unconcerned about the Rebel bullets that continued to splatter mud all around him. He got down to the tree and didn't even bother to return the salutes of his officers. In an almost matter-of-fact tone he told them the news. "General Burnside orders that the bridges must be completed whatever the cost. He thought it necessary to remind us that the whole army is waiting."

"But, sir . . ."

Woodbury ignored Spaulding's interruption.

"The artillery will chase them off. When the guns stop shooting, move out."

With no further explanation or instruction he turned and strolled easily back up the hill to observe.

Fifty cannons stationed along Stafford Heights opened fire on the buildings along the waterfront where they assumed the Rebels were hiding. They fired through the fog and the smoke from their own guns. Any shell that actually found a target was due almost entirely to good fortune. Nonetheless it was a terrible fire lasting for half an hour or more, and when the shooting stopped Spaulding ordered the engineers forward, back onto the bridge "at the double-quick." Brainerd and Ford led, but only a handful of men followed. Some cowered, some cried, and some boldly refused to go.

Woodbury went mad at the sight. He was a professional soldier with an impeccable record—not a mark against him since his 1836 graduation from West Point. But the uncontrollable chain of events over the last month had ruined all that he had worked for all of his life, and now, in full view of both armies, a bunch of cowards refused his order to attack, and he saw them driving the final nail into the coffin of his career. Daniel Woodbury was hysterical with anger. Furious and humiliated, he drew his pistol from its holster and ran down the hill screaming unintelligibly at his men and firing wildly into the air. His face was as red as a beet and his entire body was clenched so tightly that he shook. He grabbed men and pushed them toward the bridge but most still refused to budge. They preferred their chances against a madman with a gun, and maybe even against a firing squad, to the senseless suicide of the bridge.

By now the men who had followed Brainerd approached the far end of the bridge and, so far, not a single Rebel shot had been fired. After the artillery thunder died away it was quiet again and Brainerd actually held out hope that the big guns had done their job and run the sharpshooters out of their caves. It was a hope that died with the first man. The moment they reached the end of the bridge Barksdale's Rebels opened a hellish fire and half a dozen men fell almost instantly. Captain Ford took a shot in the arm and the rest, Brainerd included, hightailed it back to the shoreline without having extended the bridge a single foot.

7 A.M.

Seeing the engineers' retreat, the artillery opened fire a second time while Spaulding and Brainerd worked out a plan for another attempt. The hardest part of the plan was to find volunteers, but find them Brainerd did. The ten-man squad of lashers stood in single file waiting for the artillery to cease fire, signaling, hopefully, that the Rebels had finally been driven out of Fredericksburg and it was safe to build some more bridge. Once the lashers had secured the pontoon in place a fresh squad of balkers would replace them and extend the balks out to attach the next boat. One squad at a time—one job at a time—one agonizing step at a time until the job was done. That was Brainerd's plan.

Again the cannoneers laid down a horrible fire and this time surely not even a rat could have survived such a terrible shelling.

Brainerd paced back and forth in front of his bravest men, deep in his own thoughts, as were they all. He had written his father and made peace with his God and if this was to be his last day, then so be it. He began a private prayer that was interrupted by a boyish voice.

"Sir?"

Brainerd brought himself back to the now. "Yes, son."

The boy took off his coat and offered it to his captain.

"They might not shoot at you so much if you don't look so much like an officer."

Brainerd started to refuse and then he became choked with emotion and didn't know what to say or what to do.

"It's okay, sir. You gave it to me. Remember?"

Brainerd did remember. He remembered yanking it off the quartermaster and throwing it to the private, who looked like a scared, shivering, wet puppy. He remembered it very well. It was an enlisted man's coat and would attract no special attention on the bridge. It was a good idea.

He took the coat and put it on. It fit just fine. The boy's eyes filled with tears and then so did Brainerd's. He stood back and looked the private square in the eye and saluted him. The captain saluted the private, and it was the most wonderful moment in Billy Blakesley's young life.

The artillery ceased firing and finally Brainerd could wait no longer.

"All right, men. God be with you all. At the double-quick—march!"

Of the ten men who made the charge only five made it to the end of the bridge, and after they actually started to work it took only another minute before two more fell wounded. Billy Blakesley, Louis Wilcox, and Wes Brainerd were all that remained standing. Blakesley made himself as small as he could, kneeling in a pontoon, lashing down the side rails as quickly as he could, all the time keeping his back to Fredericksburg and to the Rebel sharpshooters only eighty feet away. Still there. Still shooting. The artillery bombardment had only made them madder. But now his job was done and it was time to get the hell off of this goddamned floating coffin. He jumped out of the boat and onto the planking and no sooner had he gained his footing than a scorching pain blazed into the back of his right knee, like a blacksmith had stabbed him deeply with a white-hot poker fresh out of the forge. He tried desperately to keep himself balanced so he could direct his fall back into the pontoon but as his leg collapsed he lost all hope of avoiding the freezing waters of the Rappahannock. The shock of the cold was worse than the wound and even worse than that was the panicking realization that his right leg was totally useless. The weight of the wool uniform and the heavy boots pulled him downward and with only one leg to kick Billy flailed wildly with his arms to get back to the surface. Yes. Just for a moment. Just long enough for one frantic gasp of air before going back under. He was on the upstream side and reached out to take hold of one of the pontoons as the currents pushed him by. He found a narrow ridge alongside one of the boats and was able to pull his head out of the water but his fingers were too cold and the river too strong and he quickly lost his grasp. He kicked with one foot, swam with one hand, and tried to grab any passing thing with the other but his clothes weighed like concrete now and blood poured out from his knee and he knew that total exhaustion was only seconds away. As he lost his last desperate chance to grab a pontoon he glanced up to see Wilcox lying on the end of the bridge reaching out to him with one of the wide oars. There was still a chance but the leg . . . *the goddamned leg won't kick*. It's only a ton of dead weight now, but with one good lunge he might grab the oar and hold on just long enough for Wilcox to pull him into a boat. "Please, God!" He looked up into his friend's eyes, pleading with him to reach out just one foot farther when Wilcox's face erupted into a red and white and gray explosion of blood and bone and brains. The gruesome sight had no time to register before Billy went under again. His fingers and toes had long since frozen beyond any use or feeling. His left leg was now as useless as his right. *Jesus, receive me.* Faces. Voices. Jenny and Mary and Pop. His body forced him at last to inhale a gallon of the freezing Rappahannock directly into lungs that urgently demanded air. Through the pain and the panic and the cold he managed to pray one last time, *Jesus, receive me,* and finally the darkness came, the struggle ended, and the pain and the panic and the cold were no more, and the lifeless, soulless body of Private Billy Blakesley sank almost gracefully to the muddy bottom of the icy Rappahannock.

Brainerd stood up, facing the Federal side of the river, and signaled that it was time to send more men but there would be no more men. Instead there was Ira frantically waving him back to the shore. Brainerd looked down in disgust and realized that he was straddling the body of Private Wilcox, the man who had died trying to pull that kid out of the water. He needed to run, but he was paralyzed by a wave of unbearable grief.

He's gone too, Brainerd thought, *that shy kid from Rome—the one who gave me his coat. For what?*

A bullet passed so close to his ear that he felt the air move. He had just started to run when the next bullet found its mark and tore through his left arm. His hand swung completely over his head before it came to lifeless rest at his side. He tried to keep running but it was a pitiful effort. The Federal artillerymen saw what was happening and unleashed a dozen more shots into the waterfront buildings of Fredericksburg and it must have worked because regardless of their best efforts the Rebel sharpshooters failed to bring Brainerd down. "Miracle" is a word that comes too easily sometimes, but not this time. Brainerd managed to stagger to safety without taking another bullet. He fell into the arms of Sergeants Simpson and Cowan, who dragged him up the hill, bullets still splashing into the earth all around them until they reached the top and managed to find safety behind a stone wall. They pulled off his coat—the one Private Blakesley had given him—and they tossed it aside before putting a handkerchief tourniquet on his arm.

"Save it," Brainerd said.

"We'll do what we can," Sergeant Simpson said, "but that's gonna be up to the surgeons."

"No. The coat. Save that coat for me, Sergeant. It's special."

STAFFORD HEIGHTS

Colonel Zook found elements of his 57th and 66th New York regiments perched safe and high on a ridge and firing blindly into the fog. He dismounted and pulled one man to his feet and pushed him down the hill. "You're wasting the government's goddamned bullets firing from up here!" Another man. Another push. "Now get your bastard asses down to the river and shoot at something you can *see*!"

"Take this key, Joe." General Meagher's cook looked like he was being handed the key to hell.

"I ain't a-takin' nothin' of a sort, Mac. General Meagher gave that key to you for safekeeping!"

Bill McCarter felt like a dog on a leash chained to a tree. He had to go. He had to. He had to break the chain and get away from this stupid tent and catch up with Stretch and the rest of the boys of the 116th. Damn the key! Damn the orders! Damn the court-martial and the firing squad. He just couldn't stay here a minute longer. The artillery fire was heavy now, and the Irish Brigade had moved out and he *had* to move out with it. He had to break that chain.

"Well, it's sure not gonna be 'safe' where it's going today!" He put the key back in his pocket, grabbed his musket and his empty cartridge box, and ran up the hill, trying to catch up with his friends in the Irish Brigade.

"Wes!"

Brainerd recognized Ira's voice and fought to remain conscious just for one more minute. Just for long enough to . . . He saw Ira's face and the poor man was pale as a ghost—like it was he who had been wounded instead.

"Wes, are you . . . ?" He looked at Sergeant Simpson. "Is he . . ."

"It's all right, Ira. The sawbones'll sew me up like an old sock, I'll be fine."

"Thank God. I . . ."

Brainerd grabbed Spaulding's sleeve with his good hand and looked into his panicked face and spoke as sternly as he could. "Ira! *Major* Spaulding. So many men have died. And many more will die." The pain in his arm made him dizzy and nauseous but he couldn't allow himself to pass out. Not yet. "If the bridges aren't finished they will all have been wasted." One more shallow breath and a whisper. "Finish the bridges, Ira." His eyes rolled back and the sleep finally came.

The sun was up and the fog was thinning. Colonel Zook had sent his men down to the riverbank, where they could see what they were shooting at. Problem was they still couldn't see the damned Rebels hiding like cowards in second-story windows, but the Confederate sharpshooters could sure as hell see them. Barksdale's Mississippians were perfectly safe and able to take careful aim at individual Yankees, and their officers quickly became the Rebels' favorite targets. First Colonel Chapman and then Colonel Bull.

A little more than a mile downstream, Lieutenant Cross watched with no satisfaction whatsoever as his engineers anchored their first pontoon to the shoreline and finally began building the bridges that General Franklin's men would cross. As anxious as he was—as cold and miserable and frustrated as he was at the delay—the young engineer was grateful for one thing. He was as glad as hell *he* wasn't going to have to cross it because he and everybody else in the army knew that Stonewall Jackson was over there somewhere—waiting for anyone who did.

Spaulding watched as Brainerd was carried up the hill where doctors would "sew him up like an old sock." "Let it be so," Ira prayed, but then Wes's final whisper returned to his mind. "Finish the bridges. . . ."

As if summoned by Ira's thought, Lieutenant George Folley appeared at his side just in time to see Brainerd carried off the field. Captain Perkins was dead, Captain Ford was wounded, and command of Brainerd's section would now fall on the shoulders of this baby-faced, scared-to-death boy. Spaulding didn't have the heart to tell him.

"You know what, Major? That spirit lady back in Washington Town said this was going to happen."

"What in hell are you talking about, Lieutenant?"

"You weren't there that night, Major, but that spiritualist told Captain Brainerd that he'd be wounded by a river."

"She said 'wounded,' right? Not killed."

"That's what she said, sir."

"Thank God for that. Now—Lieutenant Folley."

"Sir?"

"Captain Perkins is dead. Captains Ford and Brainerd are wounded. That means you are in command." Folley's expression didn't change while he absorbed the blow. "Now, Lieutenant Folley—you and I have got to finish these bridges."

"How are we gonna do it, sir? I mean we've already tried it three times—four times—hell! I've lost track of how many times—and all we're doing is dying! We can't send our boys out there again. They're just getting murdered." The words spewed out of him like bullets from a Gatling gun and he showed no signs of slowing down until Spaulding finally had to yell at him to get him to stop.

"*Folley!* You've got to stop telling me what's wrong—I *know that*! I need for you to help me figure out what to *do* about it!"

The young lieutenant was on the verge of panic and Spaulding knew that it would be a while before he could be of any help. He peeked out from behind the tree and tried to figure something out. Anything. He saw the bridge. The last pontoon just hung there, held in place only by its anchor, still eighty feet from the Fredericksburg side of the river. Dozens of engineers lay on it, some writhing but most motionless. The buildings along the riverfront were damaged from the artillery fire but still erect and strong enough to protect the Rebels. They're still in there, he thought, and there's nothing anybody can do about it. Nothing. Except commit suicide. And then he noticed the other pontoon boats—the ones not yet placed on the bridge. They were in the river but still along the near shoreline. He had an extraordinary idea. They're big damned boats and there are six of 'em. Enough to hold more than a hundred men.

"That's it!"

"What's 'it,' sir?"

"We put about a hundred infantrymen in those pontoons, row them across to the other side and let them do what the infantry does so that we can get on with doing what engineers do."

"Huh?"

"Wait here, Folley. I've got to go find General Woodbury."

8:15 A.M.

Lieutenant Cross had little to do but thank God. Regardless of his late start, his bridge at the lower crossing was progressing nicely without so much as a shot being fired. The last boat was in the water and headed for the opposite shore, loaded with a landing party assigned to prepare the exit abutment. He sent to General Franklin for some artillery—just in case they needed it.

Spaulding found Woodbury and Hunt standing nose to nose and neither too happy with the other. He didn't have time to be polite and didn't much care at this point what they might be arguing about.

"Sirs!"

The argument stopped as both generals were astounded that a lowly major would be so bold as to interrupt.

"What do you want, Major Spaulding?"

"I have a plan, sirs. I think it may be the only way that these bridges will ever be completed."

Woodbury didn't want to hear it. "The only way these bridges will ever be completed is if you get those cowards of yours off of their butts and onto the bridge!"

"Most of those 'cowards' are dead, sir!"

Silence.

Finally it was Hunt who spoke. "We have over a hundred thousand men, Major. The bridges *will* be built."

"You have over a hundred thousand *infantry*men, General. They know nothing about building bridges. Every engineer who dies takes his training with him and can't be replaced by a hundred infantrymen."

Spaulding recognized that his commanding general had lost all capacity to make rational decisions by this point so he spoke to Hunt directly. "We have six pontoons anchored by the shoreline, General. If we could load them full of infantrymen and ferry them to the other side, maybe they could get a foothold over there, sirs, and maybe they could push the Rebs back or at least occupy 'em long enough for us to get the bridges across."

All continued to go smoothly at the lower crossing. The artillery pieces arrived, the last of the pontoons was in place, and the abutment party was making progress. The sounds of battle from upstream didn't go unnoticed and the men worked like machines to finish before the Rebs got there—and they almost did it.

Totally without warning, a company of Texans appeared out of a ditch and opened fire. A half dozen engineers fell where they stood. Some of the abutment party bolted for the bridge and raced for the other side while the rest took shelter where they were and prayed. In less than a minute the newly arrived Federal guns opened on the Texans and the Rebels vanished as quickly as they had appeared.

Lieutenant Cross and his men went back to work, but this time even faster.

12:30 P.M.

According to plan at least two divisions should have been in the streets of Fredericksburg by now. Ambrose Burnside was working on less than two hours' sleep and his temper got shorter by the second. The sounds of battle only frustrated him further and the slowness of the information turned him furious until finally Ambrose Burnside exploded.

"General Hunt!"

"Sir!"

"You will bring *all* of your guns to bear on that city and batter it down!"

The artillery commander was stunned by the order. "I beg your pardon, sir?"

"You heard me, General. Every gun you've got!"

"Against the town, sir?"

"It's not a town anymore, General. It's a goddamned fort and I want it destroyed!"

FREDERICKSBURG

Jane Beale and her guests were all huddled in her cellar and actually had begun to hope that the fighting had stopped. Barksdale's men had ceased firing and, just for the moment, the afternoon was as quiet as a baby's breath. In the fresh silence Reverend Lacy began to recite the Twenty-seventh Psalm and all those gathered joined in until Hunt's guns roared to life and the entire world began to explode. Only seconds later Jane's house was shaken by a deafening thunder and the windows shattered, a beam cracked, and the cellar quickly filled with smoke and dust. Everyone in the cellar lay down and covered their heads, certain the house was about to collapse on top of them. Screaming and crying filled the room and even then Jane heard little Sam shriek above it all. She felt her way though the falling dust until she found him on the floor, whimpering and crying that he'd been shot. Jane examined him from head to toe and, thank God, found no blood. The beam had splintered and a large piece had struck the boy in the chest. He was bruised and frightened but otherwise unhurt, and to praise God for that, Reverend Lacy returned to his prayer.

Stafford Heights

Henry Hunt loved the big guns. To him there was nothing more powerful than a round of double canister ripping a hole twenty-men wide in the ranks of oncoming Rebels or throwing a shell a mile through the air and having it explode thirty yards over the heads of the enemy, sending a dozen of 'em to hell before they could get close enough to fire a shot. To this man, gun thunder was music and artillery tactics were art. He had written the book—literally. Decades ago, he had been instrumental in designing the manual on tactics that was still in use on both sides of the lines—but there was nothing in it that condoned the wanton destruction of innocent towns. On any other day there was nothing he loved more than watching the big guns at work. But not on this day.

Today he watched in pain as his orders to raze Fredericksburg were carried out. No longer was it 50 guns firing at an enemy stronghold—now it was more than 150 guns firing on a defenseless town and under orders to continue firing until Fredericksburg was rubble. He watched as a chimney collapsed into a useless pile of brick dust. A dozen houses burned throughout the town with no one able to save them. Even the churches weren't safe.

My guns, Hunt thought. *My orders.* It disgusted him to see what he was being forced to do. McClellan would never have ordered such a thing. Hell, Mac would never have *allowed* it. It wasn't a struggle for him to come up with the right word to describe what they were doing. The word was "barbaric."

Fredericksburg

While his Mississippians took refuge from the bombardment, diving into cellars, crouching behind walls, and closely hugging dear mother earth to avoid bursting shells and falling debris, General Barksdale remained mounted, riding along his lines to inspire his men with his fury.

"Those men over there—those men who are doing this to

this town—they are nothing more than uncivilized vermin!"

Even the men nearest to him weren't able to hear him over the roar of the Federal guns, but he continued shouting nonetheless. "You may kill them as you would a pack of rats!"

The burning homes infuriated him the most. *Huns. That's what they are. Savage, uncivilized, immoral Huns.* He had sent to Longstreet for permission to douse the fires but Longstreet had refused. "You have enough to do. Watch out for the Yankees." So now he had to sit and watch helplessly as an innocent town burned.

The volume of artillery fire increased and the Mississippi general was finally forced to seek refuge himself. He moved into a house that was only slightly safer than sitting on horseback in full view of the Yankee artillerists, and he set up headquarters there. He hadn't been there long before he heard the most shocking sound of the day. In the midst of battle, over the explosions that continued all around them, he heard the musical lilt of a feminine voice, calm, prim, and very Southern, coming from the parlor.

"I wish to speak with General Barksdale, if I might."

Captain Henry Ferris was astounded to see the woman standing calmly at the door and dressed as if for church. "I'm sorry, madam, but as you might expect, General Barksdale is occupied at the moment." A staff officer doing his job.

"Young man, I know that the general is a Southern gentleman, and that he would never refuse to see a lady who called on him."

Trump.

The captain turned to inform the general but Barksdale was already on his way to greet his guest—and he was not exactly in a Southern gentlemanly frame of mind.

"For God's sake, madam, go and seek some place of safety! I'll send a member of my staff to help you find one."

"I require no assistance, General." The woman was as calm as a spring breeze. She even carried a parasol, as though it might protect her from falling buildings. "I merely came to inform you that my cow has been killed in my stable." Every man in the room was totally flabbergasted.

Everything stopped while they waited to see what would come next. Barksdale didn't respond. He didn't know how. It didn't matter because the lady kept right on talking. "She is very fat and I don't want the Yankees to get her, so if you will send someone down to butcher her, you are welcome to the meat."

It took a moment, but the Southern gentleman returned just as the lady knew he must. "Ah—well— That is very kind of you, madam, and I am certain that General Lee will be most grateful. And now, I must insist that you allow Captain Ferris to escort you home and see to your safety."

"You are very kind, sir."

Captain Ferris took the lady's arm and accompanied her out onto the exploding street as though he were her escort at a social. As they left a courier entered, only momentarily distracted by the presence of the incredibly out-of-place couple.

"General Barksdale, sir. A report from Colonel Fiser, sir."

He read it quickly and smiled.

"It appears that our boys are holding firm." He had feared bad news and knew that his mission was a delaying tactic only. The slightest setback could result in orders to pull back and that was the very last thing in the world he wanted. The artillery bombardment continued without pause. It had been going on for over an hour now—nearly two—and the beautiful, historic, totally innocent town of Fredericksburg was now a burning ruin, and what William Barksdale wanted right now, more than ever, was to kill some more Huns.

"A message to General Lee."

"Yes, sir."

"Tell General Lee that if he wants a bridge of dead Yankees, I can furnish him with one."

CHAPTER 8

2:30 P.M.

Robert E. Lee stood on Telegraph Hill just watching the unforgivable barbarity. He was angry and frustrated that his guns were too far back to reply and give the Yankee gunners some trouble of their own.

He felt Longstreet's presence as he stepped up beside him. "Those people delight to destroy the weak and those who can make no defense." Now he dropped his glasses and looked at Pete. "It just suits them."

STAFFORD HEIGHTS

"It's too dangerous."

"It's no more dangerous than sending more engineers out to die on those bridges, General Burnside, and we're rapidly running out of engineers."

"You sound like you don't have any faith in your own work, General Hunt. Surely the Rebels have been driven out by now."

The artillery commander hated to think that Burnside was right, but he *didn't* have faith that even the most massive bombardment of the war had driven the rats out of their

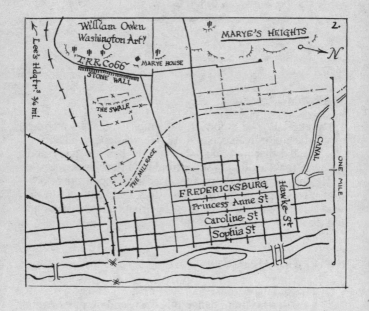

holes across the river. "Even if we have been successful, they have more men, sir."

Burnside's face was red with anger and wet with sweat. The whole plan was going straight to hell because of a handful of stubborn Rebels. A full corps should have been charging up the heights by now, before Lee had time to prepare. And another corps doing the same downriver against Lee's right. But not a soul could cross because the bastards wouldn't come out and fight like men.

Hunt took advantage of Burnside's silence to give the idea one more push. "We've got to get some infantry over there and push those people back in a hurry. Otherwise we'll still be sitting here this time tomorrow. I know it's dangerous, sir, but the boats are the only way."

Burnside removed his big, floppy hat and wiped his brow with his sleeve, giving himself just another couple of seconds to make a decision.

"Cease firing, General, and have Woodbury send the bridge builders back out. If they are met with heavy resistance then I'll reconsider . . ." He looked at Hunt sternly and pointed for effect. "But I will *only* send volunteers. Find me the men who are willing to try it and I'll send 'em over."

Marye's Heights

Along with everybody else safely ensconced atop Marye's Heights, Bill Owen and his Washington Artillery comrades had had nothing to do all day but watch the show being played out below. It was frustrating but highly entertaining.

It was frustrating because the Federal guns that were mercilessly pounding poor Fredericksburg to rubble were too far out of range for them to return fire. It was entertaining because every time those poor bastards ran out onto those bridges Barksdale's men sent 'em straight to hell. The fog was long gone and the day was downright balmy. Several of the men actually sat astride the cold barrels of their guns as if the cannon were horses, waiting to see what would happen next.

The silence of Hunt's guns signaled the opening of another act in the drama, and men who had been napping in the sun rose up to have a look. All attention was focused on the river. They couldn't see the bridges from the hillside, but every man knew where they were and the Rebels were just as interested as the Yankees to see if Barksdale's men had survived and if the survivors had any fight left in them. The suspense didn't last long. After only about three minutes of silence the roar of muskets echoed down the valley and white smoke rose up from the riverside.

Owen and an audience of about twenty thousand all stood and cheered loudly and waved their hats over their heads in ovation to the brave Mississippians who had withstood hell for two hours and given it back in two seconds.

Stafford Heights

"All right, men. General Burnside has requested volunteers to be ferried across the river in pontoons to try to push the Rebels out of the town so that the engineers can finish the bridges."

Captain Macy hadn't gotten all of the words out before the men of the 20th Massachusetts stood as one. He had prepared a long speech telling the men how important the mission was, but it just wasn't necessary. Little Abbott was the first to stand.

Macy beamed. "Very well, then. We shall follow the 7th Michigan and the 19th Mass."

The groan from his men might have been heard by the Rebels across the river. To a man they were humiliated and even angry to be relegated to a position behind the 19th. The 19th and the 20th had a not so friendly rivalry.

"The 19th?" Leander Alley was more furious than most. "That bunch of shirkers? We're only going to have to step aside to make room for their retreat!"

"That's just how it is, Lieutenant. Now, make ready, men, and we'll be following the 19th down to the boats."

* * *

The urge to volunteer wasn't nearly so strong among Ira Spaulding's decimated engineers. Even as Hunt's artillery opened again, this time focusing on the landing site, Spaulding pleaded with his demoralized troops.

"Look, men, we've got to finish those bridges! Our choices are to march out there again until every one of us is dead, or to land infantry on the other side and let them get the damned Rebs out of those buildings." He took a deep breath. He knew what he was asking them to do and even doubted that he would volunteer himself. "Now, you're the only men in this whole damned army who know how to maneuver those boats of ours, and so we've got to do it. We've got to do it because . . ." *Hell*, he thought. *There's really nothing more to say.* "Well, we've just got to do it."

He hoped that twenty men would step forward at that moment, but none did. After almost a full minute of waiting, he had no choice but to play his trump card. He had to make good on his threat.

"Very well, then. Prepare to move back out onto the bridges. We'll all be going out this time. Rowers . . . man your boats. Lashers . . ."

"I'll go, sir." One brave private. Spaulding thanked God. The others would follow very quickly.

"God bless you, Private. You may have just saved a hundred lives."

The 7th Michigan marched past them almost on cue, heading for the pontoons at the shoreline and Spaulding and his new favorite private headed down as well. Sure enough, others followed and manned their boats.

"The going will be hot, but only for the first hundred feet or so." Spaulding pointed out a landing spot upstream from the bridges. "Aim there, and that rise between the river and the buildings will protect you."

The Michigan boys began loading themselves into the pontoons, every one of them lying low. The Yankee artillery ceased firing and seconds later the Rebel infantry commenced. One of the engineer volunteers was the first to fall and most of the rest immediately lost their nerve. They bolted from the boats, leaving the infantrymen stranded, but they didn't get far. The file closers from the 7th Michigan stepped forward, rifles loaded and bayonets fixed, and the reluctant engineers returned to their boats and began rowing their way to Fredericksburg. They screamed at the Michigan boys to grab oars and help. Some tried, but it's hard to row with your head below the gunwale. The farther out they rowed, the heavier came the Rebel fire. Colonel Baxter, commanding officer of the 7th, was one of the first to fall, wounded through the chest.

But soon, as Spaulding had told them, the Rebel fire slackened, their line of sight blocked by a rise in the terrain. The Michiganders' new commanding officer stood up in the boat as they approached the landing point. "Remember your orders, men. You are to give no quarter. You are to bayonet any man with a gun who has been hiding like a coward in a drawing room and killing unarmed men. There will be no lines of battle. Move forward in small groups and force the rats out of their holes and kill 'em. MICHIGAN!"

As the prows touched the shoreline 135 men jumped out of the boats and immediately began their assault on the city. The pontoons turned and, carrying the wounded with them, headed back for the Falmouth side.

As more and more Yankees disembarked on the riverbank, General Barkesdale began slowly pulling his Rebel sharpshooters back.

The boats soon began making the crossing with little trouble and the Michigan regiment and the 19th Massachusetts were soon fully disembarked on the Fredericksburg shore. For the first time all day, it was the Yankees' turn to cheer. The engineers had found their courage and, since the Rebels now had something more pressing on their minds, they were able to complete the long-delayed bridges in only a matter of minutes. As the lead elements of the landing parties began pushing their way up the hill, toward Sophia Street, thousands of their Yankee buddies let loose with a cheer louder than the artillery had been. The boys of the 20th Massachusetts yelled the loudest, knowing they would be next, and the chore that had seemed so daunting half an hour ago now seemed like it might be a breeze.

But the men of the 20th Mass. didn't know General William Barksdale. They didn't know how angry the Mississippi general was. They didn't know how smart he was. They didn't know how determined he was to give General Lee the day he needed to get Jackson's corps fully up and in place. And they didn't know how anxious he was to kill some more Huns.

Captains Macy and Abbott led the Harvard Regiment to their boats. The bridges were done now, but their momentum carried them forward and Macy couldn't tolerate a delay. "Like a Sunday afternoon on the Charles," Little Abbott yelled as the boys from Boston pushed off. Seeing his old buddy, Alley, pulling an oar three boats away, Abbott yelled at him, "Ahoy there, matey! Keep a sharp eye out for the whales now."

The old whaler grinned and pointed up at Marye's Heights, where the Rebel army lay in wait. "Thar she blows," Alley yelled back.

At that moment the sound of musket fire exploded down from the streets of the town. Not sporadic shooting, but an eruption of hundreds of rifles all fired at one time, and Little Abbott's "day on the Charles" was over.

The 7th Michigan and the 19th Massachusetts had begun their movement off Sophia Street and up into the town, where they found Barksdale's Mississippians waiting, now concealed in the homes along Caroline Street. The volley of fire that greeted them was devastating. The two regiments were both sent reeling and diving for cover wherever it could be found. Soon they were backpedaling toward Sophia Street and the effort to clear Fredericksburg of all Rebel resistance came to an abrupt and bloody halt.

4:00 P.M.

A pounding on the door brought Jane Beale out of her prayers. Frightened to death that it might be the Yankees demanding to be let in, she was more than just relieved to hear her brother's voice shouting from the top of the stairs.

"Jane! Come on. *Now!*"

She bounded up the stairs and onto the veranda and

hugged John, who quickly pushed her away. "I've commandeered an ambulance for you—but there's only room for you and the boys. The Yankees are already across the river and there's no time to lose."

Jane couldn't even begin to think. The sunlight was blinding after hours in the near total darkness of her cellar and as her vision returned the things she saw were like something out of the nether world. The yard was filled with filthy armed men, some wounded and all sweating and anxious and shouting at one another. Tree limbs were down all around her, and she looked up to see that most of her trees had been shattered at the tops by cannon fire. The air smelled of sulfur and columns of black smoke rose up from half a dozen fires raging throughout the town. Even the church steeples were desecrated with the ugly, black scars left by Yankee cannonballs. As she took all of this in, Jane Beale prayed the oldest prayer ever whispered. "Oh, my God."

"Get on out now, missus," one of the Rebel soldiers yelled at her. "The Yankees is comin' right up that street there, and we're pulling back!"

Jane turned and ran back into the house and down the stairs. Her family and friends and servants were all still huddled in the darkness and she didn't quite know what to say. The truth is all there is.

"We have an ambulance for me and for my boys, but that's all we have space for." Her entire body began to quiver and tears welled up in her eyes. How could she leave these poor people to the Yankees, but how could she stay?

"It's all right, Jane," Reverend Lacy said in a calm voice. "You go on now. God will look after us here."

Then it was Martha who stepped forward to speak for the servants. There were tears in her eyes as well.

"Don't you worry about us, Miss Jane. You've already lost one boy to this war and there ain't no sense in risking losing any more—especially the little ones."

"That's right," another one of the servants said, with all the fervor of an "amen."

The memory of lowering Charley's young body into the

earth was more than Jane could bear, and she could no longer hold back the tears.

"Yankees won't hurt any of us," Martha continued. "If it gets too hot here in town we can just march ourselves over the river and tell 'em we want to be emancipated and they'll put us someplace safe till the shooting stops."

Jane wanted to believe it all. She had to believe it or she simply couldn't leave. "You just do that, Martha. Stay here as long as you want—as long as it's safe. But when it gets too bad, you go on over." She wiped her eyes and said, "All of you. Go on across if you have to."

"We will, Miss Jane." Martha's tears were flowing now as well. "Now you go on and get those boys on out of town now. It's gonna get worse before it gets better."

The boys of the Harvard Regiment disembarked from their pontoons and were almost immediately greeted by a river of wounded men flowing back downhill to the bridgehead. Many were being helped to the rear by two or three healthy comrades, most using their wounded buddies as an excuse to get the hell out of harm's way. Macy, Abbott, and Alley didn't take a second look at the wounded men. What frightened them was a river at their backs and a steep rise in front that they had to climb to where they knew the Rebel army was waiting. Not one of them, not a single veteran of the 20th Mass., could help but think about the disaster at Ball's Bluff. The scene was too frighteningly familiar.

The two bridges were completely finished now, and General Darius Couch began ordering his lead division to cross. The problem was there was no place for them to go once they reached the other side. The waterfront space was occupied by the bulk of the three regiments that had come over by boat. For those boys, there was nowhere to go but forward. Problem solved.

Union bands back on the Falmouth side began playing "Yankee Doodle" as Couch's regiments began their crossing and Captain Macy got his orders from Colonel Norman Hall, now commanding the brigade.

"You're to move up Hawke Street, there, reorganize the

men who are stranded along the way and push forward, Captain. Push forward. Clear this street, Captain, at all hazards!"

The officers of the 20th Mass. stood flagpole erect and brought their regiment to attention. They climbed the banks up to Sophia Street, where they ordered their men into columns by companies. As calm as parade ground cadets, the officers lifted their sabers and barked their orders, just as they had a thousand times before. "Right shoulder—shift. Forward—march!" The men of the Harvard Regiment responded without hesitation, just as *they* had a thousand times before.

They had only just begun their march up Hawke Street when Barksdale's Mississippians opened fire. The Harvard Regiment didn't flinch and continued their advance, trying as best they could to give back what they were getting, but the Rebels remained hidden, shooting from behind windows and doorways and barricades.

Only twenty yards up Hawke Street the boys from Boston came upon an alleyway and found the bulk of the 7th Michigan huddled there and going nowhere. Macy spotted their new commanding officer, Major Thomas Hunt, cowering in the alley with his men. Macy waved his saber and yelled at the men of the 7th to move out, but the badly beaten up Michigan boys simply refused to budge.

At the top of his lungs Macy yelled over the roar of battle, "You are ordered forward, Major, to clear this street of Rebels. Now I recommend you get off your cowardly fat ass and move your men up this hill!"

"I have received no such orders from my commanders and I don't take orders from captains!"

The Harvard Regiment came to a halt while Macy sent word back to Hall that his Michigan troops refused to move forward without specific orders to do so. It took only a couple of minutes to get Hall's response. "Push forward. Drive them out."

"My men will do no such thing, Captain. The Rebels are there in force!"

"Go to hell then, Major! *With* your goddamned regiment! Captain Abbott!"

"Sir!"

"Mr. Abbott, you will take your first platoon forward."

"Yes, sir!"

Little Abbott stepped forward, drew his saber, held it aloft, and shouted, "First platoon—forward—*march*!" They moved forward, directly in front of the reluctant 7th and Hunt shouted at them as they passed by, "No man can live around that corner!" Abbott and his men ignored the remark and proceeded up the hill toward Caroline Street.

Hunt shook his head and said a prayer as he watched Abbott's first platoon parade past him four abreast, into the jaws of the beast. The Rebels allowed Abbott's men to move into the intersection of Hawke and Caroline Streets before they opened fire from three sides. The dim light of dusk made every muzzle flash a visible stream of orange and yellow flame. In only a matter of seconds Abbott's lead company was virtually decimated. They broke ranks, but they didn't retreat. They bolted forward and to the left and right. They entered the buildings either to drive the Rebels out or just to escape the galling fire. Either way, many were killed or wounded. Some took prisoners and some were taken. Abbott calmly walked back down the hill, stood in front of the next men in line, and ordered, "Second platoon—forward MARCH!"

Seeing the Massachusetts state flag so far forward and in so much trouble, the boys of the stalled 19th Mass. were inspired to move back into the fight. Not in formation like the 20th, but in small groups of skirmishers fighting house to house. This was nothing like any battle any man on either side had ever seen before. It wasn't great bodies of men fighting face-to-face in elegant formations on open fields. This was a gunfight. "Black flag" orders had been issued—take no prisoners. It was a vicious feud: the Rebels seeking revenge for the immoral destruction of an innocent town and the Yanks for the cowardly murder of their unarmed engineers. Unarmed and wounded men on both sides died at the point of bayonets. Murder without honor.

There had never been a prouder moment in the life of Rebel Brigadier William Barksdale. The artillery shelling and the street fighting had reduced his numbers but he had plenty of fight left. His boys were outnumbered now, and yet they held on, fought on, and continued to hold back the whole damned Yankee army. But their foothold on Caroline Street was weakening and Barksdale was forced to yield one more block of the city to the Yankees. They moved up the hill, just a little bit farther, to Princess Anne Street, where his men could regroup, find some more hiding places, and kill some more Huns.

So when the order came from Longstreet to pull back, Barksdale thought not.

"Tell General Longstreet that my men are holding firm. Tell him that I consider a withdrawal under the cover of darkness to be the better plan."

Where Barksdale went, Little Abbott and his Massachusetts men—what was left of them—were determined to follow. Abbott was down now to fewer than two hundred men. The street behind him was heaped with bodies and every man left standing knew full well what lay ahead, and yet the young captain continued to stand tall and to rally his troops forward. Farther up the hill they moved and their arrival at Hawke and Princess Anne was just as hot as their greeting had been on Caroline.

Captains Macy and Abbott kept pushing men forward. By now the 59th New York was up and in the fight as well, but the Rebels were just as stubborn as they had been all day long and Lieutenant Lane Brandon's Mississippians were the most stubborn of the lot.

After the withdrawal to Princess Anne Street, Brandon finally had time to question some prisoners—a chore he had been trying to accomplish since he first had seen the Massachusetts flag being boldly paraded up Hawke Street.

"What is your regiment, Private?"

"The 20th Mass."

Brandon beamed. "And that would be the Harvard Regiment, would it not?"

"That's what they call us."

"Do you know an officer named Abbott?"

"I do. He's my company commander."

"Do they call him 'Little' Abbott?"

"Some do."

Brandon walked over to the second-story window to peek down on the fighting below. It took him no time at all to confirm what he had suspected for most of the evening. "Hello there, Little. I'll bet you wish you were back at Cambridge right now. If not yet, you're going to."

He turned back to the private from the 20th and smiled and said, "I'm a Harvard man myself, and an old classmate of Mr. Abbott's. And I'm about to teach him some manners he never learned at Harvard."

It was the backside of dusk before Brandon had his 21st Mississippi ready for a counterattack against his old friend and classmate. The last few men were coming into line when he was handed a note ordering him to cover Barksdale's withdrawal and pull back. Brandon only nodded and waited for the courier to vanish from sight before he ordered, "CHARGE!"

Abbott was both surprised and pleased. Surprised that at this late hour the Rebels would launch a real assault—and pleased, at last, to have something out in the open to shoot at.

Mississippi and Massachusetts battled back and forth along Hawke Street until Brandon was again ordered to fall back.

"Not a snowball's chance in July that I'm going to disengage from this fight. There is still work to do here." He screamed and physically pushed men forward. He took muskets from dead and wounded soldiers and fired into Abbott's ranks himself. His bloodlust was up and he continued pushing his men down the hill and into senseless battle. Abbott countered and Brandon countered again. By now it was pitch dark and at last a messenger from Barksdale told the defiant young lieutenant that if he continued to refuse his orders to withdraw that he would be placed under arrest.

"Better that than leaving the field in disgrace and in the hands of Little Abbott!"

"Then so be it," the courier said. "I'll have your sword." Brandon, at last, did as he was told. The last of Barksdale's Rebels pulled back to Marye's Heights and the smoldering heap of rubble that had been Fredericksburg, Virginia, finally fell quiet.

"Ma'am—you can't go over there! You'll be killed."

The corporal had grabbed the lead horse of Clara Barton's wagon team, but she was in no mood to argue. She left that to her nephew, Sam.

"This is Clara Barton, Corporal, and she is *ordered* across!"

"Ordered" was a bit of an exaggeration. But old Dr. Cutter had sent word that Massachusetts regiments were involved in heavy fighting in the streets of Fredericksburg, and that was close enough to an order for Clara. Four wagons filled with medical supplies—bandages and whiskey and the like—headed quickly for the town.

The corporal recognized the name and reluctantly stood aside. Clara's lead wagon wasn't yet half across the middle bridge before the first of several Rebel artillery rounds splashed into the river close enough to get her wet, but not nearly close enough to send her back.

THE LACY HOUSE

Captain Wesley Brainerd sat in a chair in a room filled with wounded men. The sounds in the place were worse than could possibly be imagined. Men wept or prayed or cursed as loudly as they could, each hoping to chase away the pain or attract the attention of the doctors. Brainerd's arm wound began to bleed again through the bandages, but too many men ahead of him had more serious wounds, so there Brainerd sat, waiting his turn until he finally had so little blood remaining that the room began to spin just before all went dark and he fell from his chair.

When he came to he was on a bed of straw spread out on the hardwood floor of a house some miles to the rear, the building designated by General Letterman for the wounded of the 50th New York Volunteer Engineers, and to them it might have been a deep featherbed in a fine Manhattan hotel.

As might be expected, Honest Johnny Jones, who had spent the day praying and watching from the porch of the Phillips house, was now at Brainerd's side—his gigantic, toothless smile beaming to see his hero come awake. Brainerd tried to speak, but he was simply too exhausted.

"Look you now," Johnny said in his sternest voice and his finest Welsh accent, "I know what you're a askin', and I'm gonna tell ya, but then you've gotta go right back off to sleep. Do ya understand?"

Brainerd smiled weakly and nodded.

"Your bridges are built, Captain, and the army's across."

Wesley Brainerd took a deep breath, and closed his eyes and slept.

CHAPTER 9

TELEGRAPH HILL
DECEMBER 12

While the day promised to be warm for the season, the predawn temperature was still uncomfortably cold. Cold enough that even Robert E. Lee and James Longstreet abandoned their uniforms for the warmer garb of civilian farmers. There was that, and their plans to ride far forward on this day to try to figure out what Burnside really had in mind so they could make the necessary adjustments. Lee also rode Lucy today instead of Traveler so as to attract less attention—and less fire from the ambitious Federal sharpshooters who now occupied the town.

No such caution infected Jeb Stuart, who wore his favorite gray cape lined in blood red silk, his fully festooned hat, and more gold braid than a high-toned brothel.

"Any changes, General Stuart?"

"No, sir, General Lee. It appears that the entire Army of the Potomac is directly in front of us. Sigel's corps is north, protecting Washington, but it seems that they have the six others crammed in along those heights. There are more bridges downstream, and men are crossing just below Deep Run, facing General Jackson's corps, sir. There is some activity at Skinker's Neck, but it is my belief that it is only a diversion. There are only sparse divisions posted either up-stream or down."

The dawn was only just now approaching and Lee tried to peer through the thin, foggy light with his field glasses. He saw little but didn't really need confirmation.

"Where are Jackson's divisions?"

Stuart started to answer, but was interrupted by Stonewall himself, riding up at full speed. Lee was still amazed when he saw the "ragamuffin general" wearing a uniform that would have been absolutely appropriate at a king's ball. Jeb beamed at his unlikely fashion protégé and said, "Very nice, General Jackson. At last you are properly attired for the occasion!"

"Enough, gentlemen," Lee said. "It looks as though General Burnside has elected to attack us where we are, and we must prepare. What are your current dispositions, General Jackson?"

"Powell Hill should be in position within the hour, sir, aligned in the woods beyond the railroad tracks. If time permits, we should inspect his placement."

All of those gathered recognized Jackson's comment for exactly what it was—another not-so-subtle attack on A. P. Hill's ability, but no one, not even Lee, dared to pursue the issue.

"Taliaferro's division is en route from Guiney Station. I have ordered him forward posthaste. Making good time, he should arrive sometime today."

"And Generals Early and Harvey Hill?"

Here, in Lee's mind, was the key to the whole game. Jubal Early and Harvey Hill had remained posted along the lower Rappahannock, to chase off gunboats and to guard against a crossing there—a flanking movement that could get to Lee's rear or threaten Richmond while the rest of Lee's army was busy at Fredericksburg. But he now believed it to be a highly unlikely possibility and those defenses were an insurance policy he could no longer afford. His seventy thousand men faced almost double their number, and *all* hands were going to be needed here. Quickly.

"I shall order them forward immediately, sir, but it may be tomorrow before they can get here."

Lee raised his glasses again even though he could still see little or nothing through the fog, but he didn't need to see the tens of thousands of men moving over the crest of Stafford Heights and heading down the slopes toward the bridges. He could hear them. He could feel them coming. He sighed and nodded. "Move them along, General Jackson. Tomorrow may be too late."

STAFFORD HEIGHTS

Captain Francis Adams Donaldson—the miserable, angry, and perpetually harassed commanding officer of Company H of the Corn Exchange Regiment—was, very predictably, miserable and angry. At 7 A.M., on a day when a horrible battle was beginning to take shape, his commanding officer and constant tormentor, Lieutenant Colonel James Gwyn, was drunk before breakfast, and already refilling his canteen with rum.

Donaldson nudged his manservant, George Slow, with an elbow and nodded toward the tipsy colonel. "Looks like our grand commander is pouring himself another quart of Dutch Courage to get him through the day."

Slow only nodded and smiled. He was tired of the feud between the two men. It never ceased to amaze the former slave how arrogant and stupid white folks could be. *If this is how white Yankees behave,* he often thought, *I'd just as soon take my chances with the Southerners. Always jealous of each other—always trying to hurt or humiliate each other. They're just mean and disrespectful. They're uncivilized children,* George believed, *and that's all there is to it.*

While Donaldson continued to fume at the transgressions of his lowlife colonel, a private in Company H began to sing an old hymn. Private Lorenzo Ayers loved to sing hymns, and Captain Donaldson hated Lorenzo Ayers.

"Shut up that infernal singing, Ayers!" Donaldson was face-to-face with the young soldier and yelling loud enough to be heard a thousand yards away. Ayers was visibly hurt. Here he was, maybe on the final day of his life, and singing the praises of the Lord made him peaceful of heart. He looked like a scolded puppy and almost whimpered, "Yes, sir."

A moment later, after Ayers had gone on about his chores, cleaning his rifle and packing his rations for the coming fight, Donaldson noticed the disapproving look on George's face.

"What's the matter with *you*?" Donaldson's emotions were out of control. He was about to attempt an impossible and deadly attack under the command of an idiot general and an inebriated colonel and he was not a happy man.

"Why you always gotta be so hard on Private Ayers, Captain?"

"He's a shirker and a zealot and bad for the morale of the duty-bound men of my company! That's why!"

"I don't think that's it, Captain."

Donaldson was only a little bit peeved at Slow. There may have been a time when he would have slapped him for such insolence, but George had proved himself too valuable and too loyal over the past several months and the old Negro didn't often speak just to hear himself talk.

"Just what do you think it is then, George?"

"I think that when Colonel Gwyn makes you mad, you whip Private Ayers . . ."

"Hogwash."

"Maybe it is—maybe it ain't. I just know this: that whenever a big man takes a pee, that pee keeps rolling down hill all the way till the man at the bottom of the hill gets wet. I've been a slave, Captain Donaldson, and to many folks around here I'm still 'just a darkie.' I've spent my life at the bottom of the hill. I've been plenty wet in my life and I know what it's like." He nodded toward the still pouting private who by now was almost in tears from desperately trying *not* to sing a song of praise to the Lord. "You're at the bottom of Colonel Gwyn's hill, Captain—and Private Ayers is at the bottom of yours."

8 A.M.

Bill McCarter was precisely where God intended him to be—standing in ranks with the Irish Brigade along with his buddies of the 116th Pennsylvania. He was directly behind Sergeant Stretch and next to the men he had joined up with, getting ready to do what he had joined to do—to kill some Rebels or get killed trying.

As they prepared to cross the bridge, in front of the Irish Brigade was General Meagher, and in front of him, General Hancock, and in front of him—only Rebels. It appeared to the stammering private that Winfield Scott Hancock, Thomas Meagher, and Bill McCarter were going to be the first over the bridge, the first to climb the hill, and the first to see the elephant.

A nearby band played "Yankee Doodle" and McCarter was ecstatic as they marched down the hill toward the bridge. Occasional Rebel artillery rounds exploded overhead, but, except for those who were killed or wounded, they only added to the excitement. Patriotic music, bombs exploding overhead like Chinese fireworks, and tens of thousands of armed men in blue uniforms marching off to save a nation—it was all too exciting for a lad from Derry, Ireland, to keep corked up inside. His entire face smiled and it was all he could do to keep from shouting just from the sheer joy of it all.

They had been warned *not* to march in step over the pontoons, for fear of setting them swaying, and throwing people off, so it became less of a march and more of a stroll. He was astounded to see how steady these floating bridges really were under the weight of a thousand men and a hundred horses.

Not too far ahead he saw the great green flag of the Irish Brigade. Normally there would be more, but the rest were in New York getting mended by the Know-Nothings. It was fine, though. One beautiful green flag emblazoned with a golden harp was quite enough for Bill. Quite enough to inspire him to show Americans what Irishmen could do.

As he stepped off the end of the bridge there was a silver-haired civilian in a black suit and silk hat standing off to the side, smiling a disingenuous yellow smile and handing out business cards. McCarter was astounded to see the man there and took a card just out of curiosity.

Dr. H. Shillman
Embalming and Shipping
Rest in Peace at Home
$50.00

Bill was appalled. He wadded up the card and threw it on the ground and noticed that his card joined hundreds of others in the muddy gutters of Sophia Street.

They had moved only a few yards into the town before he had second thoughts. That was when he saw his first dead soldiers—both the Rebels and the Yanks that lay in the streets and gardens of Fredericksburg. Some were covered, but some just lay there, cold and stiff and lifeless. These were real men with real faces, real families, and until only a few hours ago, real souls. Some had pulled open their shirts to see if they were gut shot and their entrails were opened and exposed for all to see. One Yankee looked all properly laid out, with his legs crossed and his arms folded across his chest. Then Bill stopped dead in his tracks. There, just off to the side of the street, was one poor, redheaded Rebel boy—with a rosary clutched to his heart. A redheaded, freckle-faced, Roman Catholic Rebel. Bill had never thought about that before, that Rebels might be Catholic. Or Irish. He fell out of ranks for a moment just to look at the boy. His body was encased in a thin sheet of frost that made him look like a ghost, or a slab of pig meat that had been stored in an icehouse. *My God,* Bill thought. *That boy is no different from me.* No older. No less loved. Obviously Catholic, but that didn't matter as much to Bill as it had back in Derry.

"Move on there, lad." It was Stretch, pushing him forward with the rest of the company, but he spoke in a soft voice. He had seen the boy too and knew what Bill was thinking. So McCarter moved on, but he didn't leave the Rebel Irishman entirely behind. He might have been from Derry. He might have had a stammer.

Two more blocks up the street another vision pulled at his heart. In what had been a lovely garden in the front yard of a pretty house were three freshly dug graves with crude crosses made from the pickets of what had once been the homeowner's fence. The names were just scribbled in pencil, and McCarter could read only one of them, Cpl. Anton Steffens, but on all three markers the other writing was clearly legible—*20th Massachusetts*—the Harvard Regiment.

Little Abbott stood in ranks with the remains of his platoon at full attention behind him. Macy conducted the roll call, officers first, and it didn't take him long to come upon the appalling silence that follows a name not answered.

"Cabot."

Nothing. For a long time there was not a sound.

"Captain Charles F. Cabot."

Still no response. Abbott felt weak and nauseous and choked back tears. He had seen his old classmate taken from the field late last night, shortly after the fighting had stopped, and he hadn't thought about him again until this very moment. But he thought about him now. He thought about the hole in Charlie's chest, he thought about their hijinks together back at Harvard, and he thought about the Cabots back home and how devastated and inconsolable Charlie's kind and elegant mother would be, and he didn't want to think about Charlie Cabot a single moment longer.

The silence after the name seemed to last an eternity. *Move on,* Abbott prayed. *Get on with it! Get on to the next name!*

"Palfrey," Macy shouted.

"Here!"

Thank God.

PROSPECT HILL

A. P. Hill had fire in his eyes. He was ready for another brawl. His men had seen no real action since their late-in-the-day heroics at Sharpsburg, when they broke onto the field after a seventeen-mile march and turned back Ambrose Burnside's corps just as they were

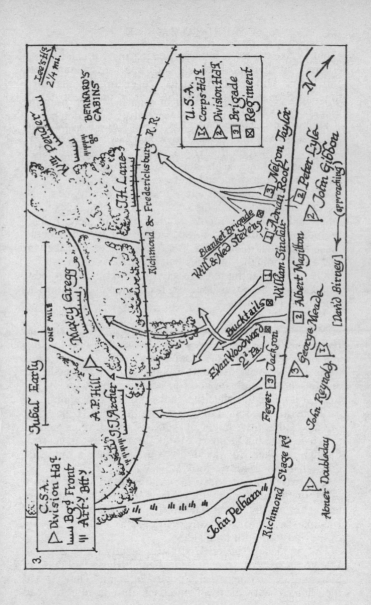

3.

CSA.
□ Division Hdq.
▲ Bgd Front>
⊔⊔ Arty. Btty.

Jubal Early

ONE MILE

Marcy Gregg

A.P. Hill ▲

J.J. Archer 🖾

Feger 3 Jackson

George Meade ▲ 3

John Reynolds 🖾

Abner Doubleday ▲

Richmond Stage Rd

John Pelham

Richmond & Fredericksburg R.R.

Wm Pendet

BERNARD'S CABINS

J.H. Lane 3

Blanket Brigade
Phil & Ned Stevens

William Sinclair □

Evan Woodward 2ª Pa. 🖾

Bucktails

Albert Magilton □ 2

Adrian Root □ 1

Nelson Taylor 3

Peter Lyle 2

John Gibbon 2
(approaching)

[David Birney] →

U.S.A.
1 Corps Hd I.
2 Division Hdq
3 Brigade
🖾 Regiment

Ireth's
2¼ mi.

N →

about to take the town and trap Lee's army with no hope of escape. But that had been almost three long months ago, and Powell Hill was anxious to prove himself, one more time, to Stonewall Jackson—the "crazy old Presbyterian fool" he worked for.

He moved his division to the base of Prospect Hill and began to survey the ground he would have to defend. He was in relief of John Bell Hood, who was being shifted left to strengthen the seam between the two corps. Hood pointed toward a spot dead in the center of the line.

"That finger of woods there, sticking out toward the river." Hood sighed and shook his head. "That's a tough spot. It's quicksand, General. A mule would drown in there. I don't see how you can defend it, but I don't see how they could make it through there either. But, left unguarded, if they *do* find a way through, your lines will be broken slap in two."

There was nothing more to say. It was Hill's worry now. Hood's work here was done, so he saluted and rode off to tend to his own men.

"General Gregg!"

Maxcy Gregg rode forward and saw immediately that Hill's blood was up. He was already wearing his "hunting shirt," the red one he wore whenever a fight was at hand. His hazel eyes were bright and he was bouncing in the saddle, as anxious as a schoolyard bully to beat somebody up—ready to go at it no matter what the Yanks might throw at him.

"General Hood says there's a swamp down there in the middle of that little finger of woods. Doesn't think we can post men there but he doesn't think the Yankees can get men through it either. So why don't you and I take a little ride down that way to have a look."

The two men were deep in slime before they were fifty feet into the woods and it didn't look like it was going to get any better anytime soon. The woods were thick, the ground was marshy, and putting any artillery there was totally out of the question—for both sides.

Hill nodded. "General Hood was exactly right, General. I'm going to post your brigade behind these woods—but there will be no one actually posted *in* them." They pushed their horses out of the muck and back onto the military road that Jackson's engineers had built through the woods along the base of Prospect Hill. There his other brigade commanders awaited their orders.

"General Gregg will post his men here. General Lane will be to the left, in the woods just this side of the railroad tracks. Archer on the right." He sat tall in the saddle. His commands were powerful and confident, but James Lane saw the flaw in the placements and didn't like them worth a damn.

"General Hill, sir, that places us well forward of General Gregg, and leaves a gap in our lines of more than five hundred yards. No disrespect, sir, but if the Yankees get far enough to meet General Gregg, we are already broken. My right flank will be in the air and under enfilade fire."

"It will not happen, General Lane. General Gregg and I have just returned. Look at our horses and you'll see how deep those marshes are. The interval cannot be breached."

He looked out in the direction of the river—toward the Union lines that he still couldn't see but could plainly hear. "It is a beautiful field, gentlemen. The approaching enemy will be caught in an artillery crossfire." He waved his hand over the indiscernible field. "When the fog lifts you will have a view of open ground and it will be full of Yankees, and you will be tempted to fire on them the moment they come into view—but *do not*!" He paused, giving each man a stern warning with a look and a nod. "Understand this and make it clear to your men—General Jackson has ordered that not a shot be fired—artillery *or* infantry—until the enemy is fully up and close at hand. We are well hidden here, men, and it is best to stay that way. The enemy has no idea of our strength or our positions and it will do us no good to give ourselves away for the sake of killing a handful of men. Do you understand?"

The men nodded. "Yes, sir."

"Even when you come under fire, you *are not* to return it. Exercise discipline on your men, Generals. Do you understand?"

"Yes, sir."

"Then make your men understand as well. Not a single musket is to be fired until the order is given, no matter how tempting the target may be."

"Yes, sir."

He nodded and smiled. They all knew what he was going to say next. He always did just before the fighting began. *"Dulce et decorum est pro patria mori!"* It was his own personal slogan: *It is pleasant and fitting to die for one's country.* "Post your men then, gentlemen. At the double-quick. We can't see them through this soup and have no idea when they plan to attack."

Lane and Archer moved off, but Gregg remained, as he and his men were already where they needed to be.

A courier came forward at full speed. Hill's face brightened. His men were moving into position. The sun was up but the fog was still thick. Information coming with such urgency must mean that the battle lines were drawn. It might bring news of the enemy's approach. In ten minutes Hill and his men would be ready. He looked at his old friend, Maxcy Gregg, and smiled brightly. "Bring 'em on," he said as the courier pulled up with a salute.

"General Hill. A telegram, sir. It's marked urgent."

Hill couldn't wait to read it. He grabbed it from the courier's hand and tore it open. For only a moment he continued to smile and then, just as though he had been shot in the chest, he doubled over in the saddle.

"Oh God! Oh, dear God—no."

Instantly tears began pouring down his face. He looked at Gregg, pleading with him as with God to do something. To make it not so.

He could not speak. His bold, commanding voice was now a choked whisper.

"Netty."

"Oh no. Powell . . ."

Hill tried with all his might to regain his composure, but it was simply not possible. His firstborn child, his beautiful, wonderful, loved, and loving two-year-old baby girl was gone. He wiped his face with his sleeve but it did nothing to stop the flood.

"I'm so sorry, Powell . . ."

Hill put up his hand and shook his head, telling Gregg to say no more. He took a breath and righted himself in his saddle, fighting a heroic struggle to regain only some small modicum of dignity, but his chin quivered and he quickly bent over again. His entire body heaved with uncontrollable grief.

"Ride back to your tent, General. We all know what we're supposed to do here, and we'll call for you when you're needed."

Hill looked at Gregg again and this time he only nodded. He forced himself to recover some semblance of a general's posture in the saddle and headed back to his tent where he could grieve alone—if only for a moment.

MARYE'S HEIGHTS

From his perspective atop Marye's Heights it looked to Thomas Cobb as though the incoming Yankees were pushing the remaining residents out of Fredericksburg. As a river of Yankees poured in, a stream of women and children trickled out. Most of them had left last week and come back—for lack of any place better to go. And now, after hunkering in darkness and fear through yesterday's bombardment, they were now more hungry, more frightened, and even dirtier than before.

Cobb was livid. "They can't find a nice, open field and fight us like honorable men. They have to come right into an innocent town and make war on women and children!"

His Georgians were now ensconced behind the stone wall that ran along the Plank Road, and they all watched in silence as the tragic procession of terrified women and frantic, often barefooted children passed slowly by in front of them.

"Don't worry, ladies," Cobb called out. "We're gonna send every one of 'em that comes up this hill straight to the devil!"

General Marsena Patrick stood on the banks of a man-made trench five feet deep and fifteen feet wide. It was a millrace—an overflow channel for the canal on the north side of town. Its banks were reinforced with stones or wood and it was almost full of water that was roofed with a sheet

of ice—and it ran slap dab through the middle of the field
the Union army was going to have to cross to get to the
Rebels up on the hill. It was deep, it was wide, it was cold,
and the Rebels had pulled the planks off one of the two
bridges, leaving only the stringers, for Sumner's men to
cross, like tightrope walkers in a circus.

Patrick looked at the significant obstacle with his hands
on his hips. At least it provided a wrinkle in the landscape,
a momentary haven for those who would have to cross it.
Thank God for small favors, he thought.

"Drain the darned thing," he told his engineers. "I don't
know what the heck else to do."

The rookies of the 27th Connecticut were assigned to build
the last bridge, this one over Hazel Run, a small but worrisome creek just on the outskirts of Fredericksburg. This was
nothing like yesterday's massive undertaking of the 50th
New York Engineers, but to the boys of the Washington Artillery the construction of this little overpass was no less re-
sistible a target. The New Orleans gunners let the
Connecticut boys get good and started—comfortable and
relaxed—before they opened fire.

The 27th Connecticut had never been fired on before,
and four shells screamed into their work party all at the
same time and a dozen or more men fell dead on the spot.
The rest dove into the creek bed and refused to come out
again until dark.

FREDERICKSBURG

The town of Fredericksburg, with a normal population
of fewer than five thousand, had suddenly become
one of the most populous cities in America. The
streets were packed with over forty thousand anxious and
angry Yankees. Many of them had started drinking before
they ever crossed the bridges, and most of those who came
across sober were well on their way to drunkenness before
the clocks struck noon. Their own rum rations were long

since gone, but the wine cellars and liquor cabinets of their recently departed hosts were still well stocked.

Little Abbott was convinced that his Harvard Regiment had done all that would be asked of them. His heart weighed a thousand pounds at the loss of Charlie Cabot and about a dozen other men from the ranks of his own platoon and when someone offered him a crystal decanter of elegant brandy, he saw no harm. His work, after all, was done, and if only one man on God's green earth needed a good stiff drink, he was the one.

By mid-afternoon it looked as though the gracious old town had been invaded by some kind of grotesque carnival. Abbott's vision was blurred by now, but what he saw was not an inebriated aberration. It was all too very real. Burly soldiers paraded down Caroline Street, along the very spot where Cabot had died, wearing hoop skirts and carrying parasols stolen from nearby homes, mocking ladies of the South with vulgar language spoken in ludicrous, falsetto imitations of delicate Southern drawls. Books and paintings; mirrors and crystal goblets crashed onto the streets, tossed from the upper windows of the Rebel homes. Furniture was hurled as well from the same windows that had concealed Rebel sharpshooters—common murderers—only the day before. On Sophia Street soldiers rolled a piano into a yard and a drunken private pounded out "Hail Columbia" and "The Star-Spangled Banner" as a company of Michiganders sang along.

All of this, Abbott knew, was wrong. Someone ought to put a stop to it—the provost or somebody, but it certainly wasn't his job, and he wasn't the only officer wandering the streets, watching and joining in the cruel fun.

The soldier at the piano concluded his concert and grandly took his bow to a raucous ovation. Another soldier then stepped up next to the beautiful instrument and took a bow of his own.

"And now a performance of a different type," he announced as he pulled from behind his back the largest sledgehammer Abbott had ever seen. The first vicious blow split the highly polished mahogany top in two. It took three

such blows before he began to take out his aggressions on
the soundboard. The ugly, discordant music of breaking
strings was accompanied by a chorus of obscene laughter,
and when at last the elegant instrument was rubble, the audience began to gather the splinters to use for firewood.

Abbott by now was as drunk as he had been since Harvard.
He decided to walk up the steps to the house to get a look at
how Southerners lived, and, as he walked in, he was again appalled by what he saw. Soldiers had taken their bayonets to
the upholstered furniture and even to the portraits that
adorned the walls. A crystal chandelier that had majestically
lighted the great room lay in shards on the floor. A dozen men
lounged on the furniture, muddy boots and all, while others
filled their pockets with whatever they could carry.

One man saw the look of horror on Abbott's face and
came over to him.

"They deserve it, sir. Every son-of-a-bitch of 'em deserves
it. There's even still a dead Rebel upstairs, right next to the
window he was shootin' out of—shot right through the middle of the eyes."

And now Little Abbott wasn't nearly so revolted by what
was happening to Fredericksburg. It might well have been
that same Rebel who shot Charlie Cabot from that very window. Lurking in a house like the murdering coward he was.

Now the blueblood from Boston stopped being an observer and suddenly joined in the pillaging of Fredericksburg. He "rescued" a book or two that Mr. Barton had left
behind—Byron and Plutarch—they were just going to be
kindling in a campfire if he didn't. But that was about all
that was left to be had from old man Barton's home, and
Little Abbott staggered back out onto the street in search of
more worthwhile trophies.

The scenes in the street were, if anything, even more out-
rageous than before. A company of men had captured a
frightened little slave boy, no more than six or seven years
old, and bound his hands and legs. They were throwing him
high in the air, catching him on a blanket, and throwing him
up again. The pitiful, helpless little boy was terrified to hysterical tears as the soldiers yelled racial taunts and threatened to throw him in the river just to see if he would float.

Abbott laughed along with the men and moved on.

He wandered almost aimlessly until he realized that he had made the full circle and was now back on Sophia Street, right where he had begun. It was quieter here now. These houses had nothing left of value in them, and the carnival had moved on to richer opportunities. The streets were still crowded. There was simply no place for the boys to go.

He ran into Macy as he turned the corner and almost fell down.

"Had a couple have you, Little?"

"Pretty well corked, George."

Macy just smiled and went on about his business. He had captured a prize or two himself.

The sun was low and the evening was cold. Abbott began to look around for his regiment but soon realized that he didn't have to look—he only had to listen.

> *I signed aboard this whaling ship*
> *I made my mark it's true,*
> *And I'll serve out the span of time*
> *I swore that I would do.*

Of course it was Leander Alley, who was "pretty well corked" himself, and was singing one of the sea shanties he loved so much from his whaling days. Abbott had heard it a thousand times before and knew the words just as well as Alley did. He stepped up next to his whaling friend and offered him a draft from his freshly filled flask. They hooked arms and together they danced the jig that went along with "A Whaler's Tale."

> *For then them whales destroyed our boats*
> *They rammed them one by one*
> *They stove them all with head and fluke*
> *And after they was done*
> *We few poor souls left half-alive*
> *Was clinging to debris*
> *I'd stake me life them fish can think*
> *As good as you and me.*

Neither man was sober enough to keep his legs beneath him but somehow they managed to stay aloft long enough for just one more verse.

> *The way them whale fish went for us*
> *It seemed as though t'was planned*
> *For each one had his target boat*
> *They played us man for man*
> *Just knowin' now they think so clear*
> *My heart says let them be*
> *I swear to God them fish can think*
> *As good as you or me.*

Now their legs got tangled and the whole package, blue-blood and whaling man, tumbled to the ground, arm in arm, laughing till they cried.

Clara Barton rode by on a wagon, holding the head of a wounded man in her arm as she headed back across the river, and saw the two drunken officers dancing and singing. After what she had seen over the last few hours it seemed like they were celebrating at a funeral. They were Massachusetts men too, making it all the worse for her. They looked like whalers in port after a yearlong hunt. When the vandalism had first begun she had actually been amused. The Rebel sympathizers—the despicable slave-holding aristocracy of the South—were getting their just deserts. But this was beyond the pale. Even conquerors— maybe even *especially* conquerors—should carry them-selves with some sense of decorum and respect.

She scowled her disapproval at Abbott and Alley as she passed by but it only made the two drunken soldiers laugh all the harder.

THE BOWLING GREEN ROAD

Ambrose Burnside crossed the river over the Deep Run pontoons to meet with Franklin and his two corps commanders, John Reynolds and William F. (Baldy) Smith. They surveyed the ground in front of them but could see very little. Jackson was over there somewhere, on that hill and in those woods, but they didn't have any way of knowing precisely where or in what numbers.

"Surely if he were there in significant strength, General, there would be more signs of it." Franklin was pushing for a massive assault. He wanted to push forward not only his two corps but one of Hooker's as well. "If we gain that military road up ahead there, just on the other side of the tracks, we will be able to wheel right, turn Jackson, and move on Longstreet's right flank."

"Moving Hooker's men into position will require time, General. The movement of a corps of men overnight could present some significant difficulties."

"Two divisions, then. Moving them would be a nuisance, sir, and nothing more. But a full corps, on this side of the river, held in reserve against any eventuality, would almost guarantee success."

Burnside nodded. "Very well, General. You may expect your orders within two hours."

RAPPAHANNOCK ACADEMY

Fifteen miles downstream General Jubal Early sat down to dinner. His servant had just poured a glass of the brandy and placed a beautiful warm steak on the table when in stormed a tired and muddy courier.

"Orders from General Jackson, sir."

Early read the note, chugged the brandy, and picked up the steak with his hands to eat on the run. "Orders to everyone—prepare to move out!"

It would be another hour before Harvey Hill, still comfortably encamped at Port Royal, an additional five miles downstream, would receive his orders to move his entire division to Fredericksburg—now.

CHAPTER 10

EN ROUTE TO FREDERICKSBURG
DECEMBER 13
1 A.M.

Moving a division of men through the dark offers challenges enough in the best of circumstances, but on this night the roads were frozen and rutted so deeply that Confederate General Harvey Hill's artillery pieces often ran aground or flipped completely over on their sides, blocking the advance of his entire column until they could be gotten out of the way. The men were sleepy and cold and many marched across the frozen ground on bare feet, but they pushed themselves forward knowing that Jackson needed them, and he needed them now. They didn't move forward "without complaint," but slowly and painfully, they did move forward.

PROSPECT HILL
2 A.M.

His staff and his corps commanders had given up hours ago and gone off to bed, but Major General William Franklin remained wide awake, waiting for the orders Burnside had promised almost ten hours ago.

With every hour that passed the grand division commander grew more anxious, more frustrated, and even more furious. Here he was, on the verge of the most important battle of his long career, maybe the most important day of his life, and he could do nothing to prepare—nothing—until he received specific orders from the commanding general. His reputation had been soiled by the pompous, incompetent blowhard, John Pope, after Second Bull Run, but McClellan had come to his rescue and he had been saved. Then he had arrived at Antietam just in time to launch the deciding assault against an obviously exhausted enemy, but Sumner had lost his nerve and talked McClellan out of sending him in. Here was a man whose career had been frustrated at every turn since the war began, standing now on the threshold of fame, and here he sat—alone in the dead of night—waiting for orders. "Within two hours" Burnside had told him, and ten hours later there was still not a word. Not a single word.

It was well past 3 A.M. when the first of Harvey Hill's soldiers began to limp down the Mine Road, just to the rear of Jackson's lines. The balance of his division stretched back down the road for miles and it would be hours before they all were up. Of course these early arrivers would have loved a nice warm fire to sleep beside, but fires were not allowed. No matter. They had been on the march for nine hours and were too sleepy and footsore to worry about fires anyway. As they slowly straggled in, each man found his own spot just off of the road, lay down in the woods, and went right off to sleep.

THE PHILLIPS HOUSE

Ambrose Burnside hadn't slept more than four hours but was up well before the sun to see to it that all of the orders for the day were properly distributed. The clerks weren't finished copying Franklin's overdue orders yet, so Burnside took it upon himself to draft a "preliminary" copy, scrawled in pencil, so that General James Hardie could be on his way to deliver it to Franklin by hand.

Burnside instructed Franklin to have his "whole command in position" to launch an assault against Jackson's corps down the Bowling Green Road. Franklin was further ordered to move "a division at least" against the heights near the Hamilton house. And, finally, "You will keep your whole command in readiness to move at once, as soon as the fog lifts."

TELEGRAPH HILL

At Robert E. Lee's observation point on Telegraph Hill, the commanders of the Army of Northern Virginia came together just at dawn. Again the fog obscured the field, but the day promised to be unseasonably warm.

Jackson was the last to arrive, still wearing his cavaliers' garb and his uncommon smile. He had been known in the past as "Old Blue Beacons" because of the way his blue eyes beamed at the slightest hint of battle—but it was not so today. He was calm and smiling and seemed almost relaxed. He was also happy to bring Lee his first good news of the day.

"Hill and Early are up, sir. Their men are tired. Some of them marched all though the night and have only just arrived, but your entire army is in place, sir, and at your command."

Now it was Lee who beamed—Lee *and* Longstreet. Longstreet now knew that this would be his day—his moment to prove what he had preached since the beginning. *Keep the army all together— Let the damned Yankees come to us.*

But his confidence was shattered very quickly when Jackson spoke again. "If we attack now, General, the fog will protect us from their guns across the river, but we must act quickly."

Attack? Longstreet couldn't believe what he was hearing. To what end? For what purpose? But he knew why Jackson wanted to charge. In Stonewall's mind a defensive fight was not a fight at all. It wasn't honorable. It wasn't manly. A defensive fight is a coward's fight, and no man would call Thomas Jackson a coward.

Almost in a panic Longstreet started to speak, but he was silenced by Lee's calm response. "No, General Jackson. We shall meet them where we stand. We will allow them to throw division after division against General Longstreet's stone wall and against your well-protected hill. We will conserve our strength. We will wear them down, and then, after they are exhausted, if an opportunity presents itself, we will attack—but not before."

Prospect Hill
7:15 A.M.

The muddy, icy road hampered General James Hardie as he rode to Burnside's left in search of General Franklin to deliver his orders. He could move only at a walk for the better part of the journey and the fifteen-minute ride took over forty-five. The sun was well up before he located the commander of the Left Grand Division.

"*. . . Send out at once a division at least.*"

William B. Franklin just stared at the penciled orders in total and complete amazement. "A *division*? That's all?"

"It says 'a division *at least*,' sir."

"I *know* what it says, General! But yesterday he said . . . Never mind. Leave me alone here while I try to figure out from this scribbled mess what I'm supposed to do. This changes everything! General Smith stays. Everyone else, wait outside."

The room emptied and the two friends were left alone.

"It does say 'at least,' General Franklin."

"But why does he say 'division' at all? How does he dare tell me what strength to put forward?"

"You are the commander in the field, sir. You do have discretion."

Franklin erupted. "So did Fitz-John Porter at Second Bull Run—and now he's under indictment and facing court-martial and a ruined career for 'exercising discretion.' They even tried to tar me with that same brush, and that arrogant bastard Pope charged *me* with disobedience when I wasn't even assigned to his army. I was still assigned to McClellan, for God's sake!"

Smith had no response.

Franklin was now shaking mad. "Let me correct myself. Porter is *not* under indictment for exercising discretion. He's under indictment for being a *Democrat* and a friend of George McClellan's! And let me remind you that I am both. Wade and Stanton are drooling over the prospect of hanging me with that same rope. Halleck told me so himself. He said that when Stanton and Chase are finished railroading Porter, that I'm next on their list—and let me *assure* you, General Smith, that that is *not* going to happen. Unlike General Porter, I intend to follow General Burnside's orders precisely and to the letter! If it's a division he wants—it's a division he shall get!"

9:30 A.M.

At long last the sun began to burn the fog away. From all of the high points around the field—Telegraph Hill, Prospect Hill, Marye's Heights, and Stafford Heights across the river—all could see that the tips of Fredericksburg's church spires were the first of the landmarks to peek out from under the blanket, almost as though they were cautiously sneaking a reluctant glance around them to see what the day might bring.

Stonewall Jackson noticed the steeples and smiled. The infamous madman, the most feared warrior since Attila the Hun, was only minutes away from entering into a horrific fight—and he sat on a cannon barrel, closed his eyes, and began to whistle a tune. His high-pitched rendition of "Amazing Grace" was interrupted by Lee and Longstreet, ready to inspect the lines.

The three men rode out together and could not believe their good fortune. On Prospect Hill, just as at Marye's Heights, the artillery was placed in such a way as to cover the ground before them like a shroud. "A slaughter pen," that young lieutenant with the Washington Artillery had called Marye's Heights, and Prospect Hill was almost as good.

They rode until they came to Maxcy Gregg's brigade, encamped behind the military road, well to the rear of Lane on his left and Archer on his right.

Jackson's pleasant demeanor vanished almost immediately.

"General Gregg—where is General Hill, sir?"

Every man who heard Jackson's voice recognized the outrage and feared what each knew was coming next. Stonewall Jackson was itching to place Powell Hill under arrest—again.

Maxcy Gregg loved A. P. Hill and absolutely despised Stonewall Jackson, and, under normal circumstances, made no attempt to disguise the fact. But these were not normal circumstances.

"A word, General Jackson, in private, if you please, sir."

Jackson nodded and the two men rode a few yards down the road, out of earshot of the rest. Lee and Longstreet watched, and when the two men returned it was as though the outburst of only a moment ago had never occurred. Jackson was no longer angry. He was somber—but not angry. "Generals Hood and Hill agree that the wetland in that finger of woods there is both indefensible and impenetrable."

"I am here, sirs."

It was Powell Hill, walking down the hill from his tent. His face was red and his eyes were swollen. Lee and Longstreet didn't notice, but Gregg and Jackson did.

Jackson spoke in a calm voice. "You are convinced, General Hill, that the Yankees will not be able to pass through those woods there."

"I am, sir, and General Hood agrees. And, if they find a way, they will feel our bayonets."

General James Archer would command the brigade on the right of the gap, and was not happy with the course of the conversation. He was, in fact, astounded.

"Sirs—if I may—if they *do* make it through those woods, both my flank and General Lane's will be in the air. They will be able to lay an enfilade fire against us and they'll come pouring through that hole like a river." He paused to give the men time to reverse their decision and put Gregg's brigade where it should be—in the middle of that damned swamp.

It was Hill who spoke. "Post pickets, Generals. In the unlikely event that they do attempt to come through there in force, a little warning will be all that General Gregg will require."

Archer looked to Jackson for help, but Stonewall only nodded and the three senior men moved on to inspect their extreme right flank.

"General Franklin, it is my belief that there is not a division of men in this army, or any other, that could take and hold that position alone!"

George Gordon Meade, the great gargoyle of a man, the "goddamned goggle-eyed old snapping turtle" that the Bucktails Regiment hated so badly, was showing his temper for all to see. Franklin, Smith, Gibbon, Doubleday, Reynolds—the entire upper echelon of the Left Grand Division—were in the room, and most nodded their heads in agreement with Meade. "We don't know what awaits us up that hill, but there are a thousand yards of open ground between here and there, all in clear view of the enemy. He has had weeks to position his men and artillery, and you can bet that whatever they have placed up there is more than a single damned division!"

"You will be supported, General Meade, by Gibbon on your right and Doubleday on your left . . ."

"With all due respect, sir, at the very least, General Reynolds's entire corps should be sent in, and more. We are repeating the mistakes of Antietam, sir, sending in little pieces of our army against all of theirs . . ."

Franklin wanted to hear no more. "Those are General Burnside's orders! And that is precisely what I intend to do!"

For all else George Meade was, he was a good soldier. The issue was decided. He was ordered to lead the assault with a single division, and lead it he would. He came to attention. "Very well, sir," Meade said, choking back his fury. "I shall go forward immediately."

"Should you not be at your post, Major Pelham?"

"General Stuart, if I may, sir?"

"What?" Jeb Stuart couldn't wait to hear Sallie Pelham's plan. Pelham always had a plan.

"Sir, it appears, or it at least sounds, as though the Yankees are massing along the Bowling Green Road."

"Yes?"

"Well, sir, if I could get just a couple of guns down the Mine Road, just to where it intersects with Bowling Green Road . . ."

"Major Pelham, that is well forward of our lines."

"I know, sir. But it is concealed, and I believe when the fog burns off, you will see that it enfilades the very spot where the Federals are massing their troops."

Stuart smiled grandly. Audacious. Even a single gun firing directly down a long line of enemy troops would be a thing of true beauty, but the danger to the gun and gunners would make such a decision out of the question—for most men.

"You know that they will turn on you—every man and every gun on the field will turn to engage you there."

"Of course I do, sir. In fact, it's the whole point."

THE LACY HOUSE

All morning long Henry Villard had followed Edwin Sumner like a tail follows a horse. It was like watching a caged animal. Here was a man who had led his corps into battle at Antietam at the very front of the line, mounted and bellowing orders. It had been a disastrous charge and it was a miracle that the old general had survived. But he had ridden into battle because that's where a general needs to be, and it was where he wanted to be right now. Today he commanded two corps—a "grand division"—and could only watch from a hilltop two miles away. Those were General Burnside's specific orders. "You are not to cross the river," his old friend had told him. And with a smile, ". . . Leave that to the younger men." And so the old officer, the old cavalryman, was chained to the Lacy house.

Villard was just as aggravated as the general but was not

under orders from anyone to stay there. There was nothing to be learned here. The most interesting note he had made so far was that Sumner had to remove his false teeth to issue orders. Villard's orders came from Horace Greeley, who expected him to report on the battle, not tell a story about an old man and his false teeth. He had to get a better view.

"General Sumner?"

"What?" Sumner didn't like reporters. He thought they were spies and he resented the interruption.

"Who will lead?"

"French."

Villard thanked the general, left the room, and headed for Fredericksburg in search of General French.

FREDERICKSBURG

Darius Couch had given William French the good news hours before daybreak. It was he who would lead the assault on Marye's Heights. Now, with the fog at last thinning, "Old Blinky" met with his brigade and regimental commanders. The first man up the hill, the tip of Edwin Sumner's spear, would be Colonel John Mason, pushing Union skirmishers forward, and Confederate pickets back. That was the way it worked. The defending army stationed thin lines of men well forward of their massed positions, just to raise a little ruckus and give a good, loud warning as the enemy approached. It was not their job to stand and fight. Only to fire off a quick volley and get the hell back to their lines. The attacking army would send up an equally thin line of skirmishers in advance of the major assault for the sole purpose of pushing back the pickets. That was how it was done. Those were the rules. But on this day Colonel Mason had a different idea.

"With your permission, sirs, I intend to move forward in strength, with three regiments. They number about seven hundred men. It is my intention to pursue them closely all the way up the heights."

The room stared at him as though not a man had understood a word he had spoken.

"To what purpose, Colonel?"

"General French, sir, if we stick with 'em, like hounds after a coon, right on their heels, sir, their defenses will be useless. Artillery and infantry alike. They won't be able to shoot at us without hitting their own men, and we'll be able to follow 'em in and breach their lines before lunch."

"And you think you can do this with seven hundred men?"

"I do, sir—if you're behind me—and I mean *right* behind me, sir, I think we'll be able to make a quick day of it."

Bill McCarter's hopes of being the first up the hill were dashed when French's division was given the honor and moved ahead of Hancock's in line. The men of the Irish Brigade at least pretended to be upset by it, but Bill, honestly, was not. The body of the Rebel Irishman he'd seen yesterday had haunted him all night long. Him and all the others. But even faced with the sickening horrors of war for the very first time, he never once considered returning to General Meagher's headquarters to resume his nice, safe adjutant's duties. No. Not today. On this morning he would see the monkey show and feel the fight and know whatever it was God had sent him here to learn. He had been ridiculed and picked on all of his life for his frail size and his incurable stammer, but today he was going to face the worst of all fears head-on. Today his life would take on meaning and tomorrow he would be a man. He had endured over two months of training for this day. He had starved and cursed and sloshed a hundred miles through freezing rain and mud. He had damned near frozen to death on picket duty, and there was no way on God's green earth he was going to turn back now. Bill McCarter was going up that hill and that was all there was to it.

The brigade was lined up along Hawke Street, waiting for the fight to begin. Everybody knew it would be some time yet, but they had to stand at the ready nonetheless, so that when French's men broke through they would be able to storm up the heights to finish off the Rebs. It was good, Bill thought. Being second up the hill today might put them first on the road to Richmond tomorrow.

General Meagher paraded himself up and down in front

of the lines. It looked to Bill like both the general and his horse were being held back by some kind of invisible, unbreakable rope that kept them from bolting up the hill and attacking the Rebels all alone.

Finally Meagher turned and faced his brigade.

"Men—'tis time again to follow the green into glorious battle." The veterans all cheered and the recruits joined, but didn't fully know why. These were the same words he had used at Antietam before the Irishmen had busted through the sunken road—the Bloody Lane the newspapers were calling it these days—and sent Lee's most stubborn Rebels hightailing it back into the town like a bunch of terrified little rabbits.

"But there's a tiny problem—we're a flag or two short. Our bonnie flags are off in New York. They've gone home for a wee bit of a rest." More cheers. "So we'll just have to make do with the flags we've got left . . ." He jumped off his horse down next to a row of boxwoods that lined the street leading up to the heights. He unsheathed his Arkansas Toothpick—a knife with a blade about twelve inches long—and cut off a sprig of the boxwoods. He climbed back on his horse and held the boxwood sprig over his head. "So this will have to do in the meantime!" He put the greenery in his hatband and lifted the hat high over his head.

"Help yourselves, lads! Each and every man! If we can't *follow* the green, well, by all the saints in heaven, we'll be *wearing* it!"

Bill thought the cheer that rose up from the Irish Brigade must have been loud enough to be heard all the way back in Derry.

PROSPECT HILL
10 A.M.

Sallie Pelham peeked out from behind the limb of a cedar tree and smiled. There, only five hundred yards directly to his front, was George Meade's division, grandly moving forward in line of battle. The flags were beautifully unfurled and the regimental bands played "Three Cheers for the Red, White and Blue." Over four thousand armed men marched toward the Rebel lines in fearsome precision, but to Jeb Stuart's daring young major they looked like nothing more than a long, straight line of blue-clad dominoes, ready to be toppled with a single nudge.

Rooney Lee had a regiment of cavalry to Pelham's rear, but other than that the young artillerist stood alone. Stuart would risk only one gun on such an uncertain endeavor, but, positioned as he was, Pelham knew he was about to cause some serious harm.

In only a few more paces Meade's first rank would be directly in his line of fire. Pelham raised his left arm into the air, alerting his gunners to the ready. He smiled as he heard his Cajun Napoleon Detachment softly whispering the *Marseillaise*.

> *Allons enfants de la Patrie*
> *Le jour de gloire . . .*

Pelham stood in his stirrups and a moment later he dropped his hand and yelled, *"Fire!"* Flame and smoke and a twelve-pound round of solid shot exploded from the muzzle of the hidden gun.

> *. . . est arrivé!*

It was like hurling a twelve-pound tenpin ball at defenseless pins all placed precisely in a row. The first man struck was neatly decapitated. A dozen or more fell to the same shot, dead, maimed, or wounded. Hundreds more fell in terror when they realized that they had yet to fire a shot and already they were flanked. Jean leaped to the front of the gun and rammed his wet sponge down the muzzle to clean it and cool it before the next powder charge was rammed home. The rest of the crew calmly but quickly reloaded, and the Battle of Fredericksburg had finally begun.

Pelham had placed his gun in a ditch in which the last of

the morning fog still lay. The muzzle was not far above ground level, making it impossible for his gunners to fire high. The ditch was further concealed behind a row of cedar trees, and Pelham's men felt as safe as babes.

The Federal artillery were all facing in the wrong direction, pointing toward Prospect Hill to their front. Those on the extreme right could not fire at all, for fear of injuring their own men with short shots. The "big" guns across the river on Stafford Heights were dug in and aimed at Prospect Hill and couldn't lower their trajectory enough to take Pelham's single gun under fire. It was almost with impunity that Pelham's gun fired round after deadly round at Meade's men, all cowering on the ground and still in their perfectly straight lines.

Brigadier General C. Feger Jackson remained calm in the face of calamity. He was not a West Point man, but he was a veteran of the Mexican War. The Pennsylvanian was almost fifty, but with a receding hairline and a graying beard, he looked even older. Most of his men had been fighting since the Peninsula and knew what to expect. He fearlessly remained mounted while his men lay in the mud with their hands over their heads. He ordered every battery he could find to turn and face Pelham. At his command his brigade boldly stood and came to attention and wheeled left, and Sallie Pelham was not nearly so comfortable anymore.

Rooney Lee sent his dismounted cavalry forward to protect the gun, but Abner Doubleday, whose job it was to guard Meade's left flank, countered with his best men—the Black Hats and Battery B of the 4th United States Artillery.

These proud heroes of Antietam made quick and easy work of the Rebel cavalry, and Pelham and his Creole gunners were not only the center of attention but were now entirely on their own.

Six Union batteries—more than two dozen guns—turned to face him, and Pelham's men began to fall, but the loading and firing never slowed. They turned their attention to the guns and back-to-back shots took out a canon from one battery and a limber chest from another. To Pelham's way of thinking, that was two guns down and thirty-four to go.

Robert E. Lee sat astride Traveler at the top of Prospect Hill watching Pelham's performance below. Stonewall

Jackson and Powell Hill pulled up alongside and all three marveled at the sight of one lone gun bringing a whole Yankee division to an absolute standstill.

"It is glorious to see such courage in one so young," Lee said.

Jackson's smile was no longer a subtle grin. It was full-fledged. "General Stuart, if you have another Pelham, I wish you would give him to me."

"Ah, 'the gallant Pelham.' I'm sorry, General, but there's only one."

"Well, if that's the case, I wonder if I might borrow him for a day."

"At your service, General."

Jackson nodded his gratitude. "With a Pelham on either flank, I could conquer the world."

By now the Union guns had found their range and Feger Jackson's infantry peppered Pelham's position with musket fire. "Do your job," Sallie told his crew, "and fall to the ground. Make yourself small until you have to stand again."

THE LACY HOUSE

The room was full of generals. Burnside, Sumner, and about two dozen others all scurried around like bees in a hive as the first sounds of battle echoed up the valley. Only "Fightin' Joe" Hooker appeared calm. He watched the activity like a stern man in a room full of clowns. His staff was astounded.

Lieutenant Colonel Joseph Dickinson was the most astounded of all. He didn't quite know how to deal with a calm Joe Hooker. Like any good adjutant, he stayed as close as he could to his general, waiting for orders or instructions, but for almost a half hour Hooker had said not a word, and Dickinson wasn't about to interrupt the rare and blessed silence.

"Colonel," Hooker finally said, almost in a whisper, "have you ever seen a greater bunch of fools all gathered in one room?"

Here it comes, Dickinson thought. *Vesuvius rumbles.* He had expected the eruption before dawn when Hooker was told that the bulk of General Stoneman's corps was to be re-assigned to cover Franklin's bridges, cutting Hooker's Center Grand Division nearly in half. But Hooker had said nothing. He expected it again when Hooker was told that the remainder of his men were to be held in reserve, leaving the fight to others. But Hooker had remained calm—at least by Joe Hooker standards. But now the sounds of battle were in the air—the fight was on and pulling Joe Hooker to it like a lion to raw meat—and Dickinson was prepared for the worst.

He didn't respond to Hooker's question—he wasn't expected to. He only shook his head in agreement.

"What is about to happen here will be an absolute disaster, Colonel, and I am quite content to have no part of it."

Marye's Heights

Bill Owen sat on the hill behind the cold guns of his Washington Artillery and watched in amazement as the Union soldiers in the town began to fill the streets of Fredericksburg. In good order they lined up cheek to jowl. "Packed" was the word that came to Bill's mind. They were crammed in there so tightly they didn't have enough room even to turn around. But it was not only the size and grandeur of the Federal army that amazed Bill Owen. It was not the idea that they were coming forward in such numbers, but the incredible idea that they were coming at all. Here were tens of thousands of men standing in line to die—for nothing.

That was what he thought—until he was handed an order signed by James Longstreet. He read it twice to make sure he'd gotten it right.

If Anderson, on your left, is badly pressed, he will fall back to the second line of heights. Conform to his movements.

Owen looked back down the hill at the massing Federal troops and realized that while he could see what looked like ten thousand men—he couldn't see them all. The lines moved back into the town, behind the buildings, and along the riverbank. Beyond that was Stafford Heights, and God only knew how many more Yankees waited on the other side of those hills. His confidence didn't completely leave him, but if Longstreet and Anderson were concerned, then maybe Bill Owen should be as well.

He took the piece of paper and loped down the hill to where General Cobb had his regiment ensconced behind the stone wall. He located Cobb and showed him the order.

Like Owen had done, Cobb read the document twice. Then he shook his head and almost laughed.

"Richard Anderson is what my momma would call a 'nervous Nellie.' There's not an army in this world that can take these heights—and, if they wait for *me* to fall back, they'll wait a long time."

Prospect Hill

By now Abner Doubleday's guns, having sent Lee's cavalry scurrying for safety, were free to turn on Pelham as well. John Pelham, with his single gun, had attracted the undivided attention of two full divisions of the Army of the Potomac. He had held them in place for almost a full hour, but now the air around him was filled with minié balls and shrapnel, and yet Pelham remained calmly mounted with his left leg draped over the pommel of his saddle as though he were having a pleasant conversation with a pretty girl on a Sunday afternoon.

"General Stuart sends his regards, sir, and wants to know how you are getting on." The courier had to shout to be heard.

"Go back and tell General Stuart I am doing first rate."

"Very well then, sir. He is sending you another gun, but he urges you to withdraw at such a time as you feel is best."

"Tell him that we will remain here for as long as our ammunition holds out, Captain."

The courier had not been gone more than a very few minutes when Captain John Esten Cooke came tearing down the road with Pelham's Blakely in tow. He pulled up well short of Pelham's position to separate the Union fire. The Blakely was unlimbered, loaded, and fired only once before it exploded into a dozen pieces by a direct hit from Meade's gunners. Half of the crew and two of the horses died after less than a minute on the field. An instant later an air burst exploded directly over Pelham's gun and Jean went quickly to the ground with a jagged piece of hot iron bigger than a man's thumb embedded in his chest.

Pelham loved the little Cajun. He was the spirit of the crew and it tore at his heart to see him go down. He dismounted and went to him and was relieved to see that he was still alive, but the relief didn't last for long. Pelham examined the wound and knew almost immediately that Jean would soon be gone.

"It hurts some, *mon Capitaine*."

"I know, Jean, but we will bandage you up and send you to the rear. You'll be back singing and swabbing before the day is out."

Jean smiled. He knew the truth as well as Pelham. The feisty little Cajun tried to speak again, but blood began to drip from his mouth and he made a dreadful gurgling sound as he fought to take a breath. Pelham put his ear close to hear what Jean had to say.

"Le jour de gloire . . . est arrivé!"

General Meade was understandably furious. He rode forward to see for himself what the holdup was and couldn't believe his eyes. He couldn't believe that this many men and this many cannons could not silence a single, undefended gun, no matter how well concealed it was. But he also couldn't see what more could be done. While his entire division cowered in the mud all around him, George Gordon Meade sat tall astride his horse, almost daring the Rebel gunners to take a shot at him. He pointed at the headless body of a Pennsylvania boy that lay at his feet.

"Bury that man. Right here. Right now. Bury them all. It's bad for morale to leave them just lying about like this."

Stafford Heights

"Colonel Wainwright!"
        Franklin's artillery chief was preoccupied in astounded admiration of Sallie Pelham's single-

handed display of fearless brilliance. The angry voice of his commanding general jarred him back to his own job.

"Sir!"

"Since you are not able to assist in ridding us of that pest on the left, you might want to consider killing some Rebels on that hill over there."

"We will open fire on your orders, sir."

"The orders are given, Colonel."

Moments later Stafford Heights spewed fire.

Prospect Hill took it.

And took it.

And took it.

Solid shot shattered trees and exploding shells hailed fist-size shards of white hot iron all along the Rebel lines. Stonewall Jackson's artillerymen chafed like tormented caged animals, angry, frustrated, and snarling to break loose to maul the tormentors.

Powell Hill had to put the images of poor, beautiful Netty out of his mind. He had to force himself not to think about Dolly back home—hysterical and grieving alone. He had to. Honor demanded it. Duty demanded it. Powell Hill would have to grieve later. Now, he had work to do.

He rode slowly along in front of his guns. Not behind. In front. His back was as straight as a beam. While all hell exploded around them, man and horse were quiet and calm.

"Hold your fire, men," he repeated time and again. "Hold your fire. Save your ammunition. Don't disclose your positions. We will pay them back with interest very soon. I promise. Hold your fire."

"Hold your fire" was the hardest order his men had ever had to obey.

FREDERICKSBURG
11 A.M.

"Move out now!"

General Nathan Kimball commanded French's 1st Brigade. These would be the very first men out of the city and up the hill. Burnside was certain the sounds of battle on his left signaled Franklin's general assault and ordered the attack against the right to commence in concert and now, at long last, after three weeks of just sitting around watching the Rebels fortify Fredericksburg—it was time.

James Mason, commanding three regiments of skirmishers, seven hundred men total, saluted his commanding officer and nodded.

"God bless you. Good-bye," Kimball shouted as Mason turned his back to Fredericksburg and his face to Marye's Heights.

To the rowdy cheers of thousands of men in line behind them, Mason's men stepped out from the protection of the town and onto the open field leading up the hill.

Henry Villard had seen and heard it all. He took out his notebook and began to write his story—one that he intended to make damned certain would *not* get lost in the mail.

PROSPECT HILL

Stuart's order to "stop firing and withdraw" was received by Sallie Pelham with a grin. There were two rounds remaining in the ammunition chest. Pelham was determined that he would return only with it empty.

A minute later they were gone, and Pelham didn't even have to issue the order. His crew brought forward the horses and limbered the gun. They lifted Jean off the ground and the gut-shot young Cajun screamed in pain. They placed him on the empty ammunition chest and whipped the horses to a full run. The road was rough and rutted and strewn with rocks and the caisson bounced violently as they made their escape. For Jean the pain became far too great and his world went suddenly black. Loss of consciousness is a gift from God to the anguished.

WASHINGTON, D.C.

President Lincoln came to the War Department telegraph room prepared to stay the day. It was a routine drill for him by now. He would sit in an overstuffed chair and spend the entire day praying for a flood of information and getting less than a trickle. This time he was prepared for the excruciating wait. He brought along a little "light reading" to keep him occupied.

It was George Livermore's book, given to him by Senator Sumner. It was entitled, *An Historical Research Respecting the Opinion of the Founders of the Republic on Negroes as Slaves, as Citizens and as Soldiers.*

He had sat in his chair—engrossed—for over two hours before the first dits and daws clicked in from Fredericksburg.

The battle so long anticipated is now progressing.

That's all it said, and Lincoln went back to his book.

CHAPTER 11

MARYE'S HEIGHTS

It was James Mason's plan to push his skirmishers forward, drive back the Rebel pickets, and stick with them all the way up the hill, using them as human shields. The Rebels were supposed to allow them to get close, then stand and fire and retreat. That was how it always worked—but not today. The men of Longstreet's corps didn't really need any warning of oncoming Yankees. They were clearly visible from a thousand yards away. The pickets were there, more or less, out of habit, but they served no real function. So, as soon as Mason's men started out from the town, the Rebels just picked up their rifles and meandered back up the hill where they fell into line with the rest of Cobb's men behind the stone wall. So now, Mason and his boys from Ohio and Delaware marched slowly up the hill, across an open field, headed directly for Colonel Alexander's slaughter pen.

A chicken could not live on that field . . .

As Mason's Yankees came into view, Bill Owen sat on the porch of the Marye house taking his lunch. The men of the Washington Artillery had managed to whip up a batch of corn bread this morning and it was nothing short of manna. He glanced down the hill and saw the Yankee skirmishers beginning their long march. He grinned and shook his head in disbelief.

"Here they come," he yelled. He pushed a handful of corn bread into his mouth as he ran to his horse. As assistant adjutant, it was his job to be at Colonel Walton's side. The commanding officer of the Washington Artillery wasn't hard to find. His horse, Rebel, was one of the largest, blackest, and most beautiful in the whole Confederate army. The two men rode down the hill and took up positions directly behind Lieutenant Charles Stocker's Napoleon. Stocker had been the lead thespian in the Literary Guild's performance of *Lady of Lyon* only a couple of nights ago, but today he was prepared to play a more serious role.

Stocker was a better gunner than he was an actor. He took his time in sighting the weapon on a spot five hundred yards down range and waited for the order to fire. The guns were loaded, pushed forward, and carefully aimed. All that remained was to pull the lanyards. All four crews stood silently by their guns and looked down the hill at the approaching Yankees. They watched with reverent awe as Mason's seven hundred began their long climb. Their huge national colors and regimental flags led the way. Their fixed bayonets glistened in the bright sunlight as they marched out of the town in a series of arrogant straight lines.

Colonel Walton watched through his glasses for a very long time until he turned to Owen and said, almost with pride, "That is the grandest spectacle I have ever witnessed. Beautiful."

Mason's men had cleared the town by now and were well on their way to the millrace, all entirely out in the open. Walton sighed, as though reluctant to issue the order.

"Attention!" He admired the oncoming regiments for one last second before he yelled, "COMMENCE—FIRING!"

James Mason, who had had such great hopes of reaching the Confederate lines with seven hundred men, watched as they began to fall, three or four at a time as shots came at them from three different directions. Huge rounds came from the left—from Lee's gigantic thirty-pounder Parrotts on Telegraph Hill. A battery of Napoleons also fired from Stansbury's Hill on the right. But the deadliest fire of all came from the guns posted on Marye's Heights, directly to their front. Those guns looked to be built into the mountain. Their muzzles would appear from behind the almost absolute safety of their breastworks, spew fire and thunder, and vanish back into the side of the hill. Less than a minute later they would appear again, roar again, and more of Mason's men would fall.

PROSPECT HILL

On the Union left, Colonel Wainwright's artillery fire against Prospect Hill fell quiet after more than an hour, accomplishing little more than tormenting the Rebels to fury. The quiet after the roar brought angry Confederates by the thousands out from the ditches and from behind the rocks and trees that had protected them from Wainwright's bombardment. Calmly and efficiently the infantrymen assumed their positions and the artillerymen manned their guns.

With Pelham out of the way, George Meade could now get back to business, the first order of which was to get his men's faces out of the mud and ready to resume their march against the Confederate lines.

Feger Jackson ordered his brigade to attention. They had been cowering under Pelham's fire for almost an hour. When they came to their feet, the fronts of their uniforms were soaked through with black, slimy goo. Many of them had buried themselves so deeply in the sludge that their faces looked to be painted black—like dancers in a minstrel show. Some laughed at the sight. They looked like an army of Africans marching off to set *themselves* free. A ludicrous thought for most.

Before they could move forward they had to redress their lines and aim them back toward the original objective—the Rebel lines that were hidden somewhere on Prospect Hill. Most of Feger Jackson's men were well-trained veteran troops and it took only a very few minutes to get them back into their lines of battle and facing in the right direction. Then the whole rigmarole started again. The flags came out, the bands played, and Jackson's men fell into line with William Sinclair's brigade immediately to their right and Albert Magilton's three hundred yards behind.

William Sinclair was a twenty-four-year-old colonel who had been in command of the 1st Brigade for less than a month. He was Regular Army but far from a West Pointer. He had come up through the ranks as an artilleryman before the war. And now, due to the incredible number of officers killed, wounded, or captured in the Maryland campaign, the young former artillery private now commanded an entire Union infantry brigade, and it was his men who George Meade ordered to lead the attack. But Colonel Sinclair wasn't worried. The Rebels had sent one gun—only one— to contest his assault. The positions on the hill had been mercilessly bombarded for over an hour and hardly a shot had been fired in return. Of course there were Rebels up there, he knew. Everybody knew that. But there didn't seem to be very many.

He sat tall and proud in the saddle, smiling and yelling encouragement, proving to his men that they were in good hands. They cheered as they passed him by, moving out toward the railroad tracks and the woods at the base of Prospect Hill a thousand yards to their front. At right shoulder shift they moved forward in perfect order, in perfect step to the cadence of the drums.

Five minutes and two hundred yards after Sinclair restarted his march, Prospect Hill erupted. The Rebel artillerymen who had felt like caged animals for the last two hours were finally *un*caged and hell fell on the advancing Yankees. Prospect Hill snarled to life and so much white smoke bellowed into the air it looked as if the entire hill had suddenly caught fire. Sinclair could see the shells coming at them from all directions as they appeared to float, seemingly harmlessly, toward them. Solid shot cut men in two and the balls that exploded in the sky spewed hot iron into the lines as if it were being thrown down at them by Satan himself. Shots that exploded in the soft ground splashed mud and body parts fifty feet in the air. William

Sinclair and Feger Jackson both ordered their brigades down, and the brave Pennsylvanians dove face-first into the slimy, black earth—again.

Bill Sinclair, the boy colonel, wasn't nearly so confident anymore. *They told me a division or two,* he thought. *They told me that I was going up against a* portion *of Jackson's corps. Well, his infantry may be stretched out from here to blue blazes, but his artillery, by God, is all right here. Right now. And there's not a damned thing that I can do to save my men.*

As the Rebel guns came alive Charles Wainwright went white. Franklin's chief of artillery had unleashed everything he had on that hill for over an hour. He had been shooting blind, but he had been certain that that much iron certainly had done damage. Right now, he wasn't nearly so certain.

"Damn!" He threw down his freshly lighted cigar. "He must *still* have a hundred guns over there!"

At least now they had something to shoot at. The Rebels had finally shown themselves, and every gun the Yankees had, both down on the field and up on Stafford Heights, opened again with renewed vigor, but this time Stonewall Jackson and Powell Hill didn't hold their gunners back, and the two opposing hills smoked and growled at each other like warring volcanoes.

FREDERICKSBURG

L ittle Abbott was sick. He was sick emotionally, for the loss of his men—especially Charlie Cabot. But he was sick physically too. He remembered telling Macy last night that he was "pretty well corked," and today the price for that had to be paid. He spent most of the morning throwing up whiskey and hardtack into the gutters of Fredericksburg that ran like a creek with the urine of thirty thousand men.

Leander Alley stood behind him and watched. Alley had

had just as much to drink, but apparently the old whaling man was better at it, for he was upright and laughed unsympathetically at his miserable young blue-blooded friend. Little looked up at him in disgust. If he'd felt better he might have killed him. The look of anger on Little's green face only made Alley laugh all the harder.

Finally the whaling man handed Abbott a canteen filled, thank God, with water. He patted him on the back and said, "At least our work here is done, my friend."

"You think?"

"I don't think anybody will have the gumption to ask us to do any more than we've already done, me hearty. There's only so much . . ."

Abbott suddenly went back to work on filling the gutters. "God willing," he said when he was through.

MARYE'S HEIGHTS

From his position behind the stone wall, General Thomas R. R. Cobb peered through his glasses and smiled. They were coming, and they were coming right at him.

"Splendid," he said aloud.

A single, overanxious soldier fired his rifle in the direction of the approaching Yankees.

"Hold your fire, men!" Cobb was in his element. Standing tall, he walked along behind his lines. The four Napoleons of the Washington Artillery were firing away directly over his head, and yet he was able to make himself heard in the pauses.

"Wait until you can count the Yankee buttons, and aim low. We've got a hot day ahead of us, men, but we are going to stay here all day—and I will stay right here with you!"

The cheers of his men could easily be heard above the artillery fire, and cheering loudest of all were his Irishmen from Georgia. He loved his Irishmen. *They work like Trojans,* he thought, *and fight like demons.*

* * *

James Mason's skirmishers continued to take a terrible beating from the guns bearing down on them from three directions, but, amazingly enough, the boys from Ohio and Delaware continued to move forward. They were slowed not only by horrible losses, but also by fences that had to be taken down before they could continue their march.

A small store stood along the way and drew men to it like sirens to the rocks. They broke down the door, which had been carefully locked to keep the Yankees out, and began dragging their wounded inside. They found their way into the cellar where a lone woman cowered and wept in a dark corner.

"Where's your well?" a sergeant barked at the terrified lady.

She could not answer. She couldn't take a breath. She became hysterical and her entire body quaked with fear.

"Where's your well?"

Still she couldn't reply. Finally the man yanked her up and pushed her up the stairs, using his rifle as a staff. Still unable to speak she pointed to the well, which was, thankfully, close to the house and at least partially protected from the Confederate cannons.

"Get back in your cellar," the sergeant said in a much more kindly voice, and this time the woman was quick to obey.

The line of march for Mason's men finally came upon the millrace—the overflow channel for the canal. It was five feet deep and fifteen feet wide and, regardless of General Patrick's best efforts to drain it, it was still floored with two feet of standing, ice cold water. There were two bridges, but the Rebels had pulled the planks off one of them, leaving only the narrow stringers for the men to cross. So into the ditch they went. Once there, many wanted nothing more than to stay, cold feet seeming a better option than hot iron. But the humiliation of being left behind by their comrades and neighbors from back home was not an option at all. If a man showed cowardice now, everybody he had ever known back home would soon hear about it, and that was a fate infinitely worse than death. And so, with cold, wet feet, they climbed out of the millrace, re-formed their thin lines, and continued up the hill while shot and shell exploded around them.

For all they had done—for all they had endured—for all the losses they had suffered so far, they still had a quarter mile to go to reach the Rebel lines.

Mason looked back over his shoulder, searching for the fresh brigades that French had promised would be close at hand, and there was no one there. There were no signs of movement. For the moment at least, Mason and what remained of his skirmishers were on the hill alone.

A hundred more yards and a hundred more wounded and yet they continued to climb. After two hundred more yards they crested a swale, a gentle slope that offered the last natural obstacle to their advance, the last tiny bit of protection in front of Thomas Cobb's stone wall.

Wait until you can count the Yankee buttons . . .

A thousand Rebels stood as one and fired as one. Along its entire length, the wall snarled and spewed fire and smoke, and with that single ghastly roar, Cobb's Rebels welcomed Mason's Yankees to Mr. Marye's hill, and the remnants of the valiant little brigade was finally shocked to a standstill.

Another desperate glance to his rear only confirmed what Mason already knew. There was no help coming soon.

"Lie down!" He repeated the order over and over again, as though it were necessary. His men took what little refuge the terrain offered behind the swale, still two hundred yards from the Rebel lines.

Lieutenant Darlington of the 1st Delaware was severely wounded by the musket fire. He had been a sergeant only a few weeks ago, and his men knew him as one of them. Several gathered together to carry him to the rear, where ambulances were supposed to be waiting. They lifted him up and moved only a matter of a few feet back down the hill when a Rebel artillery shell exploded directly over their heads, not ten yards high. When the smoke cleared these brave men were simply gone. Vanished. There wasn't enough left to bury.

FREDERICKSBURG
NOON

As the 24th New Jersey prepared to move out, James McClernan tried desperately to find his little brother lined up in the ranks ahead of him, somewhere up there with D Company, but it was hopeless. George was lost in the masses, just like everybody else. Besides, there were other things that demanded James's attention. He tried to look up the hill at what lay ahead, but he couldn't see very much. The rockets continued to explode over Mason's men and the musket fire continued at a lively pace. The white smoke from rifles and cannons lay close to the field like fog.

And then came General Kimball, parading himself directly before his men. "Cheer up, my hearties, cheer up! This is something we must get used to." He looked up the hill, trying to get a sight of his skirmishers up ahead, but the smoke covered the hillside so thickly that it was almost hopeless. "Boys, we are the attacking brigade. I shall expect you to go ahead and open the fight. Keep steady, aim low, and let every man do his duty!"

The response from the green troops of the 24th was not quite as enthusiastic as he had hoped, so he added an exclamation point sure to inspire. "Remember—you are Jerseymen!" And now the men cheered.

Rising tall in his saddle, Kimball commanded . . . "FORWARD . . ."

His regimental commanders echoed the command. "Forward . . ."

"MARCH!"

Kimball's Brigade hadn't taken more than a hundred paces before the boys of the Washington Artillery opened on them with a deadly fire. The Union file closers had a busy day pushing the men in the rear ranks forward to take the places of their fallen comrades in the front. James McClernan watched the shells floating in until they reached a point sometimes ten, sometimes fifty yards directly overhead where they would explode with a force so tremendous that he could feel the air move. Tiny white streamers burst out in all directions and smoked their way like tiny lightning bolts into the tightly packed box of men below. Twenty-five, fifty, or a hundred pieces of white hot iron shot down into the ranks like they'd been fired out of muskets, and he remembered Colonel Robertson's description of "a hole twenty-men deep in a company of men."

Twenty yards ahead he and his fellow "Jerseymen" saw the millrace. To the generals the canal was an obstacle. To the men of the 24th New Jersey, after only their first few minutes under fire, the millrace was a haven.

James McClernan lay in the cold, wet ditch along with the rest of Kimball's brigade. He looked left and right, desperate for just one glimpse of George, but there were four thousand peas in this pod and James's younger brother looked the same as all the others.

General Kimball appeared to be in command, but for those, like James, who were close enough to see, the look in his eyes was one of fear and confusion. The general was breathing heavily even though he had ridden, not run, up the hill like his men.

"James!"

Not over but below all of the sounds of war, McClernan heard his name shouted from a thousand miles away. He looked in the direction he thought the sound came from and saw a single man standing alone in the knee-deep freezing water at the bottom of the millrace. George. *Thank God.*

"George!"

The brothers made eye contact and waved and smiled, and George climbed back up the steep slope to rejoin his company.

"Look out, boys!" Kimball had caught his breath and appeared to have regained his composure. "They can't kill all of you, but they may hurt some of you."

James couldn't believe his ears. Nor, for that matter, could anyone else who heard the general's somewhat less-than-inspired speech. At this moment not even their seemingly fearless commander could find the glory in this attack, and his words said so.

"Now, drop your blankets and tents right here. Guards will be assigned so they'll be here when you get back."

If we get back, thought every man in the brigade.

After the men had shed their useless burdens, Kimball took a deep breath and yelled, "FIX . . ."

The word echoed down the line. "FIX . . ."

"BAYONETS!"

The men of the Washington Artillery had taken the past few minutes to swab the muzzles of their guns and to let them cool a bit before going back to work.

Again Colonel Walton watched the Union troops climb out of the millrace and prepare to march up the hill directly into the jaws of his clean, cool, man-eating guns. There were more of them this time, and they would come forward more tightly packed. He shook his head in disbelief, almost heartbroken just for the wasteful shame of it all, but he finally did what he had to do.

"Load canister."

They watched in amazement, reverence really, as Kimball's Brigade of Union troops marched defiantly up the hill. The Rebel cannons were loaded with double canister, each one ready to blast fifty-four half-pound cast-iron balls into the rank and file of the approaching Yankees. They sighted their guns ahead of Kimball's men and waited patiently for them to reach their premeasured spots, and when they did all four guns roared to life and opened bloody gaps in the Union lines as wide as city streets.

Men on either side of him fell in that horrific instant, but James McClernan was somehow unhurt and whispered a prayer of gratitude for himself and one of hope for George. And another prayer as well—for help to come—and to come soon.

Colonel John W. Andrews's Brigade was next in French's line to attack the Rebel stronghold on Marye's Heights. They inched forward, out from behind the protection of the buildings of the town, and waited for the order to move out.

Henry Villard, armed only with a pad and pencil, waited with them. He moved forward to get close to a regiment of

New Yorkers. Horace Greeley liked to pay extra-close attention to the home boys.

They were the 10th New York Zouaves—the National Zouaves they called themselves. Their distinctive uniforms were patterned after the French Zouaves and made them stand out like a gypsy dance troupe. They wore red shirts and dark blue jackets decorated with red garnish and light blue trousers bloused with white spats. Some wore red fez hats and some wore turbans. They had been a proud regiment with a distinguished record until Second Bull Run. On the final day of that fight, just over three months ago, they had found themselves alone and facing Longstreet's entire corps as the Rebels stormed across Chinn Ridge. No one would have faulted them had they fled the field—five hundred men facing thousands. But they had faced the onslaught and very few had survived. So the men who stood in the ranks of the 10th New York today were not the National Zouaves of old. They were either new recruits or the shaken remnants of the old 10th, and their commander, Colonel Charles Bendix, had no idea how they might perform on this day.

Villard scribbled as fast as he could, describing it all as Colonel Bendix rode boldly forward and sat astride his horse in full view of his men to keep them calm, give them confidence, and inspire them with his own fearlessness. With his entire regiment watching, a shell exploded overhead and a fragment smashed into his face and threw the colonel to the ground like a doll. The New Yorkers were appalled and certain their leader was dead until he struggled to his feet. Half of his face was gone. He tried to speak but could not. Two members of his staff rushed to his side and caught him before he fell again. The wounded colonel managed a weak salute to his men as he was carried from the field, and Henry Villard wrote it all down.

A hundred yards ahead of Anderson's men, Kimball's Brigade continued its march up the hill. In the last fifteen minutes James McClernan had seen sights no human being should ever have to witness. He saw a man with his arm blown off at the shoulder. Blood pulsed out from the stump by the gallon. He saw a hand lying in the mud like a dropped glove. The Rebel artillery continued to fire at such a pace that he thought there must be hundreds of them. They just never stopped shooting. His feet were wet and cold and the ground was muddy and slick and walking up this hill on a peaceful day would have been a chore. But regardless of all of this, he and his fellow Jerseymen continued their grisly march.

Just ahead of him was a small swale, a ridge he couldn't quite see over just yet, but on this side lay several hundred blue-coated men. Mason's skirmishers. Most of them were still, but occasionally one or two would peek over the top to fire at the Rebs.

Kimball was close behind, still mounted, and pushing his men forward.

"At the double-quick . . ."

James didn't believe it. *I can barely climb this slimy hill just walking.*

"CHARGE!"

Jesus.

James did his best, as did every other man in the 24th New Jersey. At least every man *remaining* in the 24th. The hill was steep and the footing was bad, and they were panting for air as it was. But from somewhere inside himself James found another ounce of energy and another pound of courage and he ran up the hill past Mason's men, over the top of the swale and into the hot fire of Cobb's Rebels, who leveled their rifles and poured a terrible volley into Kimball's assault and stopped it dead in its tracks.

But the general was still back there sitting boldly astride his horse and, incredibly, still urging his men forward until a Rebel infantryman found the easy target and shattered Nathan Kimball's thigh.

Their strength was gone, their courage was gone, and now their general was gone, and Kimball's Brigade fought its way backward, back down the hill, and joined Mason's skirmishers on the "safe" side of the swale.

After he'd had a moment to catch his breath and wipe his face, James looked to his left to see if he could find George, but there was no sign of him. He wanted to stand and walk down the line to go look for him, but the swale offered too little protection as it was and Rebel bullets continued to pour in and he just didn't dare. He prayed that George wouldn't either.

THE LACY HOUSE

Even from as far away as General Sumner's headquarters at the Lacy house, clear on the other side of the river, the sound of Cobb's opening volley was dreadful. Joshua Lawrence Chamberlain and the men of the 20th Maine watched the grand spectacle like a thousand theatergoers in the far back row. They seemed destined to be always in the audience and never on the stage. It was just like at Antietam all over again. Held in "reserve."

But when the fire exploded from Cobb's wall, Chamberlain winced as though he'd been slapped in the face. It stung him to see what those men had been asked to do. Irrational. Impractical. Impossible. All words from the vocabulary of a professor of rhetoric, and all perfectly applicable here. *And one more word,* he thought, not often used in his lectures at Bowdoin College—*idiotic.*

Well, he thought, *at least we've learned our lesson.*

MARYE'S HEIGHTS

The first assault had been repulsed, but Thomas R. R. Cobb saw John Andrews's Brigade coming over the swale, dressed in line of battle, and moving forward over the same ground. It never entered his mind that his stone wall was in any jeopardy. Their bravest man, or luckiest, or unluckiest, whichever he was, had not gotten within a hundred yards. The general from Georgia had only one concern.

"We're gonna need some more bullets."

* * *

Andrews's Yankees had waited in the relative safety of the millrace for the regiments in front of them to assault and carry the Rebel lines. That was the plan. The skirmishers would pursue the Rebel pickets into the line, Kimball's Brigade would follow them in and Andrews's men would come forward and force the break. That was what he had been told, and that, by damn, was what John W. Andrews intended to do. But Kimball's men were just lying there, still two hundred yards shy of their objective. They weren't doing anything but peeking up from time to time and taking harmless potshots.

While he waited, Andrews took advantage of the moment to reorganize his brigade. They had taken horrendous artillery fire while coming this far and had suffered unacceptable casualties, especially among the officers. The regiments were all mixed up and leaderless, and some order had to be put back.

While going about his job, Andrews noticed the Rebel artillery had readjusted its fire, and the canister balls weren't coming at him nearly so thickly. He thought this was good news until he looked back down toward the town and saw the reason why. Oliver Palmer's Brigade had just left the safety of the buildings around the railroad depot and were marching their way grandly up the hill.

Where will they go? Andrews began looking around like a scared rabbit until he finally understood what this meant. General French intended him to move forward whether Kimball had carried the Rebel lines or not. Colonel Palmer was coming, whether there was space for his men in the millrace or not. It was no longer Andrews's job to follow Kimball—it was now his job to lead Palmer.

Oliver Palmer's Brigade was now fully out in the open and again Confederate artillery converged on the approaching Yankees from three directions. The hottest fire fell into the leading regiment, the 14th Connecticut, and the worst of that was aimed at the color company, well ahead of the rest.

The 14th had tasted its first fight at Antietam, where they'd stood atop Roulette's Swale and took everything the Rebels in the Bloody Lane had to give. They came away bloodied and proud. They were proud of one another, proud of their regiment, proud of their state, and proud to rally behind the beautiful blue flag with the huge, angry eagle and the name of their regiment painted boldly across the bottom. It had seen only the one fight, but already this flag was a scarred and torn sacred icon, and they followed it over the two hundred yards leading up the hill to the millrace.

The artillery fire came in hot and fast and one round of solid shot found David Lincoln's legs and took both cleanly off at the knees. Two men took the time to apply tourniquets and the march slowed as men came to a stop to gawk at the poor lad.

The advance was slowing anyway because the men of the 14th had no place to go. The millrace was still full of Andrews's men, and they didn't seem to be going anywhere.

Colonel Sanford Perkins was not about to let his 14th Connecticut just stand around on open ground and die. He had to find a place to put them.

"By the right flank—*march*!"

The 14th did an abrupt right face and began moving parallel to the millrace until Perkins found what he thought was an empty spot.

"By the left flank—*march*!"

Again the regiment turned, but when they reached the ditch they found it full of gaily clad National Zouaves, all hunkered down low. All, that is, but one. Captain Winchester marched in front of his men, in full view of Rebs and Yanks alike, waving his sword over his head.

"For God's sake, Captain," one of his men yelled at him, ". . . get *down*!"

"I will stand until I am *knocked* down."

It was as though he had challenged the gods of war. One bullet or random piece of flying iron knocked the sword out of his hand at the same time another pierced his leg.

Colonel Perkins continued parading his men around the battlefield, looking for someplace to put them, marching them along the millrace until at last he found a thinly populated spot and ordered his Connecticuters to crowd themselves in.

With two more of Perkins's regiments close on their

heels and with no place for them to go, Andrews could delay no longer. He finally gave the order he had to give and
his brigade climbed out of the millrace and stood in formation, ready to march the rest of the way up the hill.

Bugles sounded the charge and what was left of Andrews's Brigade stepped off toward the swale and T. R. R.
Cobb's invincible stone wall as Perkins's men replaced
them in the millrace.

FREDERICKSBURG

"Spectacle." It was the word that kept coming into
Henry Villard's mind. He had never seen anything
like it and doubted that anyone living ever had either. He had been at Shiloh, but that fight was fought in the
woods and orchards and swamplands of southwest Tennessee. There were hills and bluffs and it was impossible
for Villard or anybody else to see the entire field. Here it
was a wide-open vista. French's men were able to line up in
battlefront formation by brigades and march up the hill with
flags flying and bands playing.

Villard was now attached to General French and when
the division commander rode to the millrace, Villard rode
with him. They were safe from the muskets but exposed to
the Rebel artillery. The reporter wisely decided that he was
there to observe bravery—not to show it himself. So he dismounted to lie down behind a bump in the earth to observe
while the general and his staff remained mounted.

The line between brave and stupid is a fine one, Villard
thought—but he didn't write it down.

Like everyone else, Villard had been horrified when the
Rebs unleashed their first volley from behind the wall.
"Like the fiery breath of an angry dragon," Villard wrote.
"But French's men didn't waver. No braver men were ever
born."

He heard horses approaching from the rear and turned to
see generals Couch and Hancock coming forward to meet
with French.

The three generals were mounted side by side, all peering through field glasses trying to see what they could of the battle raging on the hill. The smoke was thick right now and it was impossible to see, but every man there could clearly hear how ferocious a fight it was. The generals didn't speak. They didn't have to.

French was now totally committed with three brigades on the field, and Hancock's division was next. He looked back down at the town and watched as his men were funneled through the tightly packed streets of Fredericksburg. The metaphor was too easy to miss. Cattle being herded into chutes that would lead them to the slaughterhouse. Couch and Hancock had tried to stop this insane attack before it had begun. They had risked their careers and stood on the brink of arrest to tell General Burnside that an assault up Marye's Heights could only result in disaster. They had done all that they could do, but they had lost. The attack was ordered and they were soldiers. Both remembered Couch's words . . .

. . . *if I have ever done anything in any battle, I will do twice as much in this.*

Washington, D.C.

"The last news we had from Burnside was very good, Mr. Senator."

Salmon Chase and Benjamin Wade strolled down Pennsylvania Avenue from Chase's home toward a huge steak at the Willard Hotel. The bitterly cold weather of the past weeks was gone. The sky was clear and the temperature mild for the middle of December. But their decision to walk rather than take the treasury secretary's carriage was based more on a need for privacy than on the pleasant weather. Secretary Chase and Senator Wade had urgent and sensitive matters to discuss.

Like everybody else in Washington, the senator was anxious for the latest news. "Go on."

"He crossed the river yesterday without opposition. Or at

least very little. We actually expected the fight yesterday, but it apparently took him a while to get the whole army across."

Wade shook his head. "I don't like it, Sal. Lee picked the ground and has had plenty of time to dig in."

"We're told that Lee's army is spread out over a thirty-mile front. General Burnside is under *severe* pressure from Stanton and Halleck to be aggressive and he seems to be responding."

"Be careful, Sal. Too much pressure can explode backwards. The last thing we need is for the party to take the blame for another disaster."

Taking the blame, Chase thought. *That's all anything is ever about in this town. Credit and blame.* But those are the rules of the game played in Washington, and Salmon Chase and Benjamin Wade and everybody else in this swamp played by the rules. Everybody but Abraham Lincoln. And in Chase's mind that was, of course, a big part of the problem. The President was constantly riding his moral high horse and thought it honorable to place country ahead of party. What Chase knew and the President didn't was that if you're the only one playing by those rules, you are doomed to defeat—and so is the nation. Chase hoped Lincoln had finally learned his lesson from the McClellan fiasco, where he allowed a Democrat general to conduct the war in a way best suited to give Democrats credit and Republicans blame, and Republicans had taken a beating at the polls just last month as a result. McClellan's grand strategy was aimed at a political solution that would allow the South to return to "the Union as it was," with slavery intact. It was the Democrat's vision of the future, not the Republicans'. To Salmon P. Chase, the rules of the game were perhaps unpleasant but fair enough. All you have to do is genuinely believe that what's good for your party is good for the country and run the country accordingly.

"Well, let's hope *no one* has to take the blame for a defeat," he said. "Burnside seems confident."

"I wish I were more confident in Burnside."

The two men had to stop at 15th Street to allow an artillery battery to roll by. The conversation came to a stop until the noise was gone. Wade picked up where he'd left off. "Is he one of us, Sal?"

"I don't think General Burnside has an affiliation one way or the other."

The senator from Ohio couldn't conceive of such a thing. He was a man of such high-minded, moral certainty in his own party and in his own cause that it was beyond his comprehension that anyone could fail to take sides. More specifically it was beyond his comprehension that anyone could fail to take *his* side. Benjamin Wade played by the rules too. "Surely he has a stand on slavery."

"General Burnside is only a soldier, Mr. Senator, and I'm afraid not a very good one."

"Then *what is he doing* commanding our whole *army*?"

Chase saw his opening. "If the President didn't select Burnside alone, then you can bet it was Seward." Then, just to make certain his real point was made clear, "Rest assured the *cabinet* wasn't consulted!"

The treasury secretary was fishing. He wanted to know what progress was being made in the plan to force Lincoln to oust the secretary of state. Wade wasn't surprised. It was the whole purpose of the meeting. It was the purpose of every meeting with Chase these days.

"There is going to be a meeting, Sal. All of the Republican senators who are in our camp will discuss how best to proceed, but there is more to it than only ridding ourselves of 'the evil genius.' " The radical Republicans seldom referred to Seward by name anymore. He had now been dubbed "the evil genius" and "the evil genius" he would always be.

The two men turned down 16th Street and passed the White House still en route to Willard's. Wade nodded toward the Executive Mansion. "Our 'leader' needs to relinquish his dictatorship and let the Congress run the war. It's what the Constitution says and it's the only way the thing will ever be won. Getting rid of the secretary of state alone might make matters even worse . . ."

Chase didn't like where this was going. He interrupted. "I don't see how things could be much worse."

"Nonetheless . . . it is my intention that we shall demand

not only that 'the evil genius' be dismissed, but that the hiring and firing of generals come under the auspices of the Senate—'advice and consent'—and we'll never have another Porter or McClellan to deal with. The army will be commanded only by Republicans and antislavery men."

"One thing at a time, Mr. Senator. With Seward gone, Stanton, Halleck, and I will be able to keep a closer watch on Abe."

"Halleck." Wade groaned. "Put that man in charge of twenty thousand men and he wouldn't be able to scare a goose out of a nest."

Chase thought it best to disregard the senator's comment even though he agreed fully. Right now he needed to find out what he came here to find out, and he knew that if he let Wade wander too far off the subject he might never be able to get him back.

"When is the meeting?"

"Probably on Tuesday, after we see what happens at Fredericksburg. We may be looking for another new general as soon as tomorrow."

Chase hoped the senator was wrong, but was afraid he was right.

"And who will you recommend to the committee should that happen, Mr. Secretary?"

Chase heard what he said and knew what he meant. *The Committee on the Conduct of the War will appoint the next commanding general.*

Chase knew this was a battle that would have to be fought, but he decided to heed his own counsel. *One fight at a time.*

"Hooker."

CHAPTER 12

FREDERICKSBURG

As the Irish Brigade crossed Caroline Street, they passed in front of their commanding generals, and the immigrant soldiers took off their hats and waved them in the air and cheered. Couch, Hancock, and Meagher returned their salutes with shouts of encouragement that couldn't be heard over the roar.

Bill McCarter had spent the better part of two days avoiding the gaze of Thomas Meagher, afraid that the general would order him back across the river and back to his penmanship chores, but it was too late for that now, and Bill managed to catch Meagher's eye and the old Irish revolutionary recognized him and smiled and nodded and continued to point with his sword to the top of the hill.

PROSPECT HILL

George Meade had the temperament of a wasp. He was perpetually angry and ready to sting at the slightest provocation—attacking any innocent and bewildered private for any insignificant transgression. But, in the worst of times, when he had to remain calm and cool

and wholly in command, he was able to discipline his fury.
And these were the worst of times.

His division was pinned down by Rebel artillery fire, lying facedown in the mud, and until his own big guns on the
field and up on Stafford Heights could clear the way somehow, there they would remain. In the midst of all this artillery fury, George Gordon Meade strode easily forward,
directly into the line of fire of the Rebel guns.

Colonel William Sinclair had long since dismounted and
joined his men facedown in the mud with his hands over his
head, as though that might save him from a Rebel cannonball. Over the din he heard General Meade's all-too-
familiar voice. It didn't stand out because of its volume or
its rage. It stood out like a whisper in a storm.

Sinclair risked sure death to lift his head for just an instant to see where the voice came from and was astounded
to see his commanding general, fully astride his gigantic
charger, chatting with Colonel McCandless. The commander of the 2nd Pennsylvania stood alongside his own
horse, but wisely dismounted.

Meade pointed down at the silver eagle on the young colonel's shoulder.

"A star this morning, William?"

At that moment a Rebel round gutted McCandless's
horse, which went quickly down with a dying whinny.
Meade remained mounted and nonplussed.

McCandless stood and tried to wipe himself clean.

"More likely a wooden overcoat."

MARYE'S HEIGHTS

"Hold your fire."
T. R. R. Cobb continued to be amazed by the
courage of the Union men who marched over
the top of the swale and directly toward his stone wall.
These new men were the National Zouaves, clad in their red
shirts and turbans, and they were a beautiful, inspiring sight
to see. The first rank had their rifles at the "charge bayo-

nets" position, with the stocks to their hips and their bayoneted muzzles angled upward.

At two hundred yards away they were in easy killing range, but Cobb continued to hold his men back. He didn't want a single one of these incredibly brave men to survive the very first volley. He waited longer than many of his men thought he should. He waited until he heard Andrews's command.

"CHARGE!"

The blue troops hadn't run their second step before Cobb answered.

"FIRE!"

In a single instant, the entire front rank of the National Zouaves was gone. All along Palmer's attacking lines it was the same. The 10th New York . . . the 4th New York . . . the 132nd Pennsylvania . . . all faced a fire that never stopped and in less than a minute the retreat began. Those who survived turned and ran or crawled or rolled back down the hill to join Kimball's men behind the swale.

On their way down they almost ran into the color guard of the 14th Connecticut, who were on their way up.

Some of the men of the 14th Connecticut fought to preserve the Union and a few fought to free the slaves. But while marching up Marye's Heights into the face of the enemy, those huge issues became very small. Today they all agreed about why they were there, facing death and glory together. Today they fought for one another—and for their big, blue, beautiful flag. Not so much for the Stars and Stripes, though she was beautiful too, but for the blue flag with the grapevines, the eagle, and the words scrolled in gold across the bottom—"The Fourteenth Regiment." Every man in Perkins's little regiment would give his life to keep her flying and out of the hands of the enemy.

The Rebels knew this. They loved their flags too. And in the absence of a nicely mounted general or colonel to shoot at, the standard bearer was the next best thing.

They were never armed, these men who bore the pride of their regiments into battle. If one went down, or more precisely *when* one went down, the closest man would abandon his rifle, pick up the flag, and continue forward. And so it was with the men of the Fighting Fourteenth, and now it was their turn to storm the wall.

Augustus Foote and Benjamin Hirst were two ranks back, marching side by side as always, as they had in a thousand drills over the months. As they had at Antietam when they marched over Roulette's Swale and into the Bloody Lane.

The ground was still wet and slippery and it was now cluttered with the bodies of dead and wounded men. They came to the remnants of a fence that had surrounded the Fredericksburg Fairgrounds. It had been an obstacle for the 24th New Jersey, but they had managed to take most of it down. The Connecticut color guard stepped over the remaining rails and the blue flag kept moving forward. Foote was jealous of the man who carried the colors, Color Sergeant Charles Dart. What an incredible honor to stand so well forward—to be the man Connecticut followed into the worthy fight. But Dart had earned the job at Antietam and was doing it well today.

When Colonel Oliver Palmer gave the order to charge, Dart glanced back at his comrades and waved them forward. "Follow me, boys!" he yelled as he broke into a run. Foote and Hirst and all of the men of Palmer's Brigade growled and screamed and stepped over the fence rails in the same instant the Washington Artillery fired all four cannons— double-packed with canister—and over two hundred of the heavy iron pellets ripped through the ranks of the Fighting Fourteenth.

Foote and Hirst had been in the second rank, but the first rank was gone and the rest of the 14th fell to the ground. Foote saw Sergeant Dart go down and was amazed that the horribly wounded man managed to plant the flag as he fell. He speared the staff into the soft earth and leaned it against one of the remaining fence posts. The courageous color sergeant writhed on the ground for only a moment before his body went perfectly still. All of the men of the color guard were down, but the flag remained standing proudly, albeit alone and defenseless.

Foote couldn't tolerate the sight. He had to rescue her. He was just about to stand up and rush forward when a thousand muskets again appeared over the top of the stone wall and Cobb's Rebels began to unload on the prostrate Yanks. Foote couldn't stand and charge now, but he could crawl, by God. He had only ten feet to go, but it would be a hellish ten feet.

Hirst tried to stop him. "Augie—don't go!"

He grabbed the sergeant's leg, but Foote yanked it away and continued forward. He made it to within inches of the staff when one bullet struck him in the hip and another in the face.

Hirst saw his friend's body shudder with each blow.

"Nooooooo!"

He couldn't control his fury, but he knew it would be suicide to try to save him—or the flag. He aimed his rifle at the wall and sent a shot forward, knowing that it would do no good. The Rebels were just too well protected, but he fired anyway. And so did everybody else, but all they did was take small chips out of the thick rocks of Cobb's stone wall. He tried to hurry himself through the agonizingly slow procedure of reloading. While standing he could do the job in under a half a minute, but reloading under fire while lying down was awkward and dangerous and seemed to take forever. When he finally finished, he brought the weapon to the firing position, pulled the hammer back to full cock, and before he fired he heard his friend lying just ten feet ahead.

"Oh God! For the love of God. Please, somebody kill me. Somebody *kill* me! Please."

Hirst began to weep. His friend's agony tortured his soul. He couldn't save him and he couldn't kill him. All he had to do was pull the trigger, but he couldn't do it. He couldn't put his best friend in the world out of his misery.

He just couldn't do it.

FREDERICKSBURG

Bill McCarter, along with the rest of the Irish Brigade, had been given his eighty rounds of ammunition, his twigs of boxwoods, and several inspirational addresses by General Meagher. They had been shuffled from place to place within the city since early in the morning.

Whenever they had to cross one of the perpendicular-to-the-river streets, they had to run across the intersection in single file because the Rebel artillery was placed in such a way that they had clear shots down those roads all the way to the river.

But now, at last, Meagher's "little brigade" of almost 1,200 souls was in position to rush up the hill and "on to Richmond." But still they waited.

The building that served as their protection was a cotton mill or a woolen factory; Bill couldn't quite figure out what it was. Artillery from one army or the other had set the four-story building ablaze and it had been burning for hours. The bricks were hot and the roof was gone and flames jumped out of the windows to lick the exterior wall, and Bill was certain that Jericho was about to tumble down and kill them all. He was praying for God to hold up that wall when an artillery shell exploded overhead. The sound was deafening and the concussion almost knocked him down. The shell took a man's head off. Marley. It had to be Sergeant Marley. He had just been standing there, just like everybody else, not fifty feet away from Bill, when his head just exploded. His body went to its knees and paused there for a second or maybe longer, almost like it was praying one last prayer before it fell flat on the street. Bill covered his eyes and tried not to cry and not to throw up.

He hated being here, waiting, totally helpless, watching men die just standing in line—going nowhere and doing nothing.

"Let's *go!*" He didn't know whether he had said it out loud or just thought it—or maybe prayed it. *This has to be worse than fighting. It* has *to be! Nothing could be worse than this.* It filled his brain. It filled his heart. He wanted to go. He wanted to get the order to move out and come face-to-face with the enemy. *If this is to be my last day, God, then please let me die with my face to the enemy—not from a falling wall or a random shell. Please, God, don't let me die just standing here—waiting.*

He thought he had seen the worst of it when the wounded and retreating men of French's division began making their way down the streets of Fredericksburg. The men of the

Irish Brigade had to step aside to let the wounded pass through. Some limped painfully but made their way on their own. Some were being helped to the rear by friends or ambulance crews. And then there was one man—a captain— who was being carried to the rear on a window shutter. His weeping face was young and deathly white, and to the horror of everyone who saw him, his leg dangled off of the side of the shutter held to the rest of his body only by a single bloody tendon and a slender thread of flesh.

"Oh God . . ." one man cried. "Can't you just cut the damned thing off?"

His cry was ignored by the men carrying the maimed captain down the street, and another Irishman yelled, "Cut it off! It will be better for him if you just cut it off!"

It was a gut-churning sight and Bill's friend Stretch couldn't stand to watch it. He broke ranks, ran forward, and with one swipe of a penknife he cut the tendon and the captain's leg fell to the ground. The stretcher bearers continued along their way as though nothing had happened, leaving the severed leg in the middle of the street.

Bill thought he was going to faint. He didn't. Other men did—but Bill didn't.

Winfield Scott Hancock was one of the army's best cussers and at this moment he was exercising his most colorful vocabulary. In Hancock's mind there was no excuse for any whole man ever to turn his back to the enemy and yet French's men avalanched down the hill and into the town. He cursed them and belittled them and threatened them and slapped them with his sword to get them to turn around, but not a single man responded.

Finally he spotted a captain who seemed to still have his wits about him.

"Captain, did you take the wall?"

"Take the wall? Sir, we never came within a hundred yards of the wall. Their artillery killed half of us before we even got close enough to *shoot* at the wall."

Hancock looked up the hill and tried to see through the smoke. The field had gone quiet for the moment and a gust of wind blew it clear and he saw immediately that the captain was right. He saw hundreds of blue-clad soldiers lying in the mud—some moving but most still. They were scattered along the slope from the outskirts of town all the way up to the millrace. Beyond that they were packed thick on the Fredericksburg side of the swale and for only a very few yards beyond. But the ground in front of the wall was clear for a hundred yards or more—not a single Yankee body to be seen. Hancock also saw the four Rebel guns still safely placed just below the crest of Marye's Heights. It was a view that told the whole story.

We've got to silence those guns. Winfield Hancock knew a lot about artillery and most of all he knew rule number one: The only way to silence guns is with guns.

"Guns!" he yelled. "Bring up the guns!"

MARYE'S HEIGHTS

Bill Owen of the Washington Artillery was enjoying a cool moment. The Yanks had stopped coming and once again the four guns of the Marye's Heights battery fell silent. Owen congratulated himself on his foresight. He had saved a piece of corn bread and now was as good a time as any for lunch. He washed it down with just a small sip of old man Barton's finest Madeira.

The guns were loaded and the muzzles cool, and the men of the Washington Artillery waited and watched to see if the Yankees would be stupid enough to try it again. All hoped they would. It was their motto after all—"Try Us"—but they doubted that anyone who tried them once would try them again. Then Owen noticed movement on the outskirts of the town and he couldn't believe what he saw. He tapped Colonel Walton on the shoulder and pointed.

Walton raised his glasses to make certain he was seeing clearly. He was. Several batteries of Union artillery had rolled out of the town and were unlimbering their guns—out in the open, in full view and within easy range. Colonel James Walton was a very happy man.

"Your new targets will be those guns, gentlemen. Fire when ready."

It took the expert marksmen of the Washington Artillery only moments to adjust and open fire on Hancock's vulnerable guns and the fight for Marye's Heights became an artillery duel.

A Federal round of solid shot splashed down directly behind Owen. Private Kursheedt scurried up the hill and retrieved the Yankee round. Wiping the mud off it, he smiled at Owen.

"Why don't we just send this one back where it came from?" And seconds later, they did.

The Yankees along the swale saw what was happening as Rebel guns turned their attention to Hancock's guns and began to empty their cartridge boxes on the Washington Artillery. For the first time today, Owen was nervous as both artillery and musket fire roared into his position on Marye's Heights.

Corporal Ruggles was the number-one man—the rammer. He took a bullet through the back. As he had been trained to do, Perry grabbed the ramrod and took Ruggles's place, but he didn't stand there long. Owen heard the ping of a Yankee minié ball as it struck the barrel of one of their guns and saw Perry drop the ramrod and go down clutching his right arm. Privates Robb and Everett both fell in rapid succession.

As Everett was carried from the field he shouted at Owen, "It's the fire coming from that danged house over there! It's Federal sharpshooters!"

One gun turned. One gun fired. The Yankee sharpshooters ran for their lives—all except one.

T. R. R. Cobb watched for a moment and decided the whole affair wouldn't last much longer, but he also knew he had some time before his men would have to fend off another infantry assault. He took advantage of the opportunity to assemble his officers and take reports. They gathered behind the Stephens house—just for safety's sake.

Only moments after the group came together they attracted the attention of the remaining Federal sharpshooter who was still ensconced in the second story of the house. This gaggle of officers was the target he had been waiting for. He selected a single man—the tallest and most gaudily clad—sighted carefully on the Rebel officer's face and pulled the trigger.

Brigadier General John Rogers Cooke fell to his knees. The bullet had fractured his skull, but he was still alive. His adjutant caught him before his head hit the ground and lowered him gently onto the road.

"STRETCHER!"

The adjutant was wearing a sash, which he had some difficulty taking off, but he managed to wrap it around the general's head and tie it tightly before the stretcher bearers arrived.

Cobb was stunned. He had deliberately picked the single spot along his line that he decided was the safest place to meet. Cooke was a good man. All he could do now was pray, "Dear God, let him live."

Wood shattered somewhere nearby and Cobb turned to see where the sound had come from. Mrs. Stephens's door had been crashed clear through, and lying there, nearly at his feet, was a smoking Federal cannonball. He didn't have so much as a second to react. The shell exploded and Cobb was lifted off his feet by the blast. A huge piece of metal tore through his right thigh, shattering the bones from the knee up and severing the femoral artery. Blood poured from the wound before he ever hit the ground.

He somehow managed to remain conscious and he examined his wound before anyone arrived. He had seen wounds like it before, but had never seen anybody survive one.

"General Cobb!"

The Georgian looked up to see his cousin and aide-de-camp John Rutherford kneeling beside him.

Cobb took as deep a breath as he could and very calmly he said, "I shall require a tourniquet, John."

WASHINGTON, D.C.

Lincoln was distracted from his reading by the clatter of the telegraph key. This time the dits and daws lasted for a while and he convinced himself for a moment that he might be getting some significant information this time.

The battle rages furiously. I can barely hear my instrument. Wounded arriving every minute. The roar of musketry almost deafening. Nothing definite in regard to the fight.

Disappointed but not surprised, Lincoln went back to his book. He read the remembrance of a Revolutionary War officer who said, "No regiment is to be seen in which there are not Negroes in abundance; and many of them are ablebodied, strong, and brave fellows."

This was about the tenth time today he had read about the heroics of black soldiers during the Revolution.

He closed his eyes for a moment, just to give them a rest, and before he fell asleep he thought, *Maybe Greeley and Sumner and Wade and the rest are right about this. Maybe I'm wrong.*

MARYE'S HEIGHTS

Winfield Scott Hancock pulled back what was left of his artillery line. Dead men, dead horses, and a few useless piles of artillery trash were all that he had to show for his efforts to silence the Washington Artillery. But French's division was wasted—dead, wounded, in retreat, or cowering on the ground behind the swale—and it was time for Hancock to move. Zook's Brigade would lead—followed by Meagher—followed by Caldwell.

Hancock spread his men out, hoping to offer a wider front so they wouldn't be so bunched up as they left the safety of the town. They would move up three different streets and fan out into a series of lines a half a mile long. At least the Rebels wouldn't be able to kill as many of them at a time.

He pulled his horse alongside Samuel Zook, directly in front of the 27th Connecticut. Zook was a colonel with a premonition of death, and the 27th was made up of the rookies who had been ordered to bridge Hazel Run yesterday, but had spent most of the day hiding in a frozen creek bed rather than face enemy fire. Cowardice is a disease that can infect a single man or an entire regiment, and the 27th Connecticut was well on its way to becoming a coward. Spinelessness is a hard illness to recover from, and today Hancock intended to cure them of the despicable inclination.

Slowly, boldly, and calmly, Hancock rode back and forth in front of them, looking down on the rookies like a disappointed father might at a small, embarrassed child.

"You are the only Connecticut regiment in my division." Now he not only looked like a stern and disappointed father, he sounded like one too. "Bring *no dishonor* on Connecticut!"

He remained silent for a full minute to give the rookies ample time to dwell on dishonor.

He took an additional moment to look into the eyes of his brigade commanders, to see if there was anything there that might tell him how each man might perform on this day. He examined Zook especially closely but, regardless of the premonition he had confessed yesterday, he seemed confident today.

"Gentlemen—you may advance."

Zook's Brigade filed out first, followed by the Irish Brigade, two hundred paces behind. Bill McCarter, at long last, praise be to God, was finally finished waiting.

As his division moved out, Winfield Hancock continued to keep a close eye on Sam Zook. Zook seemed to have put his fears behind him, but Hancock thought it wise to keep an eye on him nonetheless. A brigade commander had too much to do to be worried about dying.

Of course Zook *was* worried but not so much about his own survival. That was up to God. He was far more concerned about the skittish rookies of the 27th Connecticut. They had embarrassed themselves yesterday and needed watching today. But they marched up to the millrace like veterans. The file closers had some trouble doing their gruesome work, but that was always true. Even in the bravest of regiments it often takes a pistol or a sword to get a man to step to the front of the line in the heat of battle. They had also made it through the second ring of artillery hell— between the millrace and the swale—without making the normal rookie mistakes. They hadn't hesitated to step over French's dead, they hadn't slowed to stare at the grotesquely wounded men who littered the field along the way, and they hadn't stopped to shoot their rifles just for the hell of it. But now they had reached the swale and the hillside was thick with French's men and the new troops needed to catch their breath and regroup for the lunge up to the wall. Sam Zook was pleased. So far the 27th had shown no fear—no signs of cowardice. Not a single man had shown his back to the enemy. But now was time for the final test.

The entire brigade lay there on the hill. Grim. Determined. They were absolutely silent as they lay there praying and waiting for Zook's command.

Never taking his eyes off of the 27th, Zook finally shouted . . . *"Attention!"*

Every man came to his feet. Every man who had cowered in the creek yesterday stood boldly in the face of the enemy today.

"CHARGE!"

Up and over the swale they poured, screaming and at a run—until the Georgians behind the wall stood and fired. Against orders, Zook's entire brigade stopped to return the fire, but a single volley was all they managed before the big guns on the hillside opened with canister fire that blasted holes ten men wide in their lines and still they held their ground, reloading their rifles to try to get off another shot. Just then the Union artillery on Stafford Heights opened fire from a mile away and their shots fell short and Sam Zook fell to the ground—his horse shot out from under him—and finally his entire brigade, not only the brave boys of Connecticut's 27th, but the remnants of the entire brigade backed down the hill to the swale.

On the outskirts of Fredericksburg, Winfield Scott Hancock had seen it all. He had seen the gallant charge. He had seen the wall of fire that brought it to a halt. And he had seen Sam Zook go down.

"I'm not coming back from this one, Win."

"Damn!"

It was all Hancock said. It was all he had time to say. Meagher's Irish Brigade was almost to the swale and Caldwell's was just behind them, and Hancock had no time to dwell on mysterious premonitions or friends lost in battle.

He just didn't have time.

"Order all officers to dismount! Every man—no exceptions!"

The efforts to stop the bleeding from Tom Cobb's shattered leg failed, but the stretcher, at least, had finally arrived. Against heavy fire from the Yankee regiments scattered along the swale, the bearers lifted him up, but remained stooped over to keep the protection of the wall for as long as they could.

Cobb continued the fight to remain conscious and keep his wits about him, at least until he was out of sight of his men.

"I'm only wounded, boys! Hold your ground like brave men!"

The guns overhead ceased firing and Cobb's Georgia boys looked behind them to see why, and what they saw was General Robert Ransom's North Carolina brigade rushing down the hill to join their ranks. The Washington Artillery held their fire to let the reinforcements pass. Bill Owen and the rest of the artillerists took off their hats and waved them in the air and cheered the new men through.

With the Rebel artillery suddenly quiet, General Thomas Meagher saw his chance to move the Irish Brigade out of the millrace.

"Colors forward!"

The color guards of each regiment climbed out of the deep ditch and came to attention. They were shy three green flags, but the National Colors were beautiful enough.

"Sound 'To the Colors.'"

The bugles sounded and the Irish Brigade aligned themselves in battlefront formation, ready at last to step forward and take the wall.

Bill McCarter looked left, right, and rear to admire the beautiful blue lines formed by the Irish Brigade and Caldwell's Brigade just behind. He wanted to take in this moment and remember it in every detail. He admired the golden harp on the single green flag posted magnificently alongside the Stars and Stripes. Ireland and America. The old country and the new. He looked into the faces of nearby men and every one of them wore the same expression of grim defiance. Not fear. Of course there *was* fear, but no one showed any. The look was of determination. Every man faced to the front.

A priest moved along the lines for the benefit of the Catholics in their midst. *"Benedicat vus omnipotens Deus, Pater, et Spritus Sanctus."*

There was movement all along the front as the officers scurried about in a hurry. General Meagher limped along and Bill remembered the lancing of the dreadful boil on the back of the general's knee. The poor man could barely stand, much less walk. General Hancock had ordered him dismounted. No officers would ride for the rest of this day—too easy a target. Zook had proved that. And so Meagher limped and grimaced with every step.

In front of them the hill leading up to the swale was strewn with the rubbish of the previous attacks. Human debris. Some wounded and some firing up at the wall, just waiting for God or the generals to tell them what to do next. And, of course, many of them were dead. *They used to be men,* Bill thought, *but now they're rubbish.* Soulless lumps. Things that have been used up and discarded. Broken parts of the war machine that need to be replaced.

He felt an elbow to his side. Stretch. "Look there, Bill." Bill looked where Stretchbok pointed some twenty yards ahead and he saw a soldier whose head had been split apart as if with a cleaver. "Look at the watermelon."

Bill pretended to be amused by his friend's callous joke, but he wasn't.

There was a sudden increase in activity among the officers as each of the five regimental commanders moved quickly to place himself at the head of his men.

Meagher raised his saber above his head. *"Fix!"*

Five voices echoed, *"Fix!"*

Two thousand men withdrew their bayonets from their cases and held them at the ready.

All along the line, hundreds of Irishmen whispered, *"Benedicat vus omnipotens . . ."*

"Bayonets!"

The ominous clank and clatter of steel against steel times 1,200.

Deus Pater . . .

Colonel Heenan now raised his saber. His hand was bandaged from a wound received from the same shell that sent Sergeant Marley to his Maker. He stood with his face to the men and one by one he repeated Meagher's commands. "Attention. Shoulder—arms. Forward at the double-quick . . ." During the pause he looked back and forth along the ranks and files of his rookies. "Now men, steady, and do your duty."

"*. . . et Spritus Sanctus.*"

He performed an about-face and waited along with every other man in the Irish Brigade for Meagher's final word.

He pointed his saber toward the swale and the stone wall beyond and repeated the final command. "*. . . March!*"

"Oh, sweet Mary."

The brogue was right off the boat. He was the first of Cobb's Irishmen to see it, but very soon they had all noticed the huge green flag of Meagher's Irish Brigade, famed even in the South by now. A moan rose up from the Southern Irishmen behind the wall, none of whom wanted to kill a fellow Irishman. But duty is duty. Their general was wounded—probably dying—and had to be avenged. And this isn't Irish soil after all—it's Virginia. This is the sovereign ground of the Confederate States of America and the men following the green flag up the hill are invaders from a foreign land. Just like the British back in Ireland.

With the addition of the reinforcements the road was now packed tight with men and muskets. There wasn't enough room for every man to have a spot of his own.

"We're four deep here now, men," General Ransom shouted. "So here's what we are going to do."

All along the wall the boys from Georgia and North Carolina paid close attention.

"The man closest to the wall will be the shooter. He will take careful aim—fire low—and hand his weapon back to the man behind him. He will then be handed another—fully loaded and half cocked. Percussion cap in place. Two men in the rear will do nothing but reload and pass forward. Do you understand?"

They all nodded, but he didn't believe them, so he demonstrated. "One shooter—one passer—two loaders—and the next poor Yankee bastards that come up that hill will find the air full of lead!"

The men cheered and raised their hats in the air, but Ransom calmed them—he had one more idea.

"Now—lay low, men. Don't let 'em see you. We'll let 'em get right up close and rise up like devils out of hell."

The Irish Brigade had long since lost the beautiful ranks and files General Meagher had spent so much time putting together. The double-quick march up the hill was interrupted by fresh fire from the Washington Artillery, and then by the thousands of Yankees, dead and living, who clung to the safe side of the swale, and then by the remains of Zook's Brigade that continued to stumble back down the hill.

Bill McCarter's kepi took a small piece of shrapnel, and the leather bill clung to the hat only by a thread. He tried to rip it off, but could not. He thought of throwing the whole thing on the ground and moving forward without it, but there was the sprig of boxwood—his own precious little piece of green. So he put the hat back on and just let the brim dangle.

As the last of Zook's men filed through, the lines of the Irish Brigade began to re-form themselves. Healed—almost by magic. As they passed over the swale, the Yankees behind them ceased firing. Fifty yards later, the Rebel artillery on the hill fell quiet. At almost the same time, the Union guns on Stafford Heights held their fire as well, and the field fell oddly quiet.

Bill's gaze was fixed on the wall that was now less than a hundred yards away, and there appeared to be no one there. There was occasional movement, but it looked to him to be no more than a handful of men. A picket line maybe.

Still at the double-quick the Irish Brigade was beginning to tire, but not to slow. They stepped over corpses and the remnants of fences along the way. Bill had to move around a pile of a dozen or more dead men gathered around a blue flag that continued to stand upright, almost defiantly, leaning against a post. The 14th Connecticut, it said. Seventy-five yards now to the wall and there were no more dead or wounded men to clutter the approach. There was nothing now between the Irish Brigade and the stone wall and those killing Rebel guns just up the hill.

Then, with only seventy-five yards to go, a thousand musket barrels suddenly appeared above the wall, leveled and hesitated only for a moment. In a single, deafening, horrifying instant, the wall exploded into two hundred yards of thunder and smoke and the entire front rank of the Irish Brigade went down. Bill actually heard the bullet hit the man in front of him. It sounded like a hammer striking a watermelon except that it was followed by an anguished scream. McCarter stepped over the wounded man to take his place in the front and not ten seconds later a thousand more muskets appeared and a thousand more bullets ripped through Meagher's little brigade. The blast was so powerful that Bill actually felt the heat against his face. The Irish poet in him knew what it felt like. *Hell's doors swung open,* he thought.

Colonel Heenan went down along with Colonel Bardwell. Lieutenant Maguire took a bullet through his shoulder and Lieutenant Montgomery stopped one with his chest. Bill began looking for an officer. Any officer. There were none. Not so much as a lieutenant. Then his heart sank. Meagher. General Meagher was nowhere to be seen.

Color Sergeant William Tyrrell had suddenly become their sole remaining leader, and he led them gallantly. He stood boldly in the face of the horrendous fire and waved his flag in defiance until a bullet lodged in his leg. But even then he went down only to one knee and continued to do his job well in front of the rest of the 116th. The banner was soon riddled with bullet holes, the staff was shot in two, and Jody Struminger stepped forward and took the flag from Tyrrell's dead hands.

Bill stopped and fired and reloaded. The Irish Brigade

had come to a stop, but as yet no one had turned to run. The wall was constantly shrouded in white smoke from the nearly incessant musket fire. Bill couldn't see the men behind the smoke, but the men behind the smoke couldn't see him either. And yet both sides continued to fire at the other as rapidly as they could. Bill lost track of how many times he'd fired his rifle. Six? Seven? He couldn't remember. He wasn't really shooting *at* anything. He was just shooting. He kept on looking for General Meagher, but couldn't find him. He suddenly felt himself alone, like he was standing in front of that wall all by himself. He looked to Stretch for some help or some comfort or some guidance as to what to do next. Hell. Sergeant Stretchbok might well be commanding the brigade by now—but Stretch . . . *My God—Oh, my dear God in heaven . . .*

"STRETCH?"

Bill looked around him. He looked on the ground at the dead and wounded Irishmen at his feet and saw a large man lying facedown. He knelt down and tried to turn him over to see if it was his friend and the man screamed in pain and Bill jumped back, startled that the soldier was alive and sorry that he had hurt him, but relieved that it wasn't Stretch after all.

Bill was terrified. General Meagher was gone. Colonel Heenan was gone. And the best friend he had ever had in this whole world was gone. The quiet, little stammering private from Derry suddenly flew into a rage at the murderers behind the wall. He would load and fire one more round and storm the wall alone if need be to get his revenge. He screamed in fury as he reached into his cartridge box and pulled out the paper packet. He put it in his mouth and ripped it open and poured the powder down the muzzle of his rifle. He had to stand to draw the ramrod and he raised it high to ram the cartridge tight when something struck his right arm close to the shoulder. He screamed again, more in anger than in pain, as his arm dropped to his side. At first he thought a fellow Irishman had accidentally butted him with a musket, but he realized very quickly that the arm was useless. He dropped his rifle and reached with his left hand to feel where he had been hit. He looked at his wet, red fingers and felt dizzy and ill and only then did the real pain of torn flesh and broken bones attack his entire body.

He was nauseous now and confused. Why had they even tried this insane attack? What was the point? What had been the chances of success? More than ever he needed his friends. He needed to see them to make sure they were alive. There were still men around him—men with sprigs of boxwoods in their hats—living men who still returned the Rebel fire, but he saw no signs of General Meagher or Stretch. He continued to look around him and up the hill at the smoke-shrouded wall where the Rebels continued to fire down on the Irish Brigade, but his vision soon blurred and everything began to fade into darkness.

Into thy hands, oh my God, I commit my soul and body.

Bill hadn't been out for more than a few seconds when he was jarred back to consciousness as another Irishman fell directly in front of him. The boy cried for his mother for only a moment before a second minié ball ended his life. The firing remained a perpetual thunder and bullets continued to strike all around Bill, splattering mud in his face. He tried to move the dead man but couldn't with only one arm, so he inched his way behind him, to use the fresh corpse as a shield.

The order sounded like it came from a million miles away, but it was still clearly heard even over the gunfire. "Fall back, men, and it's every man for himself!"

Bill couldn't fall back. He couldn't even stand up. He'd lost too much blood, and the bullets were too thick anyway. He didn't even dare to lift his head, but he did turn it slightly, just to get a look as the Irish Brigade finally turned their backs to the wall and stampeded back down the hill. Bill thought the Rebel fire would come faster and more furious if such a thing was possible. He thought that many a brave man would die from the worst of all wounds—a shot in the back. But it didn't happen. The gunfire didn't increase—it almost stopped entirely. And then, the oddest thing—the Rebels behind the wall began to cheer. They stood and lifted their hats and saluted the courage of their kinsmen.

CHAPTER 13

PROSPECT HILL

Sallie Pelham no longer commanded a single, hidden gun. A half mile up the road from his earlier position, he was now in charge of sixteen that stood out for all to see. They sent a continuous fire into Meade's frozen ranks, and Meade's and Doubleday's guns gave back all they got and more.

A screaming man drew Pelham's attention and he was surprised to see the man's wounds hadn't come from a Federal shot. He had begun to ram the powder into the muzzle of one of his Napoleons and the barrel was so hot the powder ignited and burned the young cannoneer's hands and face.

"Sponge 'em down good, now, boys. Give 'em a minute to cool!"

MARYE'S HEIGHTS

Most of the men from the Irish Brigade—at least those who could walk, run, or crawl—had made their way back down the hill to the swale where they joined the survivors of all of the previous regiments, brigades, and divisions that had gone before them. Coming

up the hill was Caldwell's Brigade—the sixth in Sumner's
line—all fresh and clean and ready to take their turn against
the wall. The Rebs stopped cheering for Meagher's Brigade
and waited for Caldwell's.

Bill McCarter still lay where he had fallen. He didn't dare
move. Some of the Rebels had decided they should finish off
any man who showed even the slightest sign of life. They
stood there behind their nice, safe wall and coolly murdered
helpless, wounded men. It was more than Bill could bear. He
was outraged and desperate to take revenge but there was
nothing he could do. His arm was limp and useless and he was
too weak to stand even if he dared. He was racked with fury,
frustration, and paralyzing fear. He didn't dare so much as
twitch a finger for fear a Rebel murderer would see it and take
aim. He was shocked to feel a hand on his shoulder. He
opened his eyes enough to see Captain Foltz, who had
crawled forward to retrieve Bill's gun. Foltz was just as angry
as McCarter and he still had some fight left in him. From a
kneeling position he quickly checked to make sure the percussion cap was in place, assuring him that the musket was
loaded. He lifted it to his shoulder and took aim at the wall but
he fell before he ever pulled the trigger, landing with his face
only inches away from McCarter's. His eyes were open but
empty, and he had a neat, round bullet hole square in the middle of his forehead.

Bill couldn't bear to look into the poor dead captain's
face. He turned his head and closed his eyes and said a
prayer for a good man's soul.

James McClernan had tolerated all that he could. His regiment had followed the skirmishers up the hill and had been
the first to face the fire from behind the wall. In the hour or
two since (he had long since lost track of time) he had lain
there and fired all of his ammunition and watched helplessly as four more brigades had marched boldly into the
face of the dragon, only to stumble and crawl back down
the hill to take cover behind the swale. And now came a
fifth. Caldwell's. *My God. This is never going to end!*
James wanted to stand up and put out his arms and shout at
the men to stop. He wanted to put an end to this absolute

madness. But even more than that, he desperately wanted to find his brother. He hadn't seen George since the mill-race and his heart was sick.

He was long since out of ammunition and was only taking up space now—contributing nothing. He devised a plan. He knew that in only a matter of seconds the Rebels would rise up from behind that wall yet again, just as they had a half dozen times before, and concentrate their horrible fire against the new attackers. In that moment, it might be safe for him to move, to crawl or run the two hundred feet or so to where George's company would probably be. He closed his eyes and waited for the thunder he knew was coming.

When the Rebel muskets exploded, James stood, and using Caldwell's entire brigade as a shield, bent at the waist and ran to his left along the lines of blue soldiers lying on the swale. There was no such thing as a regiment or a company on this hillside. There were men from twenty or more different regiments all mixed up together. It was only by the sheerest stroke of luck that James spotted a man he recognized. Douglas Davis—a boy from home.

"Douglas—" The tone in James's voice was desperate. "Have you seen George?"

Davis shook his head. "Not since the canal."

James couldn't tolerate it any longer. He stood, and over the constant roaring of the Rebel guns he shouted, "GEORGE!"

Davis grabbed the distraught young man and pulled him back down to the ground. "*James*—it won't do your momma no good if *you* get killed just looking for George!"

McClernan knew he was right, but the anguish of not knowing was about to drive him mad.

Davis put his hand on James's shoulder. "He might be here, mixed up in this mess of men. He might still be up on the hill, but even that don't mean that he's dead. Either way there ain't a darned thing you can do about it, and you'll find it all out in God's good time."

Washington, D.C.

Lincoln continued to doze in his chair in the War Office
telegraph room, and Edwin Stanton noticed the book
in his lap. It was George Livermore's book about Negroes in the Revolutionary Army. The Secretary of War was
thrilled to see the President reading it, but decided it wasn't
enough. He went to his office and retrieved a file—a battlefield report from South Carolina he'd received several weeks
ago. He only wanted to have it handy when Lincoln awoke.

Marye's Heights

Like all of the other brigadiers who had gone before him,
John Caldwell watched in horror as his beautiful regiments were violently wasted in front of the wall. He
had been so certain that *his* men would make it—that *his* men
would offer the bayonet to the Rebels on the hill—that *his*
men were sure to succeed where so many others had failed,
and yet, in less than fifteen minutes of fighting, his brigade
was finished and in full retreat—just like everybody else's.

As his men turned to retreat back to the swale, Caldwell
tried to rally them as best he could. A bullet grazed his arm
and several staff officers fell dead as they followed him
along the lines. He directed Colonel Nelson Miles to lead
two of his New York regiments to the extreme right of the
line, to ward off any potential Confederate counterattack.

Caldwell finally had to admit that he was beaten. The
flood of men back down the hill was unstoppable, and he realized at last that even *his* men—the bravest and best-trained
in the entire Army of the Potomac—that even they had been
soundly licked. No army on earth could take that wall.

As his men stormed the swale to cower there along with
the thousands of others, Caldwell found his own refuge behind the store that was now overflowing with wounded men.
It was there, in the midst of the worst disaster of his career,
that John Caldwell got one of the most pleasant surprises of
his life. There, behind the store, whole, well, and unhurt,
stood his friend Colonel Sam Zook.

"Dear God, Sam. I thought you were dead!"

Zook shook his head and grinned. "That seems to be the common perception of the day, but, as you can see, I'm still worth at least a dozen dead men."

As inappropriate as it was to make a joke at such a time and place, Caldwell couldn't help but smile, mostly just because he was so glad to see Zook alive and well.

There was an increase in the rate of fire from up on the hill, and a group of men gathered behind the store began to yell encouragement to a single soldier running toward them like the proverbial bat out of hell. It was Colonel Miles— the New Yorker Caldwell had sent to the right side of the line to protect his flank.

Miles ducked and swerved as he ran, chased by little splashes of mud squirting out of the ground in his wake, but he finally made it safely to the cheers of a hundred men who never thought it possible. He never even slowed as he approached. He snapped to attention.

"General Caldwell. Beg to report, sir."

"Go ahead, Colonel Miles."

"Sir, my men have made it to within forty yards of the wall on the extreme right flank, sir. They are protected there by a tight board fence." He ran out of what little breath he had after his dangerous run, and bent over double to take a pause to suck in some air. But he had peaked Caldwell's interest.

"Go ahead, Colonel."

He tried to continue between deep breaths. "Well, sir, we can't do it alone, sir, but I believe that a full-scale assault on the wall from my position—fully supported, sir—might be successful."

Caldwell and Zook were astounded and speechless—so Miles continued.

"Sirs—look at all these men." He pointed out over the thousands of soldiers lying on the hillside. "There's more than a full division of perfectly healthy men just lying there wasting ammunition and taking up space."

Zook knew immediately where Miles was headed and began to shake his head even before the colonel could start making his argument.

"I know what you're thinking, Colonel, but those men are exhausted and have very little ammunition left if any at all, and I don't care if you've got a million men and a billion rounds of ammunition, there isn't an army on God's green earth that can breach those lines."

"But that's the beauty of it, sir—they don't have *any* ammunition! They won't be tempted to stop and shoot on the way up! Once we get 'em all stood up, and once they get started, they *have* to go all the way!"

Zook didn't know what to say. It was as if this man hadn't just seen the strength of the defenses. He felt almost sorry for Miles, who kept on ranting like a madman.

Caldwell wanted to agree with Miles, but he just could not. "Colonel . . ."

"They're weak on the right, General. I know they are!"

"Colonel . . ."

"We can make it—my men can get around the right on their own, if you and the others will just support me!"

"Colonel!"

Miles tried desperately to think of something more to say—something that would delay the inevitable—for just one more argument that might win the men over, but his mind went blank. He saw on Caldwell's face that he was not going to be heard no matter what he said.

"First, I must say to you, Colonel, that I have no brigades left to offer you. And those who are left aren't going to stand up and they're sure as hell not going to storm that wall with unloaded muskets . . ."

Miles opened his mouth to speak—to make one more verbal charge—but Caldwell held up his hand and continued, ". . . *and*—after what they have done this day, we have no right to ask them to."

FREDERICKSBURG

Darius Couch had thrown two of his three divisions against the wall. First French, then Hancock. And now, Brigadier General Oliver O. Howard hovered around Couch's headquarters impatiently awaiting his turn.

Couch had moved into the cupola of the courthouse, an obvious target for the Rebel artillery, but Lee's guns were otherwise occupied, so it was safe enough for the moment and offered Couch the best possible view of the field. From this position Burnside's chief naysayer had watched every courageous and devastating assault. He saw no glory there. No point. No hope.

"My God," he said. "My poor boys."

He thought he had whispered it softly enough so that no one else could hear other than himself and God, but General Howard was now so close, waiting for his own orders to go forward, that he had heard it too.

"It *is* God, you know, who is responsible for this, General. It is His will." Howard spoke softly too. Not in the brash and commanding preacher voice he used every Sunday morning to bring the word of the Lord to the hearts of his men. It was a quiet and reassuring voice, but Couch snapped around nonetheless, offended at being spied upon and astounded that any man on earth could look out over this field and see the hand of God. But when he saw that the words came from Howard, it all made sense. "The Christian general" he was called. Some meant it as a sign of respect. Howard was a brand-new general, a brand-new division commander, and a good, old-fashioned, hellfire and brimstone preacher.

"Oh, it's true, General Couch."

Couch said nothing. No point.

"God is testing us. We must prove that we are worthy to carry His sword. This army will free the slaves, General, for that is God's work, but we must first be humbled before His eyes."

Howard glanced down at the place where his right arm should have been—the arm he left somewhere outside of Richmond last summer—as a subtle reminder to Couch that he had personally already passed God's stern test.

Still without a word in response, the corps commander turned his attention back to Marye's Heights and the carnage on the field. His boys.

"It is time now, General Couch," Howard said. "French and Hancock have failed, and my division is your last."

THE PHILLIPS HOUSE

Ambrose Burnside knew nothing of the fighting at
Prospect Hill, but he could clearly see the battle for
Marye's Heights. He knew that Couch had only one
more division that he could commit to the fight and he had
to be prepared for anything that might follow. If Couch's
last charge was successful, he would need a mass of men to
take advantage of that success. If not . . . ? Well, he would
still need a mass of men to try it again—or at the very least
to hold those Rebels right where they were. Whatever might
happen, Burnside needed Hooker's grand division to be in
place and ready to move.

"Order General Hooker to move his entire force across
into the town. It looks as though we are going to need every
man this day."

PROSPECT HILL

George Meade was to have started his assault with the
lifting of the fog—and that was four hours ago.
Since then his men had been facedown in the mud
while the artillery of both sides fired back and forth over
their heads. But now he was startled by a jarring thunder
from the Confederate lines, powerful enough to be heard
and felt in hell—and right behind it another, just as large
and just as loud. Two of Wainwright's gunners had found
their mark at precisely the same moment, and two Confederate caissons, loaded to overflowing with ammunition, exploded, sending huge fireballs and massive chunks of what
used to be men and cannons a hundred yards into the air.
Meade's soldiers, who were lying in the mud, all looked up
to see the flames from the massive blasts and they began to
cheer and pump their fists at the hated Rebels.

For George Gordon Meade it was a moment scripted in
heaven.

"Now, men!" he shouted. "*Now!* Up and forward. Let's
give 'em some hell!"

William Sinclair was ready. His men were ready. They had had enough of cowering in the mud. He mounted his horse and raised his saber and shouted, "Up, men. Guide on center! At the double-quick—*march*!"

FREDERICKSBURG

"Twentieth Massachusetts! Assume your ranks!"

Little Abbott had just started to feel better. He was actually able to drink water now, and keep it down. He wasn't too concerned about the orders. They could mean anything. The town was still tightly packed with men, only now many of them were wounded—walking and otherwise. The streets were filled with ambulances, speeding when they could, but mostly maneuvering slowly through the congested streets, the drivers yelling obscenities at the crowds of men who wouldn't or couldn't get out of the way. The men of the Harvard Regiment and all of the others who had cleared the town of Rebs on Thursday should have been sent back across the river long ago, if for no other reason than to get them out of the way, to make room for the divisions of men whose job it was to finish the fight.

Surely that was it. Surely they were headed back to Falmouth, and possibly even a hot meal.

He staggered into ranks along with everyone else, relieved that the urge to throw up was gone. Some of the men were still giddy from last night's drinking, and giggled, stumbled, and laughed their way into formation, but Captain Macy was deadly serious as he stood before the regiment.

"Gentlemen, you will store your knapsacks in this house here. They will be placed under guard and available for you to retrieve them when we return."

Holy Christ. It wasn't only Little Abbot who thought those words—it was virtually every man in the 20th Mass.

Clara Barton worked in the church, at the dressing station there, doing what she could. When she heard General Stur-

gis's distinctive voice shouting commands, she made her
way out onto the street, where she saw several Massachusetts flags unfurled. First she saw the 20th Mass., and wherever the Harvard Regiment stood, she knew her 21st was
nearby. She pushed her way down the crowded street toward the river until she found her boys. They were lined up
in ranks of four and facing the enemy. They had set aside
their packs and blankets and were ready to move out.

Clara hated it. She knew each and every one of these
boys. She loved them. She had cared for them for over a
year. Every face was precious to her. She knew their names
and their mother's names. She had written letters home for
some who were too hurt or too ill or who didn't know how
to write. She was good by now at fighting back tears. She
put on her best face and waved them on. Only the sight of
Thomas Plunkett marching proudly into battle filled her
eyes. He had been such a boy only a year before. Homesick
and scared. He reminded her of her brother. She had nursed
them both back to health and watched them grow from boy
to man in too short a time. Corporal Plunkett saw her standing off to the side waving her handkerchief and he smiled a
gigantic "wouldn't Momma be proud of me" smile. Clara
smiled back, but she wanted to cry.

PROSPECT HILL

His attack on the Rebel right had been delayed for
hours, but it wasn't Stonewall Jackson or John Pelham who finally ignited George Meade's fury. It
wasn't the insane orders that sent a single division against
an entire corps. No. It was none of these things. It was the
loathsome Bucktails who finally sparked his fuse—the
rough, undisciplined, uncontrollable frontiersmen who had
been the burr under his saddle ever since the day he took
command. Colonel Sinclair had left them behind to guard
the artillery. Of all the units he could have assigned to the
safety of the rear, Sinclair had picked the hated Bucktails,
and the sight of these unsoldiers leaning on their rifles and

cheering others forward sent George Gordon Meade into an uncontrolled rage. He bolted back to the Pennsylvania regiment fully prepared to arrest somebody—or shoot somebody—anybody.

"Who's in command here?"

"I am, sir."

Meade had never seen the captain before. "And who the hell are you?"

"Captain Fred Taylor, sir."

"And you're in charge of these children?"

Taylor bristled. These men had fought at Second Bull Run and South Mountain and Antietam, and he knew that he commanded some of the best fighters, if not the best soldiers, in the entire Army of the Potomac. He made no attempt to disguise the contempt in his voice. "I command the 13th Pennsylvania Volunteers, sir, if that's what you mean."

Now it was Meade's turn to bristle. "Well, command them into the fight, Captain. Now and at the double-quick." He pointed toward Sinclair's other regiments, which were well on their way to the railroad already. "You've got to cover some ground to catch up."

Taylor was now bound and determined to show the blowhard general what his men could do. He had missed the big fights in Maryland, sitting on his warm, comfortable posterior in Annapolis, still officially a prisoner and waiting to be exchanged. The Bucktails had lost most of their officers at Antietam and when he returned he found himself in command by default. His colonelcy was being held up pending approval by the Pennsylvania legislature, and this would be his first day in command of a regiment in a fight. You don't get promoted for guarding cannons.

He ordered the Bucktails into formation. Not a man hesitated.

"At the double-quick—forward—*march*!"

The going was easier for the Bucktails because, as the rest of Meade's division approached the railroad tracks and the Confederate lines, the Southern artillery fire slowed so as not to kill its own men.

Feger Jackson's Brigade was on the left, and the large
Yankee general rode his huge white horse to the middle of
his advancing troops and, as loudly as he could, he yelled
"Charge!" The bugle sounded the call and his men broke
into a run toward the tracks and just as they had built up a
good head of steam, Rebel pickets rose up from a shallow
ditch that ran along the tracks and unleashed a volley that
brought the charge to a quick halt.

True to form, the pickets fired and beat a hasty retreat.
Feger Jackson's Yankees quickly regrouped and resumed
the attack. Finally, after moving over a thousand yards of
open ground under constant artillery fire, his regiments
reached the tracks, but with their very next step James
Archer's Brigade of Rebel veterans stood and unleashed a
horrifying volley squarely into their ranks. It looked to
Jackson as though a hundred of his men all fell in one single
instant. The effect was devastating, and, once again, Feger
Jackson's assault came to a halt as the men fell into the
shallow ditch just vacated by Archer's pickets.

To Jackson's right, Colonel Sinclair's Brigade faced no
such trouble. The artillery fire had slackened and the space
directly in front of them remained inexplicably quiet. Not a
shot came at them from the finger of woods that extended
beyond the tracks, and the men of Sinclair's Brigade funneled themselves into the quiet thicket. Once out of the line
of fire they found themselves knee-deep or deeper in a
soggy marsh where there were thick stands of tall oaks and
patches of green dwarf pines—and not a Rebel to be seen.

After hours of almost constant artillery thunder, the sudden, almost churchlike quiet was ominous. Eerie. There had
to be something very wrong.

Ever since Archer's Rebels had unloaded their rifles on his
attacking lines, Feger Jackson had completely lost control
of his men. His brigade was facedown in the mud for the
third time today, this time in a shallow ditch between the
railroad tracks and Archer's fully packed and well-protected
lines. He couldn't order them back, and he sure as hell
couldn't order them forward, so he did what any sane man

would do. He ordered them to do exactly what they were going to do anyway.

"Rally men! Rally right here!"

He looked to his rear for help just as the Bucktails arrived, and they too dived into the trench. Magilton's Brigade was supposed to be close at hand, and they were. The Rebels took the new troops under fire, with very similar results. Magilton's men rushed forward to find themselves a place of safety in the ditch as well, and the confusion was doubled as each and every man tried to find his own personal haven, but there simply wasn't enough room. In the open and under fire, half of Magilton's Brigade split off to the right, following Sinclair's vanished brigade into the quiet finger of woods.

George Meade's three brigades were disorganized, stretched out, hopelessly pinned down, or vanished into the woods, and still three hundred yards shy of their target.

General John Gibbon had commanded his brigade boldly at Antietam. He had manned an artillery piece himself— Battery B of the 4th U.S.—and turned back John Bell Hood's Texans as they stormed out of the cornfield. His actions on that day had earned him his first division command, but he had almost turned it down because he hated so much leaving his beloved "Black Hats." They had complained when he had ordered them to buy the expensive and distinctive new Hardie Hats, but after Antietam they wouldn't sell them for a thousand greenbacks. They were proud of them—they were proud of themselves, they were proud of their heroic commander, and he was proud of them. But a man has to climb the ladder and a soldier has to go where he is needed. So this day was John Gibbon's first day to command an entire division in battle, but when Meade responded to the exploding caissons and ordered his assault on the railroad tracks, Gibbon simply wasn't ready. First of all, he wasn't *ordered* forward at all. His assignment from General Franklin was for his division to "support" Meade and guard his right flank. But to John Gibbon, that was not an issue. He had no intention of "supporting" Meade from the rear. When the Pennsylvanian moved forward, Gibbon intended all along to move forward with him. It was not reluctance or a lack of orders that delayed Gibbon's advance. He had greater problems than that. His men cringed under the same artillery fire as Meade's men had, and were thoroughly disorganized, and if there was one thing in this world that John Gibbon hated, it was disorganization. So he didn't bolt forward when Meade did. He got his men up and arranged them in an orderly fashion, each regiment in battlefront formation, each brigade aligned in perfect ranks and files.

But even with that accomplished he had one more thing to do before he ordered his division forward. He called his brigade commanders together—Nelson Taylor, Peter Lyle, and Adrian Root.

"Your target is that hill there—just beyond the railroad tracks." He pointed toward a rise that stood well forward and to the right of the finger of woods, *beyond* where James Lane and his Rebel brigade were well dug in. On that hill were the remains of some slave cabins—and a battery of Rebel artillery.

"We must take those guns, gentlemen—and now it is time. You are professional soldiers and, as you well know, I have taken some chances in promoting each one of you over higher-ranking volunteer officers—make-believe soldiers— so as to have you in command of your brigades on this day."

The three men all nodded. Some very powerful politicians hated Gibbon for what he had done and the professional officers were indebted to him for it.

"Prove me right, gentlemen. Move out."

NEW YORK CITY

There was a perpetual clamor in the offices of the *New York Tribune*. Reporters constantly came and went, yelling at copy boys and editors. The typesetters were in a back room, building the next issue of the *Tribune* one tiny, backwards, metal letter at a time, pounding them into the wooden body of the page with soft hammers. It was a never-ending process that created an unrelenting roar.

But when the gigantic, dignified black man entered the building, all fell silent. Well-dressed, well-groomed black men were a rarity even in the New York offices of the world's foremost abolitionist newspaper, but this man brought with him more than only a unique appearance. He brought with him a grand reputation—and when he stepped through the door, every man in the shop stopped what he was doing to catch a glimpse of Frederick O. Douglass.

They all knew his story. He was a man who escaped from slavery and then risked his own freedom to become a very public crusader against the vile institution. He was perhaps the country's most famous abolitionist lecturer, writer, and publisher. Second, of course, only to their own employer, Horace Greeley. Douglass's oratorical skills, by now, were legendary, and the social elite of New York stood in line to hear him speak.

"Everybody get back to work!"

The voice boomed down from the landing at the top of the stairs, like God thundering an eleventh commandment from on high. Of course it was Greeley, who had been summoned by the silence. The two men nodded and smiled like old friends and Greeley waved Douglass up the steps.

"I had expected you before now, Mr. Douglass."

"I've been away. Upstate talking to folks about our President's proclamation."

"And what have you been telling them?"

"That it's a notch better than a worthless scrap of paper."

"A little harsh, don't you think?"

Douglass smiled and nodded. "Of course it is, but it gets people riled up, and as you know, that's what I do best."

"There's no one better at getting people riled up than yourself, Mr. Douglass. But as a practical matter, what do you really think?"

"As a practical matter, that's *exactly* what I think, but freedom is *not* a practical matter. As a practical matter this document frees absolutely no one. As a moral issue, I'm sure Mr. Lincoln sees it as a grand gesture, but my people need more than only a gesture, sir."

"Mr. Lincoln, rightly or wrongly, sees it as a great deal more than only a gesture . . ."

"And I see it as a great deal *less*!" Douglass paused and smiled. "And a great deal more."

Greeley now recognized that this was going to be more than only a quick meeting and finally offered Douglass a chair. "I agree with you, but you must realize, sir, how difficult it was for me to get him to do this much."

Douglass was amused at the newspaperman taking nearly full credit for the emancipation of the slaves, but he didn't show it. "It is better than nothing, I grant you. It is simply such a great disappointment, couched in legal terminology and military justifications. It may be a grand gesture, Mr. Greeley, but it is a poor document."

Greeley hadn't prepared himself for an argument on syntax and didn't quite know what to say. It didn't matter though, because Douglass had just launched into his lecture circuit speech, and he was nowhere near finished.

"Had there been one expression of sound moral feeling against slavery; one word of regret and shame that this accursed system has remained so long the disgrace and scandal of the Republic; one word of satisfaction in the hope of burying slavery and the rebellion in one common grave, then a thrill of joy would have run around the world! But no such word was said."

By now, Greeley was mesmerized by Douglass's eloquent words and elegant tones. *If he weren't black*, Greeley thought, *he would be governor*. For once in his life, Horace Greeley was perfectly content to sit and listen.

"That being said, sir . . ." Douglass smiled. "It is the first step out of Egypt for my people. And it is my fervent hope that very soon we will be allowed to fight on our *own* behalf, and when that happens, sir, this war, this noble effort, will at last be sanctified. Your friend, Mr. Lincoln, has failed to do even that."

"So he has, Mr. Douglass. But that day will come."

"But there are rumors that concern me, and that brings me to the purpose of my visit."

"Rumors?"

"Rumors that Mr. Lincoln will renege on his promise. That his party's recent setbacks have convinced him to set the proclamation aside. For all of its flaws, Mr. Greeley, we cannot allow that to happen."

Greeley hesitated. He had heard the same rumors, and probably from the same unreliable sources, and he was reluctant to lend them any credence. At the same time, if there were any truth whatsoever in them, Douglass would be a powerful ally in convincing the President to hold his ground.

"I do not believe that Mr. Lincoln would do such a thing. He may be slow in deciding a thing, but once done he stands firm. Nonetheless, I have heard similar concerns. Democrats are talking impeachment—or at least accusing the President of 'high crimes and misdemeanors.' But they're just feeling their oats after their recent successes. They still don't have the votes to impeach."

"Praise God for that."

"Amen."

"And to the front, Mr. Greeley—what do we hear of Burnside?"

"The army is across the Rappahannock. I expect the fight is on."

"Let us pray for a victory then, sir. I'm not sure the President—and the proclamation—could withstand a defeat."

CHAPTER 14

MARYE'S HEIGHTS

After all Henry Villard had seen, he couldn't believe he was seeing it again. The *Tribune* reporter was beyond appalled—he was livid as he watched yet another division march forward toward the stone wall.

"Dummkopfs!"

He said it aloud as he scrawled it in large letters on his pad. Then, just in case anyone had missed it before, he said it again. Louder this time.

He recognized the banner of the 20th Massachusetts as it paraded past him. He knew who these men were. The Harvard Regiment.

Mein Gott! The reporter from Germany was heartsick for his adoptive country. *These are our finest young men—the intellectual aristocracy of America who we are sending up that hill to die, many before their twentieth birthdays.*

He finally remembered his place—he was a reporter—here to write down what he saw. But his anger refused to be set aside.

He wrote, *"Fresh brigades of valueless men vanished into a thick cloud of white artillery smoke. I do not expect to see them come back out again."*

Prospect Hill

George Meade knew that his attack was falling apart.
Feger Jackson's men were pinned down in the railroad
ditch with some of Magilton's men alongside. Others
who couldn't find a space in the ditch were on their faces behind Feger Jackson's lines, hopelessly vulnerable to the Confederates' incessant fire. Magilton himself had led the balance of his brigade into the swampy woods, following Sinclair.
Meade was angry and frustrated. He needed to be three men.
He wanted to be in direct command of all three brigades, in three different spots on the field all at the same time, and to the best of his ability, that was exactly what he intended to do.

"Lieutenant Dehon!"

"Sir!"

"Go to General Jackson and instruct him to extricate his men from that fire and move them to the right, into the woods. We shall re-form and continue the attack from there! Tell him to report to me—I'll be with Sinclair."

As Dehon rode to the left to deliver Jackson's new orders, Meade headed for the finger of woods to find Sinclair and Magilton. After the hours of constant cannon and musket fire, the scene in the wooded swamp seemed almost serene. The sounds of battle were distant and almost dreamlike. Hundreds of men quietly and cautiously inched forward, as if they were trying to sneak up on a pack of angry wolves. Most were knee-deep in cold slime and struggled with every step. With every yard Meade advanced into the woods, the packs of men grew thicker until he reached the railroad track—the only dry and stable land in sight.

He smiled when he saw Sinclair, the twenty-four-year-old colonel, moving calmly along the tracks, reorganizing his troops, preparing them to pick up the fight.

"Skirmishers forward, Colonel," Meade said. "Let them find out what lies ahead."

Sinclair was mildly irritated at the obvious instructions, but only nodded and ordered the 6th Pennsylvania Volunteers forward while the rest of the brigade prepared to follow in force.

Magilton spotted Meade and thought it prudent to check in. Meade was glad to see him. The situation was improving.

"Press your men behind the 1st Brigade as closely as possible, Colonel, and be prepared to take advantage of any success that they might have."

Conrad Feger Jackson was a giant of a man astride an enormous, white horse. In full view of his men *and* Archer's, he rode tall in the saddle. He was the favorite target of every Rebel within five hundred yards, but he ignored the swarm of bullets until his favorite charger took a bullet to the brain and went down. The general was angry but unhurt and stood up immediately, sword in hand, intent on leading a new charge against Archer's lines. Without instructions from Meade it seemed his only option.

He heard the sound of a horse approaching at a run and glanced to his right to see Lieutenant Dehon of General Meade's staff whipping his horse along the tracks.

Thank God, Jackson thought. *Help—at last.*

Dehon had to shout to be heard over the rifle fire. "General Jackson, sir. General Meade instructs that you should . . ."

The young lieutenant's chest exploded. He fell from his horse and landed facedown directly at Jackson's feet.

Shocked and now almost in panic, the general looked down at the messenger's body and cursed. The death of the young man didn't concern him. Hundreds of men were dying around him with every passing minute. But he was frustrated and furious that he hadn't gotten Meade's orders. Two seconds more and he would have known what to do, but now, with his men dying uselessly around him, he . . .

A Rebel bullet shattered Feger Jackson's skull and he fell instantly dead into the ditch with his men.

In accordance with General Meade's orders, Colonel Magilton moved back away from the railroad tracks to organize his men before moving them forward. To "press them closely" against Sinclair's leading brigade. The problem was that he didn't really have a brigade anymore—at least not one that he could find. Some of them were in the railroad ditch with Feger Jackson's Brigade over on the left, and some had wandered off to the right where the sound of muskets told Magilton that something was going very wrong. His rookie regiment, the 142nd Pennsylvania, was out of the woods and pouring a relentless volley into *Sinclair's* rear.

"Hold your fire!" Magilton was desperate to get the regiment under control and to end the savage killing of their own troops.

William Sinclair had his brigade aligned along the tracks, and prepared to march out in force through the marsh and back into the fight. The skirmishers had encountered small numbers of Rebel pickets, but no serious resistance whatsoever. The dozen or so Rebel pickets positioned in the bog reported back to their commanders—Archer on the right and Lane on the left. None bothered to report to Maxcy Gregg—dead square in the middle.

Sinclair's Brigade stepped off smartly from the railroad tracks, headed up the hill and aimed directly at Gregg's unsuspecting Rebels. Just as he ordered his men forward a Rebel minié ball smashed his left foot.

Feger Jackson was dead, William Sinclair was wounded, and Albert Magilton was desperately trying to silence the rifles of the 142nd Pennsylvania Volunteers, who he thought were firing at Sinclair's men.

They weren't.

MARYE'S HEIGHTS

It was no longer the whiskey and hardtack from last night that caused Little Abbott's stomach to churn as he marched up the hill under constant fire from the Rebel artillery. But neither was it the fear of dying. It was the fear of dying *needlessly*.

"*Winnowed out,*" General Howard will say. "*Deemed unfit to carry God's sword.*"

The Reverend General Oliver Otis Howard is a pious, sanctimonious moron, Little thought. The very idea of dying on Howard's behalf sent a new wave of nausea through his intestines.

For the Southern soldiers who were trying to kill him, he felt very little animosity. Not the way he had on Thursday in the streets of Fredericksburg when the Rebels were hiding in alleys and doorways and windows and murdering his men one at a time. The Confederates today were fighting like soldiers and only doing their duty—the same way Little himself would were the boot on the other foot. All of Little's animosity was now aimed at the imbecilic Union generals who made the Rebs' bloody work so ludicrously easy. That's what Little Abbott was thinking when a round of solid shot came lofting in from his right, scattering the boys of the Harvard Regiment. All escaped and the line quickly re-formed without Abbott even having to say a word. *Wonderful boys,* he thought. Well-trained veterans now, what was left of them, and after the disasters at Ball's Bluff and Antietam and the street fighting on Thursday, there were precious few of them left. They would be lucky if *any* would live until tomorrow.

McClellan, he thought. *Dear God, please send us back McClellan.*

PROSPECT HILL

On the left, Feger Jackson's Brigade was without a commander, hopelessly pinned down in a shallow ditch and helplessly taking bullets like practice range bull's eyes. Unable to tolerate the senseless dying a second longer, a single man stood and ran. He was followed by another and then by ten more. But these sons of Pennsylvania didn't run *away* from the murderous enemy fire— they ran to it. Following the lead of this small band of heroes, with bayonets fixed and at the ready, the 11th Pennsylvania burst out of the ditch and toward Archer's lines only to be met by a wall of smoke, a deafening roar, and a thousand bullets. Then came the Bucktails, but they had too much ground to cover and the Rebels had time to reload. They exploded another volley that sent a hundred men to the ground dead or wounded. And then, with the bad boys of Meade's division decimated and caught in open ground, on came the 5th cheering like madmen, and after the 5th, the 7th, and finally James Archer's firmly entrenched Rebel lines started to feel some heat.

The Rebel general called for a courier.

"Sir!"

"Find General Gregg and alert him that we are experiencing considerable fire here and may soon require assistance."

Albert Magilton had finally gotten the rookie 142nd to lie down and stop shooting at Sinclair's men and was on his way back into the woods to assume command of the attack when a bullet found his horse. The animal fell on the colonel's left leg and pinned him to the ground. There was nothing that Magilton could do but lie there and pray for someone to come along and help him up.

In the middle of the Rebel side of the line, Maxcy Gregg's Brigade was sunning itself.

They were posted behind the bog, between and behind Archer and Lane, and their aging, deaf, atheistic, Stonewall Jackson–hating General Gregg was perfectly content that no organized force of Yankees would be able to wade through the slimy ground in front of him to threaten his position. John Bell Hood agreed. Powell Hill agreed. Stonewall Jackson agreed. It was the only thing on which Hill and Jackson had agreed in six months or more. There was simply no way. Even if some ragged company did manage to slosh their way forward through the mire, Archer and Lane had pickets posted in there to warn Gregg of their approach. Gregg was so confident that he had even ordered his men to stack arms, to keep them from firing on Lane's men to their front left or Archer's to their front right.

But now the shooting on his right, on Archer's side of the line, was louder and closer, and Gregg's South Carolinians unstacked their arms and began firing. Gregg was terrified and furious.

"Stop firing!"

They either couldn't hear him or they chose to ignore him, so he mounted his horse and placed himself between

his own men and whoever it was they were firing at.
"You're firing at our friends!" He rode along in front of
them swearing and batting down the muzzles of their rifles,
repeating time and again that there were no Yankees in the
woods.

Maxcy Gregg was a good officer. He had led these men
through the worst of their times. At Manassas back in August, wave after merciless wave of Yankee troops had pushed
them back and back until there was no place left for them to
go. "Let us die here, my men," Gregg had shouted that day.
He had drawn his sword and stood tall, fully prepared to die
with them until Powell Hill had come to their rescue. Two
weeks later it was Gregg who had led them on the seventeen-
mile march from Harpers Ferry to Sharpsburg and won them
their glory by turning the tide of the fight at the very end of
the day, saving the Army of Northern Virginia from almost
certain destruction. These men had been through hell with
Maxcy Gregg, and if he said it, it must be so.

They restacked their arms and had just made themselves
comfortable when a thousand screaming Yankees poured
out of the woods and Gregg's beloved South Carolina
brigade began to fall by the hundreds. They scurried forward to try to grab their guns, but it was far too late already.
The general pulled his pistol but wasn't able to fire a shot
before he was jolted off his horse. He tried to remain
mounted but could not. He hit the ground hard, but it didn't
really hurt until he tried to stand and couldn't. The bullet
had nicked his spine, and the proud, scholarly aristocrat lay
on the ground, paralyzed from the waist down. A half dozen
men lifted him up and carried him with them as they got the
hell out of harm's way in a hurry.

Lieutenant Evan Woodward was lost. There were plenty of
fellow Yankees around, but not a soul he recognized. He
was only twenty-four years old, but he was already a hard-
ened veteran of the Peninsula campaign, Second Manassas,
and Antietam. He had enlisted as a private, been elected
sergeant-major, and his brand-new lieutenant's bars weren't
even dirty yet—and now he was lost in the middle of a fight.
His 2nd Pennsylvania Volunteers were God only knows

where off to his right, and the young adjutant found himself the only officer in a disorganized gaggle of strangers. When he saw the colors of the 11th Pennsylvania Volunteers, he realized that it was even worse than he had thought. Not only was it not his regiment, they weren't even from his brigade! But they were all in the same trouble now. They were ducking fire from both sides as the other Yankee regiments pressed their desperate, helter-skelter attacks. The fire "his" men were taking was as likely to be from Union rifles as from Confederate and he knew only that they had to move. He looked around for an officer. Any officer. There was not one. Now, not only was he lost and separated from his regiment—he was suddenly in command for the first time in his life, and if he didn't do something every one of these men would die.

Even though these soldiers didn't know Evan Woodward from Adam's house cat, when he ordered them to wheel left, they saw the benefit immediately and, at that moment, to them, this shave-tail lieutenant was Napoleon Bonaparte, Frederick the Great, and George Brinton McClellan all rolled into one.

Halfway through the maneuver and quite by mistake, they found themselves fully astride the Rebel's extreme left flank—looking down a hill and straight into the Rebel trenches and they laid down an enfilade fire that struck the 19th Georgia like a battering ram. The Rebels were totally defenseless, and yet Woodward's men continued taking fire. He knew damned well that it wasn't the Georgians down the hill who were shooting at him—he could see them. It had to be the Yanks in front who were overshooting the Rebs or taking his men deliberately under fire, thinking they were the enemy. He waved his blue hat in the air, to try to signal Feger Jackson's men to shoot a little more carefully, but the fire continued.

Woodward was exhausted. His men were exhausted. They were running low on ammunition and taking fire from their own friends. He had to do *some*thing, he just didn't know what. Then, to the utter amazement of his men, Evan Woodward stood bolt upright in the face of staggering fire, and ran, rolled, and tumbled down the hill directly into the

Confederate earthworks! He staggered to a stop nose to nose with a Rebel soldier, who was just too shocked to kill the crazed Yankee.

The Reb and the Yank just stared at each other while Woodward caught his breath, but in that time both men spoke without speaking. They looked at each other with pleading expressions that said, "Please, let's don't do this. Please, let this thing be over."

After a moment Woodward was finally able to speak. "Would you care to surrender?"

"We'll surrender if you let us."

The 19th Georgia handed over their colors to the brave or crazy young lieutenant and Jay Archer's Confederate brigade was suddenly one regiment short.

James Jay Archer was a Maryland man, a Princeton graduate, and a hero of the Mexican War. He had left the army after that fight was won and returned to Baltimore to practice law. But for him the satisfaction of writing a proper contract never quite matched the thrill of storming the ramparts at Chapultepec, and in 1855 he rejoined the United States Army.

Now he stood with the South, and while his men were feeling some heat, his lines continued to hold strong. Some ragtag Federal units were putting on a gallant show, trying to claw their way across open ground to his trenches, but they were falling like leaves in autumn and still had a long way to come before they could seriously threaten his men head-on. So when occasional shots began coming at him from his rear, he was considerably more irritated than concerned.

Gregg's men, he thought. He still hadn't heard back from the courier he had sent to alert the half-deaf old general, but it really hadn't been that long ago, and it was only a warning—not an actual request for reinforcements.

Apparently Gregg had come anyway and positioned his men to Archer's rear, and now they were killing their fellow Rebels by mistake. Archer prepared to mount his horse to ride up the hill to take command of Gregg's men himself and put a stop to this unnecessary killing when the fire from behind that had been a light drizzle suddenly came down in a torrential storm of lead. He glanced up the hill and saw just the very tip of a flag—not nearly half, but enough to know now that these were not Gregg's men coming to his aid. It was the flag of the United States of America and James Jay Archer suddenly realized that he was in very serious trouble.

Feger Jackson was dead, William Sinclair was wounded, and Alfred Magilton lay helplessly pinned under his wounded horse. And yet, more by accident than by plan, George Gordon Meade's single little leaderless division had broken Stonewall Jackson's lines dead in the middle.

Meade rode out beyond the finger of woods to check on Gibbon's progress and found him just moments away from clashing with the enemy on the right. He turned to his rear and saw a full Union division "parked" on the Bowling Green Road.

Birney. Just sitting there.

General David Birney's division was from Hooker's Center Grand Division, General Stoneman's corps, sent to Prospect Hill in support. Birney's men were formed up a mile to the rear and ready to move. Perfect. *If only they'll hurry.*

"Damn!" Meade bristled. *"Courier!"*

MARYE'S HEIGHTS

Little Abbott didn't have time for blame placing and name calling any longer.

The Harvard Regiment had made it more or less intact to the millrace, but by now the tattered and plankless bridges were crowded with retreaters from the previous attacks. Most of them wounded—some of them not.

Abbott had no idea how his men were supposed to get across the formidable ditch and neither did Colonel Hall. Hall knew of no command in the tactics manual that applied to his current dilemma, so he made one up.

"Make it through as best you can, boys, and regroup on the other side."

The men of the 20th Massachusetts and the rest of the men of Hall's Brigade ran, slipped, tumbled, and fell into the muddy water and, as badly as they wanted to stay there, they managed somehow to climb back out and re-form on the opposite bank.

The Rebel artillery came in now hotter than ever and it was almost impossible to hold ranks. The swale was blanketed with men, all of them just lying there, trying desperately not to draw attention to themselves. There were still the remnants of fences to be gotten around and dozens of dead and wounded horses provided safe havens for the vanquished, but major obstacles for new attackers.

Little had to keep a close eye on his platoon now, small though it was, to keep them from getting disconnected or wandering off in the wrong direction. As foolhardy as this attack was, he still had his job to do—his duty to perform.

THE PHILLIPS HOUSE

Ambrose Burnside smiled like a boy on Christmas morning as he read his latest dispatch from General Hardie, who had delivered Burnside's initial orders to Franklin hours ago, and who continued to observe the fight on Prospect Hill.

MEADE HAVING CARRIED A PORTION OF THE ENEMY'S POSITION IN THE WOOD, WE HAVE THREE HUNDRED PRISONERS. ENEMY'S BATTERIES ON OUR EXTREME LEFT RETIRED. TOUGH WORK. MEN FIGHT WELL. DRIVING THE ENEMY. MEADE HAS SUFFERED SEVERELY; DOUBLEDAY, TO MEADE'S LEFT, NOT ENGAGED.

Burnside was ecstatic. *It's working! After all the naysayers, after all the missteps, after all the delays, it's working. Sumner has to hold Lee's left in place and Franklin has to turn his right, and the whole plan will come together,* he thought, *just as I had planned it.*

PROSPECT HILL

In Archer's trenches Confederate Lieutenant Colonel James Lockert heard a tremendous commotion to his left. He didn't know what it was but he knew immediately that it couldn't be good. His 14th Tennessee had enough problems with the disorganized hordes of Yankees clawing their way toward his front and sporadic fire coming down from the rear, and now it seemed his left flank was in jeopardy as well. He moved to that side of his line just in time to see the remnants of the 19th Georgia being escorted off the field by their Yankee captors.

He didn't even have time to swear properly before the Yankees poured into his nice, safe little trench, screaming like Comanches and firing from a sure-fire angle at point-blank range. Many of his men died, some surrendered, and hundreds bolted and ran. Their only route of escape was along the rear of Archer's lines, left-to-right, behind the next regiment in line—the 7th Tennessee.

Lieutenant John Moore saw the cowards first and without so much as a thought he jumped out of his trench in a fury and started grabbing fleeing Rebels and tried to push them back down into line. He called them every vile name that came to mind. At that moment he hated them far more than he did the Yankees. The Yankees, at least, were brave men of honor and pride—these turn-tail-and-run Rebels were more despicable than Judas himself.

Soon officers and men from the 7th followed Moore's example and began to confront the cowards from the 14th but to no purpose whatsoever. The 14th Tennessee had seen enough. They knew full well what lay in store for the men who were next in line.

"You're surrounded, you danged fool!" one man yelled at Moore. "And half of the whole damned Yankee army is coming up right behind me." He started to say more, but didn't have time. He pushed Moore out of the way and kept on running.

Moore was quickly overrun by hundreds of shirkers who pushed past him like a stampede of terrified horses. His fury got the best of him and he turned and unloaded his pistol, not into the faces of the oncoming Yankees, but into the backs of the running Rebs. As he removed the cylinder to reload, a chill ran down his spine at the sound of Evan Woodward's screaming Yankees pouring down and over his line like a river from a burst dam. Men on both sides roared like angry lions as the fight degenerated into a desperate barroom brawl—a bludgeon and bayonet fight that saw faces shattered with muskets swung like baseball bats and brave men pierced through the gut, not with hot lead but cold steel. This was face-to-face fighting—look-the-other-man-square-in-the-eye-and-kill-him-anyway fighting. Ugly. Mean. Personal.

Marye's Heights

James McClernan still desperately searched for his brother, George. Whenever the Rebels were distracted, or their fire slowed for any reason, he made his way along the lines looking for him. He looked back down the hill and saw a fresh brigade cresting the swale, headed for the wall.

James couldn't just watch them march by anymore. For over two hours he had watched brigade after brigade march up the hill and in only a matter of minutes—sometimes only seconds—some of them would come tumbling back down again. But only some of them. The rest remained on the hill, dead, wounded, dying—maybe just like George. The thought of his brother lying on the ground up there next to the wall made him want to rise up and stop the madness all by himself. He watched as the regimental colors of the 20th Massachusetts passed directly by him and he couldn't watch another man go up that hill.

He grabbed a captain's coat as the man marched by.

"Don't go up there, Captain! For God's sake, don't take these boys up that hill!"

It was the last thing in the world Little Abbott had expected. He was focused on the wall now, and fully prepared to die, and suddenly here was this very sad young soldier pleading with him to stop—to turn around—to save his men from being wasted in a senseless charge. But of course he couldn't do it. He couldn't stop this attack. He couldn't even slow it down at this point. He knew the order to double-quick was only seconds away and he had to be ready. But he did steal a quick look at the man. His eyes were tearful and pleading. They were the eyes of a defeated army. This man's past was Little Abbott's future, and Abbott knew it full well—but there was nothing he could do to change it. Nothing.

He heard Hall's command and quickly he heard it again—repeated by Macy . . .

"At the double-quick . . ."

PROSPECT HILL

Fred Taylor was the most frustrated man on the field. He was still furious at General Meade for his slanderous remarks about his precious Bucktails and still wanted desperately to prove to the old snake that the 13th Pennsylvania was the fightingest regiment in his division—maybe even in the whole Army of the Potomac—regardless of their refusal to submit to the mindless rules and regulations the army loved so dearly. He also wanted to prove to Governor Curtain and the Pennsylvania legislature that he was the most qualified man in the country to command this boldly undisciplined, ragamuffin regiment. But for the past half hour he and his Bucktails had been pinned down between the railroad tracks and the Rebel lines at the base of Prospect Hill. Lead had poured in on them the entire time almost without pause. Alexander the Great would not have had the courage to stand on this field.

But suddenly the firing slowed noticeably. Captain Taylor lifted his head and was amazed to see the Stars and Stripes flying directly in the middle of the Rebel lines. The smoke had cleared and he could plainly see the hand-to-hand fighting going on in the trenches. True to Bucktail form he didn't bother to call his men to attention or arrange them in line of battle. He stood before them, mounted his horse, drew his saber, and shouted, "Thirteenth Pennsylvania—*charge*!"

They stood and ran, not in straight lines at the precisely paced, regulation "double-quick," but as a mob, as fast as they could run, screaming directly into Archer's lines to join the 11th Pennsylvania in their brawl with the 7th Tennessee.

The men of the 7th had seen their fellow Tennesseans bolt and run, but these "volunteers" had no run in them. They, by God, would stand and fight to the last man. And stand and fight they did.

Taylor led the Bucktails on horseback. He brandished his saber and fired his pistol and leaped into the Rebel lines looking every bit like an oil painting on the wall of a museum, but at the moment the Bucktails joined in the fight Archer's next regiment in line turned to face the oncoming Yankees and Taylor's horse was the first to die in the fusillade. He stood and continued to fight on foot, using his empty pistol as a hammer to beat back the determined Rebels until a bullet crushed his right shoulder. He fell to his knees and examined his wound. The arm was lost, he was sure of that. He couldn't move it and he could actually see his own shattered bones through the open wound. And then he looked at his hands. They were brilliant red with the blood of the Confederate soldiers he had whipped with his pistol. The leader of the Bucktails felt suddenly faint, but he fought it off and kept up the fight.

George Meade was a man who simply knew no fear, but he also knew he was too needed to die senselessly. He was not a commander who could sit safely on some distant hill watching the battle through a telescope and issuing orders that could take an hour to get where they needed to be. That's what corps commanders did. But as a division commander, he needed to be seen so he could be easily found if needed, a duty that came with a built-in life-or-death dilemma. If his own men could see him, so could the Rebs, and a mounted general was a most favorite target. So be it. Bullets buzzed around him everywhere he went but he made no effort to dodge them. He knew full well that a man under fire was just as likely to catch a bullet that way as to miss one. So he sat tall astride his horse just to the rear, only yards from the fight, and fought the urge to draw his sword and pull his pistol and ride forward to kill some Rebels himself.

At this moment all he could do was watch the frantic struggle in the Confederate lines and yell encouragement as though he could be heard as well as seen.

"That's the way, boys! Give 'em hell! Give 'em the bayonet!"

He watched and he smiled and he thought about how grand and handsome a scene it was. The Rebel lines that had appeared so impenetrable only minutes ago were full of the most beautiful Yankees ever to take a field. The flag waved proudly as his men raged into the enemy's midst. This is what it's all about—all the training, all the tactics, all the planning, and maneuvering are designed to get the men close enough to give the enemy the bayonet. It took all the discipline of George Meade's soul to stay back and not join in the melee himself.

God, what a beautiful thing.

He could see Gibbon's division moving grandly forward to protect him from a Rebel brigade on his right, but right now he was inches away from success on his left. He sent messengers back to Reynolds and Franklin demanding more men to finish the job and turn the Rebel flank. It was just what Burnside had planned. No one had thought it would work, but these Pennsylvania boys, Meade's men, had done with a division what even he had thought couldn't be done with a corps. One more division sent in right now, directly into those Rebel trenches, might just win the day. Just one more division.

He looked to his rear again to check on the progress of Birney's division—and there they sat—still a mile away, camped on the Bowling Green Road and going nowhere. Meade sent *another* messenger to Birney. "My division has breached the Rebel lines. Come now!"

Already angry at Birney, what he saw next exploded his temper into an uncontrollable rage. A few of his men, his beautiful Yankees, began to leave the trenches and straggle to the rear. These were not wounded men looking for help— they were cowards. Nothing more. Pure and simple. Not many. First one, then four—but trickles turn into floods—

this one was made even worse when he saw that the first coward to abandon the fight was an officer. A still wet-behind-the-ears lieutenant to be sure, but an officer nonetheless.

The general wasn't even momentarily distracted by the bullet that past through his hat as he pushed his horse to intercept the little yellow bastard.

"Back into the fight, you worthless coward, or I shall shoot you myself!"

The poor, terrified boy was covered in blood. His body shook from exhaustion and fear. He had made his decision. He had been brave for long enough and no one had any right to ask him to do any more—not even General Meade. He had stormed the Rebel lines. He had seen enough men die and may have even killed a few himself, and he just couldn't go back. He just couldn't. Without thinking he raised his rifle and pointed it directly at the outraged general's heart. Meade's fury exploded into wrath. He snarled viciously at the boy, drew his sword, and in a single motion brought the flat side down across the lieutenant's head so hard that the blade snapped in two. The boy staggered backward and dropped the rifle. Meade threw the worthless hilt of the sword to the ground and drew his sidearm. He held it not a foot from the poor child's face and pulled back the hammer.

"Go back *now,* Lieutenant, or die right here."

Pain, fear, rage, and shame filled the boy's eyes with tears, but he had just enough pride left to deny Meade the satisfaction of seeing them. He came to attention, performed a flawless about-face, and marched back to the fight.

"General Meade."

"Report."

"General Birney sends his regards, sir, and begs to remind the general that his division is attached to General Stoneman's corps, and, while he is assigned here to cooperate with General Reynolds, he is only required to respond to orders issued by General Stoneman or Reynolds. He wishes to inform the general that he has at hand only two of his three brigades, as General Robinson's Brigade is guarding the bridges and the entire army's line of retreat. He begs to remind you also, sir that he too is a division commander and is not under the command of any other division commander."

Meade was about to explode. His brave men were in a desperate hand-to-hand fight. He had expected Birney to relish the idea of "riding to the rescue," of being the man who broke the Rebel defenses and turned Stonewall Jackson's flank. He had expected Birney to come forward instantly and at the double-quick—instead what he got was a lecture in protocol.

The courier had more to say, but Meade was in no mood to listen. He put the spurs to his horse and raced to the Bowling Green Road, where General Birney calmly waited for suitable orders to arrive through proper channels. What he got was not "proper." In no uncertain terms and in language that would have made Hooker blush, Meade tore into Birney like a wolf into a lamb.

"I don't know where General Reynolds is! I don't know where General Stoneman is, and I don't have time to look for them! I know where *you* are, and I know that we're going to have only one chance to win this fight and that chance is *right now*! In ten minutes it will be gone."

Birney continued to hesitate, but if Meade was right, his options were to be the man who won the fight or the man who lost it.

"General Birney, I assume the authority of ordering you up to support my men."

Finally, after almost a ten-minute delay, Birney's division began the long march to the railroad tracks.

General Jubal Early sat in the sun warming his rheumatic bones and waiting for orders. His division was posted in reserve, well behind A. P. Hill's. He had heard from no one since Pelham had opened the battle over three hours ago and he was beginning to think everyone had forgotten he was there. That was until three messengers arrived from three different directions, all at a run and all at the same time.

"A message from General Jackson, sir."

The other two held their peace while Early got his orders from Stonewall.

"General Jackson sends his regards, sir, and instructs you to move your division to the right, sir, to Hamilton's Crossing, and to hold there for further instructions."

"Sir!" The second courier was visibly shaken and almost in a panic. "General Archer's Brigade is on the verge of collapse, sir. He begs the general to come forward with all possible speed. He fears that without immediate reinforcements he will be compelled to withdraw. He sent to General Gregg for help, sir, but General Gregg has not responded."

Now it was the third man's turn.

"General Gregg is down, sirs, and his brigade has been routed. That space between our brigades has been breached, General, and Yankees are pouring through our lines."

Jackson's messenger decided it was time to pull rank. "General *Jackson's* orders are that you should . . ."

"To arms!"

Early's men responded in an instant and very quickly the entire division was up and in formation. These were the men who had survived the freezing, sleepless, late-night march and had arrived on the field hungry and sleepy only early this morning. But they were rested and fed now, and ready for the fight.

"General Jackson's orders are probably a half an hour old, Captain." Early had made up his mind. He was already in trouble with his commanding officer from the drinking incident on the march, but that was a different issue. He would answer to Stonewall later—right now he had to answer the call to battle.

To Archer's courier he said, "Tell General Archer to hold fast—we are on our way."

Colonel Albert Magilton had been trapped under his wounded horse for what seemed like an eternity. He kept kicking the poor, tormented beast for all he was worth, but the animal wouldn't budge. The colonel endured agonizing frustration as he lay there, listening to the roar of the battle

he was supposed to be leading. He could even see the action
on his right and his frustration was tripled when he realized
that the last order he had given had been wrong. He had ordered the 142nd Pennsylvania to cease firing at the Union
troops to their right, but now he knew what the rookies of
the 142nd had known all along. They weren't Union troops
at all—they were A. P. Hill's extreme left flank—Lane's
Brigade. It was like being trapped in a ring of Dante's hell
as he lay there, unable to move, unable to call out, unable to
save his poor boys, who were dying because of his own stupid blunder. He cursed and kicked his wounded horse again
and then he prayed to God for someone to rescue his helpless men who had dutifully obeyed their orders and held
their fire. His horse didn't respond, but God, at last, did.

He thanked the Almighty a dozen times when regiments
of his own brigade, or maybe Sinclair's—who knew at this
point—came out of the woods and took the Rebel lines under fire and he almost wept as he saw the lead brigade of
Gibbon's division joining the fight at last.

It was Brigadier General Nelson Taylor's Brigade that
led Gibbon's assault against A. P. Hill's left flank, and right
now they were catching hell from a battery of guns that had
been hot all day—the one on the hill where Mr. Bernard's
slave cabins used to be before the Rebels had torn them
down to put cannons there.

Magilton helplessly watched Taylor's men parade over
the open ground as shot and shell from nine or ten or God
only knew how many Rebel guns exploded into them. But
they didn't stop. They didn't pause.

"God bless you, boys," he whispered. There was no sense
in yelling. "Now, for God's sake, hurry."

The longer he watched the magnificent march, the more
frustrated he became. He cursed as loudly as he could and
kicked his poor, wounded horse one more time.

Evan Woodward was still in the Rebel trenches along with
the exhausted men of the 2nd and 11th Pennsylvania. The
Bucktails and the other volunteer regiments had joined the
fray as well, but they just couldn't keep it up very much

longer. To the men in the fight it may have been five minutes and it might have been two weeks since they had broken into Archer's lines. The ditch was now ankle-deep in
bloody mud, and the bodies of dead and wounded men from
both sides were piled up all around him. He had no ammunition. He had no strength. He had no hope of ever getting
out of this death hole unless help came soon.

There was a commotion now, just off to his right, and he
looked that way, desperately praying that he would see Colonel Magilton at the head of a column of blue troops, but it
wasn't Magilton, and the fresh regiments to his right were
not wearing blue.

What he saw was a Confederate brigadier with a saber in
his left hand and a pistol in his right waving on the fresh
Rebel troops. The graybacks all around him started shouting, "Archer! Archer!"

Jubal Early's division had joined the fight.

John Gibbon was as proud as a poppa watching his division
march forward—holding their ranks, in perfect, well-ordered
precision—just as he had taught them. He hadn't had long to
train them—just over a month—but every day for that
month, rain or sleet or snow, it didn't matter, these men had
marched and drilled and maneuvered until they responded to
each and every command instantly and flawlessly.

Taylor's Brigade was in the lead, headed for the railroad
tracks to the right of the finger of woods. Meade's division
had spilled over to that side of the field a little bit, but most
of the fighting was to the left. He could see the Rebels
now—at least most of them. There were a couple of regiments visible to the left of a small hill, and a couple of more
to the right. What lay directly behind the hill no one knew.

At a hundred yards out, the North Carolinians opened
fire and Taylor's entire brigade hit the dirt. Some were dead,
some were wounded, but most just hit the dirt.

In the center of what had been the Rebel lines, the horribly
wounded deaf old general Maxcy Gregg sat on the ground,
leaning against a tree, unable to stand because of the bullet
in his back, but he was still able to wave his hat and urge

Jubal Early's fresh Rebels into the woods, and another wound in the Rebel line began to heal.

John Gibbon positioned himself between his two leading brigades. To his front he didn't like what he saw.

Taylor's two left-most regiments were pinned down and exchanging murderous fire with Lane's Rebels immediately to their front. Men fired and reloaded and fired again as quickly as they could. They each had been issued sixty rounds of ammunition, but fifteen minutes into the fight the 11th and the 83rd Pennsylvania regiments were running dangerously low and were already pilfering cartridges from their dead or wounded buddies. The Rebels fired at the same pace and it was a brave Yankee who would raise his hand for fear of catching a bullet. Officers went down. Color bearers went down. Any man who dared to stand would die.

On Taylor's right it was oddly quiet. His other two regiments were protected by a hill and not in the Rebel line of fire.

To his rear Gibbon's next brigade—Lyle's—was well on its way, but they couldn't get there nearly soon enough. Low on courage and out of ammunition, Taylor's two left regiments broke and ran—straight into the not so welcoming arms of their commanding general.

Gibbon and Taylor did all that they could to stem the tide of retreat, but getting Lyle's men forward took precedence.

"Forward, Colonel Lyle! Up and over that hill! Do not stop. Do not let them lie down. If they lie down they'll never get back up!"

Lyle came forward with four fresh regiments—all aimed at the quiet little hill. They picked up Taylor's 97th New York and 88th Pennsylvania and now it was six full regiments that marched boldly up the rise.

Gibbon watched anxiously as half of his division reached the top and even he was appalled when he heard the cannonlike explosion of musket fire and saw the cloud of ugly white smoke rise from behind the hill. The North Carolinians, who had been safe behind their quiet little hill all day long, stood and fired and filled the air with lead, and hundreds of Gibbon's bravest men fell—and didn't get back up.

CHAPTER 15

Marye's Heights

As he ran up the hill, Little Abbott focused on the wall ahead. There were a hundred yards of nothing between here and there. No trees, no rocks, nothing to shield him and his men from the fire that was coming. *Impossible.* Abbott knew it. Every man in the regiment knew it. And yet they kept on running, screaming and defiant, as though they were anxious to die.

Little couldn't help but admire the wall itself. It was well made of large brown, gray, and white stones, and it meandered along the base of Marye's Heights, just below a majestic white plantation house that grandly dominated the crest. In another time it might have been beautiful. But that was a thought that came and went in a second. Still with eighty or more yards to go, the beautiful wall suddenly bristled with a thousand muskets, all with bayonets fixed, all aimed directly at the brave boys of the 20th Mass. They hesitated there for an instant, almost as though it were one final warning to turn back now. A visual reminder of that poor, beaten private back down the hill.

Don't take your men up there . . .

A thousand Rebel muskets fired at once.

PROSPECT HILL

Private William A. Martin was more than happy to tell anyone who would listen that he was the best darned shooter in the whole darned Army of Northern Virginia. His buddies in the 28th North Carolina used to laugh at him when he claimed he could shoot the eye out of a flying turkey at two hundred yards, but they didn't laugh nearly so much anymore—because he could.

A fresh bunch of bluecoats lay on the crest of the hill about a hundred yards ahead and were pouring deadly rifle fire into his regiment's lines, and the brash young private crawled into a ditch along the railroad tracks to see if he could do something about it. For a moment he paused to look up the hill and admire the magnificent sight of six regiments of Yankee troops massed in front of him, shrouded like ghosts in the thin cloud of white smoke that rose up from their rifles. Only a few of them were standing—and they were the ones with the flags. For Martin, a man waving a flag might as well carry a sign that said, SHOOT ME!

An ant line of men queued back down the hillside behind Martin, each with a loaded rifle ready to pass forward to their expert rifleman. He picked out one particularly brave soldier silhouetted in the fog, gallantly standing and waving a gigantic blue banner. It was a shame to kill one so brave, but Stonewall Jackson's now famous words had long since been etched in Martin's heart. "Kill the brave ones. They lead the others."

He brought the rifle to his shoulder and rested it on the firm rails of the track. He pulled the hammer back to the full cock position and pressed his cheek against his right thumb. He inhaled deeply and held his breath while he aligned the rear sight with the front and placed the soon-to-be-dead soldier squarely over them both, aiming just a little bit low. The smoke on the hill rose straight up into the air. No wind. Beautiful. Very slowly he squeezed his entire right hand like his brother had taught him, "All nice and even, like squeezing a lemon," until the hammer released, the charge exploded, and the weapon kicked back and jerked upward. The smoke from the discharge clouded his view for an instant but he was still able to see the man— and the flag—go down.

The men behind him cheered and he smiled as he passed the empty rifle back down the line and reached behind him for a loaded one.

John Gibbon's men had made it to the railroad tracks but still hadn't crossed. Two of his regiments were in retreat and six more were stuck in the mud, lying down, firing blindly into the Rebel lines. Anyone who had the courage to raise a flag died almost instantly. Gibbon had seen a half dozen or more fall along with at least that many officers who were brave enough or stupid enough to stand up. The fire in both directions was constant and had been for ten minutes or more. The Rebels had to be weakening. They had to be.

Gibbon sent for Lyle.

"What is the enemy strength down there, Colonel?"

"A brigade is all that I can see, sir. Supported by two batteries of artillery."

"You're certain?"

"As best as I can tell, sir, but they're all dug in real well down there, General, and they're back in the woods a bit. I don't have any way of knowin' what might be behind 'em."

Then Lyle realized what the general was thinking. "It's a real strong position, General . . . we can't go down there, sir. They're . . ."

"What about their left flank . . . do they have any cover there?"

"Nothing that I can *see,* sir. Nothin' over there but those guns by the slave cabins. But we're already low on ammunition, General, and . . ."

"So are they, Colonel, and you've still got your bayonets— and I've got a fresh and fully loaded brigade not five minutes away, and they're coming, Colonel Lyle, and they're going over that hill, and they're going to cross those tracks, and they're going to take those guns, and you're going with 'em."

MARYE'S HEIGHTS

Not only had Little Abbott and most of his men survived the Rebel's opening volley, they had continued to double-quick up the hill, anticipating that it would take the Rebs a good thirty seconds to reload and fire again.

It didn't.

The second round of fire from behind the wall was more devastating than the first, but still Little managed to remain standing and unhurt.

He turned around to see how his men had fared and yes, there were a few holes in the ranks, but they quickly healed. But this time the regiment did come to a halt. They raised their rifles and returned fire, but from someplace deep in their hearts, to the man, they fought the almost irresistible urge to turn and run or to fall to the ground.

And so there they stood—face-to-face with the elephant—and now, Abbott realized, they were there all alone. The rest of the brigade had fallen or died or turned tail after the first round of Rebel fire, leaving the remains of the tiny Harvard Regiment facing the stone wall totally on their own.

George Macy turned his back to the wall and held his saber over his head with both hands—the classic command to halt.

"Back, men! Move back! Hold your lines and move back."

The Rebs could have kept up their massive and deadly rate of fire on the retreating enemy, but they didn't. Some continued to fire on the 20th as the Massachusetts men backed down the hill—slowly and in good order—but most of the men behind the wall ceased firing and rested their weapons against the stones and cheered the courage of the Harvard Regiment.

Back behind the swale they fell to ground along with thousands of others who rested there. Little found his canteen and took a much-needed draft of cold water. He then began to look around him to see who was there—or, more importantly, who was not there.

Macy was there—completely safe. A miracle considering that he had been well in front of the regiment the whole time. Little crawled over to him and the two old friends shared the horror and dismay of the past few minutes without having to say a word.

It was only then that the true horror became too very real. With panic in his eyes, Little said only one word.
"Leander?"
Macy shook his head.

PROSPECT HILL

John Gibbon was jealous of Adrian Root. Root was what Gibbon really wanted to be. He was *where* Gibbon wanted to be. Adrian Root was a brigade commander marching into the center of the fight and that, by God, was where a soldier was born to be. That's where Gibbon had been at Second Bull Run and Antietam, side by side with his magnificent "Black Hats" in the middle of a desperate, blood-boiling, life-or-death struggle, where he could breathe the smoke and smell the blood. At Antietam he had personally killed Rebels by the dozens when he took command of Battery B and pulled the lanyard himself, roaring double canister into the faces of attacking Texans not twenty feet away. That's how soldiers fight. That's where Root was headed. That's where Gibbon wanted to be.

But John Gibbon commanded a division now, and divisions are commanded from the rear, and this fight now belonged to Adrian Root.

As they got closer to the tracks, the little hill protected Root's lines from the guns on the right and from the infantry fire from the other side of the tracks. It was in good form that his men came forward and up the hill toward the exhausted lines of the Federals who had gone before them.

Along the top of the hill the 12th Massachusetts continued to exchange fire with Lane's Rebs. The Massachusetts flag was a tattered remnant. Three men had died while waving her defiantly at the enemy below. The staff had been severed twice and the banner was no more recognizable than a bag of rags. When they finally heard the cadence of drums over the sounds of battle, they turned to see the clean, new flag of the 16th Maine coming to their rescue—the much maligned Blanket Brigade. But today they didn't look like the old Blanket Brigade. They had their uniforms now. Clean and blue and proud. Not too long ago these two regiments had brawled. The Maine boys took umbrage at being called the Blanket Brigade that night and some still nursed broken noses from that glorious skirmish. They had even taken to calling them-*selves* the Blanket Brigade. It was no longer a humiliation. Now it was a badge of honor.

Dead square in the middle of the 16th Maine the Stevens brothers marched. Lieutenant Will about two paces ahead of Sergeant Ned. Colonel Tilden didn't have the foresight of Colonel Robertson of the 24th New Jersey. Robertson had split up the McClernan brothers for their mother's sake, but the thought of separating the brother tandems of the 16th Maine simply never occurred to Tilden. The Stevenses, the Souleses, and the Lyfordses were just the brother pairs from Waterville. There were more. And so, like so many brothers in both armies, Will and Ned Stevens marched forward into battle one behind the other.

They were anxious as they followed that new flag to the hill, but they beamed with pride when a Massachusetts Yankee stood and shouted, "Three cheers for old Maine!" They had fought last month, but today they cheered. The 12th Massachusetts stood aside and allowed the 16th Maine to pass through, and then they turned and prepared to leave the field. Their work here was done.

Adrian Root was astounded. He was frustrated and amazed and angry. Very quickly he found Colonel James Bates, the commander of the 12th.

"Don't retire, Colonel! We have *got* to take those guns!"

"My men are fought out, Colonel, and we have no ammunition!"

"Never mind that!" Root was desperate now. He knew he couldn't force the Rebel lines and silence the guns alone. He needed every man. "We're going to make a charge!"

Bates was a man who was neither more nor less brave

than any of his men. He had done his duty. He had cheered the Maine boys as loudly as anyone and was just as anxious to leave. He and his men had been moments away from an honorable escape and now . . .

"Did you hear me, Colonel?"

"I did, sir."

Root and Bates and Taylor and Lyle and every other officer who could still ride moved along the lines and halted any retreating man. Two of Lyle's most exhausted regiments had managed to sneak away from the fight, others had retreated or "pulled back" to replenish their ammunition. Many of Taylor's men were disconnected and more or less lost in the woods. But hundreds of weary men came to attention, fixed their bayonets, and prepared to join Root's attack, many without a bullet in their bags.

Gibbon watched as his handpicked brigade commanders did just what he had known they would do. They held their men together. They re-formed their lines under fire. They stood up in the face of the enemy and moved forward, and John Gibbon couldn't sit in the rear and watch a moment longer. He spurred his horse to a run and charged directly into the middle of his advancing columns. He and his brigade commanders managed to rally enough men to send out a seven-regiment front that rose up and over the little hill like a long, blue wave. They were less than fifty yards from the railroad tracks when the Rebels stood and fired a withering volley all across the line. The Yankees recoiled from the shock and took time to fire back, but Gibbon rode behind them yelling at the top of his lungs, "Charge, men! *Charge!* Don't stand and shoot. CHARGE!!!"

And charge they did. They growled like vicious animals and rushed toward the tracks at a full run and suddenly— and unexpectedly—the Rebels ceased firing.

They were out of ammunition too.

On the other side of the finger of woods, the hand-to-hand fight in Archer's trenches had been going on for over ten minutes, and there's only so much of that kind of brutality that any man can withstand. It was a fist to the face that finally brought Evan Woodward down. It wasn't even that violent a blow, but his knees were simply too weak to hold him up any longer. He fell on top of a dead man. He had no idea if the corpse was Rebel or loyal, but it didn't matter. He needed to lie there for just a little while, to play dead for only a minute or two while he got his strength back. But just then he heard it again—that damned yell. More Confederates coming from somewhere to his right. He glanced up and saw a man—one lone, beaten-up Yankee—crawl out of the trench and head back toward the railroad tracks. Then another. Then another.

Retreat is an army's most contagious disease. Once it infects a single man it can spread quickly into an uncontrollable epidemic.

Evan Woodward and the Pennsylvania Bucktails and all of the other Yankees in Archer's trench had simply had enough. The men who had survived the horrendous shelling on the way to the railroad tracks—the men who had charged without orders into a hailstorm of minié balls—the men who had brawled to the death with Archer's desperate Rebels had finally given all that they could give. They had marched in as a full brigade of finely trained soldiers and left like a stampeding herd. As more and more of Jubal Early's Confederates charged down the hill, thousands of brave Union soldiers turned and ran like they were escaping a burning building. They had not been outfought—they were only fought out.

WASHINGTON, D.C.

Abraham Lincoln walked slowly and alone from the telegraph station at the War Office across the lawn to the White House. He had sat in that cramped office for hours waiting for some word from Burnside. He knew the battle was being fought, but Burnside, just like McClellan, was suddenly struck mute once the bullets started to fly.

It wasn't time wasted however. While waiting for news from Fredericksburg, Secretary Stanton had shown Lincoln a document—a month old already—from an officer in South Carolina. It was General Rufus Saxton's report on a mission recently completed near the town of Darien, Georgia. It was a routine and minor effort, involving a single company of Federal soldiers. They were loaded onto boats, taken to a place where a Rebel salt works and lumber mill were active. The soldiers forced back Rebel pickets, destroyed the works, and absconded with over two hundred yards of finished lumber and hundreds of good, sharp saws that were now the property of the United States of America. The causality figures were attached: four men wounded.

This was hardly a matter worthy of the commander in chief, except for one extraordinary detail. The raid was conducted by a company comprised of white officers and black soldiers—250 or so freed slaves from St. Simons Island, Georgia, and Sea Island, South Carolina.

Lincoln had known of their existence, but very little more. They had actually existed for quite some time, but only as "volunteers" in the truest sense of the word. They wore tattered, hand-me-down uniforms, if any at all, and drilled in bare feet with broken or unreliable rifles that no one would dream of asking the white soldiers to use. They had served without pay and suffered mean-spirited, heartless, and sometimes vicious ridicule at the hands of their fellow American soldiers, and had actually been disbanded back in August for lack of support from the government. The disbanding had been deliberately done. Abraham Lincoln had absolutely convinced himself that giving rifles to slaves would result only in disaster. Another Haiti—a bloody rampage of revenge against the men and women of the South. But that was only one of his concerns. Arm the slaves and half of the white men in the army would throw down their guns in disgust and abandon the Union, and three more states would secede and go over to the other side. Lincoln had been sure of it. Montgomery Blair and others firmly believed that men who were totally uneducated and who had been systematically oppressed since birth would never be capable of soldiering. These are the things Lincoln had believed in August. Today, as hard as it was for this man to take a stand and reverse it later, he could no longer fight both the irrepressible logic of letting the

Africans free themselves and the unrelenting need for more men.

Even at this, Lincoln knew, he was ignoring the boulder that tipped the scales most heavily against allowing slaves to be soldiers. It was the "Pandora's Box" or the "can of worms"—whatever allusion one might choose to apply. Frederick O. Douglass had put it to words—powerful words that Abraham Lincoln couldn't shake from his mind.

"Once let the black man get upon his person the brass letters U.S.; let him get an eagle on his button and a musket on his shoulder and bullets in his pocket, and there is no power on earth which can deny that he has earned the right to *citizenship* in the United States."

Citizenship. Lincoln almost cringed at the thought. Other than the costing of white men's jobs, this is the thing about freeing the slaves that frightens people most—North and South. Full citizenship for the black man. The right to sit on juries, hold office, and—the greatest fear of them all—to vote. These are all things that will come. About that Mr. Douglass is right. But is the country ready for that? Are the slaves themselves ready for that? These are things unknown and unknowable, Lincoln decided, and therefore must be dismissed—variables removed from the formula.

The First South Carolina Volunteers (Colored) had tipped the scales finally in favor of an army of Americans of African descent.

Lincoln stopped and sat on the front steps of the People's House so he could think it through just a little more thoroughly. He looked around him at the soldiers whose job it was to protect the Executive Mansion and at the traffic milling its way along Pennsylvania Avenue. Mostly military traffic—hundreds of well-armed, well-trained soldiers spending the war in Washington, drinking, whoring, playing cards, and serving as little more than expensive scarecrows propped up around the city to scare the Rebels away. All perfectly good soldiers who could and should be in Fredericksburg right now were they not needed here.

Maybe the blacks can fight after all, he thought. General Saxton seems to have proven that. And they don't have to be leaders. Their officers will be white men, and the coloreds down South have been trained since birth to do as they are told—a skill the white men must be taught from scratch. And, God help us, we need so many more men. Tomorrow, after the fight in Fredericksburg, we are going to have to replace even more. And even if this one, insignificant mission in Georgia proves to be a fluke, the Negroes can be given the menial jobs—digging ditches and building roads—and guarding the White House. If we do that, it will free up these white men to fight. Thousands of them.

Two soldiers walked past the President without so much as a nod. They were accustomed to his comings and goings by now. Lincoln even knew a few of them by name, but he didn't know their hearts.

Would these men turn on me, he wondered, *rather than risk their lives for the slaves?* If they were going to revolt, they would have done it in September, when the preliminary proclamation was announced. There had been some grumbling and some threats, but very few overt acts of rebellion. A handful of officers had resigned their commissions and one regiment—from Illinois of all places—had thrown down their guns and gone home. But only one. Maryland and Missouri and Kentucky remained comfortably in the Union, regardless of his own premonitions to the contrary. The proclamation didn't apply to them anyway. *They can keep their slaves as long as they remain loyal.*

Lincoln smiled at himself, at his own illogic. *They will* all *keep their slaves.* He knew it full well. The proclamation will free no one. If you call a cow's tail a leg, it doesn't make it a five-legged cow, and if you call a slave free, it doesn't break his shackles. The Emancipation Proclamation as it stands right now is a very powerful piece of symbolism, especially in Europe, and symbols are important. But as a practical matter, it accomplishes little or nothing. By adding to it a single paragraph, allowing for the enlistment of free black men and former slaves, it will become more than only a symbol. It will become fifty thousand more armed men.

So now may be the time. He climbed the familiar stairs to his office, went to his desk, and removed his working copy of the proclamation. It had resembled chicken tracks back in September, before Antietam, and Seward had cleaned it up for the announcement and made it new again. But in the weeks since, Lincoln couldn't stop tinkering with it, changing it, adding to it. And now, with just two weeks remaining before it would go into effect, it was time, he decided, to make one more addition.

He dipped his pen and wrote, "And I further declare and make known that such persons of suitable condition will be received into the armed service of the United States to garrison forts, positions, stations, and other places, and to man vessels of all sorts in said service."

"And so it is done," he said aloud as he returned the document to the drawer. And to himself he whispered, "Maybe they can fight after all."

PROSPECT HILL

The men of the Blanket Brigade—the 16th Maine—had been in the rear of John Gibbon's initial assault, but now, through a stroke of luck—good or bad—they marched in the lead. Ned Stevens's eyes were filled with tears. Not since they had left Winterville, with the bands playing and the flags waving and the girls and children cheering, had he ever known a prouder moment. For him and his brother and the rest of the men of the 16th Maine, the time of truth had finally come. This was truly God's army, hell-bent on freedom for the slaves. Modern Crusaders with God's "terrible swift sword" at last unsheathed. Ned watched his big brother, Will, marching just to his front, his saber over his head, leading his company forward in grand style. *If pride is a sin,* he thought, *then I am surely going to hell. There is not a man in this world better or braver than Will.*

Somebody began to sing.

John Brown's body lies a-moldering in the grave . . .

The rest of the regiment joined in immediately.

John Brown's body lies a-moldering in the grave . . .

The men in front of them, the men in gray, were Satan's hordes and nothing less. Slaveholders. Abhorrent to God and all right-thinking Christians, and regardless of the death and mayhem all around them, there was no place else on earth that Ned would rather be than following Will into this holy fight.

John Brown's body lies a-moldering in the grave . . .
His soul goes marching on.

When Colonel Tilden gave the order to charge, they broke into a full run and stormed across the tracks and into the very center of Lane's lines, and again rifles became clubs and the fighting became personal. Rebels threw their unloaded, bayoneted rifles like spears. North Carolinians bludgeoned the Maine boys with rifle butts and the Blanket Brigade answered with bayonets. The Stevens boys stood side by side and fought with a fury inspired by God Almighty.

More of Root's men—the only Federals left on the field with ammunition—managed to swing around Lane's left flank and began to pour a vicious enfilade down the extreme ranks, and at last the North Carolinians could take no more. They bolted and ran into the woods and across the field toward Captain Greenlee Davidson's guns, which were still parked on the hill in the rubble of Mr. Bernard's slave cabins.

Will and Ned, who had fought back-to-back in the trenches, watched the Rebels flee and began to shout and shake their fists at the beaten demons. They looked at each other and smiled and embraced and shared their joy. Satan defeated. God victorious.

Will looked to the sky. "Thank you, God. Thank you, God. Thank you, God, for this glorious victory!"

General James Lane was a product of the Virginia Military Institute and the University of Virginia. Prior to the war he was a professor of Natural Philosophy at the North Carolina Military Institute. His was an ordered mind. He studied, taught, and lived by the laws of cause and effect. He preached the Gospel According to Sir Isaac Newton. "If *A,* then *B.*" That which is not measurable is chaos and, therefore, abhorrent to nature. In another man's eye, the events unfolding before him would be just that—chaos. His entire brigade was in full retreat through the swampy woods with Gibbon's troops shooting Rebels in the back as they ran. They hadn't begun to pursue them up the hill yet, but Lane knew that they would very soon—as quickly as their officers could calm them down and move them forward. The cool eye of Professor James Lane viewed his options in the light of science and applied Newton's most rudimentary formula. "For every action, there is an equal and opposite reaction."

He knew full well what John Gibbon had in mind. Gibbon wanted the Rebel guns. Greenlee Davidson's guns. The guns that stood on the hill amid the rubble of Mr. Bernard's slave cabins. With those guns gone, the way would then be clear to the Military Road and Stonewall Jackson's entire left flank would be in the air—vulnerable to an enfilade attack.

James Lane had to stop them and he had to stop them *now.*
"For every action . . ."

He was able to find only a single regiment that maintained any semblance of order—the 33rd North Carolina was in retreat but not in flight.

"Colonel Avery!"

"Sir."

"We must turn your men to face the enemy."

Avery's body was starved for air. He couldn't breathe. He could barely stand. He and his men had just survived several minutes of hand-to-hand combat and climbed halfway up the hill. It wasn't a very steep hill, but it was long and wet and slippery. Where the terrain was flat, it was boggy with holes and ditches that were filled with water and slime. Some were ankle-deep and some were knee-deep, and there was no way to tell which until you were already in it.

Clark Avery's face was black with powder and his clothes were soaked with freezing cold swamp slime.

"General Lane, sir . . ." Gasping for breath, he looked back over his shoulder into the woods. He knew the Yankees were coming. He also knew there were thousands of them. "We can't make a stand here, General. We would be overrun in a minute's time."

"I'm not ordering you to make a stand, Colonel."

An ominous moment passed while Avery figured out what Lane had in mind.

"Do you mean a . . . a bayonet charge, sir?"

"Give me ten minutes, Colonel. That's all I need." He gave Avery a second to come to grips with what he had just been told. "I've sent to Generals Gregg and Pender for help, and God willing they are on their way—but we *have* to stop those Yankees—we have to save those guns or General Jackson's entire line will collapse. A counterattack right now— this very instant—will hold them long enough for me to prepare a defense." He closed his eyes and took a deep breath. He knew he was probably asking Avery to give his life and the lives of what was left of his regiment as well, but there was nothing for it. "You *must* do this thing, Colonel, and you must do it *now*!"

Avery's regiment was more than decimated. They were also exhausted from a hard fight and the long escape up the slimy hill. They were out of breath, out of ammunition, and facing an attacking force three times their size.

Avery smiled. There was no man in either army more aggressive than Clark Avery. There was no unit in either army more willing to die than the men of his 33rd North Carolina. He nodded and shouted . . .

"*Attention*. About . . . *face*! Charge bayonets!"

Almost amazingly, the Carolinians did as they were ordered.

"CHARGE!"

The ragged gang of exhausted Rebels screamed down the hill, howling and yipping and snarling at the astounded Yankees. The Rebel yell it had come to be called, and it did precisely what General Lane had calculated that it would do. It stopped Gibbon's assault—again—dead in its tracks.

. . . *an equal and opposite reaction.*

First the 16th Maine—then the 94th New York—then the 104th New York collided with the advancing remnants of Avery's 33rd North Carolina. For both sides the bayonet again became the weapon of necessity. All the while Lane halted, gathered, and reorganized what he could of the balance of his scattered and demoralized command. He formed new lines halfway between the railroad tracks and Davidson's guns up on the hill and then he sent a welcome word to Avery . . . "You may withdraw."

A half a mile to the south, the fight for Archer's line was finally over. Evan Woodward and the rest of the Pennsylvania boys who had fought so bravely there, the Bucktails, the 2nd, the 3rd, the 11th Pennsylvania—at least those who could—now stumbled, ran, crawled their way back across the railroad tracks they had paid so dearly to gain. The Confederates had just kept coming at them. They never stopped. One regiment after another, they just kept on coming like a river down a mountain.

Woodward had inherited the regimental colors of the 2nd Pennsylvania Volunteers and used the shortened staff more as a crutch than anything else. All that mattered now was to keep it out of the hands of the Rebels and to get the hell away from Prospect Hill. He was tired, bruised, and mad as hell. No help. He and all of the others had fought a savage fight. Brutal. They had crossed an open field under fire. They had assaulted entrenched positions and came damned close to taking them. All they needed was help. One more push. The Rebels got help when and where they needed it. Fresh Rebel troops by the boatloads came storming into those trenches, screaming that damned Rebel yell, and all the Yanks had was one shot-up and beat-down, leaderless little brigade. And no help.

So many brave men, he thought—*just wasted.*

Most of the shooting had stopped now. The Rebs behind him were cheering and jeering and shaking their fists at the retreating heroes. But Woodward knew the hell wasn't over. They had to retreat back over the same open field they had crossed this morning and the Rebel artillery was cool and loaded and ready to fire on them again as they left.

He heard what was going on around him, but he saw little. His eyes—and his heart—were focused on the road a thousand yards away. The same road where this insanity

had begun. There he would be safe. There would be water
there.

Water.

He heard a horse running toward him. He heard a man
cursing, but he didn't care.

Water.

Then he felt the regimental colors being ripped from his
hand. His first instinct—his only instinct—was to hold the
flag fast and shoot the man who was trying to take it from
him. But his defiance turned quickly to shock when he realized that the man was General George Gordon Meade himself. He was cursing his heroes—humiliating them. He had
his pistol drawn and threatened to shoot one young officer if
he didn't rally his men and return to the Rebel lines.

Woodward just stood there, looking up at Meade as
though the general were a madman. Maybe he was. Meade
stood tall in the saddle, waved the banner of the 2nd Pennsylvania, and shouted "Rally here, men!" and to Woodward's amazement a sparse line of worn-out Yankees began
to form. First it was only a few very brave men, but others
soon joined, and before long they began to vaguely resem-
ble an army again.

Woodward continued to be pulled backward to safety and
to the water that he needed so desperately, but he just
couldn't do it. After all he had done, after all the men who
had given their lives, he couldn't turn and run before the last
hope died.

He turned around to face the enemy and drew out his
bloody saber and held it over his head.

"Rally here, men. Rally here!"

It was a thin Rebel line that "Professor" James Lane had assembled to repel Gibbon's assault. Tattered remnants of
beaten regiments. Greenlee Davidson's guns were useless
now. Their fuses were unreliable and the rounds they fired
consistently exploded short. They were more likely to kill
Lane's men than any Yankees.

The sight of William Dorsey Pender riding toward him at
full tilt was the most beautiful thing the old professor had

ever seen. Lane almost laughed. The young hero of Seven Pines riding forward at a gallop to save the day. *This is something for the history books,* Lane thought. *The stuff that glory is made of.*

"You are a sight for sore eyes, General Pender."

Pender saluted, nodded, and smiled. "Hold while you can, General Lane. Captain Latimer's guns will slow them enough, and my men are on their way."

"Hurry them along, General. My men are fought out, and there's probably not a hundred rounds of ammunition left between 'em."

"Give us five minutes, General. They're right behind me."

Lane nodded and looked back down the hill into the almost quiet woods. His worries were far from over. Avery's gallant men of the 33rd North Carolina were still down there, breaking loose from their heroic bayonet charge, and, if any had survived, they would precede the Yankees up the hill. The last thing Lane wanted was to order fire on them— not after all they had done this day. He would if he had to. He would if that's what he had to do to stop the Yankee charge. If they came up fast and well ahead of the enemy, then Lane could hold his fire, but if the Yankees were right on their heels, well . . . The professor knew what he would have to do.

If A . . . then B.

Lane was startled by the sound as Latimer's guns, posted far to the left, as they opened fire almost blindly into the woods. Shells exploded at treetop level and hot iron and tree limbs fell. On whom, General Lane had no idea. He could still see nothing as he anxiously paced behind his makeshift lines, looking down into the woods for the first signs of movement. "Hold your fire until ordered, men. Aim low and make every bullet count."

The first soldiers he saw wore gray. Avery's men. Lane whispered, "Come on, boys. Come on fast. Give me some space . . ."

Ten men—twenty—a hundred, all in gray or butternut, stumbled up the hill. They knew what was at stake here. They knew that Lane couldn't wait for them.

Then—nothing. A gap. Ten yards—twenty—thirty yards or more and the first Yankee had not yet shown himself. Lane began to cheer for Avery's boys and to wave them up the hill. Every Rebel in the line joined in and Avery's exhausted heroes seemed to take heart and move just a little bit faster.

The first blue soldier finally appeared some fifty yards away and thirty yards behind the retreating Rebels. Then came a few more. Then a blue flag with a painting of a tree on it. Maine probably. Now there were hundreds of Yankees visible to the old professor, slipping and sliding up the hill, weaving around the trees, but still trying to maintain their lines.

"Hold your fire, men. Hold . . ."

Clark Avery himself was the last of the heroes to stumble into Lane's lines, where he fell panting to the ground. Just as Lane was about to order "fire," he heard the unmistakable sound of a regiment on the double-quick coming from behind. Pender. The Yankees still had forty-or-so yards to climb before they reached Lane's lines, and Pender's men were already filing in along his flanks. The professor calculated that he could wait just a few more seconds.

"Hold your fire, men! Hold it . . . Hold it . . ."

Evan Woodward was so tired he could barely stand. He was so thirsty he could have drunk a lake. After the disastrous, hand-to-hand fighting with Archer's Rebels, everybody from Meade's division was the same. And yet hundreds of them stood in a defiant line, daring the Rebels to come on down the hill. Most were low if not completely out of ammunition. They were filthy and bloody and had every right in the world to spit in George Meade's eye and tell him to go to hell, and yet here they stood. Ready.

Elements of Birney's division were getting closer. They were ten minutes away, fifteen at the most, when the Rebel artillery opened on them, slowing their advance.

"Come on," Woodward said, talking to *both* armies of men—daring one and pleading to the other.

* * *

At this moment, it was all worth it for Will and Ned Stevens and the rest of the boys of the Blanket Brigade. The price the Maine men had paid to get here was great to be sure. The agonizing march on bare feet in the snow . . . the humiliation of wearing blankets instead of uniforms . . . the ridicule of their fellows . . . and even the losses they had suffered to Rebel guns, muskets, and bayonets . . . even those were a fair price to pay to answer God's call.

The Rebel devils were in retreat. They were beaten and humiliated and running like terrified deer. Colonel Tilden led the charge with his saber drawn, waving it in circles over his head, urging his Mainers up the hill in hot pursuit. The flags of America and Maine were beautifully unfurled and marching in the lead. Both carried bullet holes from the assault against the railroad tracks and were all the more beautiful for it. Will and Ned and the rest of the boys of the 16th Maine weren't even tired. They could chase those beaten demons from here to Richmond without even stopping to rest.

"FIRE!"

Ned heard it and couldn't believe it. It came from somewhere up ahead and sounded so close that Will might have said it standing right in front of him. But it wasn't Will. It wasn't Colonel Tilden. There was an angry, horrifying roar and men fell all around him. He was saved only by a low-hanging tree limb that caught the ball meant for his face. He tasted the bark. The line of smoke from the new Rebel lines seemed to be a hundred yards long and only thirty yards away. His soul sank from elation to terror in that one horrible instant. Both flags went down. Men cried in pain. It was an ambush. The Blanket Brigade was caught in a trap.

Without being ordered to do so, he lifted his rifle to his shoulder and got off a quick round. He reached into his cartridge box for another and realized that he had precious few left. He tore the paper envelope open with his teeth and began to pour the contents down the muzzle. He looked up to check on Will at the very instant his brother's leg exploded blood.

"Wiiiiiillllllll!"

Ned dropped his rifle and ran to his brother's side. Will looked dazed and confused. Ned checked the wound. High on the right thigh. Bullets continued to hit men and trees and kick up mud all around him while he took off his belt and fashioned a tourniquet for Will's leg.

There was no more thought of chasing the Rebels to Richmond. There was no more thought of freeing the slaves. His only mission now was to get out of this place and save his brother and himself for another day.

He helped Will to his feet.

"Stay with me, brother."

Will didn't say anything but nodded weakly.

"We're getting out of here—but you've got to . . ."

Another bullet struck a tree not an inch from Ned's ear. There was no more time for talking. Ned knelt down so Will could bend over his shoulder. The older brother screamed in pain as Ned struggled to lift him up. Blood drenched Ned's hands, making it even harder to get a grip, but there was nothing for it. Ned had to hold on and carry his brother to safety. That was all there was to it.

He slipped a few times and stumbled once or twice, but he never dropped his load. Twenty-five or thirty yards back down the hill he finally felt safe—at least for the moment. He set his brother down on a dry spot behind a tree. Will was unconscious but breathing. The tourniquet seemed to have slowed the flow of blood and Ned took a moment to thank God for that.

For James Archer and Jubal Early this was a thing of beauty. After a gap eight hundred yards wide had opened in the Confederate lines—after an entire division of Federal troops had come a stone's throw away from turning their flank—to stand here now and watch the damned Yankees finally turn and run—well, the two normally stern-faced Rebel generals were downright giddy.

A freckle-faced courier came riding up at a run to deliver the news that everyone could see for himself. But the young man was flushed with victory and couldn't hold back.

"The Yankees is fully on the run, sirs! Fast as they can go. They're gonna run clear back to Washington, I think!"

The officers just smiled even more broadly and saluted the youngster on. Early had completely forgotten that General Jackson might well be furious at him for disobeying orders. He hadn't had a drink all day long, but at this moment he felt like he had a belly full of brandy under his belt. Jubal Early felt good. Unfortunately for the wooden-faced old general, the good feeling didn't last long.

Totally without orders, Colonel Edmund Atkinson's Georgia brigade avalanched down the hill with an emotional momentum that simply couldn't be stemmed. Meade's retreating Yankees had thrown up a scrawny little line of fought-out soldiers, but directly in front of the attacking Rebels, not two hundred yards away, stood a full battery of cold and vulnerable Federal guns, just there for the taking. They couldn't be brought to bear against the Georgians because the Pennsylvanians stood in the way, and Atkinson's men were hot on their heels. Even if the gunners had the callous wherewithal to fire into their own ranks, by the time they reloaded, their guns would belong to the South, and there was no stopping Atkinson's Brigade from taking those guns.

Evan Woodward braced himself for the impact. The Pennsylvania men who had any ammunition left sent off a volley that staggered the attacking Confederates. One Rebel officer fell instantly off of his horse, but his foot was caught in the stirrup. The terrified animal tore off at a run, dragging the poor man for thirty yards before some soldiers managed to head it off, bring it to a stop, and set the wounded rider free.

One volley. That's all they had, and once again the blue and the gray came together with fists and clubs and bayonets. But there was a difference this time. These Rebel troops were Jubal Early's men. They were fresh and rested and full of fight. Meade's men had been at it all day and could simply withstand no more. The melee lasted only a matter of seconds.

There would be no more hand-to-hand fighting. There would be no more gallant rallies. Not even General Meade himself could hold back the tide this time.

It was all the heroic Lieutenant Woodward could do to crawl out of the fight and resume his odyssey back to the Bowling Green Road—back to where it had all begun.

TELEGRAPH HILL

For almost an hour Robert E. Lee had watched and worried as two divisions of Federal troops pushed their way into the woods on his right, and now, with enormous relief, he watched as they poured out again. He was amazed that these men, these fine Union soldiers, had thrown themselves against hell's gates and battered them down only to be abandoned on the threshold. He knew for a fact that at least three more divisions were ready and waiting to come forward, but none did. He could see that one was coming up now, but with the first divisions in full retreat, he knew that it was far too late for them to do any serious damage alone. One lone, fresh division was only doomed to repeat the fate of those that had gone before.

His thoughts were interrupted by a new explosion on his left and he turned to study Marye's Heights just as another brigade of Union troops felt another hell-hot blast from behind the stone wall. He was moved almost to tears by the courage of the Yankee soldiers, and almost to anger by the stupidity of their generals. He had lost count by now. It must have been two divisions at least that Burnside had thrown against that wall. Twelve thousand men or more. He remembered for the tenth time today the words of Lieutenant Owen from the Washington Artillery. "A perfect slaughter pen." Colonel Alexander had been right to station his guns on the downside of the heights—even if it *had* been against orders—against tradition. No—they couldn't return fire against the Union artillery on Stafford Heights, but against this seemingly endless flow of infantry up the hill they were flawlessly positioned, covering almost every inch of ground between the town and the wall. Brilliant. Lee remembered Porter Alexander's words as well. "A chicken could not live on that field when we open on it."

After only a few minutes of fighting, the new Union

troops were already beaten back—already stumbling down the hill to the spot where thousands of others waited, leaving piles of their dead and wounded behind. The entire hillside was blue now, except for the fifty yards immediately in front of the wall where not a single blue soldier lay. Not one.

And after all of this, at the end of the day Lee knew, nothing will have been gained and nothing will have been lost. Nothing but the lives of thousands of men. Sickened by the needless tragedy of it all, Lee shook his head in astounded disbelief, and to James Longstreet he said, "It is well that war is so terrible—we should grow too fond of it."

CHAPTER 16

PROSPECT HILL

General David Birney was very nearly in a panic as he watched Meade's men tumbling back out of the woods by the thousands. His own division was spread out over the plain leading to the railroad tracks over a line nearly a mile long. Some of his regiments marched to Meade's assistance, some to Gibbon's. He was still angered and frustrated by the ad hoc command structure. Every damned man with a star on his shoulder seemed to think he commanded Birney's division, and the men who really did—Stoneman and Reynolds—were nowhere to be seen.

And now a full brigade of Rebel troops stormed out of the woods on the run toward one of Birney's unprotected batteries. His precious guns were only moments away from capture—an almost unforgivable sin. He had to do something to stop them. A foothold here and the entire grand division would be in danger of being pushed all the way back into the river.

"General Berry!"

"Sir!"

Hiram Berry commanded Birney's 3rd Brigade, and he was simply the closest at hand.

"We need a regiment forward *now,* General, to save those guns!"

Berry looked where Birney pointed and back to his lines of men. He couldn't believe his bad luck. "Damn!"

"What is it, General?"

"The 5th Michigan is closest, sir. Gilluly's regiment."

John Gilluly was a lieutenant colonel who was bound for a star on his shoulders and a chapter in the history books. He was on a quest for glory and was perfectly willing to pay for it with the lives of his men.

Birney winced at the thought, but he had no choice.

"Send him in, Hiram. We don't have time to pick and choose."

Berry sighed heavily and the two men both shook their heads. They knew what was ahead for the poor men of the 5th Michigan. Still looking into his commanding officer's face, Berry shouted, "Colonel Gilluly!"

The arrogant colonel was at Berry's side in an instant.

"Sir."

"Move your regiment forward, Colonel, into that gap. Stop that charge and save those guns!"

Colonel Gilluly actually glowed with excitement. With a crisp salute he shouted, "Yes, sir!" and was gone.

The two generals watched as Gilluly leaped onto his horse and rode to the head of his regiment. He grabbed the regimental colors and waved them over his head as he shouted, "Fifth Michigan, *attention*! Charge bayonets! Follow me now, men, and let's give those Rebels some hell! CHARGE!"

At a run, like a *Harper's Weekly* portrait of a charging cavalry officer, he led the attack himself, well ahead of his men. With the flag in one hand and a pistol in the other, he rode past the endangered guns to meet the enemy in front. The retreating Yankees from Meade's division gladly stepped aside to let the Michiganders through.

The two generals, Birney and Berry, continued to watch.

"You had best order forward some help, General Berry. I'm afraid this is going to be over very quickly."

Berry had no sooner ordered the 3rd Michigan forward than a roar of musketry demanded his attention. He turned to look just in time to see John Gilluly's body jerk in about five different directions all at the same time. The colonel went down, the flag went down, and nearly half of the men of the 5th Michigan went down as well, and after receiving only a single volley of fire, Gilluly's men joined Meade's in the retreat.

Now it was the turn of the 3rd Michigan. They were welcomed onto the field in exactly the same manner—with exactly the same results. Atkinson's Rebels continued to swarm toward the artillery battery and it was time for the guns to limber up and pull back.

"Kill the horses!" Atkinson yelled, but it wasn't necessary. His Georgians knew what to do. On the rise, now only a hundred yards away, horses began to fall. Cannoneers in charge of each of the six guns cut the dead and wounded animals loose from their harnesses and beat the survivors without mercy to get two horses to do the work of six. They finally managed to escape, leaving only one piece behind for the oncoming Rebels.

General Berry had sent in only two of his five regiments. Those careless and desperate charges had resulted in disaster, but had saved most of the precious guns. He still had three regiments left, and the guns were no longer an issue. Instead of ordering another boisterous and reckless charge, he inched his fresh regiments up behind a knoll. He made them crawl through the cold and slimy mud up to the crest so that they would not be seen by the still oncoming Rebels.

"Quiet now, men. Lay low."

His soldiers had never heard of such a thing. Armies were supposed to march into battle, or charge like Gilluly's men had, bayonets fixed and flags unfurled. A soldier shouldn't have to sneak around and wallow in the mud. It wasn't glorious. It wasn't manly. It simply wasn't done. Some of the men resisted and walked to the top of the hill, standing tall.

"Lay down, men!" Berry had lost enough men in the last ten minutes. It was the Rebels' turn to die. "I'm here to take care of you, and I'll do it if you will let me and will obey my orders."

The overanxious men, who had managed a peek at the Rebel brigade moving along their front, saw the wisdom of Berry's commands and did as they were told. Suddenly lying facedown in the slimy mud didn't seem like such a bad idea after all. Berry alone stood at the apex of the hill, waiting for precisely the right moment.

Atkinson's Rebels, elated with their victory, came to a stop as they claimed their easily won prize and yelled and taunted the retreating Yankees until five batteries of Union guns—thirty cannons—opened on them almost simultaneously, filling the air around them with shot and shell and deadly canister pellets. The Federal gunners had been waiting, impatiently, for their retreating friends to clear the field of fire before they unleashed hell on the attacking Rebel brigade. Berry ordered *"Fire"* and his three regiments of infantry stood and unloaded thousands of minié balls on Atkinson's right flank. Other Union regiments, more of Birney's division, also rose and fired, and Colonel Atkinson was among the first hit—a flesh wound to the shoulder. He and the rest of his Georgia brigade turned and hightailed it back to the railroad tracks and dove into the safety of the ditch. Edmund Atkinson's spontaneous and unsupported counterattack came to a quick and gruesome end.

MARYE'S HEIGHTS

There was no point in amputating Thomas Cobb's leg. The best the surgeons could do was to keep him drugged enough to ease the pain. The Georgian slid in and out of sleep—in and out of delirium.

John Rutherford, the general's aide-de-camp, bent over and whispered to his dying cousin, "Hancock's assault has been repulsed, General. Your lines are holding strong."

"Thank God," Cobb said. These were Thomas Reade Rootes Cobb's final words on earth.

PROSPECT HILL

General David Birney had saved the endangered guns. His men had paid a horrible price, but they had sent the Rebels yipping back into the woods—at least for the moment. But there was no guarantee that they would stay there. They had fled back into the trenches alongside the railroad tracks and there they remained, either lying in wait for the Yankees to make another try, or regrouping for another counterattack of their own. They had fallen back, but had not really retreated. They were still on the field, still organized, and still killing men and horses by the dozens all along Birney's vulnerable lines. His division, or the two brigades of his division that were available to him, were still spread out and more a hodge-podge of individual regiments than any sort of cohesive unit. *Ten fingers,* he thought, *not attached to any one hand, in no position to cooperate with one another no matter what might come.* A single brigade of Rebel troops had come very close to overtaking the whole damned lot of them, and Birney didn't even want to think about what a truly determined counterattack by a full division—or maybe even Jackson's entire corps—might do. That was all that was on Birney's mind—how to save the army from annihilation should Stonewall Jackson come storming down that hill into the remnants of Birney's already thin and wounded defenses.

It was then that he heard what may have been the most beautiful music ever played. "Hail Columbia" covered the field, played by the gaudy brass band of Collis's Zouaves— the *Corps d'Afrique*. Birney turned to see General John Robinson's Brigade—the missing third of his division— marching onto the field.

These Zouaves were the 114th Pennsylvania, under the command of Colonel Charles H. T. Collis. He had enlisted in the army as a private early on and was elected sergeant major of his ninety-day regiment. But the three-month enlistment came and went far too quickly. So he went home to Philadelphia and raised a regiment of his own. It took him all of three days. He uniformed them after the French Algerian units of the Crimean War, with bright red trousers and wedding-gown-white turbans. They even had their own regimental *vivandière,* Mary Tepe, or French Mary, as they called her. Her mother had been French, so the tiny lady even spoke with a thick French accent—appropriate to the esprit de corps of the Zouaves *d'Afrique*. She probably weighed about 90 pounds without her uniform—and 150 with it. She was the regimental "mom" and storekeeper, and without her they would probably have to close up shop. And so French Mary marched into battle, right alongside the men of the 114th.

To David Birney's way of thinking, they stood out on the battlefield like clowns at a funeral, but he had never been happier to see anybody in his entire life.

There was, of course, still that persistent issue of protocol.

"Who ordered you forward, General Robinson?"

"Nobody did, sir." Robinson's tone was defiant. He simply dared his commander to countermand him. "I have been sitting next to that bridge all morning long, just watching and contributing nothing. When I saw you go forward—well, General—I am a part of this division and where it goes—I go."

Birney wanted to be furious, but under the circumstances . . .

"Very well, General. File into line between those two batteries and prepare to repel an assault. No one on this field knows how many men Jackson has up on that hill, but if he sends all he's got at us, it appears that our division is all that stands between him and the river."

The Rebel fire was picking up, and red pants and a marching band seemed to provide them with an irresistible new target of choice. Robinson got his men in line and ordered them to lie down, and the Rebels turned their attention back to the artillerymen and horses.

"They're coming," Birney said. "That's why they're concentrating their fire on the guns—to silence them before they attack again."

"I agree," Robinson said. "And I know of only one way to stop 'em, and that's if we attack them first."

Birney didn't want to agree, but he had no choice in the matter. Robinson was right and there was no way around it. "Make ready, then, General, and commence your attack as soon as possible."

Robinson rode calmly from regiment to regiment, instructing each commander. He met back up with Birney in the middle of his lines. The two mounted officers gave the Confederates a target too good to pass up, but the generals sat tall as shells fell around them.

Colonel Collis had one important chore to do before his unit could move forward. He had to find French Mary Tepe and order her out of danger.

"This is as far as you go, Mary."

Mary never left her post, which was virtually anywhere she darned well decided it should be. Mary marched like a soldier, worked like a soldier, was paid like a soldier, and saw absolutely no reason why she should be treated any differently from any other soldier. She cooked for them, washed for them, sold them tobacco and whiskey at a fair price, and today she intended to nurse their wounds.

She blushed and said, "Yes, sir."

She lied.

Another officer of the Zouaves turned to face his men. Over the months they had suffered the slings and arrows of ridicule for their spit-and-polish attitude, their extravagant "costumes," and mostly for their totally unearned arrogance. With their immaculately clean white gloves and spats, they performed exquisitely on the parade ground, but most had never been tested on the field of battle.

"Go in Zoo-Zoos," Lieutenant Barton yelled. "This is your chance!"

Robinson waited for the cheering to stop before he gave the order to charge.

FREDERICKSBURG

It was as if the burden of Atlas was gone from his shoulders as Darius Couch watched Joe Hooker approach.

It's over. At last, thank God, it's over.

He tapped Winfield Hancock on the shoulder and pointed toward "Fightin' Joe" coming forward at a run.

"Here comes our cover."

Hooker pulled up beside the two generals, both of whom were very glad to see him. "Welcome to hell, General Hooker."

"What am I up against here, Generals?"

Couch pointed up Hanover Street, which led from the town up to the wall. "Leave that road open so my men can pull back. We'll need artillery cover as well, General. The Rebs have the range . . ."

"Pull *back*?" Hooker shook his head and sighed. "There isn't going to be any 'pulling back,' General. I am ordered to attack."

"What?"

"My orders from the 'general commanding' "—Hooker let the sarcasm pour off of the words—"are to attack with every man I've got—which isn't very many since he's already sent most of my command to Franklin."

Hooker might as well have taken out his pistol and shot Darius Couch in the heart.

"Now—what am I up against here, General Couch?"

Couch didn't know where to begin. He took a moment and decided it was best to begin with the beginning.

"Your men will march out of the town and immediately come under artillery fire from there . . ." He pointed straight up the hill to the Marye House and the Washington Artillery dug deeply into the heights. Then Couch's finger aimed at the peak of Telegraph Hill, where thirty-pound Parrots continued to launch missiles the size of flour barrels into approaching Federals. "And from there," he added. Then he pointed to his right, where additional Confederate batteries were posted. "You will come under an oblique fire from those guns and you will lose ten to twenty percent of your force before you ever reach the ditch."

"The ditch?"

"Yes. It's a millrace that cuts directly across your approach. We've tried to keep the bridges up, but with little success. Most of your men will have to climb in and out and re-form—under fire—on the other side."

Hooker only nodded. He knew the worst was yet to come.

"Then you'll have to cover about two hundred yards of open ground. The enemy artillery has precisely calculated the range on you there, and your men will have to navigate across the remains of several fences and around all of my men who have pretty much filled up the field."

Couch was getting angrier and more desperate with every word. "Then—after you crest the swale—the Rebs'll wait until you're about fifty or a hundred yards away from a solid stone wall, and they'll rise up and begin an almost incessant musket fire. You can't take a volley and storm the wall while they're reloading. The shooting never stops. And just for good measure, they have just reinforced that line. I don't know why. There probably isn't any more room to stand back there, where they are all perfectly safe and shooting down on us like we're turkeys in a cage." Couch was almost shouting now. "Look at the final fifty yards, General Hooker." He paused to give Fightin' Joe a second to focus. "There's not a man there, General, living *or* dead. No one has made it that close. And the men who cover the next fifty yards down the hill? They're all dead. And the rest of my men, lying behind the swale? If one of them dares to lift a finger in the air, it will probably get shot off. If one of them stands, a round of solid shot will go looking for him! *That's* what you're 'up against,' General Hooker!"

Couch took a breath and calmed himself down a bit. He shifted his weight in the saddle and turned to face Hooker before he asked, "Now—do you have any questions, General?"

"Yeah—I do. How did Ambrose Burnside ever get to be a general?"

The other generals all secretly agreed with Hooker's brash comment, but none said it aloud. A moment passed while Hooker and the others just sat and stared up the hill. It was Couch who spoke first.

"Don't do it, Joe. If there's any way on God's green earth that you can put a stop to this . . ."

Hooker nodded. *"Courier!"*

An aide was at his side in an instant.

"Go to General Burnside with my compliments and tell him that I strongly recommend that the order to attack the heights be countermanded. Tell him that after viewing the field that it is my considered opinion that such an assault with the force at my disposal will result only in a useless waste of life."

There were other things that Joe Hooker wanted to say to

Ambrose Burnside, but, for once in his life, he decided against it. He only nodded and said, "Ride."

PROSPECT HILL

Colonel Charles H. T. Collis and his regiment of Pennsylvania Zouaves—white turbans, red pants, and all—marched toward the newly re-formed Rebel lines now held by Atkinson's overenthusiastic Georgians. General Robinson and his staff were well mounted and gathered together in a group so large that it formed a bull's-eye about the size of a big, red barn. They were an irresistible and unmissable target for thousands of Confederate infantrymen and dozens of Rebel guns.

An expertly timed shell exploded not twenty feet over Robinson's head. His horse was killed, his bugler was killed, two of his staff officers went down seriously wounded, and a private, who had the misfortune to be standing nearby, was cleanly decapitated by the shot, and yet General Robinson somehow survived—dazed but unhurt. He was pinned to the ground by the carcass of his dead horse, but alive—and furious. But the men of Collis's Zouaves didn't know that. As far as they could see, their brigade commander and his entire staff were dead in an instant, and the men of the 114th, most of whom had never seen a dead man before in their lives, simply froze in their tracks.

For Charles Collis, this was his moment of truth. His entire life's journey had pointed him to this time and this place. He had raised this regiment himself and there was no way in hell he was going to let them come to a stop after taking a single shot.

He charged to the front and grabbed the regimental colors from the hand of the color corporal and without a moment's hesitation he yelled, "CHARGE!" His Zouaves couldn't hear him, of course, over the gunfire, no matter how loudly he yelled—but they could see him clearly enough through the smoke, and when he bolted forward they followed—screaming and at a run. Collis's Zouaves led the way and the rest of Robinson's Brigade followed.

The Rebels stood as one and let loose another volley, and the Yanks halted and fired back. It became a stand-and-shoot battle that lasted for no more than two minutes before the Georgians, with both their ammunition and their enthusiasm exhausted, turned and ran—again. This time they weren't "pulling back." This time it was a real, honest-to-God retreat, and Robinson's Brigade set out in pursuit.

General Robinson had managed to disentangle himself from his dead horse, and the last thing in the world he wanted to see was his brigade running up into the woods where God-only-knew what might be waiting for them. He knew his mission. He knew his orders. He was to prevent another Rebel counterattack. General Birney was clear on that. Without his brigade standing by to repel whatever might come, the way to the river would be virtually wide open.

He commandeered another horse and raced to the head of his brigade. He managed to get between his men and the retreating Rebels, and somehow he was able to make himself heard. Collis and the other regimental commanders got their men under control, and the pursuit of the fleeing Rebs came to a halt.

When the jeering and cheering finally died down, a strange hush fell on the field except for one, totally incongruous sound. It was the sound of a woman—giggling. Colonel Collis knew immediately who it was. Then he saw her—French Mary—being carried off the field like a sack of potatoes with blood dripping off of her right boot and laughing like a child on her very first pony ride.

Jubal Early found Edmund Atkinson sitting down and leaning against a tree while a surgeon's assistant bandaged his wound and fashioned a sling for the injured arm.

"What in the hell were you *thinking,* Colonel, marching your entire brigade out into the open like that? Totally without orders and completely unsupported?"

Atkinson smiled up at the raging general. "I didn't have any trouble at all getting my men to fight, General, but I had a hell of a time getting 'em to stop."

Early remembered that he too had responded to conditions on the battlefield without consulting his own superior officer and, for the second time today, Jubal Early smiled. He just couldn't help it.

The past fifteen minutes had been the longest and most furiously frustrating of John Gibbon's life. He could hear the battle. He could see the white smoke lofting up through the trees. But he knew nothing. His men were deep into the woods. Against all odds they had broken the Rebel lines and pushed them back and continued the assault up the hill toward the Military Road. A foothold there, in Gibbon's mind, would change everything. It would clear those damned guns off the hill. It would offer his division an enfilade line down the Confederate lines to his left. It might even offer a line of advance against Longstreet's corps positioned to his right, behind the town. Everything hinged on the outcome of a fight he couldn't even see, much less control, and it was driving John Gibbon mad.

Twice he spurred his horse forward, and twice he held back. The fight was in the hands of his brigade commanders—Taylor and Lyle and Root. All competent commanders. All regular army men. Gibbon had seen to that. If all went well, they could handle it. If all went badly, Gibbon knew he would be needed in the rear to rally the troops, to establish defensive lines to prevent a Rebel counterattack. To hold his gains until Birney came—if Birney came.

Frustration became anguish. He wasn't much of a praying man, but now, faced with the hellish torment of powerlessness, he prayed.

His prayers were not answered.

His brigades came tumbling out of the woods, many without rifles. They had left their empty weapons behind to lighten the load and speed their escape. Others carried their wounded comrades. They weren't long out of the woods before Confederate troops appeared there, waving their flags defiantly and shaking their fists at the retreating Yanks.

Gibbon didn't have time to swear. The Rebel guns up on the hill that had been quiet for so long were being turned to face him and to take his retreating regiments under fire, and they had to be silenced. Gibbon commanded his horse to "run" and the stallion sprang forward in an instant. He headed for his own batteries to bring them to bear on the Rebel guns—at least to distract them long enough for his defeated division to survive. Gibbon may have been uncomfortable in his first battle commanding an entire division of infantry, but behind a battery of guns the West Pointer was right at home.

Rebel batteries all along the crest of Prospect Hill began to fire at the demoralized Yankees as they pulled back in absolute disarray. Gibbon made sure the Federal guns answered. The roar was ear-splitting, the smoke was blinding, and a piece of hot iron from a Rebel shell ripped into the back of John Gibbon's right hand.

FALMOUTH

A part of Joe Hooker's Center Grand Division, the 20th Maine, moved forward and down the hill from the Lacy house to the pontoon bridge that would carry them to Fredericksburg and into the fight. Joshua Lawrence Chamberlain stood out from the thousands of other men as he sat astride Prince, the wonderful white stallion that had brought him so much fame, but it hadn't yet occurred to him that this might not be a day to attract attention to himself. His professor's brain was occupied with other, more important matters. He continued to be amazed that things had been allowed to go this far. With each new assault he had tried desperately to formulate a rational argument in favor of launching another. That was his profession. At Bowdoin College he was respected for his ability to make the illogical sound reasonable and the insane seem rational. But on this day his forensic skills failed him. He could not comprehend how anyone who had witnessed the first assault against the wall could possibly order another—much less a dozen more.

Then—another distraction. A cheering began behind

him. He turned in the saddle to see what it was all about, fully expecting to see General Hooker being greeted by his men as tradition dictates. Instead he was surprised to see the commanding general himself. Ambrose Burnside was easily recognizable with his big, floppy hat and his bushy side whiskers, which wrapped around his clean-shaven chin. The road was too crowded with men for him to move easily in the opposite direction, and the soldiers gathered around him to get a closer look so that they could write home that they had seen him or maybe even touched his horse. Burnside looked nervous, maybe a little embarrassed by the attention.

"You need not crowd, boys," Chamberlain heard the general say. "There's plenty to do over there."

"We're ready for the work, General," a young Mainer hollered for all to hear, and a huge cheer rose up in salute of the grand commander.

Chamberlain couldn't join in. He felt embarrassed, and maybe even a little unpatriotic, but he just couldn't cheer Ambrose Burnside. Not today.

The first elements of the 20th began to march across the bridge. They hadn't gotten the word. Marching in cadence, it didn't take long for the floating bridge to begin to pitch and sway. Prince knew better than to step onto an unstable span and let his rider know that this was not a good idea. The men quickly resolved the problem in their own way, doing what any sane men would do. Without orders many began to run, just to get off the damned thing before it flipped over entirely, and the broken rhythm soon settled and steadied the bridge.

Chamberlain was not a man who believed in omens, but he recognized a cosmic metaphor when he saw one.

THE PHILLIPS HOUSE

Returning to his headquarters, General Burnside was greeted immediately by a courier.

"General Burnside, sir. A dispatch from General Hardie, sir!"

Burnside could see what was happening on Marye's Heights, but for the situation on Franklin's front at Prospect Hill, he had to rely exclusively on these all too infrequent little scraps of paper.

Burnside snatched the dispatch from the courier's hand. The first words hit the commanding general like a round of solid shot.

"Gibbon and Meade driven back from the wood . . . General Gibbon slightly wounded . . . General Bayard mortally wounded by shell . . . things do not look well; still we have new troops in soon."

For a long while he said nothing. He just stood there looking at the piece of paper as though if he studied it long enough, it might change.

"Gibbon and Meade . . ." the dispatch said. That's all. Just Gibbon and Meade. Two divisions. *All right,* he thought. *Maybe it's not as bad as all that.*

The assault had been late in starting, and so far Franklin had sent in only two divisions. He still had all of William Smith's corps and two divisions of Stoneman's corps "borrowed" from Hooker. Doubleday's division had been only lightly engaged. That meant that Franklin still had six full divisions packed up and ready to go. With six divisions he ought to be able to kick Thomas Jackson all the way to Richmond and back. Burnside remembered Jackson from West Point, and not very fondly. *"Stonewall," my ass.*

Burnside stole one more glance across the river and up the hill at Marye's Heights. *Hold 'em where they are boys. If Franklin does his job, that's all I need you to do. Just keep Ol' Pete Longstreet right where he is.*

"Tell General Franklin, with my compliments, that I wish him to make a *vigorous* attack with his *whole force*. Our right is hard-pressed."

FREDERICKSBURG

By mid-afternoon Colonel James Gwyn had refilled his canteen three times and was more than ready for a little fun. He had his men stationed along the banks of the river, waiting for an order to advance, but there were tens of thousands of men between his Corn Exchange Regiment and the slopes of Marye's Heights. If they were to go at all, it would not be soon, so the inebriated colonel set his regiment to drilling, knowing that it would eventually give him an opportunity to participate in his favorite pastime—the public humiliation of Captain Francis Adams Donaldson.

"Right shoulder—shift."

The regiment responded to the order as flawlessly as any rookie regiment would, and Captain Donaldson's men performed the rifle drills as well as any of the other companies, but that made no difference. Gwyn was tired of waiting for Donaldson to make a mistake.

"Why did you not repeat the command, Captain Donaldson?"

Donaldson looked to his rear to see his men all standing perfectly at right shoulder shift, just as they had been ordered. "I did, sir."

"Well, I say that you did *not*!"

"I most certainly *did*!"

"Repeat the command, Captain! As ordered!"

Donaldson was so angry that he shook. To repeat the order—again—would be admitting that he had not done so in the first place. To refuse would be to disobey the second order.

"I *said* repeat the command, Captain!"

Colonel Gwyn and his staff enjoyed the moment greatly, but their joy was cut short by a Union artillery shell that fell short of its mark and destroyed the front stoop of a nearby home revealing an entire bale of fine Southern tobacco. The regiment cheered and bolted for the treasure and Colonel Gwyn's fun came to an end. Not so for Captain Donaldson's humiliation.

Gwyn was angry at first that his regiment bolted without orders, but his tobacco tin was low as well, and he joined in the claiming of the delectable spoils of war. They resembled a swarm of bees covering a hive.

The revelry came to a sudden halt when the men heard the bugle sound "To Arms." They managed to re-form while still stuffing their pockets with tobacco.

"Are you ready for this, Captain Donaldson?"

Colonel Gwyn's question didn't have the normal sarcastic tone, but Donaldson heard it anyway. "As ready as *you* are, Colonel."

Gwyn was suddenly sober. He never ceased to be amazed that any grown man could behave so much like an arrogant, spoiled child as Donaldson. Donaldson's view was even less complimentary. *Maybe one of us will die.*

The colonel went to the head of his regiment and the captain stood, saber drawn and resting on his shoulder, waiting for the order to advance. Then, from just behind him, he heard absolutely the last thing on earth he wanted to hear. Private Ayers singing a hymn.

Donaldson spun around and found the offensive private and ran to face him. Nose to nose he shouted, "You *will* stop that infernal singing! I *never* want to hear it again! Do you understand me—this time?"

Ayers wanted to cry, but he only meekly responded, "Yes, sir."

"My only question for you, Private Ayers, is when are you going to turn tail and run? Because we both know you will!"

PROSPECT HILL

Ned Stevens adjusted Will's tourniquet and made a bandage for his brother's injured leg. Will was semi-conscious now and able to take in a little water.

At first hundreds of men came running past them. Most had dropped their rifles and their blankets and even their canteens, unloading anything that might slow them down. But Colonel Root managed to hold most of the 12th Mass. and Ned's friends from the Blanket Brigade in at least some semblance of order while they fought their way slowly back down the hill. Fresh Rebel reinforcements relentlessly pressed them back through the woods and toward the railroad tracks. A new Rebel line appeared, this time off to the side, and Ned could wait no longer. He tried to get Will to stand back up so that he could toss him over his shoulder again, but the older brother kept passing out. Ned emptied his canteen in Will's face and he came to for just long enough to stand with the help of his brother and a nice, strong tree.

"You there, Sergeant!"

Ned looked around to see a major yelling at him. He didn't know the man. He'd never seen him in his life. He didn't answer. He didn't have time.

"Soldier—I'm talking to *you*! You are ordered to leave the wounded where they fall."

"And whose orders are those, sir?"

The major was astounded that a common enlisted man would dare to question *any* order. "Mine! *And* General Burnside's!"

"Well, both you and General Burnside can just go straight to hell, Major Whatever-your-name-is, 'cause I'm getting my brother the hell outta here, and if you're gonna stop me, you're gonna have to shoot me."

He hefted Will onto his shoulder and headed down the hill as fast as he could go, wondering all the while whether the shot he was about to take in the back would come from a Rebel rifle or a Yankee pistol. It wasn't until after he crossed the tracks that he realized that it would be neither.

Praise be to God for that.

MARYE'S HEIGHTS

"General Hooker, sir. General Burnside sends his compliments with respect, sir, and instructs that your orders to attack the Rebel position stand as issued and that you should begin your attack as quickly as you can get your men into position."

Now, after a whole day of rumbling, the human Mount Vesuvius finally erupted. Hooker spewed profanities, and then using his finger like a sword he stabbed the poor, innocent messenger repeatedly in the chest and shouted, *"You go back to 'general' Burnside and you tell him I said . . ."*

The courier cowered away from the furious general as though he feared for his life. The look of shock and terror on the man's face almost made Hooker smile.

". . . Never mind, Captain. I'll tell him myself."

PROSPECT HILL

Evan Woodward limped slowly back toward the Bowling Green Road, nursing his bruised body as best he could and trying to make himself small to avoid the bullets and shells that continued to cut the air around him. His legs ached with every step and his mouth was desert dry. His tongue was swollen and he felt like his entire body was filled with sand. It dawned on him finally that he might not have to wait to get to the road to quench his almost debilitating thirst. Dead men weren't hard to find, and some of them had to have full or nearly full canteens. He began to rummage. He had never touched a dead man before, so first he had to get over that reluctance. His conscience argued that he might be stealing from the dead, but that was an argument very quickly lost. His first two corpses had no canteens at all. The third had one but it had a bullet hole in it the size of a five-dollar gold piece. He was obsessed now. Frantic. He couldn't give up. There was water nearby. He knew it. He only had to find it.

When he rolled over his fourth corpse, he finally struck gold. The canteen wasn't full, but very nearly. He unscrewed the cap and poured almost the entire contents into his mouth without stopping. His body absorbed the cold manna and his head began to spin with relief. He stopped only when he absolutely had to breathe and even then he continued to pour, letting some of the water soak his face and run down into his shirt. Almost instantly his stomach cramped itself into a knot and he threw the water back up. There was still a single mouthful left and Woodward used it to wash the vomit out of his mouth. In spite of that, he still wanted more. He would be more frugal next time and he almost immediately began to look for another canteen.

It took only a minute to find it, and the second was better than the first. He drank it slowly and even spit some of it out to give his stomach a chance to adjust and his body time to absorb. He even forced himself to save some for the walk.

He was better now and back on his way to the road when he saw a group of soldiers gathered around a wounded horse. Six men worked to roll the poor beast over until finally Colonel Albert Magilton was pulled out from under it.

The colonel had been pinned there under that horse for over an hour, watching a battle that he should have been leading. He was frustrated and furious, and the instant he was able to stand he drew his pistol and ended the animal's pain, but it was not an act of compassion—it was an act of pure, irrational, merciless revenge.

THE PHILLIPS HOUSE

Joe Hooker pulled up in front of Burnside's headquarters and didn't even wait for his horse to come to a full stop before he dismounted and raged into the house like a charging bull. He returned no salutes and, as he approached his commanding general, he offered none. He was swearing from the instant he roared into the room.

"This is the most insane damned ordered ever issued! You are sending my men to attack an absolutely impregnable position, General. You are condemning them to die for no reason and with no chance of success whatsoever!"

Hooker made no effort to appear calm or to disguise his insubordination. He yelled at Burnside like the commanding general was nothing more than a bumbling private. Burnside, Sumner, and the rest of the men in the room were simply too dumfounded to interrupt.

"You have sent two entire corps up that hill and not a single man has come within fifty yards of that goddamned wall, and since you have chosen to send half of my command to God-only-knows-where, I have even a *less* chance of success than *they* did!"

Burnside had heard more than enough. "General Hooker!"

But Hooker had no intention of stopping before he was finished. "That wall cannot be taken by any army in the world. Not today. Not tomorrow. Not ever!"

"General *Hooker*!" Now it was Burnside's turn to yell. "General Franklin is heavily involved on Prospect Hill. Meade and Gibbon have breached the enemy lines. He has been ordered to send in his *whole force,* and it is your job to hold Longstreet's corps in place, to give Franklin a chance to finish the job. If you take the wall, all the better, but, in the meantime, you are ordered to keep the pressure on Lee's left, and I expect you to do that vigorously—and *now*!"

Hooker simply stood there for a time and stared at Burnside with a look of undisguised contempt. Finally, in a slightly calmer tone, he said, "They have a name for this at West Point. You remember it, don't you, Ambrose? It's called 'reinforcing failure,' and it's the greatest sin a commander can commit."

Another tense moment passed. "You have your orders, General Hooker."

Hooker shook his head sadly, patronizingly, just to restate his scorn, and, again without a salute, he stormed out of the room even angrier than when he came in.

Edwin Sumner whispered, "You should have relieved him, General, for insubordination, right here on the spot."

"And replaced him with whom, General? They *all* want me to fail. They think that if I fail they'll get McClellan back. Just like after Pope failed at Manassas. They think that Lincoln and Halleck will go back to George—again—tails between their legs, and beg him to come back."

Sumner looked after the insolent wake of Fightin' Joe Hooker. "Joe doesn't believe that."

"No, he doesn't. *He* believes that if I fail Lincoln and Halleck will come to *him* with the job."

Sumner shook his head. "God help us all if they do."

CHAPTER 17

PROSPECT HILL

"*Attack?*" William Franklin was horrified. "General Burnside wants me to *attack*? *Again*?"

It was General Hardie's job to pass along Burnside's orders, and that was all. But he had been there all morning long and had seen that the earliest orders to send in "a division at least" had given Franklin an excuse to be timid. This latest order wasn't timid, and Hardie made sure that Franklin understood that. "He does, sir. 'Vigorously and with your entire force.' "

"What kind of force does he think I have?"

"He thinks you have two corps, sir, and then some."

"Well, I do not! Reynolds's corps is decimated and in retreat. Birney's division is fought out, and what I have left needs to stay back to protect against a counterattack and guard the bridges!"

"Very well, sir. I shall inform the commanding general that you are not in agreement and that you have refused the order to attack. Is that correct, sir?"

"*No!* For God's sake, don't do *that*!"

Visions of Fitz-John Porter appeared to Franklin for about the hundredth time today. Franklin's old friend was a very capable commander who at this very moment was being court-martialed for failure to obey another amazingly stupid order issued by another incredibly inept general. Pope at Manassas. It was exactly the same. Pope had ordered Porter to make a suicidal attack and Porter had delayed and now the promising career of a brilliant soldier was on the verge of a disgraceful end. He remembered General Halleck's warning that the Republicans in the Senate were on the warpath, looking for the scalps of all Democrats and friends of George McClellan who might be in positions of high command.

Hardie was impatient. "Then what *should* I tell him, sir?"

"I don't know. *Damn!*"

Franklin didn't have to look far to see his men—Meade's and Gibbon's men and now Birney's—crawling back over the field, or to see the dead scattered all across the plain. He didn't have to open his imagination very wide to envision Stonewall Jackson's entire corps rushing down off that hill and pushing his whole grand division, more than a third of the army, into the Rappahannock River.

What was *not* possible for William Franklin to envision was another assault against those stubborn Rebel positions concealed and entrenched in the woods on Prospect Hill.

But James Hardie needed an answer. "I have to respond, General. What should I tell him?"

"Tell him I'll do my best."

MARYE'S HEIGHTS

Joshua Lawrence Chamberlain remained mounted astride Prince and anxiously awaited the inevitable—the call to arms, the order to move out, and the attack up the hill and against the wall for the men of the 20th Maine. General Butterfield's other two brigades were already gone, sent off to the left in support of the failing Ninth Corps assault that was falling apart already after only fifteen minutes of fighting. And so it was the 3rd Brigade that would initiate Hooker's part of the fight.

Behind them would come Andrew Humphreys's division, and, as Chamberlain glanced to the rear, he saw the grand man himself parading before his brigades, absolutely exuding confidence and courage. The man beamed like a light-house. Thousands of men gathered around him, each grimly facing his own mortality, while Humphreys was a man thrilled to be standing at the gates of *im*mortality. After an hour of watching the disheartening flow of wounded men struggle by, many of them oddly wearing sprigs of boxwoods in their hatbands, Chamberlain took heart from the sight of the enthusiastic general to his rear. *If exuberance is contagious,* he thought, *please, God, let me catch it from him.*

The bugles sang the familiar and chilling call that General Butterfield had written himself back when he commanded only this brigade. He had composed it exclusively for them, to make them stand out from the rest. His men recognized the tempo immediately from the words they had given it . . . *Dan, Dan, Dan, Butterfield, Butterfield.*

The notes ran down the spine of Joshua Lawrence Chamberlain and all the men of Butterfield's 3rd Brigade. It meant "to the front." After months of drilling and marching and freezing and watching other men fight . . . after almost an hour of standing in the streets of Fredericksburg dodging artillery shells and praying for the order to go, *At long last,* Chamberlain thought, *the great question is about to be answered*—the question that had plagued Chamberlain ever since leaving Bowdoin College: *Are you a real soldier or are you still only an obscure college professor, destined to spend your life teaching young boys about the gallant deeds of others?*

Bill Owen looked over the muzzles of the four guns of the Washington Artillery as yet another brigade of men began to funnel themselves out of the streets of Fredericksburg with God-only-knew how many more lined up behind them. He had been astounded when the second brigade of the day came forward—and that was a dozen or more brigades ago. *How many damned Yankees* are *there in this world that they can afford to waste so many?* He did a quick calculation in his mind. He could only approximate the number of assaults they had turned back this day, but he knew that his guns had been busy since well before noon. Four hours or more of nearly ceaseless firing. They had to be running low on ammunition by now. He checked the boxes for all four guns and found them all wanting. There were very few rounds of exploding case shot left and absolutely no canister whatsoever. Solid shot was almost all that remained and there was precious little of that.

He sent to Colonel Alexander for fresh supplies.

Joshua Lawrence Chamberlain had come to his senses. All the officers of the 20th Maine had done the same. A single look up the hill showed them the bodies not only of thousands of men, but hundreds of horses as well. On that slope were a great many men who were still living—but no living horses. He dismounted and gave Prince a loving pat on the neck. "You go on back across the river now, boy. No sense in both of us dying."

He gave the reins to a corporal, who was much more than happy to tend to Prince and see him safely back to Falmouth.

Once dismounted, Chamberlain stood alongside his commanding officer, Colonel Adelbert Ames, and waited for the order to move out.

"God help us now," Ames said. "Take care of the right wing of the regiment."

Chamberlain saluted and moved to the right as Ames moved to the left.

The brigade was lined up well to the right of center, so as to assault the extreme end of the Confederate wall. They covered ground not as well traveled and not quite so cluttered as the path up the middle, and the artillery fire consisted primarily of solid shot rather than exploding shells. They made it to and through the millrace almost completely intact, but then they came up against a tall, sturdy board fence that no preceding regiments had been forced to deal with. It was pocked with minié ball holes and looked like it had been assaulted by a determined swarm of carpenter bees. The Rebels had seen the 20th Maine's approach and fired blindly into the fence, and any man who happened to be standing in exactly the wrong spot at precisely the wrong time might catch a bullet aimed at no one. But still the men knew it was better to be *behind* a fence and subject to fate, than to be in front of it and victims of deliberate marksmanship. To his men the fence was a haven—to Lawrence Chamberlain it was an obstacle.

"Pull it down, men . . . take down the fence!"

The men of the 20th Maine just stood there, looking at their lieutenant colonel—absolutely astounded that he would order them to do such an idiotic thing. This was Chamberlain's very first order under fire, and the men of his regiment froze in their tracks and simply failed to respond.

In that instant, as he looked into the faces of his frightened and bewildered men, Chamberlain realized that this was his moment. One way or the other—once and for all time—the greatest question of his life was about to be answered.

Soldier or teacher? Which will it be? Between him and his destiny stood an old, flimsy, bullet-riddled, wooden wall.

"Do you want *me* to do it?"

Without waiting for any response, Chamberlain attacked the fence alone. He assaulted it with a vengeance and began frantically to rip the boards away one at a time, throwing them to the ground and exposing himself to enemy fire.

There is only so long that a man can stand back and watch such an act of individual courage before he is compelled to move—one way or the other—and very quickly the men of the 20th Maine snapped out of their fear and came to the aid of their fellow soldier.

By the time the 20th got beyond the fence, the brigade lines were a shambles. They had begun their attack in the middle and now found themselves on the extreme right flank of the brigade. Ordered to "oblique left," Chamberlain and his men approached the wall at an angle, but it didn't help. The fire from behind the wall was just as thick and just as deadly as it had been all day long. But Chamberlain didn't hesitate, he didn't falter, and his men continued to follow as he led them closer.

"Colonel Chamberlain!"

Chamberlain was surprised to see Colonel Ames. He hadn't seen him in ten minutes or more.

"Sir!"

"You must continue forward," Ames shouted to him. "Those men up ahead have been trapped there all day long, and need relief, but we can't abandon the position. They are as close to the wall as anyone has gotten today, and we can't give it up. You must move your men up there, relieve them, and hold that position!"

It was only a matter of just a few more yards—but on this day they were the most deadly yards on earth. Chamberlain nodded and said nothing. He wanted to lie down and hide as much as any man there, but he continued to march forward, and his men continued to follow—and fall. Finally they reached the stranded soldiers and Chamberlain ordered them prone. Not a man alive failed to thank God that he had made it this far.

"Fire!"

The 20th Maine laid down a line of covering fire to help their predecessors escape.

Of the men on the hill, only a few were genuinely in need of relief. Most of them were dead. Of the living, only a scant few were healthy. Most were wounded to some extent or another and had to struggle back down the hill. Many assisted others too badly wounded to walk. Chamberlain specifically noticed one young man who had been shot in the arm and was limping badly. The visor of his kepi was almost ripped off and dangled beside the young soldier's face. Chamberlain thought it odd that sticking out from the band of the wounded soldier's hat was a small sprig of boxwood.

Bill McCarter hadn't limped for more than ten or twelve paces back down the hill before a Rebel bullet tore through the heel of his right shoe. It didn't draw blood but it ripped the heel off the shoe. He twisted his foot and fell back to the ground. His wounds had stopped bleeding an hour or so ago, while he was unconscious, but the exertion of the walk and the impact of the fall opened them back up again, and he had already lost so much blood that he just couldn't get back up. He was not quite as close to the wall as before, and this new regiment was now between him and the Rebs, so at least he was safer than before. A little bit. He tried one more time to stand, but his head began to spin and he was too weak now even to lift his head. He lay there for only a few seconds before God again sent sleep to rescue him from the pain.

PROSPECT HILL

William Franklin watched closely as two of his regiments moved forward on his right to plug yet another hole in his defensive lines. The hole vacated by John Gibbon's men. Regardless of General Burnside's order to attack "vigorously, and with your whole force," Franklin remained obsessed with turning back the Rebel counterattack he was certain Stonewall Jackson was about to launch. Jackson had been a plebe during Franklin's graduating year at West Point and he remembered the unrefined Virginian as a dim-witted bumpkin. George McClellan said he was "less refined than a lump of coal." But Franklin's grudging respect for his underclassman had grown with Jackson's exploits in the Shenandoah Valley and at Second Bull Run. He had left not only an army of dead men in the wake of his rise, but he ruined careers as well. Irwin McDowell. Nathaniel Banks. John Pope. And now even George McClellan himself. Everybody in the Army of the Potomac had learned firsthand how aggressive and tenacious Jackson could be.

Not quite everybody, Franklin thought. *It appears to be a lesson Ambrose Burnside has yet to learn.*

Franklin had sent the two New Jersey regiments forward as a precaution, just to have a presence in front of the tracks and alongside a creek on the right called Deep Run. They were to hold there just until General Dan Sickles could bring up his division, and Franklin watched intently as the two tiny boxes of men moved into place and as Sickles approached, not more than five hundred yards behind them.

The Jersey boys were almost there—almost to the tracks—when an entire brigade of Confederates came up, over, and down the little hill like a screaming gray wave. Franklin's pitiful regiments stood and fought for as long as they could but had to give way—quickly yielding to the sheer weight of numbers.

Franklin didn't know whether to panic or gloat. It was the thing that he feared most, but when it actually happened he knew that he was justified in ignoring Burnside's imbecilic orders to attack.

It may have been a matter of blind, dumb luck, or the gods of war playing an amusing little game, or just another example of the fortunes of war as the Rebels pursued the retreating regiments directly into the waiting arms of Sickles's oncoming division. Now only three hundred yards from the Bowling Green Road, the Confederates were suddenly and rudely met and repulsed by a full division of fresh Yankees and about a dozen batteries of Federal artillery—just as though it had all been planned.

Franklin watched the advance and the fight, which lasted no more than fifteen minutes, before the Rebs had to turn and hightail it back to the tracks, and when they were gone, to no one in particular he said, "That was a test. Jackson is probing our lines to see where we are weak before deciding where to attack."

After the smoke had cleared, through his glasses he spotted the unique figure of Dan Sickles, smoking a cigar and watching the Rebels run and, apparently, deep in thought.

"Don't do it, Dan!" Franklin yelled as though Sickles could actually hear him from a half a mile away and over the sound of the artillery that continued to chase the Confederates back to where they had come from.

Franklin knew Dan Sickles, and he knew that the impudent, glory-seeking politician would love nothing better than to chase the Rebels all the way to Richmond. It would make a magnificent headline. It was like waving a raw steak under the nose of a famished lion, and Franklin was almost certain that Sickles would not be able to resist. He held his breath briefly—waiting to see what Sickles would do. If he took out after the Rebels it could only mean disaster. Only when the division began to spread itself out along a defensive front was Franklin able to breathe again, but even then he was still not able to relax. This turn of events may have just given the Republican inquisitors from the Congress another excuse to burn him at the stake. "Failure to follow up a victory." He could almost hear Senator Wade pronouncing his vengeful verdict with the pious arrogance of a modern Torquemada. "Guilty—of heresy."

He shook his head. It just didn't matter what he did. He examined the entire length of his lines through his field glasses and found no spot where he could either launch or repel an attack. *Damned if I charge—damned if I don't.* Only when he casually noted the position of the sun did he find his rational excuse for disobeying Burnside's order. "It's too late to attack now," he announced. "We would only be doing Jackson a favor."

Stonewall Jackson watched as Sickles's division began to align itself in a defensive front. He was astounded—and pleased—when the Federals refrained from pursuit. He didn't smile. Until recently Stonewall Jackson had rarely smiled. But now his countenance changed noticeably. He sat taller in the saddle, almost standing in the stirrups. He scanned the front slowly, his mind taking in every nuance—every tiny flaw in the enemy's position. His eyes seemed to flash like a signal fire.

"Lieutenant Smith . . ."

James Power Smith was new to the staff—Kyd Douglas's replacement—and he wasn't entirely certain he wanted to hear what was coming next.

"Let's have ourselves a little ride—and a better look at what opportunities God may be offering us."

MARYE'S HEIGHTS

It had taken only a matter of seconds for the Corn Exchange Regiment to vanish before Captain Francis Donaldson's very eyes. After the first volley of fire from behind the wall, he turned and knelt, for only an instant, to help a fallen man, and when he stood back up, his company, his regiment, his entire brigade, was simply gone.

He didn't know what to do. He ran to his left, he looked to his rear. Nothing. It was as though he had been unconscious for an hour and awakened to find the whole world had changed. He drew his pistol and covered his own retreat back down the hill, across the millrace, and into the town.

Colonel Porter Alexander had moved from total elation to almost dismal boredom. This morning, as the first few waves of Union troops marched up the hill against his "masterful" artillery emplacements (even if he did think so himself), he was thrilled to see how well his plan was working. As the day wore on, however, he became more and more driven to get involved in the fight himself. He had no desire to tell his friends and family that he spent the day *watching* the Battle of Fredericksburg, and yet here he sat, commanding nine fully loaded, unused guns, whose crews were as anxious as he was to get into the fight. This was his frame of mind when Bill Owen's note arrived. *Dangerously low on ammunition. Have tenders resupply.*

Resupply, hell.

"Woolfolk—Smith—Moody! Limber your batteries and prepare to relieve Colonel Walton. Tell Colonel Walton to prepare to pull the Washington Artillery back. I will be relieving him with fresh batteries."

Even General Andrew Humphreys himself was momentarily disheartened by the sights of Fredericksburg. Beautiful buildings and homes and even churches were charred and smoldering, and along the streets was a constant flow of wounded men—some horribly so. Newly made coffins were stacked five high along the riverbank and bodies of some of the Rebel defenders still lay in the side yards of the houses. They had been there for almost forty-eight hours now and had begun to show signs of decomposition.

Humphreys wasn't distressed that these artifacts of war were there, but he was furious that they littered the streets his men would have to travel to reach the field. He didn't want his rookie brigades dispirited, so he rode ahead and ordered the roads blocked to protect his men from the carnage. The newly wounded seeking help or shelter would have to wait unseen until Humphreys's men had passed by.

Prospect Hill

Lieutenant Smith showed little concern as he rode alongside Stonewall Jackson safely behind the lines formed by General Daniel Harvey Hill's fresh division. Hill had moved his men into position to reinforce Generals Archer and Early. The lines were stronger here now than they had been even before Evan Woodbury and all the other Pennsylvania men had broken through. Stonewall had stacked his lines—one division directly behind another—so that when one became engaged, the next in line could simply roll forward. A. P. Hill had yielded to Early and Early to Harvey Hill—like rolling logs down a hill one after another.

Smith only began to show his uneasiness when his commanding general meandered out in *front* of the lines to get a better view, and offered himself—and Smith—as a target! Jackson was no longer the "ragamuffin god" who could ride out wearing his disheveled private's garb and attract little attention. He continued to wear the uniform given to him by, of all people, Jeb Stuart. He looked every bit as flamboyant as the gaudy cavalier, and it didn't take long for the two to be spotted by Yankee pickets and the bullets began to fly. Smith instinctively dodged a minié ball that, of course, had long since passed by. Jackson noticed and was amused.

"Mr. Smith—perhaps you had best go to the rear. They may shoot you here."

James Power Smith didn't care for his new job at this moment nearly as much as he thought he might when he took it over. Of course he wanted nothing more than to follow Jackson's advice and move back behind a full division of protectors, but he could no more leave the famous Stonewall Jackson here alone than he could fly to the moon.

"No, sir." He almost couldn't speak because his mouth was so dry. "I'll be here for as long as you need, me, sir," he managed to say. *Or until they shoot me,* he thought.

Jackson gave the young man an approving nod and continued his reconnaissance. The deadly bullets were of no more concern to Stonewall Jackson than an annoying swarm of harmless gnats.

MARYE'S HEIGHTS

Darius Couch was relieved to see Humphreys's division finally marching through the streets of Fredericksburg. His own men were trapped on the hillside and behind the swale and now he was absolutely convinced that the Rebel artillery was out of ammunition.

"General Humphreys! You must move forward immediately!"

Humphreys was thrilled. If he had his way his men would fix bayonets and head up that hill right this instant, without a moment's pause. Hell. If he had *his* way he would have led the very first assault at the very first hint of dawn. He'd been waiting for this order since Longstreet's first signal shots had been fired two days ago. He wanted nothing more in the world than to pull his sword and spur his horse to a run and capture that damned hill all by himself. There was no fear of the Rebels, no concern for death, no thought of defeat in Andrew Humphreys—but he was scared to death of the uncontrolled wrath of Fightin' Joe Hooker.

He shook his head sadly. "I am ordered into position here, General Couch."

Anger flashed across Couch's face, but Humphreys stopped an explosion with a whisper. "*But*—you are the ranking officer on the field, and if you give me an order to do so, I will support you at once."

Couch smiled. He understood. He wouldn't want to face an angry Joe Hooker either.

"The order is given, General Humphreys."

Much to the relief of both men, the conspiracy became immediately unnecessary as Hooker himself came up at a run.

Humphreys greeted Hooker with a salute. "General Couch has ordered my division up the hill, sir, and I have no objections. What are your orders, sir?"

Against his better judgment and regardless of his best efforts to put a stop to this madness, Hooker too had his orders, and there was nothing more that he could do. "General Burnside wants the heights taken by sundown, General. You may advance."

Andrew Humphreys glowed with excitement and anticipation. He saluted and started to return to his men, but Hooker put up his hand and held the exuberant general in check for just one more moment.

"General Humphreys—this is a mission that can be accomplished *only* with the bayonet."

Humphreys smiled at the prospect. He nodded and turned and pushed his horse hard up the hill almost to the swale, just to get a look at the ground. He saw the men and horses all around him—dead or wounded or laying low in the mud. He saw the colors of all of the regiments that had attacked the wall and failed. He saw it all, but it didn't concern him. In his imagination he saw himself at the head of his division—leaping over the wall and giving the Johnnies the bayonet. And it was good.

He turned back down the hill and returned at a walk with bullets and solid artillery shot following him every step of the way. His untested Pennsylvanians watched in astounded admiration as their division commander calmly rode through the danger.

He smoked a cigar as he rode, and when he finally came to a halt in front of his first brigade, he took a moment to fill his mouth with the sweet fumes and to savor the elegant flavor. He made a show of it.

"Three cheers for General Humphreys!" one man shouted and the division answered with shouted hoorahs. He tipped his hat to his men and bowed.

"Colonel Allabach—I want you to have every man in your brigade inspected to make certain they haven't loaded their muskets."

"I beg your pardon, sir."

"You heard me, Colonel." General Humphreys was smug and patronizing and thoroughly enjoying the astonishment on the face of his brigade commander. "I said that you should inspect your men and make absolutely certain that not a single one of them has a loaded musket. Have them drop their ramrods into the muzzle and make sure it drops all the way down. Those weapons *must* be empty, Colonel. If we send 'em up that hill with loaded rifles, they won't be able to resist coming to a halt and firing at the enemy."

Peter Allabach still couldn't believe what he was hearing. "But, General—"

"No 'buts,' Colonel. We are going to carry that wall where no one else could, and we're going to carry it because we're *not* going to stop halfway up to shoot at the enemy like everybody else did. Once we leave this place, Colonel, we're hell-bent, and we're not going to stop or even slow down until we can give those bastards the bayonet!"

He took another long and loving draw from his cigar. He blew the smoke out of his mouth and inhaled it back through his nose, adoring the aroma. "Southern tobacco." He grinned. "This is why we can't let them leave the Union."

Allabach smiled. *There is not another man in the world with the calm self-assurance of Andrew Atkinson Humphreys and these men will follow him anywhere.* The colonel wasn't sure that empty muskets was a good idea, but those were his orders, and if Humphreys said it, it must be right. And so the inspection began.

PROSPECT HILL

Daniel Harvey Hill stood poised and ready. His Confederate division was stacked up deep in the woods, well above the railroad tracks in a line two hundred yards long. Every man was loaded and ready because Hill knew his brother-in-law better than any other man in this army, and he knew that Stonewall Jackson had stood still and taken enough blows this day. He had wanted to start the day with an attack, but Lee had turned him down. The only question in Hill's mind was the time of day. It was late and the sun rested near the horizon. The precious daylight was almost spent. And yet somehow Hill knew—darkness be damned—that Stonewall Jackson was about to launch a massive counterattack against the wounded and unenthusiastic Union lines.

Hill admired the gallant Stonewall second only to God Himself. If Jefferson Davis had a brain the size of a pea in his tiny Mississippi head, Jackson would be commanding the Army of Northern Virginia and Robert E. Lee would be back in Richmond, where he belonged, shuffling papers around a desk and polishing Davis's boots. Lee had stained Hill's brilliant career after Malvern Hill, and at South Mountain he had left Hill with a single division to hold back the entire Army of the Potomac. It wasn't anybody's fault, really. That darned lost dispatch told McClellan everything he could ever want to know about where the Confederates were and what they had in mind. But General Lee had gotten it into his mind somehow that Hill was at fault for some darned courier losing an important piece of paper. It was Hill's copy that was lost, but *he* didn't lose it. What should have been Hill's glory day, the day he held back five full corps of Federal troops with a single torn-up division of barefooted Rebels—well, the glory was tarnished, and the man from South Carolina knew how to carry a grudge.

From fifty yards away Hill could see that he had been right. Jackson wouldn't be pushing Little Sorrel so hard just to ride up here and tell him to hold his position. With little more than an hour of daylight left, maybe less, Stonewall Jackson was about to order an attack.

"Forward, Harvey," Jackson told him. His face was red and his tone urgent. "We're going to drive them into the river yonder. I'm sending in every man, Harvey. The whole corps is to go forward the instant the artillery ceases firing! Do you understand?"

"I do, sir!"

"God be with you, sir!"

"And with you, General Jackson!"

MARYE'S HEIGHTS

Humphreys's division reached the millrace easily. A few rounds of solid shot from the Rebel artillery found their mark, but, compared to previous assaults, Humphreys's approach was a cakewalk.

Joe Hooker watched from the outskirts and was amazed at the ease of Humphreys's approach. Then it dawned on him. "They're out of ammunition!"

Hooker instantly shouted, "Bring up the guns!" He sent every available man on his staff out on a mission. Every gun they could find was to be ordered forward to take the wall under fire before Humphreys launched the final leg of his attack. If they could go in man against man—infantry against infantry—without the deadly fire from those damned guns up on the hill, then this idiotic charge might actually work!

Captain John Hazard had been there before. He had responded when Winfield Hancock had tried the very same thing earlier in the day. He had rolled his battery forward, gotten off one shot, lost a half dozen men and a pair of horses, and pulled quickly back. He wanted no part of going back.

"General, a battery cannot live out there!"

"Then they will have to die out there! Now, move out!"

Edward Porter Alexander was suddenly in the greatest danger and the biggest hurry of his life. His three batteries of guns had to get to the pits along Marye's Heights to relieve the Washington Artillery and the other batteries posted along the ridge. His only approach to the position was along a stretch of the Plank Road, parts of which were open to Federal fire—all types of Federal fire. Sharpshooters had a clear shot at them. Thousands of infantrymen stacked along the swale saw them clearly and opened fire. And now, more and more Federal guns were being rolled forward and they had clear shots at the road as well. But at this moment, with all of the minié balls and artillery rounds pouring in around him, Alexander was concerned with one artillery shell and one shell only—because he could *see* it and it was headed his way. It hadn't been fired at him but at the wall. It hit its mark but failed to explode and the ricochet sent it tumbling end over end—*like a thrown stick,* Alexander thought—and it was coming directly at him, slowly enough that he could see it, but too fast for him to get out of the way.

His mind screamed for him to react—to duck, to dodge, to run—but his body suddenly weighed a thousand tons. He instinctively pulled his horse to a stop. He deeply inhaled his last breath on earth. He turned his face away from the incoming shell and closed his eyes—either to brace himself for the impact or to utter a very quick, final prayer—or both. A half second later he heard a soggy thump as the shell passed directly under his horse and splashed into the muddy bank behind him. He remained frozen in that spot for another moment, waiting to see if it might yet explode. His skin bristled with exhilaration and, as soon as he realized that he was safe, his heart pounded with relief.

He looked back at Captain Haskell, who rode only a length behind him. Haskell was holding his breath as well, and his eyes were as big as a cow's. After an instant of silence, both men began to laugh, almost hysterically. "Thank you, Jesus," Alexander said through the laughter, and then, almost calmly, he went on about his work.

Bill Owen was steamed. His commander, Colonel Walton, was fuming. The Washington Artillery had asked for more ammunition—that's all. They didn't *need* relief. They didn't *want* relief. All they wanted was more ammunition—pure and simple. Porter Alexander's fresh batteries forcing their way up the Plank Road were anything *but* a welcome sight. The New Orleans boys had started this fight, they had won this fight, and by damn they wanted to *finish* this fight. Walton was fully prepared to risk court-martial by telling Porter Alexander precisely what he thought of an officer who would pull rank at the end of the day so that he could take the credit for another man's victory.

As Walton rehearsed his speech, Hooker's cannons rolled forward and began to find their mark, and the Washington Artillery, with the ammunition chests almost completely dry, couldn't respond as they had earlier in the day. Within minutes three men fell dead and another twenty or more were wounded. The task of repositioning the guns after every recoil became a nearly impossible chore as their numbers shrank to a precious few.

Walton and Owen, observers until now, were forced into dangerous manual labor as every available man had to put his shoulder to the wheels and tails of the heavy guns, to shove them back through the churned-up ground into their redoubts to fire just one more precious round of solid shot. Every effort cost more men.

Owen stood behind gun commander Charlie Squires as they and nine others heaved with all their strength to get the number-one gun back into place. The footing was worse than sloppy as a day of rocking heavy guns back and forth over the soft, wet earth made the nearly impossible job that much harder. Squires slipped and fell and Owen tumbled on top of him as his feet got tangled with Squires's legs. He pulled himself up by a wheel spoke and offered Squires help up, but the captain held his hand over his shoulder and shook his head.

"Send for Galbraith to take command. I'm wounded."

Only then did Owen see the blood.

Now the sight of Alexander coming up the road with nine fresh guns, each with full crews and packed ammunition chests, wasn't such a bad thing after all.

The Federal artillery fire increased with every passing moment and Walton began to worry if he would have enough men left to pull the guns over the hill and out of the fight.

"Bring up the horses and limbers!" He turned to Owen, and a little more quietly, he said, "It's time to get the hell out of here, Bill."

The exuberant General Andrew Humphreys could not believe his good fortune. As his men fixed their bayonets to their unloaded rifles, the Rebels on the hill began to pull back. He could see it clearly. The artillery battery on the ridge, just above the wall, was limbering its guns. The four cannons that had given the previous assaults such deadly hell all day long were suddenly in retreat.

"Gentlemen! I shall lead this charge." Then, with a smile the size of Pennsylvania, he added, "I presume, of course, that you will wish to ride with me!"

Then Andrew Humphreys struck a pose. There's no other way to describe it. Shoulders back, sword in hand, tall in the saddle, and facing the enemy, he shouted, "Officers to the front!" No one would "lead" this attack from behind. The officers joined Humphreys, fully intending to be the first over the wall.

"*Forward . . .*"

Colonel Allabach echoed, "*Forward!*"

"*March!*"

Two thousand, three hundred men stepped out of the mill-race with bayonets fixed to empty rifles and began their march up the hill. General Erastus Tyler's Brigade remained in the millrace, under orders to follow two hundred paces to the rear.

PROSPECT HILL

The Confederate artillery fire began with Sallie Pelham's guns on Jackson's right, and sparked its way like a lit fuse completely around Prospect Hill to Greenlee Davidson's guns a mile away on the left. Facing the Rebel guns, Franklin's Union artillery was stacked deep on the plain and supported by the thirty-pound Parrotts across the river on Stafford Heights. The duel at dusk was every bit as furious and deadly as the morning fight that had set the whole thing off.

In the darkening woods of Prospect Hill couriers set out in all directions in a desperate search for Jackson's generals with orders for them to prepare for the all-out assault. A few were easily found—most were not. While some of Jackson's men prepared to attack, others began to dig in or to build cooking fires, and many were left just wondering what in the hell was going on.

TELEGRAPH HILL

For the first time today a surge of panic attacked the heart of Robert E. Lee. He yelled at Longstreet, but the artillery posted all around Telegraph Hill fired almost continually down onto the Union positions under Prospect Hill in support of Jackson. Longstreet heard not a word. Even though they stood side by side Lee had to tug on Pete's sleeve just to get his attention.

"Look there!" He pointed to Marye's Heights and to the Washington Artillery limbering its guns and pulling away. "What does *that* mean?" Lee shouted.

Now it was Longstreet's turn to panic. Furiously he grabbed the nearest staff officer and yelled into his ear, "Major Fairfax—go and order Walton back into position and tell him that my orders are for him to *stay* there!"

Fairfax only had time to mount his horse before both Lee and Longstreet saw Porter Alexander's guns moving into place—ready to replace Walton as soon as the space was cleared.

Longstreet didn't have time to enjoy his sense of relief. Jackson's guns continued to pound away on Franklin's positions at the base of Prospect Hill, and Longstreet knew precisely what Stonewall Jackson had in mind. With the shadows now longer than the trees, he knew that the only way they could be beaten on this day was for Jackson to risk his entire corps in some foolhardy attack.

Marye's Heights

General Humphreys and the officers of Allabach's Brigade were now riding totally alone—beyond the swale and before the wall. Allabach turned in the saddle to wave his men on and was horrified to see that his men, or at least most of his men, had marched as far as the swale and simply decided that this was as far as they cared to go. The wreckage of the previous assaults and the thousands of men lying on the hillside had been more than enough to break up their formations, and the survivors had implored them not to go forward, and, to the Pennsylvania rookies, it seemed like excellent advice.

"Son-of-a-*bitch*!" Humphreys and the rest of his officers turned their backs to the enemy and moved back down the hill to rally the men. He was furious and frustrated. Here were thousands of men—more than enough to take that wall in five minute's time—all cowering under the limited

protection of a shallow dip in the earth. If they all stood—
every cowardly one of them—and ran screaming to the
wall with bayonets fixed and at the ready, the heights would
easily be theirs. He couldn't spare the time to separate his
men from the remnants of General Couch's beaten divisions and began to berate every man within the sound of
his voice.

An unknown major from some whipped division was the
first to feel Humphreys's wrath.

"Either get your men up to face the enemy and move forward with me, or get the little yellow bastards the hell out of
my way!"

The astounded major wanted to shoot the arrogant bastard. The man was crazed. He had no idea what these men
had done—what they had endured for the past four hours—
and even less of an idea about what would greet them if
they were stupid enough to stand. That was what the major
thought, but it was not what he could say.

"I have no orders beyond the holding of this position,
General, and that is precisely what I intend to do."

Humphreys wanted to pull rank on the little coward, but
he just didn't have time to argue. Allabach had located the
heart of his brigade and was desperately attempting to get
the men up and moving forward again. Humphreys saw him
and rode to his aid.

Mounted on his gigantic charger and almost silhouetted
by the red light of the setting sun, A. A. Humphreys looked
to be more than only a man. He appeared almost godlike—
and he knew it. He felt it. He relished it. He believed it. He
was not behind his soldiers, pushing them ahead like a mortal man might. He rode boldly in front—confident of success and impervious to fear.

"Rally, men," the general shouted. "Up—up and forward!"

The guns on the hill were gone, and the rifles behind the
wall were quiet, and every man was able to hear the order.

A cheer rose up—and, incredibly, so did his men.

Fredericksburg

In his notebook Villard had written the words "gallant" and "valiant" probably a hundred times. The flags waved and the bands played and the brave officers on horseback pushed those boys up the hill for no other purpose than to be killed or maimed. Another word: "Glory." The wind would occasionally blow the smoke off the field to offer the spectators the grandest of all panoramas. Everything was on a massive scale. The flags were huge and beautiful. The guns seemed to fire in a constant thunder and the men—thousands upon thousands of them—continued to march against the dragon as though there were an endless supply of expendable boys. Angry blue ants storming out of a just-stepped-on mound. Villard looked back at the words he had written so many times and decided they were simply wrong.

No. They're not wrong. It's not the adjectives that are wrong. It's the object. These aren't "gallant charges," or "valiant assaults." They are gallant *men*. They are *stupid* assaults ordered by stupid men. *Dumme Männer! Sheisskopfs.*

He watched now as more "gallant" men filed out from the town and prepared for another "stupid" charge and he just couldn't do it. He couldn't stand there and watch it happen all over again like some kind of horrifying recurring nightmare. He couldn't bear to see another brigade march up the hill until the dragon spewed another breath of fire a half a mile long until the "valiant" brigade was dead. He just couldn't watch it again. He mounted his horse and headed for the town.

CHAPTER 18

PROSPECT HILL

Stonewall Jackson deflated. He was astounded that the response of the Federal artillery was so massive and the guns so expertly positioned. Like most West Pointers, Jackson was first and foremost an expert in artillery. It was the subject he taught at the Virginia Military Institute, but it didn't take an expert or an instructor to appreciate what his men would be up against if he sent them out now. Any plebe could look over this field and see that an attack over this open ground, against such devastating artillery fire would be nothing more than a waste of thousands of good men—men who he would need tomorrow.

"Call it off."

Smith barely heard him. "I beg your pardon, sir."

Jackson took a breath and slouched in the saddle. "I said, 'call off the attack,' Lieutenant."

Smith waited for an explanation, but it was futile. He was still new enough to Stonewall's staff that he hadn't learned yet that Jackson never explained anything—to anybody.

A new batch of couriers went out carrying the new orders. They had no better luck in hunting down Jackson's generals than the men who had been sent out ten minutes before—the ones carrying the orders for the attack to begin.

Marye's Heights

Porter Alexander had his guns parked behind the casements and well out of sight of the approaching Yankee brigade. All nine guns—the four in the center and the five positioned along the flanks—were primed and loaded with double canister.

The timing couldn't have been better. The swap between his guns and the Washington Artillery had gone much better than anyone had a right to expect. Alexander himself had survived the near miss on the Plank Road. He had lost four men and a dozen or so horses—acceptable losses under the circumstances. They had arrived only a matter of minutes after the Louisianans cleared the ground and just as a fresh Yankee assault began its march up from the swale.

He started to roll the guns forward when the enemy was a hundred yards out, but he decided to wait for them to come in closer. The longer he waited, the more devastating and demoralizing the fire would be. Five more yards—ten more—and still he waited. At fifty yards out, Alexander only nodded.

He became a little nervous when his men lost their footing in the mud, and it took them longer than expected to roll the guns into place, but the second try pushed them nicely into the redoubts.

Every man on all four crews was now in position. The guns were aimed, the lanyards were set, and everyone looked to Alexander, anxiously waiting for the order to fire. He took one more moment to admire his enemy.

God, what courage! The general leading the charge was finely mounted and well out in front of his men. His soldiers came forward in almost perfect order, following their flags and their officers and marching shoulder-to-shoulder with bayonets fixed and at the ready. It was a long line of men, only two ranks deep, and it may have been the most beautiful sight Porter Alexander had ever seen.

He raised his glasses to get a better look at the brave general in blue.

"Well, I'll be damned." He didn't know why he was surprised. As long as this war had lasted, it was bound to happen eventually—at least to anyone from the old army.

Eventually men who had known each other would have to come face-to-face.

"Andrew Humphreys, as I live and breathe."

He hadn't known Humphreys well, but they had served together long ago, before they had to choose sides. A good engineer and a fine officer. And one more thing . . .

"Still as arrogant as ever, huh, Andrew?"

Alexander watched as Humphreys raised himself high in the stirrups and lifted his hat in the air, ready to give the order to charge, and Alexander could admire the man's phenomenal courage no longer.

It's one thing to give the order to fire into a mass of faceless strangers, but quite another . . . damn!

"Fire!"

Standing ten feet behind the guns, Alexander felt the hot air hit his chest and warm his face. The sound was that of close thunder times four and it left his ears ringing. The ground shook beneath his feet. For the first time today the approaching darkness made the orange-hot flames clearly visible as the fire blasted fifteen feet out from each barrel. Each gun weighed over two thousand pounds and yet the force of the explosions sent them bouncing into the air and recoiling up the slope like kicked toys.

The gun commanders all ordered *"load!"* almost at the same time. Alexander continued to hold his breath, waiting for the curtain of thick, white smoke to rise so he could see if his incredibly impudent Yankee friend had survived.

He hoped he had.

He hoped he hadn't.

He remembered General Jackson's cruel credo: *Kill the brave ones. They lead the others.*

PROSPECT HILL

A. P. Hill got the word. Jubal Early and John Bell Hood got the word. Stonewall Jackson's full-corps assault was canceled.

Daniel Harvey Hill *didn't* get the word.

The instant the Confederate guns fell silent, Hill ordered

his division forward through the woods and toward the railroad tracks, believing that three or four more divisions were directly alongside. Men got lost and confused in the darkened swamp and regiments got separated and it was a disorganized bunch that finally reached the tracks and began to move forward across the plain—alone.

"I *knew* it!"

William Franklin was vindicated. "I *knew* Jackson was going to attack! Every gun is to take those men under fire—*now*!"

It was like ordering fish to swim. Hundreds of Federal guns of all shapes and sizes opened on the advancing Confederates before they were twenty yards out of the woods. Daylight returned as the darkening sky became noontime bright, illuminated by the flames of hundreds of exploding shells. It was now the Rebels' turn to dive for their lives into the mud and sludge, just as Meade's Yankees had done six hours before.

Only moments later and in good order Hill's men retreated back to the safety of the woods.

For the first time today William Franklin was a very happy man. The Rebel counterattack that he had predicted—the attack he had prepared for and defended against—was repulsed in only a matter of minutes. His actions were now completely above reproach. Not Benjamin Wade—not Ambrose Burnside—not Henry Halleck . . . no one could now question his refusal to launch a suicidal assault.

I would have lost my whole army if I had done that, he thought. *The whole damned thing—horse, fort, and dragoon.*

MARYE'S HEIGHTS

Charley was dead, and Charley was General Humphreys's favorite horse. The gigantic charger took four of the deadly canister pellets in the first artillery blast, but his rider survived without a scratch. Only one horse survived and Humphrey's son rode her.

"Give me your horse, Lieutenant, and find yourself another!"

Lieutenant Henry Humphreys did as his father and commanding officer ordered. Before mounting, the general patted his son on the shoulder.

"I'm proud of you, son. You're a chip off the old block!"

Henry beamed.

The general mounted and turned to his dispirited men. Not a soul remained standing and Humphreys couldn't tell who was wounded and who was dead and who was still healthy and able to continue the charge. He knew only this: that if he didn't charge, nobody would.

His men, who had been ordered to attack without ammunition, had somehow found time to load, and were firing up the hill, wasting time and effort and ammunition.

"Dammit, don't waste so much ball!"

They had all seen Humphreys go down with his horse in the first blast. The animal had reared like a fighting stallion and man and horse had fallen together. And yet here he was—either alive or an apparition—back in the saddle and even more fearless than before. To his men, General A. A. Humphreys had just returned from the dead.

"Give 'em the cold steel—that's what the rascals want!"

He ordered them to attention and most of those who could stood, only to be greeted by a second blast from Alexander's guns, this time accompanied by a thousand minié balls from behind the wall. This time even Andrew Humphreys knew that Allabach's Brigade had climbed the hill as far as they could.

"I'm off for help, men. Hold your ground!"

Tyler's Brigade, which was supposed to be two hundred paces to the rear of Allabach's, was still stuck in the millrace, pinned down by the guns on Alexander's flanks. Allabach's men had been gone for ten minutes, and General Tyler and his friend Colonel Quay, the man who was half dead of pneumonia only yesterday, had had no luck in getting the men reorganized and ready to move forward. The mere sight of the gallant Humphreys riding casually down from the wall was enough to inspire a dead man. Tyler rode out to greet him, expecting to be welcomed by a harangue of foul language. Instead he was astounded to hear his bold commander whistling as he rode.

"That's a happy little tune, General."

"It is, isn't it?" Humphreys answered, just as casually as if they were walking home from church. "That's even what it is called, I believe. 'Gay and Happy.' It's one of my wife's favorites. Now, Colonel Tyler, what seems to be the problem here?"

"Those guns, sir, particularly the ones on the right, are holding us down pretty good, sir."

"Call your color guard to attention and have the bugler sound 'To the Colors.' That should do it."

It did. Tyler's Brigade of two thousand men stood and stepped forward onto the uphill side of the millrace while the worrisome artillery battery on the right redoubled their efforts. The men were still nervous and ducked and bobbed as every round of solid shot approached.

"Don't juke, boys! By the time you've seen it, it's generally too late anyway!"

At that moment, right on cue, a well-aimed round came lofting in directly toward the general's head—and Andrew Humphreys "juked." The round missed by several feet, but the tension of the moment was broken and several close-by soldiers were even able to laugh, and Humphreys laughed right along with them.

"All right," he said with a bit of a giggle and a Humphreys-size smile. "It's all right to juke the *big* ones, but don't mind the little ones!"

FREDERICKSBURG

Over the past two hours Clara Barton had worked at the church, at the town hall, and out in the streets helping the surgeons dress wounds, administer opiates, and amputate limbs. Now she stood at the intersection of Caroline and Hawke Streets greeting the most seriously wounded as they streamed back down the hill from the most recent assaults against Marye's Heights. Her attention was wholly focused on a young man with a flesh wound—it was something that she could do by now in her sleep.

"Clara!"

It was Cornelius Welles—the best surgeon's assistant in the 21st Massachusetts, and, as far as Clara was concerned, the best in the whole Army of the Potomac. He and Colonel Clark were headed her way carrying a stretcher.

"It's Thomas, Clara!"

Oh, dear God. Please let it be nothing. Please!

Thomas Plunkett looked dead. His face was whiter than a steeple and she saw no movement. Welles knew what she was thinking.

"I think he's still alive, ma'am. I gave him a mess of opium." They set him down, right there on the street directly at Clara's feet. "Miss Barton—it was the damnedest thing—the darndest thing I ever saw, what he did up there."

She pulled back the blanket that covered the boy and, regardless of all that she had seen in the last few months from Bull Run to Antietam, this wound shocked her. Maybe just because it was Thomas, but even for a stranger it would have been ghastly. Both of his hands were gone. Both of them. Cornelius had applied tourniquets to both forearms and had managed to slow the effusion of blood, but not stop it.

"Bring him into the church."

Sergeant Welles and Colonel Clark lifted the stretcher and did as they were told. Clara led them through the line of wounded men, all waiting for their turns under the surgeon's knife. Even ahead of the officers. She would wait for Dr. Noland to finish his current amputation, but not a moment longer to get Thomas on his table.

She began to prepare him while she waited, so that Noland could get right to work. While she cut off the sleeves of Plunkett's uniform, Welles continued talking.

"It was horrible up there, Clara. They should never have sent us up there. A million men couldn't take that wall."

Clara put a wet cloth in Thomas's mouth. Conscious or not, she knew the boy needed to take in some water somehow. She saw Welles looking at the bucket of water and offered him a sip as well. He accepted it gratefully and went on.

"He picked up the flag when it fell—the national colors—and waved them right in the faces of the damned—darned Rebels. And just then a shell went off right in front of him. That's what took his hands. But he didn't fall down and *he didn't even drop the flag*! He hugged it to his chest with his arms! He wouldn't let it fall!"

Clara looked up to check on Dr. Noland's progress. It was a leg amputation, and the limb was just now cut loose. A surgeon's assistant took the leg away, removed the boot—it was still a perfectly good boot—and tossed the leg out the window. There was still work to be done—another five or six minutes before Thomas would get his turn.

"Look at this, Clara." Colonel Clark had the flag with him. There was no white on it. Even the stars were red from Thomas's blood.

"Next!"

The amputation was done, and Welles and Clark lifted Thomas off the stretcher and put him on the surgeon's table. It was only a door, really, and blood was pooled in the depressions. No matter.

Dr. Noland examined the corporal's wounds and indicated the tourniquets and bandages. "Who did this?"

"Sergeant Welles, here, Doctor."

Noland looked at the crusty old sergeant and nodded. "Very nice work, Sergeant. I think you may have saved this man's life—a least for the moment."

MARYE'S HEIGHTS

Colonel Quay filled his lungs for the first time in weeks. Months more likely if he were honest with himself. The infernal coughing had stopped hours ago. His blood was up and he felt young and invincible with bullets and cannon shot whizzing by and colliding with the earth all around him. He would love to see one of those so-called "surgeons" now—the ones who had him packed up and headed home to die in bed.

"Up, men! Up and in formation!" His voice was as strong and loud as a steam horn. He felt as if he could dismount and run alongside his men, all the way up the hill and on to Richmond. He never felt better or more full of life.

A. A. Humphreys heard him even over the din, and admired the man. An entirely different man than the one who had come to his tent, begging for a chance to fight one last fight. It was not a good or pleasant thing to think, but remembering the violent cough that racked the man that night, it occurred to Humphreys that it might serve Colonel Quay better to die here—today—rather than to live another month, only to die of pneumonia. *Quay's words deserve a spot in the history books: "I would rather* die *and be called foolish than* live *and be called a coward!"*

Live and be called a hero, Humphreys thought.

Quay pulled up next to Humphreys and Tyler. "They'll follow *me,* sirs—I have their pay in my pockets." Both generals grinned. "At least they won't leave my bones on the field."

The sun had vanished and they were only moments away from total darkness. Humphreys held out hope that Tyler's Brigade would pull up alongside of Allabach's and the two could then sprint together up the hill under the cover and relative safety of darkness.

Tyler sat mounted before his brigade. "Boys—we are ordered to take that stone wall and we must do it with the bayonet."

Humphreys raised his hat over his head and the men began to cheer. The order to *"forward march"* went unheard in the roar, but was instantly understood when the hat came down.

Behind the wall and on the hill, the Confederates heard the commotion. The infantrymen cocked their hammers and the artillerymen set their lanyards, and all waited for the order to fire.

PROSPECT HILL

Ned Stevens stood in the doorway of the field hospital stunned and frozen. After all that he had seen this day he didn't think that he could ever be shocked again, but what he saw before him was nothing less than Dante's innermost ring—the place Satan reserved for those who deserved the worst. The windows were all covered with blankets to keep the light from attracting Rebel fire, and the orange glow of fifty candles gave the room a fiery light, making the long, narrow space look even more like the true hell his daddy preached about.

As he stepped into the doorway the first thing he saw was an arm as it rolled off the amputation table and fell to the floor with a muffled thud. A doctor picked it up and removed the wedding ring and placed it in the poor soldier's pocket before he tossed the limb onto a tarp, adding it to a pile of bloody arms and legs and hands and bare feet. There was blood pooled everywhere on the floor, and wounded men lined the walls. Those waiting for attention prayed or wept, and those who had already been cared for were mercifully drunk on ether or morphine or opium and they groaned mournfully through their stupors.

The doctor who had thrown the arm onto the pile now folded the tarp and threw it over his shoulder like Santa's bag of toys and came toward Ned, who remained fixed in the doorway.

"What have you got there, Sergeant?"

"Huh?"

"I said, 'What have you got there?' " He indicated Will's unconscious body still slung over Ned's shoulder.

"Oh. It's my brother, sir. He's been shot."

"Seems to be a lot of that going around," he said. "Let's have a look."

Both men set their bundles down and the doctor wiped blood off his hands with a rag. He pulled a box of matches from under his apron and relighted his exhausted cigar before he went to work. He cut off Will's pant leg and examined the wound.

"Well, he's shot sure enough, but he ain't shot bad. Looks like the bullet went clean through." He took the cigar out of his mouth and flipped the ashes on the floor. "No bone damage that I can see. Just set him down in the corner over there and we'll stitch him up in a minute."

"Is he gonna be all right, Doctor?"

"If he hasn't lost too much blood and if the gangrene don't get him, he'll be fine. Now, Sergeant, you've gotta get back to your unit."

Ned had never really taken his eyes off the poor one-armed man who had been stitched up in a matter of a minute and was now being placed on the floor, alongside the other groaners.

"Sergeant!"

"Oh—yeah—I mean, yes, sir."

Ned kissed his big brother and left the room but hadn't gone far before he fell to his knees to give thanks for sparing them both and to ask God's pity on the poor men back in that dreadful room. And then, a final thought . . . a pledge to his Maker. "We're still gonna do it, God," he said. "We're still gonna free the slaves, Will and me. I promise. You'll see. Amen."

MARYE'S HEIGHTS

A. A. Humphreys couldn't see a damned thing. His plan to pull Tyler's Brigade alongside of Allabach's was well on its way to hell in a handbasket. Thousands of men cluttered the entire hillside between the millrace and the swale. There were still remnants of fences that were made worse in the dark because they were invisible. Men—even officers now—pleaded with Humphreys's advancing troops to stop and lie down—to go no farther. His men stumbled and fell and wandered off.

There could be no more hand signals. The charge would have to be called with voices and bugles. As the obstacles thinned, Humphreys assumed he was close to the wall. He was almost certain. So he ordered the bugler to sound the charge.

The notes that ordered his men to the double-quick served also as the order for the Rebels to open fire blindly into the darkness.

From fifty yards ahead the wall exploded with a long line of red flame, and from higher up the hill, four more eruptions—larger—angrier—louder. His second horse fell from under him, but, as though protected by the hand of God Himself, Humphreys stood up—again—totally unscathed. But his brigades were gone. Allabach's and Tyler's regiments both bolted back down the hill, the slower and weaker of them, and some of the wounded, got trampled in the rush to get away.

God sent Humphreys another horse. He may have had to kill another man to provide it, but there she was, all saddled up and healthy and ready to ride. The general mounted and tried to rally his men for another attempt, but they were all too far gone. Halfway to Falmouth by now.

Andrew A. Humphreys's glorious day was over. He and his newfound horse walked slowly down the hill toward the swale and again the favorite song popped into his head. Last time he had whistled, but this time he decided to sing.

> *Some folks say that I'm not handsome:*
> *Lest this slander round should buzz,*
> *I can prove that I'm a beauty*
> *For "handsome is that handsome does."*

It was storming outside, with frequent claps of thunder, but Bill McCarter was in his own home with his beautiful young wife, cuddled up next to the fire. The fire seemed to give off no heat, and his arm ached for some reason he couldn't remember, but no matter. He was comfortable and content.

And then, suddenly . . .

Holy Jesus! Where in the hell?

. . . He was gripped by a wrenching pain and a horrible panic. Instantly he was yanked from his perfect dream and cast into a grotesque nightmare—hurled into some kind of bizarre, freezing-cold hell. He had no recollection of the battle or the charge or of his desperate search for General Meagher or Stretch. It took only seconds for the horrors of the day to come back to him when he saw the bodies around him and felt the cold mud underneath. He remembered getting shot in the arm and . . . he tried to lift it, but it was still useless. The bleeding seemed to have stooped, and so, for the moment, had the shooting. He had to get away from this place. He had to try it again. He stood up slowly and felt a bit dizzy at first but managed to keep his balance. Once he gained his feet he actually felt surprisingly strong and decided he could make it down the hill and back into the town.

He made it almost to the swale before he fell the first time. He tripped over the leg of a wounded man who groaned first and then cursed him. "S-s-sorry."

He tried to get up again, but another soldier grabbed him and whispered, "George?"

Bill had never seen James McClernan before, but in the last light of the day he easily saw the disappointment in the poor man's eyes. He had urgently wanted Bill to be "George," whoever George was.

In the past six hours James had endured a lifetime of anguish. He had watched twenty regiments or more march past him toward the wall. He had tried for a while to stop them, but only a handful of men had yielded to sanity. It tore at his heart to watch each man go by, but his greatest agony came from not knowing if his brother was alive or dead. It was the not knowing that tortured him almost to madness. He had resigned himself to the fact that George was up on the hill somewhere, but he had convinced himself that most of the men up there were still alive. Wounded maybe—probably—some horribly. But a lot of them had come back down. James had tried to look every man in the face and he had prayed for every one to be George. He suffered another wound of the heart when each man turned out to be a stranger.

But it was dark now, and the fight was over and at least most of the shooting had stopped. He knew he should wait. He knew that it was stupid to move up there again—up close to the wall. Even in the dark the Rebels could still see movement and were not even a little bit reluctant to shoot anything that moved. But he couldn't wait. Not a moment longer. He knew better than to stand and walk, so he crawled through the mud toward the space where he thought George might be. He crawled around and sometimes over the bodies of a hundred dead and wounded soldiers just to get there. When he thought he was near the spot where the 24th New Jersey had received the Reb's very first volley of the day, he began looking every man in the face. Most were wounded—many were dead—none was George. His most recent disappointment was this young, dazed private with the visor of his kepi hanging loosely off to the side of his face and a sprig of boxwood in the band.

The two men just looked at each other for a moment, each feeling too sorry for himself to feel pity for the other.

Without another word, Bill McCarter continued his mission down the hill—and James McClernan continued his mission up it.

Porter Alexander had worked up one hell of a thirst. It had been a half hour since the last Yankee attack had been repulsed, and the field was dark and quiet. A few individual rifle shots were fired from time to time, just for the hell of it—or to keep the other guys in place, but Alexander's guns were cool. All were loaded and ready, and the crews were fully alert, but he was almost certain now that the day was over. He was proud of himself. He was proud of his men, and the Washington Artillery boys—the work they had done this day—but mostly he was proud of his placements. His plan had worked just as he had anticipated, maybe better, and even over General Lee's objections. *Teacher learns from student,* he thought with a smile.

Alexander decided he should indulge himself with a nice, long, self-congratulatory toast. He found his horse tied behind the Marye house and opened the saddlebag. He pulled out a nice bottle of fine whiskey given to him by the friendly townsfolk. He had wrapped it in a blanket for safety's sake and was very pleased to see that it had survived the day intact. It wasn't the best ever concocted, but, drunk as a toast to himself, it was the best he'd ever tasted. He decided to toast General Lee as well. And General Longstreet.

When he noticed that his lips were numb, he decided that he really couldn't afford to toast anybody else, so he reluctantly returned his prized possession to the safety of his saddlebag and headed back down the hill to his guns. The night was clear and cold and getting colder. It was a moonless night so far and the sky was brilliant with a billion stars.

"Charge!"

The unmistakable roar of an attacking army rose up and Porter Alexander was quickly as sober as a judge.

His men were confused. They could see nothing, but the sound seemed to come from the right.

"Tails left!" he ordered, hoping against hope that what he heard wasn't an acoustical anomaly—a lying echo.

Corporal Longwood aimed the gun at nothing and stepped back and ordered *"fire."* Alexander grabbed the arm of the number-four man before he could pull the lanyard.

"Corporal—another couple of turns down on the screw! You might be aiming directly into our boys down there."

Longwood stepped forward to twist the elevation screw, but fell to the ground before he ever got there, shot through the stomach. Alexander didn't have time to sort out who was next in line as gun commander, so he stepped forward and raised the elevation himself.

"Fire!"

The gun roared and the crew went quickly back to work. The colonel had no idea where his rounds of canister had struck, but he was certain he had overshot the Confederates down behind the wall. Problem was, he may have overshot the Yanks as well.

From a point fifty yards away, a line of red flames pinpointed the enemy for him. He stepped forward, gave the screw one more turn, and ordered *"fire"* again. The infantry below had also seen the muzzle flashes and they had the range as well, and even though the Rebels fired blindly into the night it still took only minutes to send the fresh Yankee assault scurrying back down the hill.

"Damn," Alexander said to no one. "If they hadn't yelled, they would have been in our laps before we ever knew they were coming."

Little Abbott climbed the hill, bolt upright, back up to the spot where Leander Alley lay dead. For some reason no one on the Confederate line bothered to shoot him. He was one man walking slowly up the hill and a threat to no one. Nonetheless a thousand men could have killed him easily, but none did.

It took Abbott only a minute to find the old whaler's body

and lift it up in his arms. He wept the whole way as he carried the cold body of his dearest friend back down the hill. As he walked through the human wreckage of the day, softly he sang . . .

> *For then them whales destroyed our boats*
> *They rammed them one by one*
> *They stove them all with head and fluke*
> *And after they was done*
> *We few poor souls left half-alive*
> *Was clinging to debris*
> *I'd stake me life them fish can think*
> *As good as you and me.*

FREDERICKSBURG

General Humphreys found General Hooker just on the outskirts of town. There was a group gathered around as always. He was happy to see Tyler and Allabach there.

"Gentlemen—your men did gallant work today. And how are you, Colonel Quay?"

"Quite well, General!" He took a huge, deep breath, just to show that he could. "I feel like a boy of sixteen!"

Humphreys was surprised that Quay had survived. He had put himself in front of the enemy and dared the bastards to shoot him. To Humphreys it had seemed the perfect time for God to take him home. *Mysterious ways.*

"And how about yourself, General Humphreys? How are you?"

The general laughed. "I felt like a young *girl* of sixteen at her first ball. I felt more like a *god* than a man."

General George Sykes, who commanded Hooker's last unused division, joined the men surrounding the Center Grand Division commander.

"General Hooker, sir, my division of *regular* troops is available and at your command, sir."

Hooker noticed the emphasis on "regular" troops. It was

the standard West Point prejudice against volunteers and the unquestionable assumption that ten "professional" soldiers could do easily what a thousand "amateurs" would die trying. Hooker had believed it himself—until today. Today he had watched tens of thousands of "amateurs" march up that hill against the most savage enemy fire he had ever encountered, most knowing full well that they had no chance in hell of gaining their objective. Farm boys and store clerks from across the country marched against the wall, held their formations, and died for their flags and their friends and their country. They had changed Hooker's mind about "volunteers." The "ninety-day boys" who died today were no less soldiers than a West Point–trained twenty-year "regular" veteran.

Hooker sighed and shook his head. "No, General Sykes. I have lost as many men as my orders require me to. But be ready in case Lee decides to come down off that damned hill."

Sykes saluted and rode away to position his men to cover a retreat or repel an attack, leaving Hooker alone, still looking up the hill. "I hope you do, Bobby Lee, you incompetent little lieutenant. Why don't you come on out from behind that wall, and let's have us a real fight?"

A thousand dollars, Bill McCarter thought. *I'd give a thousand dollars for only one sip of water.*

He was safe now from Confederate fire, but his tongue was swollen twice its normal size and stuck to the roof of his mouth. He was dizzy with the loss of blood and scalding hot with a fever. The wounds had reopened and he was once again too weak to stand. He had made it as far as the swale and beyond, but the millrace and the town seemed to be getting farther away with every step.

Give me water, God, or take my life. Here and now.

Not another step. Not another . . .

He went down to his knees, just to rest. A small fire. He saw a tiny flame not too very far away. A candle lantern. Two men making their way up the hill. Ambulance corpsmen, he hoped. Or just anybody with a canteen. An answered prayer.

He tried to call to them, but his mouth was too dry and his tongue too large to move in his mouth.

One of the two men spoke—in a recognizable voice. *Another dream—the dreams are all so real when you're dying. But they're all so nice, and warm and comforting.* He knew it couldn't be true. He *had* to be dreaming that it was Stretch coming up the hill. But the voice was so real. In his dream he was able to will just a single drop of saliva into his mouth, and just enough air into his lungs to speak—softly—pitifully—a single word.

"Stretch?"

"Bill!"

In less than a minute Sergeant Stretchbok—the man who had saved him from freezing to death only last week—came to his rescue again. This time with a canteen full of cold, clean water, and a stretcher to carry him home.

Joshua Lawrence Chamberlain lay flat on the field with the rest of his boys from the 20th Maine. The occasional flashes from the Rebel muskets were visible as they fired down the hill, killing the wounded. Chamberlain retreated inside his thoughts. *They're only murderers now.* Survived the day. Now to survive just an hour or so longer waiting for the order to withdraw. Burnside is probably only waiting for the cover of total darkness to move the covering troops into place and pull us all back. Another hour or two at the most.

Chamberlain had thought ahead enough to bring a biscuit of hardtack with him but no canteen, no blanket, no coat. The plan was to be on the top of the heights by now, or back in Fredericksburg. Or dead. He lay as still has he could. Why risk attracting the attention of a Rebel rifleman up there, safely hidden behind his damned stone wall just waiting for some poor bastard to move?

The sunset excited the wind just to make the night even colder and the men even more miserable.

It's so cold. Just let the wind stop. It wasn't only Chamberlain's prayer. Ten thousand men on both sides begged the Lord to make it stop. God omnipresent had to have heard those thousands of prayers, but if He did . . . What? A rhetorical debate worthy of a classroom. Did God answer

"No"? Did He turn His back on thousands of dying men? Did He not hear or did He not care? Or is this too much agony even for God to bear?

A single rifle shot and a dull thump. The God-awful sound of a bullet insulting the body of a boy already dead. The Rebs are just shooting into the darkness now. Just for fun. The firing slacked off to the point where each individual shot could be heard. Chamberlain punched the man in front of him just to make absolutely certain he was dead. No response. He rolled the body over on its side to give him some protection in case one of the random bullets headed his way. Total darkness now. So cold his bones hurt. He punched the man to his left, then the man to his right. Both dead. One was wearing a coat and Chamberlain managed to wrestle it off the corpse that was already growing stiff. He pulled both of the bodies closer to him to try to keep the wind away. The uphill man, the one guarding him against rifle fire, was wearing a coat as well and the colonel managed to pull the flap over his face. He used the man's leg as a pillow. He was surrounded by thousands of moaning, crying, pleading men. The noises they made were more animal than human. Chamberlain tried to drown it all out by retreating into his mind, seeking a peaceful haven but he found no refuge even there. The pleadings of ten thousand tortured souls could not be ignored. *Tortured souls.* The unsummoned thought chilled his spine. For the college professor who questioned everything, about this there was no question.

This is what hell sounds like.

Eventually, regardless of the cold, regardless of the corpses and of the mournful sounds of the thousands of anguished men around him, Chamberlain's exhausted body surrendered to sleep. Thank God.

James McClernan couldn't cry. He just couldn't. He fixed his brother's body as best he could, laying him out nicely with his arms crossing his chest. He took a cloth out of his pocket and wiped the mud from George's face and removed a couple of letters from his pocket to save them for the family. He wrote a note that said, simply, *George McClernan, 24th New Jersey, Camden, N.J.,* and fixed it to a button on George's uniform so the burial detail would know who he was and could put him to rest in a marked grave so that the body could be retrieved later and returned to the family plot. He kissed his brother good-bye and, forgetting the danger, he stood and began to walk back down the hill to Fredericksburg. He wondered while he walked why there were no tears, but he decided it really didn't matter.

I'll cry tomorrow, he thought. *Right now I have to find Dad and tell him. There will be time to cry tomorrow.*

THE PHILLIPS HOUSE
9 P.M.

Generals Burnside, Hooker, and Sumner sat quietly as enlisted men cleared the table. The canned salmon and peas were gone, but the fresh coffee kept coming. To Sumner it looked like Burnside was moments away from passing out from exhaustion and lack of sleep. The commanding general was drinking coffee by the gallon—the hotter and blacker the better.

General Franklin finally arrived and refused the coffee—refused a chair—refused to stand still. He made it clear that he could not spend a moment more than necessary away from his command.

"Apologies, sirs, but my corps commanders cannot be spared. My lines are weak and the Rebs have already shown signs of a willingness to attack in darkness. They simply can't be spared."

Burnside concealed his irritation.

"Very well, then. Recommendations for tomorrow's plan of attack."

Plan of attack? The grand division commanders were dumbfounded.

Burnside was expecting to have to mediate between three different approaches. He thought the men would be yelling at one another by now, each trying to press his own men to the front. Instead he was greeted with silence. Total, dumfounded silence.

"Nothing?"

Of course it was Joe Hooker who burst first.

"General Burnside—I told you several hours ago that your order sending my men up that hill was tantamount to murder—I *have not* changed my position. I will be happy to offer you a plan for covering our *retreat,* but another attack tomorrow will gain us nothing more than a longer causality list!"

Burnside bristled, but this was Joe Hooker, and it was to be expected. More frustrating than Hooker's insubordination was the timid silence of the other two men.

"General Sumner?"

Sumner only shook his head.

"General Franklin?"

The same.

"Very well, then." Now Burnside was furious. He couldn't tolerate even being in the same room with any of these cowards. They were a small pack of McClellan-loving backstabbers. Even Sumner. *Et tu?* He stood and looked briefly at each man.

"If none of you has the courage to lead tomorrow's fight, then *I shall lead it myself*! Have the Ninth Corps ready to move forward as soon as tomorrow's fog lifts, and meet me back here at ten o'clock in the morning. That is all."

FREDERICKSBURG

Henry Villard found a beautiful, brick home on the outskirts of Fredericksburg that as yet seemed untouched by the battle. No looters were throwing things out of the upper-story windows, no artillery-inflicted scars. The roof and windows all seemed to be intact. In fact there was no one around. The reporter pounded on the door several times and no one came out; it seemed to be empty so he tried the door. Locked. He stepped back to see if there was another way in when a terrified slave opened the door just a crack.

"The Massah ain't here. He says you go away."

Villard almost laughed. *"Scheisse."* Somebody had left

this poor, scared-pissless Negro here and told him to keep the Yankee army out. Now Villard had to deal with the man.

"Ich sein müd und ich benötigen ein Platz zu schlafen. Jetzt, hinausgehen von mein Weise." It meant, "I'm tired and I need a place to sleep—now get out of my way," but Villard figured it would shorten the argument if he said it *auf Deutsch*. It was a tool he used frequently and it generally worked on just about anybody.

He pushed his way in, found a comfortable chair, and plopped down as though he were in his own home. In only seconds Villard was asleep and the slave had resumed his guard duties.

10 P.M.

It had been hours since Francis Donaldson had seen a single white man he knew. He was still amazed that an entire regiment could just vanish and be nowhere to be found. He had managed to find his man, George Slow—or, more accurately, George had found him. But the Corn Exchange Regiment was missing in action. The whole damned thing. Hell, at this point he might even be happy to see Colonel Gwyn. He was certain they were not in the city. That left only two alternatives. Either they had retreated all the way back to Falmouth, which wasn't likely, or they were still up on the hill somewhere. But he had looked there, diligently, he thought, during the height of the fighting before retreating alone to Fredericksburg. If that was the case, if they were still up there, living or dead, it would look to the world as though he were a coward. As though he had turned his back and skedaddled in the face of the enemy. Colonel Gwyn would love that.

A horrible vision flashed through Donaldson's mind of the drunken, arrogant son-of-a-bitch relieving him of his sword, breaking it over his knee, and ordering him to the gallows to be hanged for cowardice in the face of the enemy—and laughing the whole while.

And then—there they were. Just as though they had stepped out of his nightmare, they came marching off the hill and into the town. With the hellish vision still fresh in his mind, Donaldson wanted to make himself very small, but he couldn't. He just stood there, with George at his side, as though watching a parade on the Fourth of July.

"Well—if it isn't Captain Donaldson!" There was no sarcasm in Gwyn's voice. This time it was genuine loathing. "May I ask where in the hell you have been keeping yourself while your company was fighting?"

Donaldson wanted desperately to grab the bastard by the throat and strangle him to death. "I was with them, Colonel. And if you take exception to my conduct, then my sword is at your disposal."

"I don't want your damned sword, Captain. We will discuss this matter later."

The Corn Exchange Regiment continued to pass by and Donaldson watched closely for anyone from his own company.

"Captain Donaldson!" one man shouted. Several broke ranks and gathered around him, genuinely happy that their captain had survived. Then came a soft voice out of the pack. Private Ayers. "Captain—I have been at the front the whole time!"

For the second time in five minutes, Donaldson wanted to strangle a man to death. He started to yell at the religious little fellow, just out of habit, but George nudged him slightly, telling him gently that this was not the time. He swallowed his pride—which was a seven-course meal for a man like Francis Donaldson—and nodded and smiled at the poor, picked-on lad.

"Well done, Private Ayers. Well done."

CHAPTER 19

Chamberlain hadn't been asleep nearly long enough when the coat flap that covered his face was roughly pulled away by a soldier who was even more startled than Chamberlain.

"Oh! Sorry, sir. Thought you were dead."

"Thankfully not."

The man turned away and casually continued his search for a coat that some poor boy didn't really need anymore.

It was impossible now for Chamberlain to return to sleep with a thousand brave men weeping around him. On this field, on this night, not even this man of reason could silence his angry thoughts. *This is how we reward valor? Stage a gallant charge, we tell them—perhaps the most gallant in the history of the world. And if you should take a bullet in the leg or the arm or the gut for your country, we will leave you for hours on a frozen field to cry and beg for just one final sip of water. The newspapers, and even the textbooks, will give it a name. They will call it "glorious."*

He could no longer lie there just listening to his own rage. He had to do something. He got up and followed the sounds to what seemed to be the worst of it. He started searching bodies for canteens. Most, of course, were empty.

Some were frozen. He spent an hour searching for them and giving them away. Where he could he would apply a tourniquet or reposition a broken arm or leg to make the poor soul more comfortable. With those who could speak he took names and hometowns and promised to write to wives and mothers and children to tell them that their hero had died valiantly—"gloriously"—with his face to the enemy.

It finally became too much to bear and after a while he somehow managed to find his way back to his gruesome bed. He lay back down with two bodies as side rails and another as a headboard, pulled the flap of the top man's coat over his face, and tried again to find sleep.

FREDERICKSBURG
2 A.M.

General Couch was equally as exhausted and far more comfortable lying in a real bed in a real house, but he couldn't sleep either. The wounded men just outside his window were *his* men and in their heart they were pleading to him for help. Not to God, but personally to Darius Couch—the man who had sent them there and the only man who could call them away. He pictured himself on the field picking up each and every son and carrying him to safety himself.

He heard a commotion in the front of the house and managed to sit up just before Burnside crashed into the room.

"Report, General Couch."

It took him a second or two to bring himself to the moment. Maybe he had been asleep after all. Couch made his report in as much detail as he could remember, from the opening moments of the fight all the way up to Humphreys's final, gallant, disastrous charge. Burnside never interrupted. He never changed his expression. He listened until Couch had nothing more to say.

In the silence that followed Couch thought that his commander was almost zombielike. Sleepwalking. He didn't move. He didn't blink. He didn't respond.

What in the hell is he thinking? Couch couldn't figure it

out. He thought that Burn might collapse right there. Still nothing. Not a word. Then a horrible thought. *Does he think that I let him down—on purpose?* He remembered the meeting where every man in the room had to swear allegiance. He remembered his own words: *"If I have ever done anything in any battle, I will do twice as much in this."* Surely Burnside can't be thinking . . .

"General Burnside, you must know that everything that could be done by troops *was* done by the Second Corps."

Burnside seemed to awaken. He smiled slightly and looked at Couch as though he were a favorite son. "Couch, I know that. I am perfectly satisfied that you did your best."

With that the commanding general turned and left the room without a word about tomorrow.

My God, Couch thought. *What does he have in mind for tomorrow?*

3 A.M.

It was amazing that Henry Villard was able to force himself awake at 3 A.M., but he had to get away from Fredericksburg to file his report. His revered and "legendary" predecessor, George Smalley, had made himself a hero by leaving the Antietam battlefield and "spurring" his way to Frederick to file his report. Villard had heard the story far too many times, but now he had the same opportunity to follow suit and to scoop the world as Smalley had. So, well ahead of the sun, exhausted, cold, and hungry, he began to "spur" his own way to Aquia Creek, where he hoped to wire Washington. The problem was that there could be no "spurring" involved. The night was so dark that he might as well have been a blind man on a blind horse. The road to Aquia Creek at one time had been corduroyed but had since been used by supply trains and heavy artillery and had fallen into deplorable disrepair. The logs used to construct the road were no longer tightly packed and the recent rains made the earth beneath them a slimy quagmire. Most of the time Villard couldn't swear to the fact that he was on a road at all. He wished for one of those Mexican cowboy saddles so that he could have something to hold on to.

Oddly enough Villard found himself thinking about the horse and what *he* must be going through. *He must be thinking that I am the stupidest man on the face of the earth. He may be right.*

At that moment a log half rolled and half squirted out from under the poor animal's left front leg and with a panicked whinny he fell shoulder first into the mud on the left side of the road. Villard managed to push himself off just before the last instant when his leg would have been crushed between the horse and God-knows-what might be lying in the mud. What ended up lying in the mud was the *New York Tribune*'s prized senior war correspondent. His mouth was full of mud and his clothes were covered and soaked with the wet, cold, slimy goop. He wanted to cry until he realized that he wasn't hurt and then he was just grateful that no one had been around to witness the fall.

By the time he had spit out the sizable mouthful of muck and wiped it off his face and out of his eyes, the horse, in no better shape than Villard himself, had managed to regain his own footing. The reporter went over to calm the poor beast, which let out an angry snort and spit out his own mouthful of mud.

"You're absolutely right, boy," Villard said, patting him on the snout. "I am a total idiot."

THE YERBY HOUSE
5 A.M.

Maxcy Gregg had to stay awake. His blood-starved body wanted sleep—demanded sleep—but he knew that once he surrendered to it he would never wake up. At this moment there were thousands of men nearby spending their dying moments in prayer, making peace with God and preparing for their life after death, but Gregg had been a scientist all of his adult life and had long ago set aside religion as illogical, irrational, and unprovable. Somewhere between an agnostic and a downright atheist he had never been afraid to say so. Even now, faced with the horrific alternatives of hell or oblivion, it was not Jesus that he sought—it was Stonewall Jackson.

The wait hadn't been long, but by this time Gregg no longer had any rational concept of time. Fighting off death is a full-time chore. To him it seemed like days when it actually had been only hours since he had pleaded with Kyd Douglas to summon Jackson to his bedside. Through the veil of drugs and exhaustion he saw a gigantic figure of a man standing over him and heard a kind and friendly voice that he struggled to recognize. It was soft and gentle and almost loving, but it was, nonetheless, the voice of Stonewall Jackson. Gregg tried to rise up, to come to attention, to address his commanding officer in a proper manner. He wanted desperately to make up for the dozens of times over the past year when his careless posture and his flippant salute had demonstrated far more contempt than respect. When he couldn't rise, he fell back hard onto the pillow and tried to speak through his approaching tears. He muttered something about a document. No disrespect. Forgive me.

Jackson sat down and took Gregg's hand in his and spoke softly. Gently. "I know nothing of those things, General. I know only of the great things that you have done."

Gregg went limp and tried to focus his eyes and his thoughts. He tried again to speak, but Jackson interrupted in a whisper. "The doctors tell me that you have not long to live. Let me ask you to dismiss these matters from your mind and turn your thoughts to God."

Now the tears flowed. He mouthed the words "thank you" but his voice couldn't be heard. He tried again to salute but Jackson lifted the hand to his lips and kissed him good-bye. Only after Jackson had left the room was Gregg able to speak aloud. "Thank you very much—sir."

Ten minutes later, Maxcy Gregg was dead.

Somewhere Between Fredericksburg and Aquia Creek Landing

The sun still hadn't shown itself, but the hint of blue light made the going easier for both Villard and his horse. His trip should have been over by now but he figured he wasn't halfway there. He passed the time thinking about the reporters for the competition papers who were probably just now rising, and he smiled at the thought of them arriving in Washington just in time to read his headline: DISASTER IN FREDERICKSBURG! The smile faded when he saw it in his mind and began to write his lead. He remembered the carnage. He remembered the futile and idiotic charges against the impenetrable stone wall. No. "Impenetrable" isn't the right word. "Impregnable." "Unapproachable." Worse than Shiloh. Much, much worse because Grant was *being* attacked in Tennessee and couldn't call it off. Burnside should never have ordered it to begin, but even after he did he could have stopped it at any time. But he didn't. Regiment after regiment; rank after rank of beautiful and brave young men marched to certain failure and almost certain death— the ones who followed not getting a single foot closer than those who had led. He saw the men piled up on the sloping ground leading up to the wall, just as he had left them. Many dead, many more wounded, and many more just lying there cold and scared, afraid to lift their heads for fear of getting them blown off.

Now the sun was over the edge of the earth, but the brightness didn't chase the vision from Villard's mind. The men were still there, waiting. Waiting for what?

Waiting to retreat? They had still been there at three in the morning when Villard left. If a retreat were to be called, it would have been in progress by then. Was Burnside waiting for a truce that the Rebels would never allow? Or was he waiting for another attack against the dragon? *Oh, my God,* Villard thought. *Another assault? Another day of that? There won't be a whole man left in the entire Army of the Potomac if that happens.*

Oh, *mein Gott.*

Now Villard's way was lighted and clear and he had to get to Aquia Landing as quickly as horse and man could move. Now he wasn't only trying to beat the competition. Now he was trying to save lives. Thousands of them.

MARYE'S HEIGHTS
5:30 A.M.

Porter Alexander hadn't been asleep for very long when he was nudged awake by a man he'd never seen before.

"Sorry to wake you, sir, but I have urgent information from General Longstreet."

Groggy two seconds ago, Alexander was fully awake now. "Go ahead."

"General Longstreet sends his regards, sir, and begs to inform you that a Yankee courier has been captured and that he had in his possession orders from General Burnside to prepare to renew the attack as early as practicable today."

"Renew the *attack*?" Alexander was astounded.

"That is what I am told, sir."

"Received and understood, Captain."

Alexander pulled on his boots and roused the men and prepared for another day of killing.

PROSPECT HILL
6 A.M.

The words meant nothing to John Pelham, but they brought tears nonetheless.

Indulgentiam, absolutionem, et remissionem peccatorum tuorum tribua tibi omnipotens et misericors Dominus.

The men looked over the crude casket in which Jean lay. As the priest made the sign of the cross they all responded, "Amen."

Someone had drawn a crude French flag on a white piece of cloth and placed it in Jean's hand, and as the body of the spirited young Cajun was lowered into the ground, they all sang, softly and slowly . . .

> *Allons enfants de la Patrie*
> *Le jour de gloire, est arrivé!*

WASHINGTON, D.C.

Lincoln made the short trek across the street to the War Office and wandered into the telegraph room almost unnoticed. Edwin Stanton walked in just behind him.

"What news?" Lincoln asked the telegrapher.

"One message, received at four o'clock this morning, sir."

"Go ahead, Sergeant. Read it."

"Our troops are all across the river. We hope to carry the crest today. Our loss is heavy—say five thousand."

On the heels of Antietam, where McClellan had lost almost thirteen thousand men, five thousand didn't seem so much to Lincoln anymore—until he thought about it.

Five thousand men. Five thousand husbands and sons and brothers.

He knew he couldn't think of it that way—or at least he *shouldn't*. If they break through and open the way to Richmond, then lives may actually have been *saved* today. Fifty thousand. A hundred thousand. There was no way of knowing. It was the gruesome arithmetic again. *If the Rebels out-kill us four-to-one every day—we win.*

Keep them as numbers, Abe, he told himself. *Otherwise you'll go mad.*

MARYE'S HEIGHTS

From his position behind the stone wall, Sergeant Richard Kirkland had spent most of the night with his hands over his ears trying to block out the horrible sounds coming from the wounded Yankees on the hill below. It wasn't lost on him that he had probably shot a dozen of those men himself. Maybe more. The cries of one man in particular taunted him. Separate and apart from the thousand other voices, Kirkland seemed to hear one above them all, as though this lone individual were pleading to him and him alone. There was one Yankee soldier he remembered clearly. Maybe too clearly. He remembered the man's expression as he marched so boldly, so proudly up the hill. He had to be frightened to death, but no fear showed on his face. Determination—with every step. Determination to get just two feet closer. That's what showed. Kirkland remembered placing the beardless boy in his sights and pulling the trigger and after the smoke cleared he wasn't there anymore. Richard Kirkland remembered it all and couldn't stop thinking that this man—this one Yankee—was still alive and suffering tortuous pain, and called to him for help.

"I've got to go down there."

"What?" Doug Counts, Kirkland's best friend since childhood, didn't understand what Richard had said. He must have heard him wrong, or he meant something other than the obvious.

"I've got to go down there," Kirkland repeated. "I've got to help those poor men."

"You can't go down there! They'll kill you sure as God made apples."

"God just spoke to me, Doug. He told me to go down there and I've got to go."

FREDERICKSBURG

This time Little Abbott only observed the sacking of Fredericksburg. He delivered Leander's body to Dr. Shillman for embalming and shipment back to Massachusetts. He signed an IOU. Now, again, he wandered the streets of the town and watched the cruel carnival that seemed to have picked up right where it left off on Friday. The troops lucky enough to have stayed the night in the town now proceeded to steal breakfast and resume their interrupted rampage against Fredericksburg. Pigs were stolen and slaughtered, mirrors shattered, elegant crystal chandeliers cut down just for the fun of watching them fall and shatter on the floor. And, of course, there was still enough wine and liquor to go around.

What the hell, Abbott thought. The goddamned people who lived here had let the Rebs hide in these very houses so they could murder our bridge builders and all. And murder was all it was. Pure and simple. Unarmed men! Helpless men just trying to do their jobs. They'd murdered Charlie Cabot while hiding in these houses. Then they had run up the hill to hide again, this time behind a wall, and murdered Leander too. They're cowards and barbarians—all of them—and they deserve to be *treated* like barbarians. So to hell with all of 'em! Have another drink mates, and pee on the goddamned rug.

AQUIA CREEK LANDING
9 A.M.

It had taken Henry Villard six hours to make the three-hour ride to Aquia Landing. He looked like hell, thanks to the time he'd spent wallowing in the mud. Even so, he was the first reporter to arrive, and this was a very good thing. The morning got even better when the commanding officer offered him a hot breakfast courtesy of the United States Army. The *Tribune* reporter should have been exhausted but a four-egg breakfast along with the anticipation of a major scoop had him buzzing.

He told the men gathered around him all about the events of yesterday's battle. Truth be known he was trying out his story on them and got the exact response he anticipated: speechless horror. Perfect. He was still chewing his last bite of bread when he said, ". . . and now if you'll kindly direct me to the telegraph office, I've got a story to send." He beamed at his admirers almost as though he expected a round of applause. It didn't come.

"Sorry, sir, but the telegraph office is off limits for all business except official military matters."

"Shit!"

"I appreciate your disappointment, sir, but not your language."

"Of course, Lieutenant, it's not your doing, but goddamn it, there *is* a such a thing as the goddamned First Amendment!"

"Well, I don't know anything about that, Mr. Villard, but I do know my orders, and . . ."

"Never mind! Just trade horses with me and I'll be on my way."

The lieutenant blushed, totally embarrassed by what he had to say next.

"I'm sorry, sir, but I can't do that either."

"But my horse is exhausted and can't . . ."

"It's not the horse thing, sir. I can't let you leave here."

"What?"

"Those are my orders, sir. No one attached to the army may proceed north without a pass from General Burnside's headquarters."

"I'm not attached to any goddamned army! I'm attached to the *New York Tribune*!"

"The orders specified reporters, sir. It may have even said 'especially' reporters."

Villard was loaded and primed to fire a volley of profanities at the young officer when even worse news, if there could be such a thing, interrupted him. Coffin, the correspondent from the *New York Times,* exploded into the tent.

"Gather round, boys! Have I ever got a story for *you*!"

Suddenly the *Tribune* reporter was unbearably tired.

FREDERICKSBURG
10:15 A.M.

The Ninth Corps, Burnside's old command, the men who had followed him across his already-notorious bridge at Antietam, assembled in formations in the town where they waited for orders to resume the assault against Marye's Heights.

Still sleep-starved, Burnside marched boldly into the Lacy house fully prepared to show his reluctant subordinates how to lead a charge and finish the job. His old friend Edwin Sumner saw the swagger and it almost made him weep. There was no rational explanation for what Burnside was about to do. Sumner thought it through as best he could. *He has either convinced himself that snowballs can survive in hell, or he is determined to kill himself—to die on the field of honor rather than face the disgrace of defeat. Suicide by gallantry.* He knew that it would be easier to stop an order from being issued than to rescind one already given, so he interrupted Burnside before he even began.

"General, I hope you will desist from this attack."

Burnside was stunned. "What do you mean, 'desist'?"

Quietly Sumner proceeded, trying not to sound condescending or insubordinate in any way. "I mean, sir, that I do not know of any general officer who approves of it and I think it will prove disastrous to the army."

Sumner had been Burnside's best friend and most ardent supporter ever since he had assumed command, but now, apparently, even Sumner had gone over to the other side. But the commanding general wasn't ready to surrender.

"General Sumner! We have made progress on all fronts. Franklin found the weakness in Jackson's line that we will be able to exploit today with just one more push, and on the right we are just feet away from success—and all this with fewer than five thousand casualties!"

Now it was Sumner's turn to be stunned. He addressed his old friend quietly and casually, to make it personal. "Burn—I do not know where you get your numbers, but I can tell you without question . . ." He didn't know any way to lessen the blow, so he shot out what Burnside had to know without pity. "Burn—I may have twice that number of casualties in my command alone. And they are not 'feet away from success,' they are a hundred yards away from success and it might as well be a hundred miles."

TELEGRAPH HILL

As the heart of Lee's command, the greatest of his generals, stood atop Telegraph Hill, looking over the battlefield, A. P. Hill was not among them. Off to the side and alone, Powell Hill sat on the wreckage of a caisson with his shoulders stooped and his head low.

The commanding general noticed and thought it more than odd. Hill was among his fiercest and most aggressive commanders and to see him sitting off alone, away from the rest, told Lee quickly that something was wrong. He feared that Hill might be wounded, for only such a thing as this could pull him down. He had not performed well yesterday. The gap left in his lines had very nearly proven disastrous, but the plan had been approved both by himself and General Jackson. Nonetheless, the man sitting off alone was not the A. P. Hill Robert E. Lee knew.

Colonel Taylor caught Lee's glance at the morose general and saw the concern on his face.

"It has been a bad week for General Hill, sir."

"Yes. The loss of General Gregg . . ."

Taylor shook his head. "I'm sure that is part of it, General, but he has also just learned of the death of his daughter as well."

Netty. Lee was her godfather. He had played with her, tickled her feet, and felt the God-sent joy that comes only from a little girl's giggle.

Annie.

Lee's heart broke all over again as his own recently passed Annie visited him for an instant, saying, "Go to him, Daddy."

Normally where Lee went, twenty men followed, but this time they all seemed to know that the general was on a private mission and they stood back and watched him go. As he approached, Hill stood, as protocol required. There were no tears on Hill's face, but they were clearly visible in his heart.

"God is in all things, General Hill." Lee put his hand on Hill's shoulder and gently turned him so that they could have their backs to the rest. "He knows far better than we who is best prepared for heaven, and He takes only those."

Now the tears flowed freely and Hill began to sob without shame. Lee wanted to embrace him, but could not. It would not be proper. But he did touch the general's arm and said, "It is God's will that has been done, General. Remember that always. It is God's will and must, in God's eyes, be good."

MARYE'S HEIGHTS
10:30 A.M.

Chamberlain still lay between the bodies that had sheltered him all night. The day was warming now, the dense fog thinning away, and it was again dangerous to move. The killing had resumed but it was on a much more personal level; one man at a time. Only an occasional shot fired into the body of some poor boy who caught a leg cramp and had to move, pinpointing himself for the Rebel riflemen behind the wall. It wasn't only Rebs killing Yanks. A few Confederates were dumb or unfortunate enough to keep their heads above the wall for just long enough for the Union sharpshooters to draw a bead.

All of this made the single Rebel soldier walking boldly down the hill just that much more improbable. Yankees on the swale and sharpshooters in the houses opened fire on him as though he were a one-man counterattack. A hundred shots were fired and not a one found its mark.

Chamberlain turned his head, slowly, to get a better view of the bulletproof idiot. The soldier then knelt down next to a wounded man, maybe one of Chamberlain's own, and placed a canteen to his lips.

The shooting slowed.

He unrolled the wounded man's blanket and covered him with it, like a mother tucking in a child at bedtime.

The shooting stopped and, slowly, men on both sides began to cheer.

My God. An angel! An angel on a battlefield! Chamberlain was convinced that he had become delirious. College professors don't see angels. But if they ever did, he decided, on this field, at this moment, would be the time. He continued to watch as the Rebel angel moved slowly from man to man down the hill until he got close enough for Chamberlain to hear his conversation.

After a sip of desperately needed water, the nearby wounded Yankee asked, "Who are you?"

"Name's Kirkland. Richard."

"Where are you from? Are you from heaven?"

"Guess you could say," Kirkland said, smiling. "South Carolina."

Another swallow. "Why are you here? Why did you come down here? You could've gotten killed."

"God told me to come. He wouldn't send me down here just to get shot, I don't reckon."

"He sent me *up* here just to get shot."

"No—*He* didn't. Some stupider-than-mud general sent *you* up here."

Amazing, Chamberlain thought. Try as he might, the professor of rhetoric couldn't think of a single argument against that simple, childish logic.

FREDERICKSBURG
NOON

"A million bullets were fired, George! A million of 'em! And not *one* found the right targets!"

Macy tried to calm Little Abbott down, as he had been trying to do for hours, but Little would hear nothing. It was a rage on the verge of driving the young captain mad.

"One found Leander! One of the finest men ever to walk the earth! One found Charlie Cabot! But if our sanctimonious son-of-a-bitch commander is right, and those bullets were guided by God, then God is a *damned* poor marksman!"

"There's no need to blaspheme, Little."

"It's not blasphemous if it's *true,* George. If God had a hand in this, then one of those million bullets would have found that pious jackass General Howard or Burnside, or, better yet, Halleck, who was fifty miles away, probably in a nice warm house eating bananas with Lincoln and his other baboons!"

The image made Macy smile—even under the circumstances. But for Little Abbott, no humor was intended. "Henry Halleck is a useless piece of furniture and A. E. Burnside a high-minded donkey and they're *both* still walking around today safe and warm while we have to put Leander Alley in the ground."

There was a moment of quiet, but only a moment. Abbott was at least a little quieter when he spoke again.

"I'm sending him home, George. This hellish place is going to become some sort of sacred ground, dedicated to the honor of men like Burnside and Howard."

"More likely Lee and Longstreet," Macy said, but Little chose not to hear.

"They will get statues and, if I left him here, Leander would get a cheap government stone—if that."

He paused again and shook his head and the tears began all over again. This time when he spoke, it was almost in a whisper.

"I'm sending him home, George. I've already arranged it. I signed an IOU. I'll figure out how to pay for it later. If I have to sell the farm, Leander's going back home to his mother, where he will be laid to rest far away from this place. Close to the ocean. Leander Alley will not lie at the feet of a statue of Ambrose Burnside!"

AQUIA CREEK LANDING
1 P.M.

Henry Villard waited until he was certain that Coffee, the *Boston Globe* reporter, was genuinely sound asleep. Then he sneaked off to the docks surreptitiously looking to hitch a ride up the Potomac on a steamer. There were four boats moored there and only one was destined north, and that one not until tomorrow. Well out in the river, however, there was a constant flow of water traffic passing Aquia Landing by, and bound for the capital.

"Hey! Uncles!" Villard shouted to two Negroes who were fishing out of a small rowboat twenty yards offshore. "Come in. I've got a proposition for you."

Moments later their boat touched the shore.

"A dollar apiece if you'll row me out and lend me a rod." This was a ruse intended for any army personnel who might be eavesdropping. "I would very much enjoy drowning a worm or two myself."

In all probability the men would have sold him the boat,

fishing rods, and all for such a grand sum. Villard stepped in and the men began to row.

"Now that I've got your attention," Villard said after they had gotten back out to their original spot, "I am not even the slightest bit interested in fishing."

The fishermen knew it was all too good to be true, and became suddenly nervous about what might be coming next.

"Five dollars each if you'll row me out into the Potomac and get me close enough to catch a ride to Washington Town."

Five dollars! Each! The men rowed like they were being chased by savage Indians.

A half hour later, the *Tribune* man paid a fifty-dollar fare (a bribe really) and was on his way to Washington on a steam-powered side-wheeler. He was sixty-two dollars poorer—not to mention the loss of his exhausted, muddy, left-behind hero of a horse—but at least he would beat Coffee to the story.

He found a quiet corner and began to write.

Marye's Heights

There was nothing Lawrence Chamberlain could do but lie low and watch and wonder. The Rebels continued to shoot any man who made any effort whatsoever to stand up—even those who just wanted to stumble back down the hill to Fredericksburg. All along the Federal "lines" men had followed Chamberlain's example and built their own ramparts of corpses to hide behind. They reread old letters. They rummaged through the packs of their dearly departed buddies in hopes of finding a biscuit of hardtack or a bit of bacon. Up on the hill, the Rebels seemed content to stay right there, and down in Fredericksburg, it looked to Chamberlain as though no one intended to come up either.

So there he lay. Watching and wondering. *What in the hell will happen next?*

THE PHILLIPS HOUSE
4 P.M.

"It is up to a vote then."

Ambrose Burnside looked each officer in the face. Sumner, Franklin, Hooker, and a half dozen corps commanders sat in somber silence, waiting for the decision to come. Each had spoken out against Burnside's plan, but, for some reason, the commanding general insisted that it be put to a vote.

"All in favor of resuming the attack, raise your right hand."

Not a hand went up.

Not one.

BEHIND THE STONE WALL
6:15 P.M.

"You're a hero, Richard! What you done was ... heck, I don't know what it was, but you're a hero now—in *both* armies!"

Doug Counts was amazed and grateful and proud of his dearest friend in the world. Richard Kirkland was now the pride of South Carolina after his mission of mercy to help the poor, wounded Yankees down on the hill.

Kirkland was grateful too, but he was neither amazed nor proud.

"I didn't do nothin'," he told Counts. "I only did what God said."

At that moment Counts would have sworn that his friend began to glow with some kind of heavenly radiance. Heck, maybe the man *was* what everybody was calling him. Maybe Richard Kirkland *was* an angel. But glowing or not, Richard got a confused look on his face and pointed to the north.

"Look at that, Doug. I ain't never seen *nothin'* like that."

Counts turned and looked and now he was more amazed than ever.

The dark northern sky was curtained with brilliant streamers of light in every color ever seen, from pale yellow to blood red and everything in between. The colors themselves danced in thin air. They seemed to rise up out of the earth, bound for heaven.

"What do you suppose it is?" Kirkland asked his friend.

Counts thought for a moment before he figured it out. "God has put up flags," he said. "We've won this fight, and God is celebratin'. That's what I think it is."

The two men watched the Northern Lights in total amazement. Neither had ever heard of such a thing—much less seen it.

After a while, Kirkland shook his head. "I don't think that's it."

"Well, you got a better idea?"

"It's all those Yankee souls all goin' up to heaven all at the same time."

Counts knew that wasn't right. "Stonewall says Yankees don't go to heaven. Stonewall says they all go straight to hell."

Kirkland knew that he was about to blaspheme a national hero, but even national heroes are little or nothin' next to God.

"Well, you'll pardon me for sayin', but General Jackson's wrong about that. Jesus died for Yankee souls too."

WASHINGTON, D.C.
8 P.M.

The mud on his clothes was dust now, almost fifteen hours after he had fallen off his horse trying to get to Aquia Creek. But a bath and a change of clothes would still have to wait. Henry Villard had a story to file.

"You look like hell unwashed!" Bureau Chief Sam Wilkeson had just returned from dinner at the Willard and was half an ounce away from drunk.

"I *feel* worse. Here's your story."

A single paragraph in and Wilkeson was sober.

"We need to get this telegraphed out right now, Sam. Coffee is right behind me and God only knows where the *Globe* man is . . . or the AP correspondent."

"We ain't telegraphing anything, Henry. Stanton has closed down the telegraph office for anything other than 'official military business' again."

"Schisse!" Villard began to rant about the sons of bitches in the War Office and the Freedom of the Press—all of the usual ravings of a journalist who's just been censored. But Wilkeson shook his head.

"Henry—there's not much point in sending this story anyway. Greeley's never gonna print this."

"What?"

"You heard me. And you remember First Bull Run. Look at these words you've written here . . . *'great, general defeat'* . . . *'inexcusable blunder'* . . . *'the greatest disaster yet suffered.'* Horace Greeley will never publish those words."

Villard did remember First Bull Run, and the watered-down version of his story that Greeley had printed, afraid that an *honest* report would stir the nation to surrender. Greeley had been wrong then—and he would be wrong now.

"It's *not* Horace Greeley's job to decide the truth! *Ich war dort! I was there!*"

"Henry—if this is true . . ."

"What do you mean, *'if'* it's true? I'm telling you, Sam . . ."

"Henry! Listen to me! If we print this, and it turns out to be even a little bit exaggerated, or if Burnside has renewed the attack today and the situation has changed, the damage done to the paper *and* to the nation will be incalculable."

"If Burnside renewed the attack today, then he lost *another* ten thousand men and the news is even worse. His men never got within a hundred yards of that stone wall, Sam. Every general I spoke with agreed with me that a hundred charges against that wall would come no closer than the first."

Wilkeson was out of arguments.

"All right, Henry. Whatever you say. We'll send this out on the next train. But it will do no good. Our leader will never print news *this* bad until it has been verified."

9 P.M.

Herman Haupt couldn't believe what Lincoln had just told him. Five thousand casualties? The numbers must have gotten jumbled somehow when the telegraph was deciphered.

"Five thousand is a very conservative estimate, Mr. President."

Lincoln wanted to cover his ears, like a child might, afraid to hear what General Haupt was going to say next. He couldn't bear it.

"In fact, sir, I would estimate that many casualties at Marye's Heights alone, and that was only half of the fight."

"How can you say that, General? How can you know?"

"I was there, Mr. President."

Lincoln wanted to challenge Haupt, just to shut him up so that he wouldn't have to hear any more. But Haupt was one of the few generals in the army who Lincoln genuinely respected. Here was a man who built railroads overnight it seemed, and kept them running. For Herman Haupt nothing was impossible and Lincoln trusted him implicitly.

The President grimaced. It wasn't only from emotional pain, but from a very real, physical blow that felt like a gunshot to the head. And again—worse this time. His entire face contorted and he put his hands over his face to keep his skull from exploding.

Haupt felt like he had just shot the man. The real news was actually worse, but Haupt admired the President, and even loved him, and just couldn't bring himself to describe yesterday's events in all their horrid and hopeless detail. It might kill him. As it was he thought that Abraham Lincoln might be suffering an attack of apoplexy right now.

The President felt the dark curtain being drawn closed around his heart again—the first sign of the debilitating, black despair that haunted him—the despondency he hadn't felt in its full force since Willie had died. He had to fight it back. He couldn't surrender. He uncovered his face, wiping his eyes as he did so and hoping that Haupt wouldn't notice.

"We must go to General Halleck."

For three blocks Haupt almost had to run to keep pace with Lincoln's gigantic strides. Not a word was spoken.

Halleck's house was lighted up like the French court and H Street was lined with double-parked carriages, but Lincoln didn't notice. He wasn't even surprised when he walked in to find the house packed with well-dressed ladies and uniformed officers drinking and laughing as though the world *hadn't* just come to an end. He stepped into the doorway and the party slowed to a halt. The revelry trickled away to silence as every conversation ended in mid-sentence and the house became ominously quiet. All of Halleck's guests turned as one to look at the clearly distraught President of the United States. No one failed to notice the look of urgency and distress on Lincoln's face. They all knew about the big fight going on in Virginia and it wasn't hard for them to guess why their President was there.

The young and beautiful Terry Clack stood in the center of the room on the arm of her father, since her incredibly handsome soldier, her gallant husband to be, was away—at Fredericksburg. When she saw the President's ashen and somber face, she spoke for the whole room—for the whole nation—when she very softly whispered the oldest prayer known to man.

"Oh, my dear God."

She watched, horrified, as the general in chief made his way through the throng of silent guests to greet the President and General Haupt. Short and squat and balding, she thought Halleck looked like one of Mr. Barnum's dwarfs alongside the towering Lincoln.

"Mr. President?"

"I need to speak with you—privately if I may, General."

Halleck nodded and led the two visitors into a small room—nothing more than a pantry really—so that they could speak in private.

"Tell General Halleck what you just told me, General Haupt."

The railroad man repeated his story of the Battle of Fredericksburg—continuing to soften the blow even now. But when he came to the number, the horrific total, there was no way to make it smaller. "Ten thousand killed and wounded is my estimate—I believe it to be a far more accurate number than the five thousand you have been told."

There was silence in the little room. There was even silence on the other side of the door, in a house filled with people. Finally Haupt continued. "I am afraid *that* number may even be small."

Halleck continued to say nothing. Like no other before, Fredericksburg was his battle. He had played a role in its design—and even pressured Burnside to press on after the pontoon debacle that Burnside was already trying to blame on him—regardless of the strength of the enemy positions. The public and the President might actually hold him responsible for Burnside's failure—if Burnside failed.

"General Halleck . . ." The President's voice was strong again. "I want you to telegraph General Burnside to withdraw his army."

Still Halleck didn't speak, so Lincoln did.

"General! We cannot tolerate the loss of *another* ten thousand men! And, if General Haupt is correct, another attempt will only bring the same results!"

For the first time since he had set foot in Washington, Henry Halleck decided it was time to take a stand. With his own reputation at stake now, Burnside *had* to be given another chance to succeed. He *had* to. The general in chief decided that now was the time to draw a line that should have been drawn a long time ago—he simply could not let this backwoods civilian—this militia lieutenant for crying out loud—continue to command professional, West Point–trained professionals in the field—no matter who the general may be. Especially now—especially with so much on the line. He had to screw up his courage for once and stand up to the President.

"I will do no such thing!" He was so panicked his voice almost squeaked. Haupt thought he looked and sounded like a terrified mouse. "If such orders are issued, you must issue them yourself!"

Now it was Lincoln's turn to be struck dumb. Halleck realized that he might have taken a step too far, but he was bound and determined to stand by his argument. He softened his tone.

"I hold that a general in command of an army on the field is the best judge of existing conditions."

Lincoln turned to Haupt. "Is this your view as well, General?"

"Mr. President, I was a witness to the events of the fight, but I was not privy to all of the information that General Burnside may have. The situation may have improved since I left. If we were there, and had up-to-the-minute information, then perhaps we would call Burnside off. But from Washington, acting on stale information . . . well, Mr. President, I think that it is still best left to General Burnside."

Lincoln looked at his feet while he thought it over and, again, Haupt decided to soften the blow.

"Mr. President, I witnessed much of the fight around Fredericksburg, but very little of the battle on our left. I have heard that General Franklin may have had some success there."

Lincoln nodded. He knew that Haupt was offering only a straw of hope for him to grasp and nothing more, but grasp it he did. "Very well then. What you say gives me a great many grains of comfort."

But all the grains of comfort in the world couldn't calm the cannons exploding in the President's brain.

The story was on the train and safely on its way to New York. At least Villard hoped it was safe. *Please, dear God, at least let it get there this time.*

But it was out of his hands now, and a warm bath and a hot steak were only feet away as he walked into the lobby of the Willard Hotel. It was like passing through the pearly gates—heaven was in his grasp.

"Villard!"

He pretended not to hear. He didn't even know who it was who called him—he didn't care. He cared only about the bath and the steak and didn't want to be delayed another second, but the man was too close and too persistent. He caught up with the reporter and put his hand on his shoulder and turned him around.

"Villard, right? The *Tribune* man?"

"That's right."

The well-dressed and apparently clean and well-fed gentleman put out his hand. Villard recognized him now. Henry Wilson—the abolitionist Republican senator from Massachusetts. "Good to see you, Mr. Senator."

"And you, sir. I assume you've just returned from the front." Villard didn't even have time to respond before the questions came racing out. "What's the news? Have we won?"

The pearly gates slammed shut in Villard's face. He knew this was going to take a while.

"You must understand, Mr. Senator, that anything that I might tell you is the property of the *New York Tribune,* and I will tell you nothing except in the strictest confidence. Is that understood?"

The senator was irritated at Villard's pompous attitude. The whole damned game was at stake and all he cared about was his damned scoop.

"Yes, yes—of course—now tell me . . . Have we won?"

In a hushed and secretive tone Villard told Wilson the whole deplorable story.

Wilson was appalled and speechless. He doubted the reporter's sanity for a moment, but only for a moment. He suddenly had trouble breathing.

Villard continued. "I have told you this for a reason, Mr. Senator. I think that it is urgent that you go directly to the White House and tell the President what I have told you. You may tell him that your information comes from me—he will believe me. You should also tell him that if he has heard otherwise from *any* other source, that he is being lied to. What happened—what *is happening* at Fredericksburg, is nothing short of the worst disaster in the history of the Republic. And tell him this as well. Tell the President that he should order General Burnside to retreat his army back across the river immediately—before he does something stupid—again."

Wilson remained speechless, telling Villard that his work here was done—and his steak beckoned. The reporter nodded and turned to enter the bar, but Wilson grabbed his arm again.

"No. *You* tell him!"

Prospect Hill

"God Almighty, damn it's cold!"

The boys of the 7th Tennessee, after yesterday's heroic fighting and today's burial details, were now curled up in the woods and freezing their rear ends off. No blankets—no coats—and in some cases no shoes. At least they had been fed. Hardtack and bacon grease. There wasn't any bacon, but there was plenty of grease.

"You know what? There's about a thousand perfectly good coats out there just lying on the railroad tracks goin' to waste. They sure as heck ain't keepin' their dead owners warm any more."

"And shoes," another man added.

"And underwear!"

Most of the men hadn't thought of that, but the man desperately in need made no apologies. "Shoot—I can't afford to be proud no more."

It started with just these three men, sneaking out beyond the Confederate lines and onto and over the tracks. Then a dozen more. Then a hundred more. Dark shapes in the night scavenging the Union dead like vultures. In only a matter of minutes there was nothing more to steal. No coats. No shoes. No underwear.

"Hey—look at *me*, boys," one man whispered as they scurried quickly and quietly back to their lines. "I'm a gosh-darned Yankee *general*!"

Behind them, on the rise leading up to the tracks, lay the totally naked bodies of Union General Feger Jackson and about a hundred of his men.

Washington, D.C.

Senator Wilson only observed as Lincoln grilled Henry Villard for over a half hour, pressing him hard for details about the Rebel positions and Union casualties and any possible chances for success. Unlike General Haupt, Villard held back nothing. With each disheartening response the President's head throbbed more violently and the black curtain of his mind continued to close around him. He took a seat and placed his hands flat on the table in front of him. He looked down as though studying something that lay on the desk, but there was nothing there. When he finally spoke, it was almost in a whisper. It was almost a prayer. "I hope it is not so bad as all that."

"I'm afraid it is much worse, Mr. President." Villard saw the President's discomfort just as clearly as Haupt had, but he didn't feel the same compassion. Not for the President at least. His concern was for the men of the Army of the Potomac, so he continued to beat Lincoln with the horrible truth and without pity.

"Mr. Lincoln, I know it is not for me to offer you advice, but success is impossible. A renewed assault will result only in the greatest disaster ever to befall the Army of the Potomac."

The President's gaze remained fixed either on his hands or on some imaginary document. He didn't look up, he didn't shake or nod his head—he just sat there absolutely motionless.

Villard saw it as permission to continue. "You cannot render the Republic any greater service, Mr. President, than to order General Burnside to withdraw his army back across the river into Falmouth if he has not already done so."

Villard was done. He waited for the President to speak, to argue, to call him a liar, or to yell at him to mind his own business—anything. But the President did not.

After a short eternity of silence Senator Wilson touched Villard's shoulder and said, "Thank you for your time, Mr. President."

Lincoln nodded almost imperceptibly and the two men left him to his misery. He shifted his gaze to the glowing embers of a dying fire as he surrendered to the total darkness of profound despair.

FREDERICKSBURG

Clara Barton saw to it that Bill McCarter's wound was bandaged and that he was given all the water he could drink. She wrapped him in a warm blanket, placed him on a straw bed, and told him that his arm had been saved and that tomorrow he would be put on a train to begin his journey home. "There's one more thing," she said before she moved on to the next man. "You're very fortunate to have a friend like that big fellow who brought you in here."

"Y-yes, ma'am. You're r-right about that."

James McClernan found his father sleeping by his cannon on Stafford Heights and told him about George, whose body still lay a hundred yards away from the wall. In his father's arms, he now had time to cry.

Little Abbott sat beside Oliver Wendell Holmes in a field hospital well to the rear. Holmes was almost recovered from the dysentery that may have saved his life. Abbott told him everything. He told him about the street fighting and Charlie Cabot and the idiotic assault up Marye's Heights, and about sending poor Leander's body home for burial. For the first time in Little's memory, Oliver Wendell Holmes had nothing to say.

Along with thousands of other Union soldiers, Lawrence Chamberlain continued to "hold his position"—as ordered—on the swale below Marye's Heights where he had been for over thirty hours. They were still waiting for orders—forward or back—it made little difference at this point. The groaning and pleading from the wounded was less now than it had been—a great deal less—and it didn't take a college professor to figure out why.

CHAPTER 20

THE PHILLIPS HOUSE
DECEMBER 15

Corporal Finous Burr knocked on Ambrose Burnside's door precisely at sunrise as ordered, but the knock didn't do it. Burnside had sent his telegram to the War Office at 4 A.M. and gone to bed for the first time since his two-hour nap in the wee hours on the day of the fight. He hadn't had four hours' sleep in the last thirty-six, and not a great deal before that.

Burr had to enter and shake the general awake. When Burnside finally sat up, Burr handed him his coffee and helped him on with his boots. The commanding general then just sat there on the bed—dazed—probably still asleep until the corporal offered him a hand and physically helped him to stand. The general was so exhausted and sleep-deprived that he walked like a drunkard, almost falling as he maneuvered down the steps. He spoke to no one. His horse was saddled and ready to carry him to Sumner's headquarters for a better view of the field.

As he rode off, Burr hoped that his commanding general wouldn't fall off his horse along the way and break his danged-fool neck. *That'd be a helluva way for a general to die,* he thought. He shook his head as he watched Burnside go and whispered under his breath, "God-danged idjet."

Burnside and Sumner peered through their glasses at the Confederate lines atop Marye's Heights. In his exhausted state, Burnside had genuinely hoped that he would rise this morning to find the positions evacuated and the Rebels on the run, and the road to Richmond open. Instead what he saw were stronger fortifications that had been improved overnight and made even more intimidating than before. Yesterday all he had needed was one friend—one good man ready to resume the fight—and not a single soldier stepped forward. Looking at Longstreet's newly improved lines he knew that there would be no found courage on this day either.

"It is time for me to offer my resignation, Edwin. I have lost this fight and the confidence of my generals and my men."

Sumner didn't know what to say. He certainly couldn't argue that Burnside was mistaken.

"They deserve better, General Sumner."

Then Hooker came to Sumner's mind. The intolerable heir-apparent.

"You must not think such a thing, Burn. You need sleep. You've needed sleep for a week or more. And you can't tell by looking from here what may be true over there."

"You're right, Edwin. I need to cross the river, to have a closer look."

WASHINGTON, D.C.
6:30 A.M.

The pounding on the door was urgent—almost like someone had come to warn the Chases that their house was on fire. Kate was irritated that someone—anyone—would come calling well before the appropriate hour. One of the servants rushed to the door, but Kate grabbed him by the sleeve so as to make the rude caller wait. When she finally allowed the door to be opened, she wasn't surprised to find Senator Wade on the other side—red-faced and panic-stricken.

"I must see your father immediately, Kate."

She offered him a beautiful smile and a brief curtsy that

would stop a train, which was, of course, exactly what she was trying to do. "Of course, Mr. Senator, if you'll be so kind as to wait in the . . ."

"Never mind the formalities, Kate," she heard her father say from the drawing room, "I'm here."

She hated it when he did that. She had told him time and again that absolutely everyone should be kept waiting, especially if they arrived unannounced. The more important the personage, the longer the wait, so that the proper order of things might be understood. But there was no controlling Salmon P. Chase—even if he was your daddy.

"Could I interest you in some lemonade, Mr. Senator?" She didn't offer coffee. It was her subtle way of informing the senator that she didn't approve of callers before breakfast.

"Thank you kindly, Miss Kate, but no."

"Very well, then. I shall leave you gentlemen to your important affairs."

She escorted him into the drawing room where she offered her hand to the senator, who was thus compelled to take it for the obligatory and proper kiss. She smiled and turned and left the room—but she didn't go far. She hid herself just outside the door and listened as Senator Wade briefed the Secretary of the Treasury on the events of Fredericksburg.

"I spoke at length with Senator Wilson and he tells me there are ten thousand dead and wounded, and the Rebels haven't budged . . ."

Kate had to stifle a gasp when she heard the number.

". . . and he tells me one more thing. He says that General Franklin, with more than two full corps at his disposal, committed only two *divisions* to the fight!"

Wade paused to let Chase catch up with the significance of what had just been said. He knew he didn't have to explain it. William Franklin was a Democrat and a McClellan man. General Pope had accused him of complicity—treason really—after Second Bull Run. Franklin had refused to take orders from Pope, saying that he was still officially under McClellan's command, and had left Pope and his army to fend for themselves. Fitz-John Porter was being court-martialed for failure to respond promptly to Pope's orders on that day and the proceedings were going well, but somehow Franklin had weaseled his way off the hook and now, here he was again, holding back men—apparently *still* awaiting orders from George Brinton McClellan!

During the silence, Kate sent a telepathic message to her father. *Seward, Daddy. Point the gun at Seward!*

"Do you find it at all odd, Mr. Senator, that I am learning all of this from *you*?"

It was Chase's turn to pause for effect. "Do you find it odd that I am not at the White House this very minute, ensconced there with the cabinet, discussing these issues with Stanton and Halleck . . . and Seward?"

They continued to plot for another hour and before Wade left, plans had been made to rid the nation of *both* of the scoundrels who were *clearly* responsible for the debacle at Fredericksburg—William Buel Franklin and William Henry Seward.

Kate Chase was very pleased.

New York City

Frederick O. Douglass could tell by the look on Horace Greeley's face that the news was not good. Douglass was in town for another speaking engagement and always dropped by for a visit with his friend at the *Tribune*. He had gotten to know Greeley well, and had never seen the editor so distressed.

When Greeley finished reading only the first few paragraphs of Henry Villard's dispatch, he couldn't speak. He looked up at Douglass with a pleading expression, as though Douglass could make it all not so. He handed the first page across the desk for Douglass to read.

"Great, general defeat" . . . *"inexcusable blunder"* . . . *"the greatest disaster yet suffered."*

"This cannot be." Douglass was thunderstruck.

Greeley went to his office door and yelled down the stairs. "Gay! Smalley!"

The two editors ran up the stairs. They were conditioned to respond without hesitation to Greeley's bellows from on high.

The four men poured over Villard's story and three of

them refused to believe it. The fourth was George Smalley, the only man in the room who had ever witnessed a battle close up. Smalley knew full well how incompetent the Union generals were and the idiotic way this war was being fought. He had known since the moment Burnside was given command that this day would soon follow. He argued that there was no reason to doubt Villard's account.

Greeley was ready to shoot the messenger. "We can't print this. The nation cannot withstand it. The people are almost ready to sue for peace anyway—to give up the struggle and let the Rebels go on their own merry way! And if we print *this* . . ."

He didn't finish.

The room was silent until Douglass spoke and made matters even worse.

"The proclamation."

His people were two weeks away from freedom, but a blow this hard could force Lincoln to withdraw the Emancipation Proclamation and keep them in chains forever.

They had to do something. They had to print a story, Smalley knew, but just not *this* story. "It's not the facts—it's the verbiage."

Greeley looked at him with a spark of hope. Smalley pointed at the key paragraphs. "Look—it's not a 'defeat'— it's a 'repulse.' It's not a 'disaster'—it's a 'setback.' "

"Get on it, George! Do a rewrite and calm it down. Sydney—I want biographies of every general who saw action—fill the pages with heroes."

WASHINGTON, D.C.

Lincoln had stood up only twice during the night— both times just to put another log or two on the fire. This is what he did in the dark times. He had suffered bouts of debilitating melancholy before in his life, but they generally hit hardest following the death of a loved one. First his mother. Then Ann Rutledge, his first true love back in Illinois, and of course his sons, Eddie and Willie. These were the worst, but there were others. Sometimes the emotional paralysis lasted only for a few hours, but the serious attacks could lock him in a dark place for days. He called it "living in the tombs." And now there were so many.

Hay and Nicolay served as Lincoln's private secretaries, valets, and confidants. Other than Seward, Lincoln believed them to be his only friends left in the world. He called them the two Johns. They called him the Tycoon. Both had been with him since the campaign of 1860 and they loved him like a father, protected him like a child, and worried about him like a pair of dotting old spinster aunts.

On this day, when he found the President gazing into a dying fire with his bed unslept in and his coffee untouched, Hay knew that the Tycoon was living in the tombs again. Whenever anyone asked for the President, the two Johns simply told the seekers that he was away—probably at the War Office or visiting the Soldier's Home—sending them on a wild goose chase and hoping the Tycoon would be "back" when they returned, but it was a charade they knew could not be kept up for long.

"George McClellan and his minions are going to hound me to my grave!"

The Secretary of War was ready to put William Franklin against a wall and shoot him right this instant. No charges. No trial. Just take the man out and shoot him.

General in Chief Halleck was cautious by nature and wanted to pull Edwin Stanton back from whatever it was he was about to do. He just couldn't believe what Salmon Chase had just reported—third hand—about Franklin deliberately holding back troops. No general in the history of the world, at least no West Point general, had ever deliberately lost a fight to prove a point. But he knew that Chase and Stanton believed it. It was what they *wanted* to believe. For the last six months these men had jumped on any opportunity—any excuse—to rid the army of what they considered to be Democrat, McClellanite, antiabolitionist traitors. Halleck needed to calm Stanton down.

"Right now these are only allegations against General Franklin, Mr. Secretary—from a reporter . . ."

"But it's certainly true to form! He did it at Bull Run and

we let him get away with it, and now he's done it again. First Pope and now Burnside—and he will just continue to sacrifice men by the thousands under some insane impression that failure in the field will somehow get him his precious McClellan back!" Stanton had trouble taking a breath. His asthma tended to flair up in concert with his temper.

Chase took advantage of the momentary silence to interrupt. "Edwin—we must deal with this thing properly. Let Senator Wade and his committee deal with Franklin. We have greater fires to put out."

"Like what?"

Chase pointed at the quiet telegraph station. "You know that the next telegram to come across those wires will be General Burnside's resignation. He's going to accept the blame. That's just his nature. Every man in the army is going to blame him, every newspaper in the country is going to blame him—and if *he* gets the blame, *we* get the blame."

Stanton knew immediately that Chase was right, but that made it even more important that Franklin be publicly disciplined and they didn't have time to wait for any damned committees. Then he had a thought. *Let Burnside do it.*

"General Halleck, send a message to General Burnside. Tell him that he has our full support and that he shall be sustained in any measures he may take in regard to any . . ." He hesitated just long enough to find precisely the right euphemism for "traitors." "Unreliable officers."

FREDERICKSBURG

The ceremony was the oddest event Sergeant John Stretchbok had ever witnessed. It was a morose celebration if there can be such a thing. All the right ingredients were there. There was a band, and food for everyone—the surviving officers and even the few enlisted men who had been invited to participate as the guard of honor. Generals Meagher and Couch and Hancock were all there and made eloquent speeches. The band began to play—Garryowen, of course—and Stretch and the other members of the guard marched into the room carrying the freshly repaired green flags of the Irish Brigade, back from their dates with the seamstresses of New York, just as promised. They were beautiful. Clean and whole again. Unwounded.

There was very little cheering.

Ambrose Burnside slouched in the saddle, weary, sleepless, and beaten. Defeated by Robert E. Lee and his army of Rebels, yes, but also by Hooker and Franklin and even Edwin Sumner. A brigade commander or two had urged him to pick up the fight—told him they'd follow him anywhere— but the corps and division commanders were unanimous. The Battle of Fredericksburg was lost and any thought to the contrary was nothing more than a desperate and dangerous forlorn hope.

The sights and sounds of a beaten army followed him wherever he went. The hoorahs and three cheers that traditionally greeted a commanding general were nowhere to be heard. He had warned them. He had told them to pick someone else. He had told them a dozen times that he was not capable of leading an entire army in battle, but they hadn't listened and now the army—the entire nation—had paid the price.

He rode slowly through the town and up to the middle bridge—Wesley Brainerd's bridge, the one that so many engineers had died building—the bridge that was so late arriving—*Halleck's fault*—and ruined the whole plan before it ever started. He sat there for some time, well off to the side so as not to be noticed, and watched ambulances and buckboards filled with wounded soldiers as they crossed the Rappahannock, headed for the hospitals on the Falmouth side. Other wounded men were being carried across on stretchers or on doors that had been ripped off the houses of the town. These were the worst because Burnside could see their faces—and their blood. He pulled his slouch hat far down over his eyes so that his army might not see the tears as he inched his horse into the flow of traffic and made his way very slowly to the Phillips house, where his grand division commanders continued to wait, just as they had all day long.

He wanted no more discussion. He didn't want to hear another arrogant "I told you so" from Hooker. He didn't want any more excuses from Franklin or sympathy from Sumner. He didn't even stop as he walked through the room. He said, simply, "Pull 'em back," and continued up the stairs to bed.

Under the cover of darkness it was now safe for the Federal soldiers on Marye's Heights to move again. Using bayonets, pocket knives, sharp pieces of exploded Rebel shells—whatever they could—many of them began digging shallow graves for their fallen friends.

Lawrence Chamberlain was about this same work when Colonel Ames tapped him on the shoulder.

"Colonel Chamberlain. I've just been given orders to pull back into the town."

Chamberlain didn't know whether to damnation or praise the Lord. "Very well, sir."

"Quiet is the word, Colonel. Every man is to secure his bayonet, his canteen—anything that might rattle and attract the attention of the Rebs—wrap them in blankets or, hell, just leave them behind as far as I care. But we're sneaking away, Lawrence. Like a bunch of scared mice."

Chamberlain said nothing.

"Well. In about an hour or so then, Colonel. Pass the word."

FALMOUTH
DECEMBER 16

As a wet dawn began to light the day, Ira Spaulding stood in the deluge watching the Army of the Potomac as it quickly and quietly crossed back over the bridges he and his men had paid so dearly to build. It had been raining hard for over three hours and a stiff wind gusted into his face—all to the advantage of the army, blowing the sounds of retreat away from the Rebel lines. The skedaddle was very nearly accomplished and, so far, thank God, not a shot had been fired.

It was not the same army that had crossed in the opposite direction five days ago. Those men were tall and proud. These were slouched and miserable as they limped back to where they had come from. But it was done now. The history books were already being written in a thousand diaries and ten thousand letters home. Soon the official reports would come in and every colonel and general on the field would glorify himself and his men while pointing the finger of blame at someone else—anyone else. Spaulding knew that a hundred of those fingers would point at him.

"If the engineers had gotten the bridges here on time, before the Rebs got here . . ."

If I had gotten my orders in time . . . If the biggest winter storm of the century hadn't hit . . . If . . . If . . . If.

But the *ifs* would have to wait for tomorrow. The last of Burnside's army was across, and it was time for Spaulding's engineers to pull back their bridges. The men had been waiting on the Falmouth side for hours now, hoping, praying, that the retreat would be finished before sunrise, but it wasn't. So now they had to step back out onto the spans in the soft light of the morning, in full view of the Rebels across the river. Every man remembered what had happened the last time they had stood on these bridges in daylight, and not a one took a step before making his final peace.

"Make certain they're well anchored on this side and then just cut 'em loose on the other," Spaulding ordered. "Let the currents pull them to us."

Still without a shot being fired, the bridges gently floated home and the 50th New York Engineers began to disassemble them, wrestle them up the hill and onto their wagons.

Spaulding glanced up toward the Lacy house, and standing there on the road, looking back down at him were two men, one with his arm in a sling and leaning heavily on the other. Honest Johnny Jones and Captain Wesley Brainerd. It took him a moment to recognize his old friend because he wore the plain topcoat of an ordinary private. But there he was—*stitched up like an old sock*—and Spaulding was never happier to see anyone in his life.

They were too far apart to speak, but they didn't have to. They felt the same emotions and thought the same horribly painful thought. *All for nothing . . .*

Wesley Brainerd nodded and offered a respectful salute to Major Ira Spaulding.

WASHINGTON, D.C.
DECEMBER 17
NOON

Senator Preston King exploded into the Executive Mansion and marched right past John Hay, bound for the President's office. Hay was up in a flash, placing himself between the senator and the door.

"May I help you, Mr. Senator?"

"You may either get the President or get the hell out of my way, young man. I have just come from a meeting with Secretary Seward and have urgent business with Mr. Lincoln."

Hay knew King well. The senator from New York was well respected among radicals *and* conservatives, Republicans and Democrats, and was always welcome at the White House. But Hay had only recently been in to check on the President, and the Tycoon was still slouched in his chair—unmoving.

"I'm afraid the President isn't in, sir. May I suggest you try the War Office?"

"Mr. Hay—no one has seen the President in over two days. He's not at the War Office. He's not at the Soldier's Home. He's 'living in the tombs' again, according to Secretary Seward, and it's time for him to come out."

Hay couldn't believe his ears. He thought the euphemism was a secret kept between the Tycoon and the two Johns. But if anyone else would know of it, it would be Seward. Still, he didn't know what to say, so he just stood there, blinking.

"John . . ." King held up an envelope. "This is Secretary

Seward's letter of resignation. He just gave it to me and asked me to bring it to the President. There is a conspiracy in the Senate to *dictate* to the President who is to serve in the cabinet and who is to command the army. I attended a meeting of the conspirators yesterday and I know. Now, either you must retrieve the President from his 'tombs' or I will."

Hay had known that a time like this was coming, but he and Nicolay had done nothing to prepare other than to hope and pray that by the time the blow fell the President would be able to stand and take it. It was not to be.

Hay inhaled deeply and nodded. "Please wait here for just a moment, Mr. Senator. I'll see what I can do."

He entered Lincoln's office without knocking only to find the President still in his chair—still gazing into a now dead fire. He pulled up a chair of his own and placed it between the President and the fireplace. He touched Lincoln's knee softly.

"Mr. President. We need you."

Lincoln began to breathe a little more noticeably. Hay noticed his cheeks were swollen and his eyes were horribly bloodshot.

"Senator King is here, sir, and insists that he be allowed to see you." Hay now had to deliver the blow himself. There was no other way. "He has brought with him Secretary Seward's resignation letter, sir, and news that the Senate is going to make certain demands of you."

Hay was relieved when Lincoln lifted his head slightly and looked into his face. The President took a very deep breath, slouched deeper into the chair, and rubbed his eyes, and then, for the first time in over two days, he spoke to his young friend.

"John—if there is a place worse than hell—I'm in it."

FREDERICKSBURG

Stonewall Jackson was outraged. His entire body shook in anger as he looked around him at what had been done to the city of Fredericksburg. He saw the pianos and the works of art and the crystal chandeliers smashed and ruined on the streets. He saw elegant furniture that had been wantonly vandalized and the remains of leather-bound books that had been burned for kindling. But it was the churches—the *churches*—that infuriated him most. Houses of God were pocked with bullet holes and charred by cannon shot. This was a crime against God—a despicable blasphemy—and it very nearly made him weep.

Dr. McGuire, who was seldom far from Jackson's side, shook his head in revulsion. "What can we do about this kind of barbaric behavior?"

Jackson's voice trembled. "Kill 'em," he said. "Kill 'em all."

WASHINGTON, D.C.

"Mr. Secretary, I beg you to withdraw this letter." The secretary of state wasn't surprised to see the President in his home. It had taken him only a few minutes longer to arrive than Seward had expected.

"And I beg *you* to accept it, sir."

"I cannot!"

"Mr. President, Senator Wade and his colleagues want my head, and are prepared to demand it of you. You cannot yield to those demands—it would be too serious a wound to the presidency. If, on the other hand, you accept my resignation *before* it is demanded, then they have no demands left to make. They get what they want, and the presidency escapes unscathed."

"You are only the whipping boy," Lincoln said. "The head they really want is mine—and sometimes I am half disposed to gratify them."

"And that is something else you cannot do. The only thing you *can* do, Mr. President, is accept that letter."

"That will do very well for you, but I *can't* get out."

Senator John Sherman held the floor and was not about to turn it loose. This was their second meeting of the day, and Senators Wade and Sumner and the rest were hell-bent on lynching the wrong man, and he had to stop it.

"It's Seward who's the puppet. The difficulty is with the

President himself. He has not the dignity, order, nor firmness to do the job we have entrusted to him!"

The other senators listened impatiently for Sherman to have his say and sit down. They knew he was serving as his brother's mouthpiece and William Tecumseh Sherman was no angel himself. He and his friend out West, Sam Grant, were generally known as "the madman and the drunk." Besides, the goal was already determined and it was only the proper method of ridding the nation of Henry Seward that was left to be decided.

But it was Sherman's turn to speak and the others sat quietly waiting for him to run out of words.

"You are correct that we must visit the President and demand immediate changes, but he himself must be brought on board. We must inform him that he is deficient; we must remind him that this is a Republican war, a war against slavery, and nothing less. We want *only* antislavery men in the cabinet, *and* in command of the army—*and in the White House!*"

Sherman received the obligatory "smattering" of applause and a polite "thank you" from the chair, and the senators went back to the real business of the day. They had to decide how best to confront the President with a demand that Seward be let go along with all Democrat generals—all McClellanites—or the war would never be won.

A document was proposed and approved. A committee of nine senators was appointed to deliver the Wade manifesto to the President. John Sherman was not on it.

FREDERICKSBURG
DECEMBER 18

For five days the bodies had been lying in the mud, disrespected by rain and cold and Confederate scavengers desperate for coats and shirts and shoes and underwear. Now virtually every Union hero who had given his life in the futile assault lay totally naked on the cold and muddy field.

The generals had finally agreed on a truce to allow for

Union troops to return to the place of their own humiliation to put the dead in the ground where they lay.

Trenches were dug. Not graves. Trenches. Some of the bodies were wrapped in blankets before being dumped into the holes, but most were tossed in naked, one on top of six others.

The last man buried was one of the first men killed. His brother had written a note on the night of the battle and attached it to a button on his uniform to tell the burial detail who he was and where he was from so that his grave could be marked and his body retrieved later. But he was as naked now as the day he was born and the note was gone, and the anonymous body of George McClernan was tossed onto the pile along with a thousand other unknown soldiers.

WASHINGTON, D.C.
7 P.M.

Abraham Lincoln felt like a dying deer surrounded by a pack of famished wolves. Senator Wade and his committee attacked him with accusations of carelessness and disloyalty to the cause of freedom. He had "lavished important commands on bitter and malignant Democrats." He had disgraced good Republican generals like Frémont and Howard while encouraging the McClellans and Porters of the world—men who were proslavery Southern sympathizers with no desire whatsoever to bring the South to its knees. They laid the recent defeats—both military and political—directly at the President's doorstep. The malignancy was not only eating away the heart of the army, but it had found its way into the cabinet as well. With an abundance of "good" Republicans to advise him, it seemed that the President ignored the antislavery men like Chase and Stanton in favor of the counsel of the one man who was the weakest—the one man who was willing to compromise on freedom. They had it on good authority that he no longer consulted with anyone *other* than Seward—the greatest turncoat since Benedict Arnold.

Good authority, Lincoln thought. *That would be Chase. Without a doubt.*

He had Seward's resignation letter safely tucked away in his coat pocket. All he had to do was take it out and hand it to Senator Wade. Then he could return to the tombs, where he most desperately wanted to be. But he didn't. He couldn't.

For three hours they harangued him, and Lincoln just sat there and took the beating like a dazed and exhausted prize-fighter. He didn't have the energy to fight back. He didn't even have the desire. He even thought for a while that they might be right. Maybe it *was* all his fault. He reached into his pocket and touched Seward's letter.

But then Senator Wade delivered the President of the United States an ultimatum.

Seward must go. Seward and Franklin and anybody else not totally committed to complete and immediate emancipation. The Committee on the Conduct of the War would advise him on all future military appointments—and Democrats need not apply.

How dare they? Lincoln was livid. How dare they dictate to the President of the United States who his advisers should be? How dare they dictate to the commander in chief of the Army and Navy of the United States who his generals and admirals should be? How dare they demand that he abdicate the constitutional powers of the presidency to them? He wanted to take each and every one of them— the most powerful leaders of his own party—and grab them by the collar and belt loop and heave them out of the second-story window. He wanted to kick each man hard in the seat of the pants and send the whole pack of wolves whimpering down Pennsylvania Avenue like a litter of spanked puppies. He wanted to, but he didn't.

"Gentlemen, you have given me a great deal to ponder, and I promise you that I shall. With your permission, we shall meet back here at the same time tomorrow. Does that meet with your approval, Senator Wade?"

Wade was disappointed. He had to leave for Falmouth in the morning along with the Committee on the Conduct of the War and he had wanted to leave here tonight with Seward's scalp hanging neatly from his belt. But he knew Lincoln was a beaten man. He could tell by looking at him. The other senators could be here to accept Seward's resignation, and he could head for Falmouth—and return with General Franklin's scalp as well. Today would have been better, but tomorrow will be fine.

THE PHILLIPS HOUSE
II P.M.

Ambrose Burnside didn't know what to make of it all. When he'd heard that the general in chief was coming to Falmouth, he was certain that Halleck would make that trip for one reason and one reason only—to fire the commanding general. But he hadn't. He hadn't fired him. He hadn't accepted his resignation. He hadn't even chastised him for his humiliating defeat. None of that. Instead Halleck had warned him that the Committee on the Conduct of the War would arrive tomorrow and he had spent most of the evening instructing Burnside on what to say to whom.

"You are the world's most passionate advocate of abolition, Ambrose," he had said. "George McClellan is a fool, a coward, and a traitor and you are a dyed-in-the-wool Republican. Your entire goal in life is the total conquest—the absolute destruction—of the Rebel states and all of their deplorable institutions. Do you understand me?"

Burnside was smart enough to know that while it was Henry Halleck's lips that were moving, the words were coming from Stanton and Chase. Of course he wouldn't accuse George of treason. Or Porter or Franklin or anybody else. He hated politics and, frankly, had little concern for the slaves. But now he was under orders, and he was still a soldier.

Halleck had left him moments ago with one more piece of "advice."

"Don't go into winter quarters, General. The damage that

has been done to the nation here must be undone. And quickly."

With that the general in chief left Ambrose Burnside standing alone, staring at a six-foot-long map and wondering what in the hell he was going to do next.

CHAPTER 21

The sunrise service was mandatory. Oliver Howard's men had spent Sunday on the field and "the Christian general" had missed his weekly occasion to share the Word of the Lord with his flock. They had been too busy every day since, so Sunday would be on Friday this week. It was his earliest opportunity.

Little Abbott and a thousand other beaten Yankees sat in the dark on the cold ground waiting for the arrival of the sun and their pious commander. As scripted, both arrived at precisely the same moment. The men stood to attention as protocol required.

"Congratulations, my brave boys!" Howard yelled, still mounted on his huge, black stallion. "You have been tested by the Lord and He has found you most worthy to carry His sword! You have been spared by God! *You*, my men, are the *chosen ones*!"

Howard had expected a rousing cheer at this moment, but none came. His men were obviously too deeply moved to hoorah.

Abbot was certainly not moved. How dare this man even so much as imply that Charlie Cabot was somehow *unwor-*

thy in God's eyes? How dare he even suggest that Leander Alley was chosen by God only to die—to be tossed onto a rubbish heap like some worthless scrap of God's garbage?

He whispered to George Macy, "This sanctimonious son-of-a-bitch can kiss my Yankee ass."

Macy closed his eyes and shook his head. He prayed for Abbott to shut the hell up.

Howard still wanted his cheer and he knew a foolproof way of getting it. It was obligatory.

"Three cheers for General Burnside!"

Had it not been for the singing of the birds, there would have been no sound at all. A thousand men stood before him as quiet as statues. "The Christian general" was first confused, then angry, then humiliated. He looked like a suddenly trapped animal, searching desperately for a way to escape or a safe place to hide.

From the back of the crowd Little Abbott filled his lungs and at the top of his voice he yelled, "Three cheers for George McClellan! Hip hip . . ."

The hoorays exploded like cannons.

WASHINGTON, D.C.
7 P.M.

As they were ushered into the room, the senators were stunned to find the President's cabinet gathered and waiting. All except Seward. The cabinet was equally surprised to see the senators and no one was more surprised than Salmon P. Chase.

After an incredibly awkward moment, the President entered the room, standing tall and commanding the attention of all.

"Gentlemen—these respected senators believe that Mr. Seward is unenthusiastic about the war and opposed to emancipation. They have demanded that I dismiss the secretary of state. I have assured them that they are mistaken on both counts. They are also under the impression that I do not consult with you on matters of national importance. Secretary Welles, do you find that to be the case?"

Lincoln spoke to the Secretary of the Navy, but all the while he stared directly at the treasury secretary. Chase knew instantly what was about to happen. He began to squirm in his chair and Lincoln smiled. *Trapped in a cage like the conniving little weasel that you are,* Lincoln thought. He almost laughed when he saw Chase's face begin to turn a brilliant red and he remembered his earlier description of the pompous secretary whenever he got angry—"a tomato with ears."

He could have called on Chase next, after Welles was finished assuring the senators that they were, in fact, consulted on all matters of an urgent nature. But Lincoln was having too much fun watching his old rival squirm. He would let him wallow in anguish a little while longer.

"Mr. Blair? Do you agree with Secretary Welles?"

"I certainly do, sir, and may I add for the benefit of the distinguished members of the Senate, that Mr. Lincoln is the President of the United States, and he may consult or *not* consult with anyone he chooses."

Bates agreed, as did Smith and even Stanton.

And finally, it was time. "And Mr. Chase . . . what are the views of the Secretary of the Treasury on this matter?"

There was total silence. Not a person moved. Everyone in the room knew Chase's dilemma. If he supported the President, he had lied to the Senate. If he supported the Senate, he had conspired against the President.

"Mr. President, I want you to know that I would not have come here tonight if I had known that I would be arraigned before a committee of the Senate . . ."

"Your views, Mr. Secretary, are all I ask. Has there been any time during which Mr. Seward has suggested that we pursue any course other than all-out war?"

On this cold night Chase's red face and balding head were suddenly beaded with perspiration. "No, sir, he has not."

"Were you or were you not consulted on the issue of emancipation?"

"We were."

"Other than to recommend a delay to a more opportune time, has Mr. Seward ever suggested that the Emancipation Proclamation be weakened or dispensed with?"

Lincoln was having a wonderful time. He was back in

Springfield, standing before the bar, cross-examining a reluctant, hostile witness. He was in his element. His time in the tombs was over.

"No," Chase said. "I only regret, Mr. President, that we do not have a . . . a more thorough consideration and canvass of every important measure in open cabinet."

The words were spoken weakly—apologetically—and the once skyrocketing political career of Salmon P. Chase came to a humiliating end in a sad and pathetic sputter.

DECEMBER 20
7 A.M.

The President had barely swallowed the last bite of his huge breakfast before his Secretary of the Navy came to call.

"Father Neptune! What brings you here so early in the morning?"

Gideon Welles admired and respected Abraham Lincoln probably more than any other member of his cabinet other than Seward. But, like Salmon Chase, Welles too had problems with the Secretary of State. He was meddlesome and arrogant and wielded far too much influence with the President. Seward's resignation should have been a blessing, but Welles was irate over the events of last night. He had lost sleep thinking about it, and the more he thought, the angrier he became. He was outraged that a committee of the Senate would actually attempt to force the President of the United States to abdicate a grain of his authority to anyone in the legislative branch. What the senators had attempted was nothing short of a coup d'état, and it had to be stopped.

"I had to come here first thing, Mr. President, to share with you my conviction that you should not—in fact you *cannot* under the current circumstances—accept Secretary Seward's resignation."

"And why not, Gideon?"

"I have difficulties with Mr. Seward, Mr. President, as do many within your cabinet. I have difficulties often with the way you seem to disregard the rest of us in favor of the Secretary of State. But to accept Secretary Seward's resignation in the light of what happened last night would be to surrender the presidency to the Senate."

Welles had practiced what he had intended to say, but what came out was nothing like what he had rehearsed. It was better. It was perfectly honest and unhedging. "It is my view, Mr. President, that for the good of the country, you cannot yield one iota of presidential authority to the Congress."

There. It was done. It was done well and easily and Welles was relieved. "You have not sought my advice on the matter, Mr. President, but that is my position, and I felt compelled to come here first thing this morning to share it with you."

"Your advice is *always* welcome, Gideon." Lincoln recognized the irony of that statement at this moment and it made both men smile. "And I fully agree. Have you expressed these thoughts to Secretary Seward?"

"I have not."

"Well then, may I suggest that you do?"

ALONG THE BANKS OF THE RAPPAHANNOCK

"Hey—Johnny Reb! You got anything to trade today?"

The pickets had been facing each other across the Rappahannock long enough now that they should have known each other by name, but Johnny Reb and Billy Yank worked good enough. Newspapers, Southern tobacco, Northern coffee, and small cargoes of other valuable commodities filled the holds of tiny, homemade boats that did a thriving commerce across the river and between the lines.

"Got a Richmond newspaper that tells how bad y'all got licked!"

"Seen enough of that. You got anything else?"

"We've got a good-for-nothin' swaybacked, lame ol' mare over here, not worth eatin'. What'll you give us for her?"

"Will you take General Burnside?"

WASHINGTON, D.C.

"He said *what*?"

Senator Benjamin Wade was madder than a *hive* of hornets. His trip to Falmouth to investigate the battle had been a worse disaster than the battle itself. The damned generals had circled the wagons so they could pat one another on the back. Hooker was the only one who broke ranks. He called Burnside everything but an idiot, but even he wouldn't say anything about Franklin's treachery. And Burnside—what a shock Burnside had been! He took most of the blame himself. Even when asked point blank about Franklin's performance, he blamed the Rebels. He said Franklin failed because of Lee's "great strength" and his "accumulation of forces there."

It would have been easy enough to come away with Burnside's head, but damned if he didn't turn out to be one of the best antislavery men in the whole damned army.

And everybody, even Hooker when it came down to it, blamed the whole fiasco on the pontoons. And whose fault was *that*? Every finger in the room pointed to Halleck!

And now, back in Washington, he had just been told about Salmon Chase's shameful performance at the White House last night.

"You heard me, Ben!" Senator Charles Sumner was still furious at Chase almost twenty-four hours later. "He sat right there and told everybody that he had been lying all along. A dozen senators, the cabinet, except for Seward, and the President himself—we all heard it."

"But what did he say specifically?"

"He said that Seward had always favored an aggressive prosecution of the war, that he *favored* the proclamation, and that the President had consulted the cabinet on every issue of importance. I swear to God, Ben. You can ask anybody."

"Jesus God in heaven. And Seward remains in the cabinet?"

"The President has his resignation—at least that's what everyone is saying—but I doubt at this point if he will accept it."

"Well, he'll damn sure accept Chase's! Hell, Charles. We're worse off now than when we started!"

Wade fumed for a minute while he considered his options, trying to find something—anything—that he could salvage from the wreckage of his failed scheme. There was nothing. He had to smile. "The old rail splitter just outmaneuvered us," he said. "We had him surrounded and he escaped. Amazing."

Then another sudden moment of panic. Wade thought his heart was going to explode.

"What about the Emancipation Proclamation? Is he still going to do *that* at least?"

"Only God Almighty and Abraham Lincoln know that, Ben," Sumner said. "I sure as hell don't."

Gideon Welles returned to the Executive Mansion to find Chase waiting to see the President. But it wasn't really Chase. At least this wasn't the arrogant, indignant, self-righteous Salmon P. Chase who had been blustering around Washington for the past two years. He was quiet and soft and looked almost embarrassed to be alive.

Thankfully for both men they had only a brief, awkward moment to exchange meaningless pleasantries before the President entered the room. He spoke first to Welles, virtually ignoring the disgraced Secretary of the Treasury.

"Have you seen the man?"

Welles was hesitant to answer with Chase in the room, and was made even more so by Lincoln's referring to Seward as "the man." He decided to remain clandestine in his response.

"I have, sir, and he has assented to my views."

The President smiled and nodded and turned to Chase.

"The matter of the Senate's disapproval of my choice of advisers is giving me great trouble."

"I hope it will be less so now, Mr. President."

Chase reached into his coat pocket and produced an envelope. "This is my resignation, sir. I wrote it this morning and want you to know . . ."

It was all Lincoln could do not to leap across the desk.

"Let me have it!"

He leaned across the wide table—his long right arm striking like a snake—and, to Chase's visible astonishment, the letter was yanked away in a flash. He clearly had more to say, some kind of speech or apology or denial he wanted to make, but Lincoln seized the document so quickly as to leave Chase stammering. He ripped the envelope open like a child tearing into a Christmas package, smiling the whole while.

He quickly read the letter, looked back at Welles, and laughed. It was an uncontrolled giggle—still the little boy at Christmastime.

"*This* cuts the Gordian Knot!"

If it were possible for Chase to be even more humiliated than he already was, the sight of the President of the United States laughing and rejoicing over his resignation bordered now on blatant ridicule. Especially with Welles in the room. Chase's face began to redden.

Then, to the further amazement of both Welles and Chase, Lincoln said, "Return to your department, Mr. Chase. I cannot do without you—just as I cannot do without Mr. Seward."

Now totally bewildered, Chase looked as confused as a mouse in a maze.

"You see, Mr. Chase, I need to hear from all sides of every issue. To isolate myself from opposing views would prove disastrous to me, to the party, and to the nation." The President's glee calmed itself to only a boyish grin. "A man cannot ride with only one pumpkin in his pocket—he must have another for balance or he will fall." He held up Chase's letter in one hand, and Seward's in the other. "Now I have a pumpkin in each pocket, and I can ride a straight line again."

To make his meaning even more clear, the President took both resignation letters and placed them in the drawer of his desk. Then, with a bit of a flourish, he closed the drawer—and locked it.

FALMOUTH
DECEMBER 21

S o far, this night differed from no other since the fight. The grand division commander and his staff gathered, dined, and complained.

"General Burnside has written a letter," Franklin said as he speared a nicely fried steak. "A very *public* letter—accepting full responsibility for the failure here, and it is going to be published in every paper in the nation—North *and* South— before the week's end." He had suddenly become the commanding general's greatest friend since Burnside had defended him before the Committee on the Conduct of the War. "It's not fair. It wasn't Burnside's fault." Any references to the late and vague orders of the morning of the battle were set aside—not forgotten—only tucked away for later use if need be. "He says in the letter that he wasn't ordered to attack, but I'll tell you this—it was only because they *knew* better than to *order* him to cross in so many words, but they let him know, by God, that they *expected* him to move forward as quickly as possible. You mark my words."

Generals John Newton and John Cochrane were among the lower-ranking men in William Franklin's inner circle, and they sat, as usual, at the far end of the table, nodding their heads and soaking it all in. Newton was a West Point engineer who looked like a slovenly politician and Cochrane was a politician who looked like a spit-and-polish West Point engineer. They had become best friends.

Franklin reached for a bowl of mashed potatoes and plopped a giant spoonful onto his plate. "Henry Halleck deserves to be hanged!"

Now he had the attention of the room. Hanging Henry Halleck was a flashy new addition to his well-worn repertoire. "*He* pushed this army into the fight after *he himself* had failed to send the pontoons in time, knowing full well that Lee's entire army was ready and waiting on the other side." He shook his head in disgust. "That's criminal incompetence, my friends, and that's a hanging offense. Henry Halleck is a fool and a liar."

The room was getting angrier and angrier—especially

Newton and Cochrane. The whole idea of such quality leaders as Franklin, and McClellan for that matter, being under the tyrannical thumbs of idiotic, make-believe generals was frustrating and infuriating, especially when it repeatedly cost so many thousands of wasted lives.

Dinner was over and a squad of enlisted men cleared the table, poured brandy, and passed out cigars. It took only seconds before the large room filled with blue smoke, and the dinner conversation turned into an impromptu staff meeting.

Franklin continued to hold court. "Now here, gentlemen, is the real news of the day. It looks as though our friends in Washington are about to make the same mistake all over again."

There were twelve men in the room and all fell silent, waiting for Franklin's other shoe to drop.

"General Burnside is looking for another place to cross the river."

A dozen men—a dozen expletives. Each man competed with all the others to show himself the most incredulous and angry. Franklin held up his right hand for silence.

"Agreed. It is insane. But it is nonetheless. General Burnside is incapable of saying 'no' to these imbeciles. General McClellan refused them and General McClellan got fired. These are the new rules."

John Newton by now was no longer content to sit in the amen corner and listen. "We *must* do something to put a stop to this! It doesn't matter *where* we cross, Lee's army—his *whole* army—is still sitting over there *waiting*! The results will be no different!"

"We all know that, John," Franklin said, a little too patronizing for Newton's liking, but—

"And General Smith and I have come up with a plan—an alternative."

The room was quiet once again.

"We have sent a letter to the President suggesting another attempt at attacking Richmond from the south."

John Cochrane was only a brigade commander, far and away the most junior man in the room and as such he was expected to sit and listen and nothing more, but a suggestion to resurrect the old plan brought a roll of the eyes and an involuntary groan.

"General Cochrane—you have an objection?"

Cochrane was embarrassed. He really hadn't intended to make his opinion known and wasn't comfortable arguing with his grand division commander.

"It's okay, John. You have served in Congress—*as* a Democrat, I believe . . ." The room laughed because Franklin expected them to. Cochrane saw no need to correct the general. He had been a Democrat, but he was a convert to the antislavery cause. He remained quiet and let Franklin continue. "I know you have friends in Washington. Your opinion is important to me."

"Very well, sir. The administration will see it as McClellan's Peninsula campaign all over again. It is a strategy tried and failed."

"We anticipated that. It is different in that we will unite all of the armies of the East and will storm Richmond with an army a quarter of a million strong. They will never be able to resist such strength."

"And what about Washington, sir?" Cochrane knew that Lincoln would never in a million years leave Washington unprotected. A trade of Washington for Richmond would be a queen for a pawn.

"If we unite our armies, Lee will have to unite his."

"I'm sorry, sir, but you asked my opinion, and my opinion is that the administration will never allow it. General Burnside can demand it till the cows come home, but they will never agree."

Franklin grimaced slightly before he let the cat out. "Who said anything about General Burnside?"

MARYE'S HEIGHTS
DECEMBER 22

Porter Alexander and Bill Owen leaned against a freshly filled caisson eating corn bread. Alexander had absconded with some butter and Owen, a proud son of New Orleans, was seldom without a nice bottle of some sweet vintage. In the days since the fight the two had grown tired of congratulating each other on the placement and the fighting of the guns. The men of the Washington Artillery were settling into winter quarters and were already planning their next stage production. Maybe even Shakespeare this time.

"Don't get too comfortable, Bill," Alexander warned. "General Lee isn't convinced that this fight is over yet."

"Surely they won't come back. Not after what we did to them last week."

"Like I said, Bill, General Lee isn't convinced. And all those Yankees we killed? Abraham Lincoln can replace that many men in a week. They've got millions of 'em."

"Shoot. Do you think they'll give us till Christmas at least?"

Alexander smiled. "Three days? Yeah, Bill. I think we're safe till Christmas."

CHRISTMAS DAY
NANTUCKET, MASSACHUSETTS

Leander Alley's body arrived back in Nantucket, Massachusetts, appropriately, by boat. A large crowd gathered at the pier. There were his old whaling mates gathered around an honor guard arranged by the governor at the request of Little Abbott's very influential father. Townspeople of all shapes, sizes, attire, and even color stood reverently watching, the ladies dabbing tears and the men with hats in hand, as the casket was carried down the gangplank and loaded into a flag-draped hearse. As it left the wharf pulled by a single, black horse, the honor guard fell in behind and the town followed until they reached Leander's family home. The modest house was draped in black crepe and his mother stood weeping on the porch as the soldiers escorted the coffin into her parlor.

FALMOUTH

Sergeant Stretchbok had a Christmas tradition that many of his comrades of the Irish Brigade had never seen before. He had managed to find a pretty decent tree that hadn't already been chopped up for firewood. He dug it up by the roots and dragged it into camp, where he stood it up for all to see. Then he began to gather things. Just things. Preferably shiny things. Steel cups. Tin cans. Belt buckles and buttons. He worked all morning long just hanging his shiny things from the limbs and when he was done he made his bold announcement to *lads of the alt sod*.

"It's a Christmas tree! Very popular back in my old country."

"What's it for?" one man yelled.

It took Stretch a moment to think it through. He'd never really thought about it before. He had just always had one.

"Well, if you've managed to brew up a keg or two of Knock 'em Stiff, it's for drinking under!"

They proceeded to put Stretch's tree to its rightful purpose and within an hour not a man among them had a sober bone in his body. They Indian-wrestled and played a little football. They even managed to find a single, terrified pig, which they lathered up with bacon grease. Men paid a dollar apiece to chase the poor animal and the soldier who finally caught her won half the pot. The rest was to be sent to a New York orphanage. A thousand men of the Irish Brigade ran and stumbled and fell, and more than only a few fistfights broke out before the creature could be cornered. The men had been rolling in the mud and were dirtier than the pig and, of course, that's when General Meagher came riding in to announce a review and a parade in honor of General Burnside, who had just dropped by to pay his respects.

Stretch was filthy head to toe and so drunk he could barely stand. "Wonderful," he said as he stumbled to his feet. "This should be a grand salute if ever there was one. There's not a man here who wouldn't punch old Sideburns square in the jaw if given half the chance, and every mother's son of us is as drunk as an owl."

New York City

Newspapers get published even on Christmas, and newspapermen go to work. Henry Villard had been back in New York for a day or two, lobbying to be sent South to watch yet another newly promoted Federal general at work. William Rosecrans was now in command in Tennessee, and Villard hoped—prayed—that Lincoln had at last found his man. Villard met with Horace Greeley and George Smalley and told them that Stanton and Chase were frantic for a victory and had lost all confidence, justifiably, in Burnside. He was convinced that irresistible pressure was now being placed on Rosecrans to move in western Tennessee and if that was where the next fight would be—that's where he wanted to be.

His case was a good one and Greeley agreed.

"Catch the next train, Henry."

Villard left the office but came to an abrupt stop at the top of the stairs. The *Tribune* office below was packed tight with people. Mostly poor people.

"Was die Hölle?"

George Smalley joined him on the landing. The two lorded over the masses crammed below.

"What the hell is *this* all about, George?"

Even the cynical Smalley was moved by the sight. "We've just posted the most recent casualty lists from Fredericksburg. They're here to see if their sons or husbands are on the list."

Villard's heart went out to them. It was a part of the story seldom told by the press—the stories of those left behind. He hadn't even thought about it that much, but now he saw it for himself. To see all those people corralled into a single room, all trying to elbow their way to the front, each desperately praying not to see a name printed in agate type in a long column of others. Several broadsheet pages were tacked to the wall. The mass pushed forward as a single flood of humanity, but trickled back toward the door one at a time. Most came away happy but trying not to show it—trying not to gloat. The rest left weeping. One poor woman fainted. Some men helped her up and tried to push their way through the crowd to get her out to the street for some air. Villard had no way of knowing which way her prayers had been answered—whether she had found that her beautiful son was living or dead.

He had seen a lot since First Bull Run, but this sight on this day may have been the most tragic of all.

With only a hint of sarcasm he whispered very softly to George Smalley—"Merry Christmas."

PROSPECT HILL
DECEMBER 26

"I must know what those people are doing over there, General Stuart."

Robert E. Lee was convinced that the Yankee army was not going into winter quarters. Something was up—he just didn't know what. There was nothing to lend credence to his suspicions other than simple intuition, but with General Lee, intuition was often enough.

"I need for you to take another one of your famous excursions, General." Stuart smiled. There was nothing in the world he loved more than circumnavigating the Army of the Potomac and creating havoc along their lines of supply and communication. Bridge burnings and train derailments were fun too, and it didn't hurt that these little picnics never failed to get his name in the papers.

Lee pointed casually at his map. "They can move freely behind those heights and I am blind. So I need for you to cross the river, General, have a good look and report back to me."

THE PHILLIPS HOUSE

The grand division commanders sat around Ambrose Burnside's big map table like three pouty children. Their mission, to their great disgust, was to hear the commanding general's plan for the next offensive. All three of them had told him time and again that the plan was doomed to failure, but Burnside would hear nothing of it.

"The infantry will cross here—at Muddy Creek, twelve miles downstream from where the enemy is encamped," he told them. "The cavalry will cross at this point well upstream, where they will be able to close down the enemy's supply and reinforcement lines from Richmond. This time there will be no delays, gentlemen. The pontoons are already here, and a rapid march will catch the Rebels still encamped around Fredericksburg.

"It will work this time, gentlemen."

"No," Hooker said. "It won't."

Burnside looked to Franklin, who only shook his head. Then, almost pleadingly, he turned to his old friend Edwin Sumner. Sumner too shook his head and said nothing.

Et tu?

Burnside began to shake with fury. *To hell with 'em all.*

"Have your men cook up three days' of rations and load up ten days' worth of supplies. Bring up a herd of beef cattle to last twelve days and issue each man sixty rounds of ammunition."

He looked back at Sumner, Franklin, and Hooker and saw three portraits of treachery. Brutus—Arnold—and, in the face of Joe Hooker, Judas Iscariot himself.

"Have this army ready to move in twelve hours."

DUMFRIES
DECEMBER 27

Sergeant Robert Crow was almost asleep in the saddle as he and six troopers from the 12th Illinois Cavalry rode slowly down the Telegraph Road, which ran between Chopawamsic Creek and the small town of Dumfries, Virginia. Stationed safely in the rear, these men had only read about the Battle of Fredericksburg in the papers. They were in the business of guarding a short stretch of the telegraph lines that ran from Fredericksburg to Washington, and that's about all. And that's all they were doing on this rather pleasant Saturday morning before the world exploded around them.

Crow hadn't even lifted his head before his horse whinnied

and fell. The first heart-stopping volley of rifle fire was followed instantly by some kind of blood-curdling Comanche
scream. The Yankee sergeant rolled into a shallow ditch and
had the presence of mind to keep rolling into the woods only
about ten feet off the side of the road. He hid himself in some
deep scrub before he looked back out to see what was happening. Coming straight toward him was a bearded man on a
beautiful horse. He wore a Hardee hat plumed with ostrich
feathers and a gray cape lined with blood-red silk.

Jeb Stuart. Crow knew damned well that's who it was,
and the son-of-a-bitch came to a stop not ten feet in front of
him. And there Crow lay, totally unarmed. His carbine remained in his saddle holster, still strapped to his dead
horse. *Son-of-a-BITCH!*

He watched as five of his men surrendered. The others
lay facedown in the road.

Son-of-a-BITCH.

STAFFORD HEIGHTS

Reluctantly, the grand division commanders supervised
the Army of the Potomac's preparations for the coming offensive. The rations were cooked and the ammunition was parceled out, but well after General
Burnside's twelve hours had passed, the orders to move had
not yet been given.

DUMFRIES

Jeb Stuart's cavalry rode into Dumfries with sabers
drawn and pistols blazing. The bluecoats skedaddled
and Stuart's boys chased 'em clear out of town until
they were greeted with hot fire from a long line of entrenched infantry supported by several pieces of well-
placed artillery.

"Does it feel a little warm to you, Major Blackford?" Stuart asked with a smile.

"Yes, sir. Maybe just a bit too warm—if you're askin'."

The Rebel cavalry pulled back, dismounted, and waited for the Yankees to come out. A few did. Most didn't.

As darkness approached, Stuart ordered his men to build fires, just to make the Yankees think they were going to stay the night.

They didn't.

BURKE'S STATION
DECEMBER 28

Early on this quiet Sunday morning, the Yankee telegraph operator dozed at his switch until the door exploded open like a cannon shot.

"Touch that key and you're a dead man!"

The Union private, scared as a rabbit in a pack of hounds, leaped out of his chair next to the telegraph key with his hands in the air, desperately wishing he'd had time to rip the contraption out of the wall and destroy it before the Rebels got their hands on it, but the Rebel cavalrymen had burst in so suddenly that he didn't even have time to disconnect the thing, much less send off a distress signal. As the private was ushered out of the Burke's Station telegraph office, Jeb Stuart entered.

"Well—look what we have here!" As he looked around the room his eyes sparkled. "Tell the boys to leave the lines up for a moment. I intend to have a little fun while we're here."

He began to rummage through the stack of papers and it didn't take him long to find something important.

"Take a look at this, Major Blackford."

Stuart's adjutant read the dispatch that said elements from Heinzelman's corps were en route south to deal with the Rebel cavalry.

Stuart pointed at the Union general's name. "Heinzelman is coming down from Washington, Major. That means no one is coming *up* from Fredericksburg, and that tells me that Burnside is busy. He is not in winter quarters—but has something else in mind."

As usual, Blackford was impressed with Stuart's ability to find information that other men might never see.

"We'd better head home, Major, and let General Lee in on this—but *first* . . ." Stuart pointed at the telegraph key. "Where is Corporal Shepard—that kid that knows how to use this thing?"

The corporal was quickly located and brought to the telegraph office, where he made himself comfortable at the switch.

"Send this telegram for me, young man."

The corporal placed his hand on the key and waited while Stuart composed his message.

"To General Montgomery Meigs, Quartermaster General of the United States Army—Washington.

"My Dear General Meigs; I have recently come into possession of several of your wagons and mules. While the wagons are first-rate, I must register a complaint regarding the mules. They are of such poor quality that I shall be embarrassed when I present them to General Lee. I will expect you to provide better quality animals in the future.

"Sincerely, your most obedient servant, James Ewell Brown Stuart, Major General, Confederate States Army."

When the dits and daws came to a halt, Stuart clapped his hands together. "Now—let's cut some telegraph lines, blow up a bridge, and head on home."

CHAPTER 22

With a mischievous smile, Abraham Lincoln looked directly at Salmon Chase as he said, "I have called you *all* together to review the document one last time before it is unleashed."

Chase nodded, but he didn't smile.

The Emancipation Proclamation was laid out on the long table for the entire cabinet to see.

"You will each be receiving your own copy. Take it with you and review it for the purpose of proposing any changes that you might find appropriate."

Along with the others, Chase examined the proclamation—and now he smiled.

"The recruitment of colored troops!"

"It is a matter of military necessity," Lincoln said. "It is *all* a matter of military necessity, issued by me as commander in chief. It can be no other. Keep this in mind as you review the document. If any other motive can be seen in it, it will be an unconstitutional scrap—as worthless as the pope's bull against the comet."

"So it is done then?"

Lincoln hesitated. "It will be done when it is done. Peter denied his Master. He thought he wouldn't, but he did."

STAFFORD HEIGHTS

W illiam Franklin was more disgusted now than ever. He had just returned from a personal reconnaissance of the proposed Muddy Creek crossing site favored by General Burnside and he was not pleased.

"It's open enough now, but once General Woodbury puts his pontoons in the water, a single Rebel observer could have Jackson's entire corps there before the bridges could ever be finished and the whole rigmarole will just start over. The whole thing is senseless."

As usual for General John Newton, the longer he listened, the madder he got.

"Have you received a response from Lincoln yet on your plan to come at Richmond from the south?"

"Yes." The word was coated with bitter sarcasm. The thought of it made Franklin steam even hotter. "He said just what General Cochrane said he would. It has been tried and failed, and he would never consider leaving Washington so 'vulnerable.'"

A spattering of expletives ricocheted around the room.

"Hell—Washington is the best-guarded fortress since Troy!" Franklin spat. "The minions of hell couldn't storm those gates."

"What are we to do then?"

"Well, General Newton, unless there is someone in this room with more influence in Washington than *I* have"— Franklin looked directly at John Cochrane, the former two-term Democrat Congressman from New York—"then I'm afraid there's nothing left to do but follow orders."

Newton and Cochrane knew instantly precisely what their commander had just "suggested" that they do. Franklin wanted them to go to Washington and pressure members of Congress to intervene. He wanted these two lowly brigadier generals to commit blatant insubordination—to circumvent the chain of command and challenge the competency of the supreme commander of the largest army in the world.

The two friends looked at each other as they considered their unacceptable options: to risk court-martial or to stand idly by and allow another meaningless slaughter. There seemed to be nothing in between.

Cochrane was the first to nod.

"Very well, then," Franklin said. He took out a pad and pencil and wrote out two passes. Newton and Cochrane were on their way to Washington within the hour.

STAFFORD HEIGHTS
DECEMBER 30

"General Burnside, I cannot in any stronger language tell you how adamantly opposed I am to undertaking another offensive at this time."

Burnside had come to Franklin's headquarters for one last try at gaining an ally, but it was simply not to be. A fatal card was about to be played and Franklin had one last chance to stop it. He knew that Hooker and Sumner were on record as well. Ambrose Burnside stood alone in this and, especially in Franklin's mind, so it had to be. This time there would be no doubt as to where the blame should be placed.

He was afraid that Burnside was on the verge of collapse. The beleaguered general wouldn't—or couldn't—look Franklin in the eyes. His shoulders were slouched, his breathing was short, and his gaze was fixed on nothing.

"You have no idea, General Franklin, the pressure I am under. The administration is in a shambles. The nation is depressed. To hear Stanton talk you would think that the people are fully prepared to surrender. They are desperate for any little bit of success that they can take to the people."

Franklin genuinely felt badly for him. He spoke softly— as a friend might. "If we cross that river, General, I'm afraid it will not be a success that they will report. I firmly believe, sir, that it will be another disaster—maybe even worse than the last."

Now Burnside closed his horribly bloodshot eyes and his chin fell to his chest like a man who had just dozed off in church. He remained in that pose long enough for Franklin to believe that the man had actually gone to sleep until Burnside whispered, "You know that I've offered to resign, but they turned me down."

Franklin didn't respond. He didn't know what to say, so he said nothing.

"Very well, then." Burnside took in a deep breath and, still avoiding Franklin's eyes, he said, "As everyone seems to stand against me on this, I will take another day to reconsider."

He then remembered who he was talking to and what Franklin had done—or not done—during the first fight. "But, General Franklin, you should know this—if I give the order to go, I shall expect you and all the others to go full out. To hold nothing back. We will not be beaten by timidity! Not this time."

Franklin was stung by the words—the thinly veiled accusation—but he fought back the urge to challenge Burnside on the issue. That he would save for a later time. Right now William Franklin wanted nothing more than to stop the insanity.

He kept his tone friendly. "I know it's hard, Ambrose, but right now winter quarters is the right choice." He could see that Burnside was a beaten man and tried to ease the moment for him. "It will save thousands of lives, General, that would have been lost for no good reason. Tell the politicians to go to hell."

WASHINGTON, D.C.

Generals Newton and Cochrane were astounded at how empty the nation's capital was. Cochrane was a little embarrassed as well. After serving four years in the Congress, he should have remembered that every December the legislative branch stampedes out of Washington like horses out of a burning barn.

"You could fire a thirty-pounder in the Capitol and no one would notice."

"Sorry, John. It just never occurred to me."

"Well—it's an easy enough mistake. Hell—*we've* got to work. Why should *they* get to go home?"

"A bunch of 'em are lame ducks anyway."

"But the question is what to do now."

"Well, nothing bad ever happened at the Willard." Cochrane smiled. He remembered his days—and nights—spent there. They had to walk around piles of marble building stone lying about. The workers putting the new dome on the Capitol were still at work at least. "Anything that ever gets done in Washington gets done at the Willard. If there's a living soul left in this town, we'll find him there."

No sooner had they walked in the door of the hotel than Cochrane spotted an old friend from New York.

"Henry! You old Republican SOB! What's new in the world of governing?"

Newton wouldn't have been more surprised if Cochrane had hugged the devil himself.

"How are you, John? It's good to see you."

"John Newton, allow me to introduce you to our Secretary of State. Henry Seward, this is my good friend and commanding officer, General John Newton."

Newton was able only to stammer out a "Pleased to meet you" before Seward and Cochrane headed for a quiet table—which wasn't hard to find.

"Henry, I need your help."

"Anything you want, John."

Cochrane was a Democrat, but an antislavery moderate, making him a much favored person in the Lincoln administration, even though he no longer served in the Congress.

"I want to see the President."

Newton almost choked.

"About what?"

Cochrane took a deep breath. From this point forward, there would be no turning back. Insubordination.

"Henry, General Burnside is about to make a horrible mistake."

"Oh?"

"He's determined to try to cross the river again. Nothing has changed, Henry. Lee is still over there with his entire army, and it is the opinion of just about everybody, *all* of the grand division commanders included, that the results of a fresh offensive would be Fredericksburg all over again."

It was the last thing on earth Henry Seward wanted to hear. He had just come within a hair's breadth of losing his job for meddling in the affairs of Secretary Stanton and others. The dust hadn't settled on that fight yet, and here he was being asked to involve himself again.

"This is an issue for Secretary Stanton, John. He's in town and all you have to do is knock on his door. I'm sure he'll be happy to hear you out."

Cochrane was shaking his head before Seward ever finished his sentence.

"We can't go that way, Henry. I'm sure you understand that we are taking a very large personal risk here by circumventing the chain of command. It cannot get back to General Burnside that we were ever here."

Seward took a while to answer. He knew that he was meddling again, but he also knew John Cochrane. He would not have come here, he would not have considered for a moment ruining his career, were it not an issue of life or death on a grand scale.

"Very well, John. Wait here. I'll see the President and see what I can arrange."

It wasn't a half hour later that Secretary Seward returned and came directly to their table.

"He's waiting for you. Good luck."

The two generals stood and started to thank Seward, but he interrupted. "And, John . . . I had nothing to do with this."

"Understood, Henry."

As they crossed the street, Newton was still shaking his head. "Are you sure we want to do this, John?"

"There is nothing else *to* do."

When they entered the President's office, Lincoln did not stand to greet them. He looked angry.

"What can I do for you gentlemen?"

Newton, being senior, spoke first.

"Mr. President, we thought that you should know firsthand the situation as it exists on the Rappahannock."

"Go ahead."

"The Army of the Potomac is totally demoralized, sir. General Lee has joined his entire force on the Fredericksburg side of the river and is able to move freely from there west to the Rapidan, or east to Aquia Creek."

He paused and waited for Lincoln to speak. He did not.

"Mr. President, a second failed attempt . . ."

"Why are you *here*?" Lincoln's temper had been simmering ever since Seward had knocked on his door. Everybody on God's green earth seemed to know better how to run the war than the commander in chief, and for two brigadiers to barge into his office with their knives drawn and pointed directly at the back of their commanding general was more than Lincoln could tolerate.

"Get to the point, General, unless you are here to injure General Burnside, in which case I suggest that you leave now, because if that is your purpose I will have your stars before the sun sets!"

"No, sir!" Both generals responded at once, even though that was, in fact, their purpose. Or it had been ten seconds ago.

Newton was a career military man—Cochrane was an experienced politician. It was Cochrane's turn to talk.

"Mr. President, let me assure you that no such thing has entered our minds." Lincoln unclenched and Cochrane continued. "We come here as patriots, wholly loyal to the government. Our whole purpose here is to warn you that the Army of the Potomac will not be able to withstand another setback like it suffered at Fredericksburg. It would not result in defeat, but in the *destruction* of the Army of the Potomac. We believe, sir, as do a great many senior officers, that another defeat of those proportions will have a ruinous effect on the cause and the nation. We are here, sir, to express our firm belief that the very existence of the country is at stake and to ask that you take the condition of the army into account before you allow another fight. We are here, sir, simply to suggest that you proceed with the utmost caution."

Lincoln sat still and quiet for a long moment before he nodded and said, "You have risked much to come here and I will take your observations into account."

The generals waited for more—hoped for more—and Lincoln saw it in their faces. "I'm glad that you have come here and I assure you that good will come of it."

Newton and Cochrane left the President's office with knees shaking, happy to still have stars on their shoulders. A few moments later Lincoln, too, left the White House and headed for the telegraph station at the War Office.

"Send the following telegram to General Burnside over *my* signature," he told a telegrapher.

"I have good reason for saying you must not make a general movement of the army without letting me know."

THE PHILLIPS HOUSE

"Good reason!" Ambrose Burnside wanted to throw something. He wanted to kick things. He wanted to take about a half dozen generals out and have them shot. "I wonder where Mr. Lincoln might have come upon his 'good reason'!"

Members of Burnside's staff, who had been with him since the very first days of the war, were astonished at their general's fury. They had never seen him so angry. He was a man who seldom lost his temper, but this telegram from the President had launched him into a fury worthy of Joe Hooker.

"I will not stand for this backstabbing and conniving a moment longer!" He slammed his hat hard against a table three times. "Those conniving little sons of bitches have gone behind my back directly to the President, and as God is my *witness* I intend to have every one of them drummed out of this army or be damned!"

He looked around the room at his stunned staff. Not a man said a word.

"Arrange a steamer for me. I'm going to Washington. They want me to testify at Porter's court-martial anyway, and apparently I don't have anything *else* to do!"

One man responded, timidly, and only because he had to. "When would you like to leave, sir?"

"*Now, dammit!* Right damned *now*!"

"General Burnside! A pleasant surprise to find you here!"

"I'm here to testify in the Porter affair, Mr. President, but I received your telegram and think it important that we talk about our future plans."

The President remained standing. "Very well, General. What *are* our future plans?"

"I will tell you honestly, Mr. President, that your message halted the army dead in its tracks and as a result I have no idea where we are going or what we are going to do when we get there!"

Burnside thought that his temper had cooled overnight, but the very thought of the whole affair set him off again. *So be it,* Burnside thought. *It's time to play all the cards and end the petty games one way or the other.* "The generals around me are so bound and determined to undermine anything that I might attempt that I can't even order a squad to clean the stables without getting an argument from *some*one. And apparently now some of my so-called subordinates have come directly to you with their complaints and you have allowed them to stab me in the back!"

"General Burnside, I have done no such thing."

"Then what is your 'good reason' for halting a campaign, Mr. President?"

"There are those who believe that another attempt to cross the Rappahannock will meet with the same results as the first."

"And who are these people, Mr. President? Who is it that has told you this? Secretary Stanton? General Halleck? They are the only people on this earth who know the details, and they both tell me that they favor the plan! So it must be someone else!"

Lincoln was trapped. Burnside was right and he knew it.

"General Burnside, I will not give you any names, but I am told that none of your highest-ranking officers supports your planned movement, and that the army is dispirited and demoralized."

Burnside could feel the heat rushing to his face and the sweat beading on his forehead. His heart began to pound and his hands balled themselves into fists as he thought about the three Judases. Hooker. Sumner. Franklin. And even—maybe especially—Stanton and Halleck for their failure to support him as they had promised. Hell—it was Stanton and Halleck who were relentlessly *pushing* him to move, to attack, to give the government a victory at any cost. They were the ones that the generals of the Army of the Potomac really hated.

He forced himself to come to attention and look directly to his front, and not at his commander in chief. "If that is the case, sir, that the highest-ranking officers of my command have no faith in me, and the army is as dispirited as you say, then it is appropriate that I should relinquish that command. But I see it as my duty, sir, to point out to you that those same officers whose opinions you so respect have even less confidence in Secretary Stanton and General Halleck than they do in me, and for the greater good, they should resign as well."

Lincoln's eyes slammed shut in disgust. He had just dealt with Seward and Chase and now his highest-ranking general was pushing to get rid of Stanton and Halleck.

"I must go to the War Office now, General Burnside. General Rosecrans is active in Tennessee." The President grabbed his coat and hat off the stand by the door. "Come back tomorrow, and we shall finish our talk."

A hundred thoughts rattled in Ambrose Burnside's mind as he rode the nearly three miles from the White House to the Capitol. First was the view of the uncompleted Capitol dome. To his depressed mind it looked more like a ruin than a hope for the future.

The meeting he'd just left and the one he was about to have got all mixed up together. He was on his way to testify *on behalf* of Fitz-John Porter—a man accused of failing to support his commanding general at Second Bull Run. The irony of it almost made him laugh. Porter and Pope—

Franklin and Burnside. Porter is being court-martialed and Pope is in Minnesota, relegated to fighting the Indians.

As he walked into the room his frame of mind did not improve. It was obvious to Burnside that this was a packed court if ever there was one. Every man on the panel was either a Republican or someone with a personal grudge against either Porter or McClellan. There was no love lost between Burnside and Porter, but the poor man was being railroaded—he didn't have a snowball's chance in July of surviving this Edwin Stanton Inquisition.

As he stepped forward and placed his hand on the Bible, a debate raged in Ambrose Burnside's heart. A man must follow orders. Porter should have. Franklin should have. The dishonorable discharge of Fitz-John Porter would send a message to the Hookers and Franklins of the world to do as they were ordered—and to do it without pause, regardless of what they might think of the orders or the man who issued them. But then came the words, "the whole truth and nothing but the truth."

When the question came, Burnside did the only thing a man under oath could do. The truth and nothing but.

"I do not think it was the impression of the officers generally that General Pope was fully up to the task of conducting so large a campaign, but I have never seen anything to lead me to think that General Porter was anything but a zealous, faithful, and loyal officer."

Washington, D.C.

Clara Barton walked into the room where fifty soldiers lay, recovering from their wounds. Just the sight of her made Bill McCarter smile. She was the kindest and most beautiful woman he'd ever known. Of course nothing would ever come of Bill's infatuation with his nurse. He had a beautiful wife back home and seeing her again was almost all Bill ever thought about. The most frustrating thing in the world was that he wasn't able to write her. For weeks the man famous for his letter writing couldn't draw a line with a ruler.

Clara was furious when Bill told her that the surgeons back in Falmouth had wanted to cut off his writing arm. "I t-told 'em 'Nix to that! If this arm goes, I'm goin' right along with it.'"

Bill's brogue always made Clara smile and she found the slight stammer nothing but charming. Here was a beautiful boy with the soul of a poet and the hand of an artist. He had shown her some of his penmanship from before he was wounded and it was as beautiful to her as an Eastman Johnson painting. "Graceful" was the word that came to mind. She took it upon herself to help him get the use of his hand back. She worked with him every day, forcing him to grip first a Bible, then a baseball, and finally a pencil. Anything to get strength and control back to his right hand.

The going was slow, but at least he could guide the pencil now. The writing was a poor imitation of what had gone into General Meagher's book, but it was still better than most.

Clara walked toward him with a sly grin. She sat by his bed, reached into her purse, and took out a clear, corked bottle filled only halfway up with a lovely light brown liquid.

"It's a fine brandy, Bill." Then she whispered, as though she were confessing to a felony, "It was confiscated from a general's dinner table." She patted him on his good arm. "I thought you might want to toast in the New Year."

Bill grinned and accepted the gift—with his *right* hand. "I'll be delighted, ma'am, to kick 1862 in the seat of his pants and send him on his despicable way."

He pulled the cork and held up the bottle. "To 1863. May it be a darned sight better." He took a short swig and enjoyed the elegant warmth. "Aye. The year 1863 is looking better already."

After Clara had left he uncorked the bottle again and this time he raised it to the small jar he kept with him at all times. It held a sprig of boxwood.

"And here's to you, lads. If there's to be another wall in your future, may ya be behind it."

The Willard Hotel

While the rest of the Yankee world celebrated the demise of 1862, Ambrose Burnside sat alone in his hotel room and wrote a letter to Abraham Lincoln.

The White House
January 1, 1863

General Burnside couldn't have been more surprised if he had walked into the President's office and found Jeb Stuart there. Both Stanton and Halleck waited along with the President to ambush him the moment he opened the door. He made a quick decision simply to ignore the Secretary of War and the general in chief. He walked directly to the President and handed him the letter he had written last night and stood in silence as Lincoln read it.

He watched carefully for any reaction to his resignation, to his distrustful view of the leadership within the Army of the Potomac, to his insistence that the officers who had demonstrated blatant insubordination be summarily dismissed, and finally to his formal recommendation that Stanton and Halleck should follow him out the door. He studied Lincoln's face intently as he read, but Lincoln showed him nothing. There was no anger, no disappointment, amusement, frustration—nothing. When he was finished, he simply folded the document and handed it back to the general without a word.

"General Halleck, what is your opinion of General Burnside's plan?"

The trap set for Burnside suddenly snapped shut on Halleck and the general in chief visibly writhed for a moment in the pain. If he supported the plan and it failed, he would be blamed—and it appeared that virtually everyone in the world other than Burnside himself believed that it would fail.

"Mr. President, as I've said before, the general commanding in the field is the best judge of such things."

"Then what are we paying *you* for?"

The uncharacteristic explosion staggered Halleck. Neither Stanton nor Burnside came to the general's defense and Halleck was left blinking.

"If you do not help me in this, you fail me precisely at the point where I need you most!"

Halleck was dazed and unable to defend himself, and Stanton and Burnside surely were not going to step into the line of Lincoln's fire.

"Go to Fredericksburg, General Halleck. I want you to survey the ground, consult with General Burnside and his subordinates, and come back here and tell me that you *do* or that you do *not* approve the plan. Your military skill is useless to me if you will not do this."

There was even more silence. "Now go, Generals. I want General Lee's army destroyed. Go to Fredericksburg now and decide how best to do it. Mr. Stanton, you stay here for the moment. We have a document to sign."

Halleck and Burnside left as the rest of the cabinet filed in.

BOSTON, MASSACHUSETTS

Underneath the bandstand a small group stood gathered around a hastily installed telegraph station. On the parade grounds hundreds of men and women, black and white, stood in silence, most with their heads bowed in prayer.

After an hour or more of silence the machine began to click and the telegrapher began to write and Frederick Douglass began to weep. He read the transcription over the man's shoulder as each series of clicks was converted into words—words that, at long last, would set his people free.

And then, just when he expected to see the name of the President at the end of the document, there came more. More than he had really even dared to pray for.

"And I further declare and make known that such persons of suitable condition will be received into the armed

service of the United States to garrison forts, positions, stations, and other places, and to man vessels of all sorts in said service."

Without so much as a thank you, Douglass pulled the transcription away from the telegrapher and bounded up the steps to the top of the stands and triumphantly held the paper over his head. The silent crowd erupted into an ecstatic roar that went on for ten minutes or more. Douglass finally had to silence them, and when he at last succeeded he said, "Your prayers have been answered, and America is soon to be cleansed of the great sin and shame of slavery!"

The crowd exploded again, and again Douglass had to silence them.

"There is more!" he shouted. "There is *more!*"

What more could there possibly be? Those in the back pushed forward to hear. Douglass then read them the order to begin accepting colored troops into the United States army and navy, and this time the crowd was too moved to cheer. Instead, after a moment of grateful silence, they began to sing.

In the beauty of the lilies Christ was born across the sea,
With a glory in His bosom that transfigures you and me:
As He died to make men holy, let us die to make men free;
While God is marching on.

Washington, D.C.

Bill McCarter handed Clara Barton a note written on a tiny scrap of paper. The note was two words only. "Thank you" was all it said, but each finely crafted letter was its own tiny work of art.

Clara looked at it in amazement and came very close to tears.

"Did he do it, Miss Barton? Did Mr. Lincoln free the slaves?"

"Yes, Bill. He did it."

"Then I guess it w-wasn't all for nothin' after all then, huh?"

"No, Bill." She patted McCarter on his good arm and smiled. "It wasn't all for nothing at all."

POSTSCRIPT

THE MUD MARCH
JANUARY 16

Ira Spaulding wondered how many times a single soul could be condemned to hell. Back in November fouled-up orders had gotten him and his pontoon bridges off to a late start and then the winter storm of the damned century stopped them dead in their tracks. For all of that he had been threatened with prison. Then had come his first real tour of duty in hell—the day he was ordered to build bridges across an almost frozen river with enemy sharp-shooters picking off his men from hidden positions not a hundred yards away. And for all of this it seemed the whole country blamed him for their humiliation at Fredericksburg.

And now, only five weeks later, here he stood again, stuck chest-deep in the slimiest mud God ever concocted, with heaven pouring an endless ocean of rain and sleet on his men, his wagons, his mules, and his precious pontoons.

Yesterday, when Burnside had ordered the army west for another attempt at crossing the river, the weather had been fine and the roads hard. But late in the afternoon the skies darkened and the rains came with an Old Testament vengeance and the roads broke open. The hard crust that covered them literally shattered under the weight of the army like ice on a pond, uncovering a stagnant river of mud that seemed to have no bottom. Cannons vanished and horses and mules drowned. Not an occasional horse or mule here or there—the poor animals died by the hundreds, clogging the roads even worse.

It had rained hard all night and late in the second day Spaulding couldn't believe it was all happening again. The genuine nor'easter continued without a hint of abatement. A team of eight mules and two hundred men couldn't pull a single wagon out of its muddy pit. And still the rains came.

As his men struggled to move his pontoons through the rain and mire, Spaulding was finally able to glance across the river to get his first sight of their intended crossing point, and there, hoisted on tall posts at the top of a rise was a gigantic tent fly. It had drawn on it an absurd caricature of Ambrose Burnside, ludicrous muttonchops and all, and the words BURNSIDE—STUCK IN THE MUD. It was even signed THE ARMY OF NORTHERN VIRGINIA.

Over 120,000 men were grateful when Burnside ordered them to return to Falmouth—but none more grateful than Ira Spaulding.

WASHINGTON, D.C.
JANUARY 23

For Abraham Lincoln, Ambrose Burnside had become a recurring caricature of himself, showing up repeatedly at the White House, resignation in hand, and insisting that he be permitted to go home. This time it flashed through the President's mind that the file containing Burnside's resignations must be thicker than a Bible by now.

But this morning was different. Today the general brought two documents.

"I must insist, Mr. President, that you accept my resignation, or agree to this."

Lincoln looked at the second paper. It was headed, "General Order Number 8," and it was a cannon fired in the White House. It relieved Joe Hooker from duty, calling him "unfit to hold an important commission." But that wasn't all. Lincoln was almost amused to find Generals Newton and Cochrane discharged for sharing military secrets when, to the best of his knowledge, those secrets had been shared only with the commander in chief. Generals Franklin and Smith would be cashiered for "open and public" opposition to the general commanding. General Order Number 8 was a wholesale firing of the entire high command of the Army of the Potomac save Edwin Sumner.

When Lincoln looked up, Burnside made his demand as sternly as he could. "You must accept one or the other, Mr. President. We cannot go on like we are."

"I think you are right, General Burnside. Come back tomorrow, after I have met with my advisers, and I will give you my decision."

"If you meet with them, Mr. President, it will not be done."

"Be that as it may, General, I must meet with them."

JANUARY 25

It wasn't a hard decision for Stanton or Halleck to make. Every Republican in Washington had been badgering them for weeks to fire Burnside and put Hooker in charge. He was a fighter and an antislavery man who had no ties to George McClellan whatsoever.

"So Burnside is gone," Lincoln said. "And that's a shame. He's the only man yet with only the interests of the nation at heart, and I'm afraid I will be able to find no other."

The two men left without a decision. Again, just like with Pope and McClellan, this was for Lincoln to decide. And Lincoln alone.

Sometimes he debated with himself on paper, and at other times he invited one of the two Johns to sit and talk. Listen really. And on this night it was John Hay's turn.

"Who are you considering, sir?"

"Franklin and Hooker."

Hay knew better than to press the President. This was a time to sit still and be quiet and let the man think. After only a minute of silence Lincoln nodded. He agreed with himself. He'd made up his mind.

"Franklin seems timid and Hooker fights well. Franklin

is a McClellan man and a Democrat. Hooker is a Hooker man and a devout member of whatever party might be in power."

"Does it not concern you, sir, that Hooker has conspired against every general he has ever worked for?"

"As do they all. Burnside was the only one who didn't and they killed him for it. Hooker participated in the Burnside coup, but Franklin led it."

Another moment, another nod, and another commanding general for the Army of the Potomac. Its sixth.

January 26, 1863
Major General Hooker;

I have placed you in command of the Army of the Potomac. Of course I have done this upon what appears to me to be sufficient reasons. And yet I think it best for you to know that there are some things in regard to which I am not quite satisfied with you. I believe you to be a brave and skillful soldier, which, of course, I like. I also believe you do not mix politics with your profession, in which you are right. You have confidence in yourself, which is a valuable, if not indispensable, quality. You are ambitious, which, within reasonable bounds, does good rather than harm. But I think that during General Burnside's command of the army, you have taken counsel of your ambition and thwarted him as much as you could, in which you did a great wrong to the country, and to a most meritorious and honorable brother officer. I have heard in such a way as to believe it, of your recently saying that both the army and the government needed a dictator. Of course it was not for *this reason, but in spite of it, that I have given you the command. Only those generals who gain successes can set up dictators. What I now ask of you is military success, and I will risk the dictatorship. The government will support you to the utmost of its ability, which is neither more nor less than it has done or will do for all commanders. I much fear that the spirit which you have aided to infuse into the army of criticizing their commander and withholding confidence from him will now turn upon you. I shall assist you as far as I can to put it down. Neither you nor Napoleon could get any good out of an army while such a spirit prevails in it.*

And now, beware of rashness. Beware of rashness, but with energy and sleepless vigilance, go forward and give us victories.

Yours very truly,
A. LINCOLN

LITERARY LICENSE

The facts of the Billy Blakesley story are these: He was a raw recruit in the 50th New York Engineers; he was from Rome, New York, and he was killed while trying to lay the bridge at Fredericksburg. Captain Wesley Brainerd was wearing an enlisted man's coat so as not to draw the attention of the Rebel sharpshooters in Fredericksburg. All else is from my own imagination.

Lincoln's words, "If there is a place worse than hell—I'm in it," were probably not spoken to John Hay. The literature says only "to a friend."

Senator Benjamin Wade did not attend the December 18 meeting at the White House. He was already en route to Falmouth with the Committee on the Conduct of the War. I have placed him at the White House meeting simply to avoid having to introduce an entire new cast of characters.

William McCarter was nursed back to health by a caring, nameless lady, who was probably *not* Clara Barton. He recovered the use of his arm, but his *Life in the Irish Brigade* was over.

AFTERWORD

HENRY LIVERMORE (LITTLE) ABBOTT ultimately commanded the Harvard Regiment. At the Battle of the Wilderness, with General Hancock's flank turned and in jeopardy, Little Abbott boldly held his regiment in line long enough for Hancock to re-form—and for this heroic act, Little Abbott gave his life.

JANE HOWISON BEALE returned to her home to find it in much better condition than many of her neighbors'.

WESLEY BRAINERD survived the war and wrote a wonderful memoir with a bad title: *Bridge Building in Wartime*.

AMBROSE BURNSIDE was given command of the Department of the Ohio, where he successfully defended Knoxville against James Longstreet. Following the infamous crater episode at Petersburg, he was accused of failing to exploit the gap in Confederate lines. After the war, he served three terms as governor of Rhode Island and was twice elected to the U.S. Senate from that state. He died early in his second term.

JOSHUA LAWRENCE CHAMBERLAIN was the Hero of Little Round Top at Gettysburg and received the surrender of the Army of Northern Virginia at Appomattox Courthouse. He served four terms as governor of Maine.

Salmon Chase: In 1864 Lincoln accepted Chase's resignation because they had reached a point of "mutual embarrassment" in their official relations. Nevertheless, when Roger Taney died in October of that year, Lincoln appointed Chase as Chief Justice of the United States Supreme Court.

Darius Couch had even less faith in Hooker than he did in Burnside. After Hooker's debacle at Chancellorsville, he asked to be relieved from service. Because he was a Democrat and a McClellan devotee, his resignation was accepted.

Captain Francis Donaldson and Lieutenant Colonel James Gwyn continued their feud through actions at Chancellorsville, Gettysburg, Bristoe Station, and Rappahannock Station. A year after the Battle of Fredericksburg, in front of the entire regiment, Donaldson called his commanding officer an "incompetent, drunken, immoral coward and tyrant." Colonel Gwyn went to draw his sword, but Donaldson drew his pistol first, saying, "If you draw your sword on me, I will shoot you down like a dog." He was, of course, arrested, court-martialed (he offered no defense), found guilty, and sentenced to be dismissed from the service, which was precisely what he wanted. It was his intention all along to appeal any decision of the court directly to President Lincoln. He did so on March 3, 1864, and the President arranged for his discharge to be honorable.

William Franklin was relieved of his command by President Lincoln in the same order that gave Hooker the command of the Army of the Potomac. From that point forward, Franklin's situation only grew worse. The Republican-dominated Committee on the Conduct of the War needed a scapegoat for the debacle at Fredericksburg and looked no further than the highest-ranking Democrat—William Franklin. He was not discharged from the army, but relegated to Louisiana. He finished the war as president of an officer's retirement board.

HENRY HALLECK is one of the most maligned persons in American history. Halleck's reputation went from "Old Brains" before the war to "Old Wooden Head" during. His ineptness may be the only thing on which George McClellan and the Lincoln administration agreed.

WINFIELD SCOTT HANCOCK advanced to corps commander and received the brunt of Pickett's Charge at Gettysburg. Urged to dismount on that day he replied, "Sometimes a corps commander's life does not matter." Shortly thereafter he was severely wounded but survived. Following the repulse of Picketts Charge that day, his men began chanting, "Fredericksburg Fredericksburg" at the retreating Rebels.

AMBROSE POWELL (A. P.) HILL was killed at the Battle of Petersburg.

JOSEPH HOOKER took command of the Army of the Potomac and moved it across the Rapidan and Rappahannock Rivers in the spring of 1863. He engaged Lee's army in the Battle of Chancellorsville. Well planned and coordinated at first, a counterstroke by Stonewall Jackson turned it into a rout. Hooker was replaced by George Meade three days prior to the Battle of Gettysburg.

OLIVER O. HOWARD seemed to come out of every scrape smelling like a rose regardless of some seriously bad decision making. The religious fanatic may have cost Hooker Chancellorsville and came close to costing Meade Gettysburg, but nonetheless he finished the war in command of the Army of Tennessee under William Tecumseh Sherman. After the war, his political connections earned him the Medal of Honor for heroism in the Battle of Fair Oaks that cost him his arm.

ANDREW ATKINSON HUMPHREYS, regardless of his "odd" behavior at Fredericksburg, went on to become one of the most respected officers in the Union army. His men fought heroically at Chancellorsville and Gettysburg, and he was promoted to command of the Second Corps.

THOMAS ("STONEWALL") JACKSON was wounded by "friendly fire" at the Battle of Chancellorsville, and died of complications resulting from the amputation of his left arm. One of the great unanswerable questions of American history is, "What if Lee had had Stonewall at Gettysburg?"

RICHARD KIRKLAND is known as "The Angel of Marye's Heights" for his humanitarian acts at Fredericksburg. While he is honored with a statue there, he was probably one of many.

JAMES LONGSTREET was a man before his time. His defensive tactics won acceptance and were widely applied in WWI. He was reviled in the South after the war and ultimately became the scapegoat for questioning Lee's tactics at the Battle of Gettysburg.

JAMES MCCLERNAN was killed at the Battle of Chancellorsville.

GEORGE GORDON MEADE replaced Hooker as the commanding general of the Army of the Potomac three days prior to Gettysburg. While he won the battle, he failed to pursue Lee's retreating army (à la George McClellan), which infuriated Abraham Lincoln. Ulysses S. Grant was placed in command of all Union armies and attached himself to the Army of the Potomac, making Meade's command "nominal."

THOMAS FRANCIS MEAGHER was much more Irish than American, and after the Irish Brigade was disbanded he attempted to resign from the service entirely. His resignation was not accepted and he finished the war serving under William Tecumseh Sherman. He survived the war and was appointed acting governor of the Territory of Montana. He fell off a steamboat and drowned.

WILLIAM OWEN survived the war and wrote *In Camp and Battle with the Washington Artillery of New Orleans.*

JOHN (SALLIE) PELHAM. "The Gallant Pelham" was mortally wounded at the Battle of Kelly's Ford in March 1863.

FITZ-JOHN PORTER was found guilty of all charges against him and discharged from the service (and prevented from holding any public office) on January 21, 1863. Sixteen years later another commission vindicated him, and in 1886 President Grover Cleveland reinstated his name on the rolls of veterans.

WILLIAM HENRY SEWARD remained Secretary of State throughout the Andrew Johnson administration and is, of course, famous for a real estate purchase known at the time as "Seward's Folly." He bought Alaska for the United States.

IRA SPAULDING was eventually promoted to Lieutenant Colonel. According to his pension records he received a wound that affected his health for the remainder of his life.

MARTHA STEPHENS (OR STEVENS) is a bit of a riddle. Did she remain in her house at the stone wall throughout the battle? No one claimed to have seen her there, but she insisted until her death that she never left.

WILL STEVENS was wounded again and captured at Gettysburg. He was exchanged and returned to action and was killed June 19, 1864, at Petersburg. His younger brother, **Ned,** was killed two months later, August 18, at Weldon Railroad, Virginia.

JOHN (OR JACOB) STRECTHBOK (or Stretchabok or Stretchabach) vanishes from the record after Fredericksburg. He is not listed among the dead, wounded, missing, deserted, or even on the "mustering-out rolls."

EDWIN SUMNER asked to be relieved from duty rather than serve under Hooker. He was reassigned to the Department of Missouri but died of natural causes before he could report.

HENRY VILLARD continued as a reporter for Horace Greeley throughout the war after which he made successful investments in several railroads and became one of the nation's most successful financiers—even lending a helping hand to a young inventor named Thomas Alva Edison, who wanted to start a business called Edison General Electric. Villard died in 1900, a very wealthy man.

EVAN WOODWARD was (belatedly) awarded the Medal of Honor for capturing the colors of the 19th Georgia at Fredericksburg.

PRIMARY RESOURCES

While this is far from a complete bibliography, these are the works I relied upon most heavily while researching No Greater Courage.

Abbott, Henry L. *Fallen Leaves.* Robert Garth Scott, ed. Kent, Ohio: Kent State University Press, 1991.

Alexander, Edward Porter. *Fighting for the Confederacy.* Gary W. Gallagher, ed. Chapel Hill: University of North Carolina Press, 1989.

Beale, Jane Howison. *The Journal of Jane Howison Beale.* Barbara P. Willis, ed. Fredericksburg, Va.: Fredericksburg Foundation, 1979.

Brainerd, Wesley. *Bridge Building in Wartime.* Ed Malles, ed. Knoxville: University of Tennessee Press, 1997.

Chamberlain, Joshua Lawrence. *Bayonet! Forward.* Gettysburg, Pa.: Stan Clark Military Books, 1994.

Dalton, Cyndi. *The Blanket Brigade.* Union, Maine: Union Publishing, 1995.

Donald, David Herbert. *Lincoln.* New York: Simon & Schuster, 1995.

Donaldson, Francis Adams. *Inside the Army of the Potomac.* J. Gregory Acken, ed. Mechanicsburg, Penn.: Stackpole Books, 1998.

McCarter, William. *My Life in the Irish Brigade.* Kevin O'Brien, ed. Campbell, Calif.: Savas Publishing, 1996.

Marvel, William. *Burnside.* Chapel Hill: University of North Carolina Press, 1991.

O'Reilly, Francis Augustin. *The Fredericksburg Campaign.* Baton Rouge: Louisiana State University Press, 2003.

Rable, George C. *Fredericksburg! Fredericksburg!* Chapel Hill: University of North Carolina Press, 2002.

Snell, Mark A. *From First to Last: The Life of Major General William B. Franklin.* New York: Fordham University Press, 2002.

U.S. Congress. *Report of the Joint Committee on the Conduct of the War.* Washington, D.C.: Government Printing Office, 1863.

Villard, Henry. *Memoirs, Vol. 1.* New York: Da Capo Press, 1969.

Warner, Ezra J. *Generals in Blue.* Baton Rouge: Louisiana State University Press, 1964.